Shakespeare and His Social Context

AMS Studies in the Renaissance: No. 10
ISSN: 0195–8011

Shakespeare and His Social Context

Essays in Osmotic Knowledge and Literary Interpretation

Margaret Loftus Ranald

AMS Press, Inc.
New York

PR
2991
R36
1987

Library of Congress Cataloging-in-Publication Data
Ranald, Margaret Loftus.
  Shakespeare and his social context.
  (AMS studies in the Renaissance, ISSN 0195-8011; no. 10)
  Bibliography: p.
  Includes index.
  1. Shakespeare, William, 1564-1616—Characters—Women.
2. Shakespeare, William, 1564-1616—Political and social
views. 3. Shakespeare, William, 1564-1616—Contemporary
England. 4. Women in literature. 5. England—Social life and
customs—16th century.
  I. Title. II. Series.
PR2991.R36 1987   822.3'3   83-45279
ISBN 0-404-62280-1

Manufactured in the United States of America

Second Impression: 1989

For Ralph and Caroline

Contents

ACKNOWLEDGMENTS

The happiest task in finishing a manuscript is acknowledging those who have helped. First, I thank the late James E. Phillips of UCLA, who always had faith in this material. The Henry E. Huntington Library very early gave me assistance in allowing, to a Fulbright Scholar, reading privileges not then usually allowed a first-year student. The Folger Shakespeare Library honored me with a Senior Fellowship which introduced me to that fine fellowship of friendly, generous, supportive, and social Shakespeareans who frequent it. To my colleagues, both there and at Queens College, I owe more debts of friendship than can be acknowledged in notes. William Green I thank for information on the Order of the Garter, Richard McCoy for comments on chivalry, Malcolm Goldstein for listening. Eugene M. Waith (Yale University), made probing comments on individual chapters as also did Arthur F. Kinney (University of Massachusetts, Amherst), Anne Parten (UVa), and Paul A. Jorgensen (UCLA). Theodore Shapiro, M.D., of Cornell Medical Center, gave me some useful information on psychological aspects of twinning. To Dr. William B. Long of AMS Press, I am indebted for wisdom and consideration. Mrs. Pearl Sigberman, Mrs. Wendy de Fortuna, Mrs. Fay Diamond, and their colleagues in the Queens College Word Processing Unit, Jefferson Hall Division, did a superb job in typing a difficult manuscript.

The editorial boards of *English Literary Research, Essays in Literature, The Huntington Library Quarterly, Shakespeare Quarterly,* and *Topic* kindly allowed me to reprint, with revisions, material they had previously published. The Renaissance Seminar of Columbia University, New York, heard and commented on the *Lucrece* section as it was being developed. I am grateful for their comments. I also thank my students, both past and present, who allowed me to try some of these ideas on them and who were always ready to offer criticism and fresh insights. Special thanks to Robert M. Tannenbaum who showed me how to index by computer.

Lastly, I thank my family: my daughter, Caroline, our two cats, Demelza and Roxelana, and particularly my husband Ralph, for love, consideration, patience, companionship, and help in proofreading that went far beyond the call of matrimonial duty. Without his encouragement this book could never have been finished.

NEW YORK CITY

July 1985

GENERAL INTRODUCTION

The late R. P. Blackmur in private conversation once defined historical criticism as "putting in the explanations the author left out," because they were not needed. This comment describes to some extent the approach followed in this collection of Shakespearean essays. My intent is neither to supply a proliferation of footnotes, at times lamentably necessary, nor to assert the discovery of new sources, which sometimes instinct requests, but reason and scholarship reject. My focus always remains the dramatic text and my approach aims to illuminate that text by placing it in the context of a shared background of knowledge and assumptions which were familiar to the playgoers of Shakespeare's day, if not our own.

This kind of common knowledge can be found today, even in a pluralistic society such as the United States. It is the sort of information that is obtained not through conscious effort, and not necessarily from instruction, but somehow absorbed. This is osmotic knowledge, which in my definition of the term, describes the information, the moral and behavioral assumptions that a "reasonable man," that delightful legal fiction, should somehow have learned, or at least understood. That such knowledge should very frequently be concerned with manners and *mores* should come as no surprise. Even now the state laws and customs relating to marriage, divorce, cohabitation, desertion, drug use, drinking, welfare and unemployment have currency far beyond the limits of law books or law courts. Both educated and underprivileged persons also have a very clear understanding of their "constitutional rights," frequently obtained without benefit of any civics course. And again, despite a growing informality of behavior and dress, "the correct thing" is still being advised on and discussed in tabloid newspapers, while Emily Post, that bible of social behavior, has a new, albeit revised, edition. Finally, the social activities and misdeeds of the wealthy are fully reported, often with gleeful voyeurism, in "popular" newspapers and magazines.

From these and similar sources derives osmotic knowledge, which enables individuals to understand, even if they cannot share, the life styles of others. No reasonable person would presume a single, monolothic American public opinion on almost any subject, and surely the same was true for "the Elizabethans," whether the topic be Copernican astronomy or the rule of Queen Elizabeth. What was possible for the citizens of London, and even elsewhere, was a sense of shared identity, of cultural background, of chauvinism, and to a very large extent, a shared religion. This last is highly important, because on many subjects one must look to the Established Church of England as a socio-political as well as a religious institution for both Elizabethan and Jacobean periods. Through compulsory attendance at services, absence being punishable by fine, the English people were skillfully indoctrinated by officially composed and officially designated homilies on topics ranging from the necessity of obedience to authority, proceeding through the horrors of whoredom and adultery, rebellion, and civil disturbance, and reaching heights of theological reinterpretations of the doctrines of repentance, forgiveness, and the necessity of good works. And lest one draw attention to the existence of recusants, crypto-Lollards, and other hidden religious nonconformists, the fact remains that since the *via media* approach of the Church of England had left much of the Old Religion in place, recusants could understand the nature of the new revelation, and other nonconformists would continue to oppose some of the same things they had disapproved of before the Reformation. Further, since religion was literally a burning question, individuals needed to know something of religious orthodoxy in order to avoid, or commit, heresy.

It may be objected that my modern examples presuppose some literacy and some access to newspapers, magazines, and mass communication media, impossible in the sixteenth and seventeenth centuries. But those years were also media conscious, though the manner of communication was different. Queen Elizabeth herself was a most astute exploiter of the public appearance—in particular the Royal Progress (the equivalent of the modern "photo opportunity"), by which she made herself visible to large crowds of her subjects to elicit demonstrations of loyalty. At the same time she thriftily saved money by residing with selected nobles at their expense while her own houses were being "sweetened." In this way, as well as through hortatory speeches and proclamations on threatening as well as joyous occasions, the Queen not only united her people, but also taught them. In England today, the Royal Family is still a paradigm of the individual British family whose members participate avidly in royal marriages, births, deaths, and other ceremonials.

The educational aspect of leadership which Elizabeth I pursued with such skill has, however, become the province of elected officials. In England, Winston Churchill comes to mind, while in the United States Franklin Roosevelt's mantle of "great communicator" now rests easily on the shoulders of President Ronald Reagan.

Other public occasions which helped unite Elizabethan society, particularly against threats of foreign intervention, were the frequent public executions for treason or heresy, rituals of horror in which the crowd took a very active role. Accounts of the death of Roderigo Lopez (1594) speak of the people's bitter hostility and desire to prolong the agony of a man who was probably innocent. Conversely, and unexpectedly, in the case of Father Henry Garnet, of Gunpowder Plot fame (1606), the crowd called successfully for him to be left hanging until dead. On another occasion, when the condemned man had some public support, the execution took place at an unprecedentedly early hour to avoid mob violence. The lesson of retribution for treason and incitement to disloyalty was also taught with visual reinforcement by the solemn quartering of traitors, with their parboiled and tarred quarters sent for display to four principal cities, while the exhibition of traitors' heads on London Bridge was a grisly reminder of the power of justice. An Elizabethan crowd, it is clear, understood the limits of punishments, whether it was the dishonoring of a knight by reversing his coat of arms, or the hanging, drawing, and quartering of someone condemned for high treason.

Communication by means of symbol was also important in the days before public address systems, as the white smoke of a Papal Conclave still indicates. Sentences in capital crimes were usually announced visually by the way in which the executioner's axe was held when the accused criminal appeared after sentencing. On one occasion the watching crowd nearly rioted in protest when it misread a sign of double axes, the first with the blade turned away from, the second with the blade turned toward a prisoner acquitted of high treason but sentenced to death for a lesser included offense.

Appearance was another form of communication among the upper classes, and many a country gentleman is alleged to have nearly bankrupted himself to put fine clothing on his back to make a good showing at court. But above all, one's identity among the nobility was enshrined on a coat of arms, an escutcheon one feared to blot with pusillanimity and whose possession one needed to ratify by individual deeds of nobility. Similarly, craftsmen wore their badges of office in the tools and dress of their trade, while sumptuary laws forbade the wearing of certain luxurious fabrics to those below certain social classes—as much to keep people in their place as to stimulate the local cloth industry. As a result, Malvolio's yeomanly cross-gartered yellow stockings would be more amusing to an Elizabethan than to a modern audience. As a member of the professional servant class he may well have come from humble origins, and his willingness to resume the garb of his former class indicates the depth of his folly.

Along with a certain amount of social mobility came books of behavior and manners, the native English ones pragmatic and factual, the foreign ones frequently philosophical, romantic, and idealistic. Some of these books also aimed at the crafts and servant classes, as well as members of the bourgeoisie, the mercantile class with more money than social polish, who wished to pass over into the realm of the landed gentry, if not the aristocracy, by means of marriage to an impoverished member of it. These persons needed books of conduct, and they were literate enough to read them. Indeed, one should realize that the majority of London's working inhabitants came from the mercantile or craft classes, and craft guilds usually required functional literacy for full membership.

To be sure, there were no newspapers to keep London's 190,000 inhabitants informed, but penny broadsides proliferated, ballads on current events were common, Royal Proclamations were frequently made, public notices and handbills distributed. In short, the general public was kept suitably informed and propagandized. Elizabethans were also familiar with the vagaries of the law, as their extraordinary litigiousness indicates—a phemonemon that transcended social class. And above all this was word of mouth, together with the religious and political orthodoxy purveyed by censored public entertainment from public playhouse to public progress. Heresy, whether political or religious, was sternly excised from the theatre—witness the abolition of the Mystery cycle performances in 1576 as something that smacked too much of the Old Faith.

This is the nature of the osmotic knowledge I attribute to both playgoers and public in Shakespeare's day. Some of its strictures were certainly "more honored in the breach than in the observance," but basically it formed a shared cultural frame of reference, something that could be taken for granted in the shorthand of dramatic dialogue. Needless to say, some members of the audience understood more than others, but such is the genius of Shakespeare that the entry level of his work, even today, is not restricted to specialists. It can be achieved by almost everyone, from the immediate reaction of a streetwise teenager to a human situation, to the sophistication of the interpretive scholar. In

short, Shakespeare's role as a specialist in the art of Elizabethan media communication should not be overlooked.

My aim in these essays is to demonstrate Shakespeare's use of some of
this shared cultural experience through a study of several different aspects of
manners and *mores*. Thus the first sections of each part develop some background for Shakespeare's use of matrimonial law, precepts of feminine behavior, the rules of siege warfare and the laws of chivalry. From these topics new
theses and foci emerge. Part One develops the idea of high-spirited women as
teachers of love during the period of courtship, even engaging in cross-dressing for that purpose. After marriage, as Part Two shows, women are expected
to become more conformable, a topic that is treated in both comedy and tragedy. Part Three continues with this theme, but it introduces the use of siege
warfare as structural device in *Lucrece* and shows that words are the weapon of
the powerless, which is illustrated by three women in the English history
plays. Finally the laws and rituals of chivalry are shown in Part Four and applied to *Richard II*, while the last section shows their relevance to the motif of
unclothing in several plays.

As this study has evolved, so too has scholarship on the status of women
in law and society. Lawrence Stone's *The Family, Sex, and Marriage in England 1500–1800* (1977) is an indispensable sociological study, while feminist
scholarship in Shakespeare achieved solid academic recognition in the 1980
anthology, *The Woman's Part: Feminist Criticism of Shakespeare*. Since that
time the book-length studies of Irene G. Dash, Coppélia Kahn, Suzanne W.
Hull, Linda Woodbridge and others have contributed differently: Dash,
through her emphasis on theatrical performance, Kahn through her psychological approach, and Hull and Woodbridge through their analyses and bib-
liographies of "the woman question." The pioneering work of Juliet
Dusinberre, *Shakespeare and the Nature of Women* (1975), should not be overlooked, and neither should Carolyn G. Heilbrun, *Toward a Recognition of
Androgyny* (1973), when one is investigating the trouser roles of Shakespeare's women.

Such a welcome explosion of scholarship has rendered my original,
comprehensive chapters on law and the status of women supererogatory.
Therefore I have confined myself to a few specifically relevant aspects of this
varied material. Elsewhere, as in Parts Three and Four, I have been more
expansive. In other words, some of the shared common knowlege available in
Elizabethan England has been rediscovered by feminist scholarship.
Perhaps, with the growth of women's studies, and popular discussion and

debate on the place of women in history and society, this material will again become osmotic knowledge.[1]

I now welcome the soubriquet "feminist" as a computational facet of the *MLA International Bibliography*. Nonetheless, I do not believe that Shakespeare was in effect a feminist before the feminist movement. Similarly, I do not believe that the Protestant Reformation offered any great improvement in woman's status—sometimes the reverse, particularly in education. I have tried to present my findings in a neutral manner, refusing to consider Petruchio and Bertram solely as male chauvinists, or Kate and Isabella as masochists. But certainly I welcome modern scholarship's newly raised consciousness which has enabled me to state opinions more forcefully and use material more directly than was possible in those not-so-distant days when such studies were dismissed as "just the kind of topic a woman would work on."

NOTE: Unless otherwise specified, all Shakespearean quotations and citations are from *William Shakespeare: The Complete Works*, gen. ed. Alfred Harbage, The Pelican Shakespeare (Baltimore, Md.: Penguin Books, 1969).

Part One

THE PATHWAY INTO MARRIAGE.

CHAPTER I

Matrimonial Law and the Education of Lovers

SECTION 1
Introduction

M atrimonial impediments, clandestine marriages, secret spousals, enforced marriage, infidelity (real or imagined), antenuptial sexual unions, mistaken identity, elopements; where would Elizabethan and Jacobean drama be without these situations? In fact a full understanding of the action of many plays during this period depends largely on a knowledge of the complexities of contemporary English matrimonial law. However, of those dramatists who make considerable use of the law, only John Webster is believed to have completed legal training at the Inns of Court,[1] and therefore they were writing as laymen for a popular, non-specialist audience which must have understood the material, otherwise the plays would have failed. But matrimonial law, and some of the situations detailed above are matters which one discovers through osmosis rather than through formal study. Even today, almost any randomly chosen group of laypeople can usually compile a fairly accurate account of state laws relating to marriage, divorce, and abortion. In the sixteenth and seventeenth centuries, however, the requirements of canon law were consciously and officially imparted by the Church of England in its prescribed homilies on matrimony, whoredom, and adultery, so that dramatists were able to depend on the existence of an audience that had sufficient information to follow the intricacies of a fairly complex legal plot.

Sexual morality was also a constant concern of the Church and attempts were made to enforce a rigid code. Parish priests were expected to report breaches of matrimonial law occurring among their flock; ecclesiastical visitors always inquired after such matters, and apparitors were appointed to bring offenders to the attention of bishops and the ecclesiastical courts, which had jurisdiction over matrimonial causes. Public penance was frequently imposed

3

for sexual offenses, and since it was usually performed before the church at Sunday services where attendance was compulsory, with penitents exhibited as an example to all, the lessons of the pulpit were given visual reinforcement.

As for Shakespeare himself, the circumstances of his own marriage, and his participation on the 1610 Belott-Mountjoy suit (concerning the arrangements of a marriage contract) indicate that he had at least a well-informed layman's knowledge of English marriage law.[2] It is also certain that he read Holinshed's *Chronicles* and Foxe's *Actes and Monumentes*, both of which contain extensive matrimonial material. And he may have had professional advice, the source of which has as yet defied discovery. Be that as it may, almost all the matrimonial situations used by Shakespeare and his fellow dramatists suggest *common knowledge* rather than specialized study of English canon and civil law. For the purposes of their plays they merely transferred English law to foreign settings.

Throughout his works, Shakespeare uses matrimonial problems as plot devices, frequently in ways not dictated by his sources, and which show the ease of long acquaintance with the material. Immediately the allied problem plays of *Measure for Measure* and *All's Well That Ends Well* come to mind, for they mandate some understanding of English matrimonial law for their interpretation.[3] The history plays are concerned frequently with matters of precontract and the resultant impediments as causing problems with legitimate succession. Richard III alleges a precontract to argue the bastardy of the children of Edward IV and Elizabeth Woodville.[4] Henry VI is also shown potentially liable to this impediment in his marriage with Margaret of Anjou,[5] and there is more than a hint that this is one of the reasons for his downfall. *Henry VIII*, the last play in which Shakespeare had a hand, is also concerned with matters of affinity arising from the king's initial marital adventure. The comedies, of course, are replete with matrimonial problems, practices, and situations—from public spousals, recitation of the marriage ceremony and secret marriage, to forced marriage in *A Midsummer Night's Dream* and *The Merry Wives of Windsor*. Among the tragedies, *Hamlet* and *Othello* deal very specifically with matrimonial matters.[6] The romances also offer a variety of such situations: incest, attempts to enforce marriage, alleged infidelity, elopement, and finally careful preparation for a chaste union in *The Tempest*.

Clearly, some account of the canon law of marriage in England and its relation to Shakespeare is necessary before proceeding to a discussion of the imaginative manner in which he makes use of this material. At first blush, the statement that he is concerned with the laws current in England in his own day seems supererogatory and simplistic. But paradoxically, in describing English practice he almost always approximates the matrimonial customs and laws of Roman Catholic Europe prior to the Council of Trent (1547–1563). Despite the popular belief that the English Reformation was precipitated by a marriage, it did not permanently change the matrimonial law of Shakespeare's day which remained "a continuation of the canon law of Rome as it existed prior to the Council of Trent."[7] Thus Shakespeare and his fellows, by using the English law of marriage to dramatize events in Vienna, Paris, Venice, or Padua, approximate to the pre-Tridentine Roman Canon Law.

This connection between English and Roman canon law remains to this day, and is enshrined in the statutes passed by parliament to rule the Church of England as the established religion. The noted jurist, Sir Frederic Maitland commented in 1898 that "in all probability large portions (to say the least) of 'the canon law of Rome' were regarded by the courts Christian in this country as absolutely binding statute law."[8] This leads to the curious possibility, now being explored by theologians seeking unity between English and Roman churches, that the English Reformation was not really necessary and that English orders may still be valid in the eyes of Rome. If, as Anglican canonists suggest, the medieval English episcopal synods had by long custom and the silent acquiescence of Rome, chosen only those parts of the Roman canon law they considered applicable, then the English church had long been essentially self-governing. In that case the English church in fact had the right to take independent action to reject the authority of Rome.

By this argument the differences between England and Rome were those of authority rather than doctrine. Further, Henry VIII, though repeatedly empowered to undertake a major reform of English canon law. did not do so. A new code is believed to have been compiled, but not adopted, before Henry's death in 1547, and revisions continued. In 1571 a commission, headed by John Foxe, developed the *Reformatio Legum Ecclesiasticarum*, which was never presented to parliament because it was considered too radical. Some of its provisions were, however, incorporated in the *Constitutions and Canons Ecclesiastical* of 1604, which, by Canon 100, required the consent of parents or guardians for the marriage of persons under the age of twenty-one.

The matrimonial law of the Roman Catholic church had been developed on the basic premise that marriage was a sacrament and the union was indissoluble. The sacrament, however, consisted not in the religious ceremony but in the act of physical consummation which properly should take place after the church ritual. This distinction between *matrimonium initiatum* and *matrimo-*

nium ratum continued to hold in English canon law, as did the concept of indissolubility. But the Anglican church rejected marriage as a sacrament, while still accepting the idea of its sanctity and divine origin. The 1559 *Book of Common Prayer* refers to it as "an honorable estate, instituted of God in paradise in the time of man's innocency, signifying unto us the mystical union, that is, between Christ and his Church."[9] The Puritan wing, on the other hand, considered marriage as a civil contract, a concept not embodied in English statute law until 1653.[10]

One very fruitful area seized on by dramatists and exploited in almost endless variety was that of impediments, both prohibitive and diriment. Prohibitive impediments merely obstructed marriage and, though subjecting offenders to ecclesiastical punishment, did not annul the union. Offenders were subject to dispensation by the Pope, or in England, by the law as interpreted by the ecclesiastical courts. Diriment impediments, on the other hand, not only obstructed marriage, but also rendered it null and void *ab initio*, even to the extent of bastardizing the children born of the union. Officially, diriment impediments were not subject to dispensation, though exceptions were made.

The prohibitive impediments that commonly appear in drama are those of antenuptial immorality (if the couple were already betrothed), and lack of parental consent. The first, of course, was easily cured by means of paying a fine (in York it was 2/6), public penance, and recelebration of the union in the church, before a priest. Usually in the drama, lack of parental consent was coupled with secret marriage or elopement and it will therefore be discussed later.

The diriment impediments that dramatists most frequently employ make up a longer list (not surprisingly, because there are more of them in the canon law). They are: mistaken identity, disparity of religion (*disparitas cultus*), marriage between baptized and unbaptized persons; criminality, especially when preceded by adultery and the promise of marriage on the death of the obstructing person; fear caused by threats "such as would affect even a strong man" (*metus qui posset in constantem cadere*); reverential fear (*metus reverentialis*), the moral compulsion of parent or guardian; prior marriage or contract *de praesenti* (in words of the present tense); relationships within the forbidden degrees of consanguinity or affinity.[11]

Shakespeare makes use of every one of these impediments, sometimes on more than one occasion, ringing interesting changes on them. In *Twelfth Night* he exploits the dramatic device of mistaken identity through the sworn spousals of Olivia and Sebastian, but reveals the truth before their wedding.

This impediment also has some importance in the final revelations of *All's Well That Ends Well*, and to a lesser extent in *Much Ado About Nothing*. Marriage between baptized and unbaptized persons becomes a possible impediment in *Othello* (but he is later spoken of as having been baptized), and it offers a logical reason for Jessica's decision to change her religion in *The Merchant of Venice*.

Hamlet presents us with an array of diriment impediments: marriage within the forbidden degrees, possible adultery, and certain criminality. Through affinity, the marriage of Gertrude and Claudius is clearly null and void *ab initio*;[12] however, there is some legitimate doubt about the exact nature of the adultery. The Ghost's verbal attack on Claudius as "that incestuous, that adulterate beast" (I.v.42) need not indicate Gertrude's adultery with Claudius during the lifetime of her first husband, but rather to her current marriage.[13] In addition, by murdering his brother, Claudius falls within the purview of the impediment of criminality, in killing a party who obstructs a marriage. Hamlet's disgust with his mother's remarriage, even before the Ghost tells him of the murder, can thus be explained through the impediment of affinity. Revulsion against Gertrude's sexuality is only part of Hamlet's horror: his mother and uncle are living in a union which most Elizabethans would probably have instantly recognized as totally invalid, whether or not Gertrude bears any guilt in the murder of her first husband.[14]

Affinity, together with the impediment of "public honesty," which arises from an unconsummated contract, forms the basis of the conflict in *Henry VIII* where the whole divorce case rests on the question of whether Katherine of Aragon's prior marriage to Henry's brother, Arthur, had been consummated. If, as Katherine argued, her marriage with Arthur had never been consummated, the papal dispensation to marry Henry should have been given on the grounds of public honesty: "but not least in order to ensure the princess's dower rights, . . . the Spanish ambassador . . . agreed with the English that a dispensation should be sought from the impediment of affinity in the first degree collateral, . . . which could have arisen only from physical union of the parties [Arthur and Katherine]."[15] Curiously, in his marriage to Anne Boleyn Henry was again involved in the impediment of affinity, this time as a result of his earlier, illicit, and consummated relationship with Anne's sister, Mary. For this reason the "Act for the Establishment of the King's Succession" (25 Hen. VIII, c. 22) was passed, listing the degrees forbidden by Leviticus, and declaring the legality of the king's marriage with Anne.[16]

Enforced marriage and reverential fear form the basis of the plot of *All's Well That Ends Well*, to be discussed in detail later, while in other plays, such as *The Taming of the Shrew* and *Cymbeline*, the problems are solved by elopement or flight. Enforcement quite obviously is the theme of George Wilkins's *The Miseries of Inforst Marriage*, but that play also includes the additional impediment of prior marriage, or prior contract in words of the present tense. This second impediment is employed as plot device in *The Two Gentlemen of Verona, Much Ado, Measure for Measure, All's Well That Ends Well*, and to a lesser extent, *The Taming of the Shrew*. In all of these plays, the existence of a marriage contract (in *All's Well* a marriage), publicly performed, helps to explain the acceptance of apparently unworthy men by the women they have wronged. In *Troilus and Cressida*, the fact that Shakespeare arranges a witnessed exchange of vowed love increases the culpability of the disloyal Cressida. To be sure, this is a classically-based play, but the moral judgment of the audience remains conditioned by medieval and Elizabethan laws of matrimonial contracting.

This brings us to other matters often exploited by dramatists—precontract, and type of contract. Precontract obviously means a prior commitment to a match other than the one that is currently being negotiated. The exact force of the earlier vows, however, depends on the nature of the words spoken, whether they were couched in words of the present tense (*per verba de praesenti*) or the future tense (*per verba de futuro*). The former constituted an agreement to enter immediately into the married state, while the latter was merely a promise to marry at some later time—a specific date was not necessary.[17] Contracts to marry, or "spousals," as they were called, could also be made subject to conditions, as long as these were not frivolous, and on the fulfillment of the conditions they became binding. Nonfulfillment nullified the contract.[18]

Spousals, whether *de praesenti* or *de futuro*, did not, however, confer all the physical rights of marriage.[19] Betrothals had to be recelebrated publicly, *in facie ecclesiae*, according to the *Book of Common Prayer*. The Church of England required publicity to avoid the scandal resulting from secret contracts and clandestine marriages. Shakespeare's Prospero enunciates the orthodox position very clearly when he warns Ferdinand and Miranda, after he overhears their vows and grants permission for their marriage:

> If thou dost break her virgin-knot before
> All sanctimonious ceremonies may,
> With full and holy rite be minist'red,

No sweet aspersion shall the heavens let fall
To make this contract grow; but barren hate,
Sour-eyed disdain, and discord shall bestrew
The union of your bed with weeds so loathly
That you shall hate it both.

(IV.i.15–22)

Nevertheless, the recalcitrance of human nature meant that some persons ignored these attempts to legislate human behavior and acted as if spousals (whether or not vows were exchanged before witnesses) were the equivalent of marriage, "and on sexual relations taking place [they] became what was called a presumptive marriage."[20] In this manner an indissoluble contract was created and ratified to form a union that was irregular but valid, according to Elizabethan and Jacobean law.[21] The civil law, however, attempted to discourage such clandestine unions by ruling that certain property rights, including the wife's right to dower, and her right to administer her husband's estate after his death were forfeit unless assigned "atte churche dore" according to custom, or unless a woman could produce "some tangible documentation of her marriage, or an acceptable witness to it."[22] In this case, her property rights were equal to those arising from a public ceremony.[23]

After the Council of Trent (1547–63), Roman and English canon law diverged completely on clandestine marriages, though dramatists paid no attention to this fact. In its decree *Tametsi* the Council attacked the practice, while not nullifying existing unions "so long as the Church has not declared them invalid."[24] It then laid down a rule which required public celebration of marriage in church after formal publication of banns (which could occasionally be dispensed with). However, and most importantly, this decree was not promulgated in any country that was mainly Protestant, and thus England was exempt from its provisions, presumably in order to preserve the canonical validity of marriages contracted by recusants unable to find a Catholic priest.[25] Thus in Elizabethan and Jacobean England the old law on clandestine marriages remained in force for both Catholic and Protestant, and free and unforced consent still formed the basis of matrimony, even in unwitnessed unions, providing that both parties would swear to the marriage. Elsewhere in Catholic Europe, marriage celebrated *in facie ecclesiae* alone became the rule thirty days after the decree *Tametsi* was promulgated from the parish pulpit.

But Elizabethan and Jacobean dramatists do not seem to have known this, and consequently Webster's Duchess of Malfi contracts a marriage with Antonio that was valid in English law (though it could have been disputed), but

invalid in Italy. Similarly, Claudio and Juliet in *Measure for Measure* contract a union that would have been valid in England, but not in Vienna. John
Wilkins, in *The Miseries of Inforst Marriage* is quite correct, for his setting
is England, and Clare is rightly concerned that Scarborowe, in submitting to an
enforced marriage, is in effect committing adultery as a result of his precontract
to her.

Other aspects of matrimonial law and ritual have their place in drama, and
Shakespeare is shown as having knowledge of them. His lovers almost invari-
ably exchange vows and rings in the proper canonical manner, and the use of
rings is more than a mere device of romantic recognition. It is a statement that
a legal contract has in fact been made, for even in the most secret marriages, a
ring was provided, if at all possible.[26] In Shakespeare, for instance, Julia and
Proteus in *The Two Gentlemen of Verona* exchange rings and *de praesenti*
vows; Portia and Nerissa in *The Merchant of Venice* exchange rings with
their men; in *Twelfth Night*, Olivia and Sebastian do the same; and in *Richard
III*, Anne Neville *accepts* a ring. The rituals of marriage are also those of
Elizabethan and Jacobean England, though of course a full ceremonial is never
shown onstage since this would be a kind of blasphemy. Nonetheless, in *The
Taming of the Shrew* Shakespeare has the reported scene of Petruchio's marriage to Kate, and in *Much Ado*, the "maimed rite" of Hero's wedding, while
public spousals are endemic in the comedies. The rituals which surround the
preparation of the bride and groom are those of England, and so too is the
conclusion of *A Midsummer Night's Dream* where the blessings of house and
bridal bed parallel very closely the priestly blessings given in pre-Reforma-
tion England and preserved in the Sarum Missal, one of the basic source
documents of the *Book of Common Prayer*.[27]

Throughout his career, and most particularly in the comedies, Shakespeare made considerable use of matters matrimonial to provide a contemporary foundation for his plots. Certainly he was not the only playwright of his
time to do so, as the final scene in Ben Jonson's *Epicoene* indicates by found-
ing its *dénouement* on a complete summary of matrimonial impediments, culminating in *error personae*. What is noteworthy is that Shakespeare goes beyond mere display of knowledge or conscious didacticism and uses this material as major plot device, character development and revelation, and as frame of
reference. As a result, if we are to understand his plays fully, and particularly
the comedies, we must look at the ways in which he used this particular aspect
of his own milieu.

SECTION 2
Much Ado About Nothing—From Legalism To Love

Much Ado About Nothing is the first play in which Shakespeare employs matrimonial law as the mainspring of the plot and an essential component in character drawing. At the same time he presents a recurrent theme in the comedies, the education of the male characters by women. The men of the comedies need to be taught the true nature of love so that they can mature into suitable social and sexual partners for their women. Thus the women of Shakespeare's comedies "are extraordinarily proficient, socially and sexually: they are the arbiters of social relations, deeply in harmony with the biological needs of the race."[28] And since courtship is the area of life in which women control the action, their role in the comedies is more active than in those plays which deal with post-marital conduct, for by both Elizabethan law and social custom, the man was expected to be dominant in a marriage.

This play, the first of Shakespeare's mature comedies, has generated a variety of critical opinions. King Charles II in his personal Folio retitled it as "Benedick and Betteris," thereby signifying his preference for the battling lovers, and many critics have followed suit. Nonetheless one often reads that the two plots of the play are incompatible, that the scene of Hero's accusation is out of place in a comedy, and that Beatrice and Benedick are very difficult to play on stage today.[29] Thomas Marc Parrott suggested that this plot was grafted on to the tale of Claudio in order to provide comic relief from the near tragedy of the main plot,[30] a theory that was carried further by J. Dover Wilson's suggestion that Shakespeare had revised an earlier play.[31]

In general, critics have tended to treat the two parts of this play as discrete, thereby giving the impression that it lacks a unifying principle. Careful examination nonetheless reveals that *Much Ado* is indeed a unified play, a comedy of manners, and that the unity is provided by the contrast between the two different marriages and the characters involved in them.[32] Opinions differ markedly over the person of Claudio, one critic seeing him as "a kind of romantic Orlando brought face to face with dismal fact"[33] while another maintains that he is a rather calculating young man out to improve himself economically by marriage to a wealthy wife.[34] Here the suggestion of Charles T. Prouty that the two marriages of the play demonstrate different antiromantic approaches offers an explanation for the apparent divergence. The match of Claudio and Hero typifies the conventional Elizabethan method of matchmak-

ing, while that of Beatrice and Benedick operates on a different emotional
level:

> . . . The former [Claudio and Hero] follow the way of the world where
> marriages are arranged by patrons or parents in contrast with the idyllic
> unions which literary convention followed exclusively. On the other
> hand, Beatrice and Benedick are interested in an emotion which is real and
> a relationship based on reality instead of convention.[35]

Claudio, then, undertakes marriage as a businesslike arrangement, and is
discomfited, but finally forgiven. On the way to that outcome he is re-edu-
cated, in part by Hero, but more particularly by Beatrice and Benedick until he
reaches enlightenment through the revelation that he has been deceived and is
forced to reassess himself and his behavior. Hero is a passive educator, but
Beatrice operates actively. The play also develops the general theme of education into love, with the maturing of both Claudio and Benedick into love-
worthiness.

One significant aspect of *Much Ado* is its setting. As Sherman Hawkins
has pointed out, there are two worlds in Shakespearean comedy, "the green
world" of Northrop Frye's happy phrase, and the closed world of society.[36] In
The Merry Wives of Windsor, for instance, the action moves from one area
to another, and this movement is very common throughout Shakespearean
comedy. However, to some extent the term "green world" is a misnomer, for
such movement is not confined to the "forest primeval." There is almost always a journey in Shakespearean comedy in which one or more parties is temporarily deracinated and forced to act alone without complete understanding of
the *mores* of another group. This revelatory journey may be simply the move
from Padua to Petruchio's country house in *The Taming of the Shrew*, from
Venice to Belmont in *The Merchant of Venice*, or the voyage to Ephesus in
The Comedy of Errors. In *Much Ado*, however, there is no such external
journey, and the inward journey toward enlightenment, the movement of spirit,
if you will, that the characters undergo, takes place in the closed world of a
ducal court.

The fact remains that there is an advance in the characters themselves, as
Barbara Lewalski comments:

> . . . the principal characters in both of the plots arrive, after some false
> starts, at the "state" of true love, and in that idealized condition achieve
> heightened perception needed to dispel error and to reorder the confusion
> rampant in their world.[37]

I agree with these conclusions, but part company on the road to reaching them. The characters do not necessarily achieve enlightenment and maturity by means of Christianized Neoplatonism; they can take a different route by way of rationality and questioning of the *mores* of Shakespeare's own time. In this approach the play is even more specifically a foray into the art of the comedy of manners, set in the relatively limited world of of the court of Messina, which, of course, is a microcosm of the world of human behavior.

The basic theme, and the shaping force of the play is that of education into suitability *for* love and the development of a capacity *to* love. This topic also demonstrates the growing power of women in Shakespeare's comedies as the movers and shakers of this social world. They are the moral center of the play and through them and their example their men become better human beings. But this enlightenment does not culminate in a neoplatonic union with the Ideal, but in the accommodation of individuals to marriage, the ultimate harmony of human existence in Shakespeare's comedic world. Structurally, the play is built on counterpoint and contrast, with individual characters acting as foils for each other. Each of the four major characters moves from some kind of excessive behavior to a middle ground where reason and passion are in balance and a successful sexual union is about to be consummated. One curious aspect of this play's structure is the reverse emphasis, which is repeated in *Twelfth Night*. The motivating force, the action plot of the play, is less interesting than what is officially the subplot. Thus, the action arises from the Hero-Claudio material, but the emphasis of wit and wisdom is on Beatrice and Benedick who almost take over the play.

Much Ado opens with an arrival that spurs conflict and wit-combat and concludes with a dance, following the comedic pattern noted by Neville Coghill,[38] in which the characters move from trouble to joy. But the dance is also important, symbolically; it is not merely a method of clearing the stage, but (along with music) a symbol of marriage, of the harmony of human existence and the embodiment of the earthly ideal of human love. One also recognizes a stock figure from *The Two Gentleman of Verona*, the scoffer at love, but this time both the woman and the man share the honors of misogyny. As Benedick asserts "truly I love none," and Beatrice replies, "I had rather hear my dog bark at a crow than a man swear he loves me" (I.i.112,116–118), the outcome of this plot is clearly telegraphed in advance. However, with this introductory skirmish of wit, the battle of the sexes as a theme is temporarily dropped for the much discussed match of Claudio and Hero.

This is the motivating matrimonial situation of the play, and it should be taken as representing the norm for marriage, based as it is solidly on those Elizabethan social conventions according to which marriages were arranged for money rather than ideals of love and compatibility. If this is so, then Claudio is no romantic lover, but a shrewd, handsome, somewhat impecunious young opportunist who wishes to marry for wealth, and hopes to advance at court. Hero is also a type character, an excellent portrait of the ideal Elizabethan maiden according to the code of behavior promulgated by the writers of courtesy and conduct books. She is virtuous in report, looks, apparel, and companions, possessing in addition the virtues that Benedick extols as necessary for *his* ideal lady:

> Rich she shall be, that's certain; wise, or I'll none; virtuous, or I'll never
> cheapen her; fair, or I'll never look on her; mild, or come not near me;
> noble, or not I for an angel; of good discourse, an excellent musician, and
> her hair shall be of what color it please God.
>
> (II.iii.27–32)

Hero is rich, since she is her father's sole heir (I.i.262–263), modest (I.i.146), virtuous (I.i.197–198), beautiful (IV.i.98–106), tractable (II.i.45–48), silent unless addressed (II.ii.270ff.), and noble, since her father is the governor of Messina. By these qualities she is shown to conform not merely to the code of conduct books in general, but to the strictest of them. She does not develop to the same extent as the other major characters of the play, though by the *dénouement* she does speak without prompting. Her educative role in the play is pursued entirely in a passive manner. She exerts the power of moral suasion without taking overt action, allowing others to use her and make her decisions. This modesty is the first attribute to strike Claudio's attention, and since at that time in the play she has spoken only once, and that before Claudio's entrance (I.i.35–36), she is established as a self-effacing personality of the type described by Barnabe Rich:

> The woman of modestie openeth not her mouth but with discretion, nei-
> ther is there any bitterness in her tongue: shee seemeth in speaking to
> hould her peace, and in her silence she seemeth to speake.
>   Her very countenance doth preach modesty, sobrietie, bashfull-
> nesse, continency, temperance, stayednes, humilitie, grace and good-
> ness: . . .[39]

Thus Leonato and her uncle Antonio can confidently assume that Hero will follow instructions and be ruled by her father:

> Daughter, remember what I told you. If the Prince do solicit you in that
> kind, you know your answer.
>
> (II.i.57–59)

This admonition is based on the misapprehension that Don Pedro is wooing for himself instead of for Claudio. Hero is expected to accept whoever asks for her, and love appears irrelevant to the situation. This is the same as the mercenary matching practised by Baptista in *The Taming of the Shrew*. Certainly, from a material point of view, the master, Don Pedro, is a better matrimonial investment (with both a title and money) than Claudio, the young, apparently impecunious soldier of fortune, and Hero's family is taking good care of her financially. As for the young woman, she epitomizes the chaste, silent, and obedient ideal, saying nothing throughout the negotiations for her future, like the maiden praised by Juan Luis Vives:

> . . . it doth not become a mayde to make any signe, that she wolde fayne be maryed, or that she loueth any yonge man to wedde. For if she loue him afore she haue hym, that it be knowen, what shall he thynke but that she wyll as lyghtly loue an other as she hath done hym, whom as yet she ought to shewe no loue vnto: neither he wyll beleue, that as she loueth hym alone seynge there is as great case to loue other. And if he shulde mary her, he wyl thynke she wyll haue as good mynd to other as hym selfe, whā she is so light of loue.[40]

Parents know much better than their children what constitutes a good marriage because they will not be turned aside by sensual desire and make a match without regard to degree or income. Affection is irrelevant; love will come after marriage and it will be mandated by duty. Woe to those who allow themselves to follow their hearts. Vives again thunders against such folly, quoting the old proverb

> . . . *they that mary for loue, shall leade their lyfe in sorowe*. For it chanceth by many, that after the heate of loue is ones paste, there foloweth great hate which thynge ofte times maketh wondre and talke among the people, when they tell, how so great louers within iii. or iiii. dayes fal at debate, and begynne to deuorce or the bryde cake be eaten.[41]

Claudio, unlike his bride, is drawn in such a subtle and ironic manner that his true nature is not immediately apparent. From outward appearance and reported behavior he would appear to represent the ideal Renaissance gentleman whose active characteristics were considered to be valor and honor gained through arms. Claudio has displayed both of these excellencies and by their means has advanced in the favor of Don Pedro, his lord (I.i.8–15). If Beatrice is to be trusted, he is "the noble Claudio" (I.i.77), and the bastard Don John also refers to him as "a proper squire" (I.iii.45), and Borachio uses his title of Count (I.iii.56). Claudio has also validated his lineage by deeds of valor,[42] and has shown himself willing at all times to follow his lord and to serve him. One assumes him handsome, and though nothing is said of his economic affairs, he has status in the good graces of Don Pedro. So far he appears to be a gentleman, but all these qualities are those of outward appearance, not those of moral worth which such courtesy writers as Castiglione, Ducci, Giraldi, Guazzo, and Romei considered essential.[43] Virtue, then was the true nobility, proceeding from the mind and soul of the possessor, with the exterior merely a reflection of philosophical and moral excellence. In the character of Claudio, Shakespeare exploits the contradiction between appearance and reality: the handsome exterior hides a morally flawed human being, and the major action of the play is concentrated on teaching the young man the error of his judgment, leading him through repentance to forgiveness.[44]

Claudio is shown at the beginning of the play to be a very cautious young man, unwilling to commit himself to love, and very much concerned with his own advancement. Admittedly he claims that he was first struck with the modesty of Hero (I.i.146), and praises her as "the sweetest lady that ever I looked on" (I.i.166–167). This may sound like love at first sight, but it also indicates a preference for a malleable maiden of meekness whom he can control. At the same time there is a curiously mercantile and pejoratively sexual quality about the language of both Benedick and Claudio:

> *Benedick* Would you buy her, that you enquire after her?
> *Claudio* Can the world buy such a jewel?
> *Benedick* Yea, and a case to put it into.
>
> (I.i.159–161)

And the exchange continues with Benedick cynically twitting Claudio for his excessively rational understatement. Claudio's caution is further demonstrated when Benedick informs Don Pedro of the young man's interest in Hero. To the Don's comment that "the lady is very well worthy" (I.i.196–197) Claudio replies "You speak this to fetch me in, my lord" (I.i.198), a sentiment that hardly sounds like true love, since *to fetch in* also means to cheat or beguile. That *worth* for Claudio means cash rather than moral virtue is emphasized in a later exchange:

> *Claudio* Hath Leonato any son, my lord?
> *Pedro* No child but Hero; she's his only heir.
>
> (I.i.262–263)

Only after this assurance does Claudio launch into any speech that might be construed as a romantic avowal of love, but even here he commits himself no further than "Saying I liked her ere I went to wars" (I.i.279), despite his admission that he does feel "fair and delicate desires."

Altogether his love is grounded more on magisterial approval than deeply felt passion; this is confirmed by Claudio's reaction when the bastard Don John erroneously informs him that Pedro is wooing the young woman for himself. He barely laments, is instantly resigned to this change in his fortunes, notes the deleterious power of feminine beauty and recalls the frequently repeated warning to lovers, "Wooe not by Embassadour:"[45]

> Friendship is constant in all other things
> Save in the office and affairs of love.
> Therefore all hearts in love use their own tongues;
> Let every eye negotiate for itself,
> And trust no agent; for beauty is a witch
> Against whose charms faith melteth into blood.
> This is an accident of hourly proof,
> Which I mistrusted not. Farewell therefore Hero!
> (II.i.157–164)

So now, Hero, through her beauty, is being blamed for Don Pedro's apparent disloyalty. Claudio certainly is no true lover, but rather a poseur, and his reputation as a romantic lover comes only from the reports of Benedick which make him so stereotypical that one cannot take them seriously:

> . . . I have known when there was no music with him but the drum and fife; and now had he rather hear the tabor and the pipe. I have known when he would have walked ten mile afoot to see a good armor; and now will he lie ten nights awake carving the fashion of a new doublet. He was wont to speak plain and to the purpose, like an honest man and a soldier; and now is he turned orthography; his words are very fantastical banquet—just so many strange dishes.
> (II.iii.12–20)

If in fact Claudio is acting in this manner, it indicates another aspect of his self-centeredness: he is in love with the idea of love rather than the lady herself. This attitude is reinforced when he offers to accompany Don Pedro back to Arragon as soon as his "marriage be consummate" (III.ii.3–4). Such willingness to leave the marriage bed to follow his master argues sycophantic ambition rather than true love. Claudio suits his behavior to the occasion without the heart's commitment. Blinded by his own self-love he cannot penetrate beneath the appearance to perceive the truth beneath; judging others by his own selfishness he can easily believe in the apparent falsehood of Don Pedro, and later of Hero herself. Obviously this unromantic, materialistic young man needs some education in love so that he will eventually be worthy of Hero.

Shakespeare treats the negotiations leading to Claudio's marriage with extremely careful attention to the details of English practice, according to the principles of canon law and conventional pecuniary arrangements. Claudio is espoused twice in the course of the play, and in both cases the ceremonies are public and *de praesenti*, with vows exchanged in words of the present tense, before sufficient witnesses, and in the house of the bride with her father performing the ritual. We are not told of the financial negotiations in the same detail as in *The Taming of the Shrew*, but to judge from Leonato's words, satisfactory arrangements have been made. Don Pedro has apparently gained Hero's consent, but Beatrice has already indicated that her cousin will follow the dictates of "duty to make cursy and say, 'Father, as it please you'" (II.i.45–46), while Leonato has also taken her consent for granted when he believes that Pedro was a candidate for her hand (II.i.57–59). The matter-of-fact wording of the initial espousal shows the businesslike manoeuvring that has gone into this match, and one wonders how it can ever have been taken as anything other than an arranged *mariage de convenance*, with money as a major object.

The self-centeredness of Claudio is again demonstrated in his part of the spousal; at first he says nothing, but prompted by Beatrice, he claims to be overwhelmed with emotion:

> Silence is the perfectest herald of joy; I were but little happy, if I could say how much. Lady, as you are mine, I am yours. I give away myself for you and dote upon the exchange.
>
> (II.i.274–277)

To be sure, the comment on silence is a delicate compliment, but then he claims instant possession of the lady, speaking as a superior to an inferior; giving himself—but in exchange. Even here he does not state full and loving commitment to Hero. Logically, she should reply to her future husband with an avowal of love, but the modesty of Hero is such that she says nothing. Again, Beatrice takes command and suggests:

> Speak, cousin; or, if you cannot, stop his mouth with a kiss, and let him not speak neither.
>
> (II.i.268–269)

Hero then kisses Claudio, and Beatrice gives the impression, confirmed by Claudio, that her cousin has whispered her consent in his ear. Of course, the doctrine that "silence means consent" can also operate here, especially since Hero apparently *offers* her lips to Claudio in a spousal kiss, to signify her "free and unforced consent." No rings are exchanged, but this is not an absolute requirement of a spousal, though it was customary.[46] The words of betrothal have been spoken in the present tense, and hence the state of marriage exists immediately, and to all intents and purposes Hero and Claudio are husband and wife. Despite this fact they should not anticipate the rights of marriage and seal the bargain with physical consummation before the church ceremony, or they "*synne deedly*."[47] This particular betrothal is completely legal and indissoluble, despite the existence of a few minor irregularities, and there is now but one cause for the dissolution of the contract:

> . . . for Spousals *de praesenti*, though not consummate, be in truth and substance very matrimony, and therefore perpetually indissoluble, except for Adultery."[48]

The day of marriage is chosen, and Claudio claims that the next day is for him the desired one, for "Time goes on crutches till love have all his rites" (II.i.317–318). For the first time Claudio appears to be an ardent lover, but in III.ii he again disappoints by putting ambition before affection. He will leave his bride to languish while he escorts Don Pedro home; but the Don refuses the offer.

So far Claudio has shown himself ambitious, self-centered, and eager to match with a wealthy wife—nothing really to blame here—but now he moves into reprehensible action. He is far too quick to condemn Hero on the basis of very little evidence, and his decision to shame her publicly is highly vindictive. The pride of this rather selfish young man is hurt, and he instantly plots a suitable revenge. Nonetheless he was within his rights in refusing to go through with the marriage. As Don John obviously is shown to understand, the contract would be nullified

> . . . if either of them be formerly betrothed, or haue committed adulterie after the contract, or be alied, or a kin, or for any other cause not at libertie to marie.[49]

Thus Hero's supposed adultery would have constituted a breaking of the marriage contract and a diriment impediment to the marriage itself, unless Claudio decided to forgive her fault and take no action. Such a course is impossible for Claudio at this stage of his moral development:

> . . . If Hero has a clandestine lover she has affronted all the properties. Unchastity is but one of her sins, the others being a deliberate flaunting of the arrangements of her father and Pedro and an attempt to pass herself off to her proud young husband as undamaged merchandise. In the eyes of the aggrieved, she was not only a wanton but an intentional perpetrator of fraud.[50]

So, filled with the righteous indignation of a duped bridegroom, Claudio decides to inflict public humiliation on Hero, in the church, before witnesses. This action does seem to be rather extreme for comedy, and it clouds future audience reaction to Claudio. Shakespeare has also run counter to his source in Matteo Bandello, where Timbreo renounces Fenicia by letter. Undeniably the scene of renunciation is highly dramatic, and as Nadine Page notes, Claudio is not being unnecessarily cruel, for his action is quite in accord with Elizabethan conventions. Only by public defamation would a deceived Elizabethan bridegroom feel he had been suitably revenged and absolved of all responsibility for the marriage-breaking.[51]

Shakespeare introduces this scene skilfully, leading his audience slowly into it by showing the preparations, taking some pains to observe the old customs of his day. For instance, the gloves which the bride is to wear are the gift of her future husband. This is entirely proper, for gloves, along with jewelry other than rings, were about the only article of wearing that a maiden could with propriety receive from a young man. Hero is also led in procession to the wedding between bridemen. Presumably she is "in her haire," with her hair unloosed about her shoulders to signify her virginity.[52] Visually this would act as dramatic counterpoint to Claudio's vicious verbal assault on her chastity. The ceremonial follows the form laid down in *The Book of Common Prayer* and in Leonato's initial remark we may find a mild comment on the fact that wedding sermons in Elizabethan England were sometimes regarded as things to be endured, rather than exhortations of interest and importance:

> Come, Friar Francis, be brief. Only to the plain form of marriage, and you shall recount their particular duties afterwards.
>
> (IV.i.1–3)

The suspense of the scene is increased by the fact that Claudio does not immediately denounce Hero when Friar invokes the formulaic

> If either of you know any inward impediment why you should not be conjoined, I charge you, on your souls, to utter it.
>
> (IV.i.10–12)[53]

Initially Claudio interrogates Hero, and on receiving a negative reply from her and also from a puzzled Leonato, he refuses her on the grounds of dishonesty and antenuptial immorality, committed after the making of the contract.

Well-versed in law, Leonato instantly thinks of a way out. If Claudio, Hero's espoused husband, has had sexual intercourse with her—but Claudio cuts him short with

> . . . If I have known her,
> You will say she did embrace me as a husband,
> And so extenuate the forehand sin.
> (IV.i.46–48)

In other words, ecclesiastical law, while forbidding espoused persons to

> . . . flesshely meddle togyther as man and wyfe: afore suche tyme as that matrymony may be approued and solempnysed by our mother holy chyrche. . . .[54]

nevertheless recognized that a consummated spousal was valid and indissoluble marriage, though recelebration in *facie ecclesiae* was required and ecclesiastical penalties exacted. Claudio speedily disabuses Leonato by attacking Hero, who is shocked into near silence by his verbal onslaught.

Angered by the failure of his prudently approached marriage, and humiliated by the affront offered to both himself and Don Pedro, Claudio is blind to the truth. Even Hero's beauty becomes for him a snare:

> O Hero! what a Hero hadst thou been,
> If half thy outward graces had been placed
> About thy thoughts and counsels of thy heart!
> But fare thee well, most foul, most fair! Farewell,
> Thou pure impiety and impious purity!
> For thee I'll lock up all the gates of love,
> And on my eyelids shall conjecture hang,
> To turn all beauty into thoughts of harm,
> And never shall it more be gracious.
> (IV.i.98–106)

Leonato, with even less reason, since he has no "ocular proof" continues the accusation, even after Hero swoons, showing the same preoccupation as Claudio with deceiving appearances. He repeats the possessive pronoun "mine" time after time, as he berates his formerly beloved daughter whose matrimonial value has now fallen. As in the case of Lucrece, death for the lady is preferable to the dishonor of her family.

Both Leonato and Claudio are enraged that Hero's apparent actions are an attack upon them, but their motivations are slightly different. Leonato is a loving father, a traditional-minded one, who believes in the priceless value of his daughter's most precious jewel, her chastity. Claudio, however, looks upon Hero as a piece of private property, and in asserting his right to exclusive possession of his wife's body he cannot under any circumstances now go through with the marriage; if he were to condone the offense he might cast doubt on the legitimacy of both the marriage and any children yet to be born of it. He thinks only of himself and the failure of an investment, for his understanding of love is no deeper than his own self-contemplation and ambitious self image. In his lack of self-knowledge he is unworthy of Hero, and of love. He must undertake his own personal journey into the heart of self and be educated in order to find enlightenment and become love-worthy through the attainment of a charitable generosity that "seeketh not her own."

Despite these charges Hero acts with remarkable restraint and respect (IV.i.60ff.). She behaves as she has been taught, following the manner of a courtesy-book lady, and when her emotions become too overwhelming she swoons. She speaks only when spoken to; it is not her place to defend herself; this is not the time for a woman to argue; it is the place of men to rail, and a woman defends herself best by remaining silent, showing by her self-control and shamefast demeanor that the charges preferred against her are false. She follows the behavior of "the virtuous and godly Susanna," one of the most popular mirrors of feminine conduct in this regard. As Vives tells it:

> Saynte Susan excused her selfe of the cryme of adultery with sylence, and
> nat with wordes. Nowe let vs here Saynt Ambrose.
>   The holy woman Susan helde her peace and ouer came her enemyes:
> for she defended nat her selfe with reasonyng of wordes, nor with speche
> of any atturney, but the holy woman her selfe holdyng her tonge, her
> chastitee spake for her.[55]

It is as a result of Hero's shamefastness, together with his skillful observation of her behavior before her swoon, that the Friar decides to trust his instincts and become the champion of her innocence. Significantly, as a Christian believer, he would be expected to have some understanding of the virtue of *caritas* and a concomitant ability to pierce through appearance and comprehend the honesty within.

The plan for teaching and testing Claudio then commences, and Leonato, though not fully convinced, agrees to the deception that Hero is dead. At this point she becomes the passive agent of Claudio's education into love rather than an active principle. She is the catalyst who also brings en-lightenment to Benedick and Beatrice, by testing their affection for each oth-er. She is now the reference point for the play and around her reputation and fate the rest of the play revolves.

What, however, of Benedick and Beatrice, and what education in love does each of them require? To begin with, Benedick, in his account of the ideal lady claims to be just as conventional a character as Claudio, but he has gone further to become a cynical scoffer at love. Women, he claims, are by nature unchaste and certain in their infidelity, and therefore in his pride and self-love, he wants noth-ing to do with them:

> That woman conceived me, I thank her; that she brought me up, I like-wise give her most humble thanks; but that I will have a rechate winded in my forehead, or hang my bugle in an invisible baldrick, all women shall pardon me. Because I will not do them the wrong to mistrust any, I will do myself the right to trust none; and the fine is (for which I may go the finer), I will live a bachelor.

> (I.i.212–219)

He sees himself as a thoroughly rational misogynist, so aware of feminine faults that he will never bow under the yoke of matrimony. He wants perfection in womankind, and since he has deluded himself so far as to insist on this, he will not love. He must learn tolerance, to settle for the unpredictable joys of human imperfection.

Throughout the play Benedick is shown to be a gentleman, by contrast with Claudio. Early in the play Don Pedro assigns to him the specific Eliz-abethan attributes of the perfect gentleman,

> . . . of a noble strain, or approved valor, and confirmed honesty. . . .
> (II.i.336–337)

These are the outward signs: good lineage, and a ratification of that inheri-tance by valorous deeds and the moral virtue of unsmirched honesty.[56] In the possession of some of the moral and philosophical virtues of a true gentleman Benedick differs from his friend Claudio. For instance in the first scene of the play, the messenger notes that Benedick is "as pleasant as ever he was" (I.i.32–33), a remark which indicates the quality of benevolence, or kindness to his inferiors—high praise indeed. Likewise, Benedick is never shown as doing anyone a wrong; his pranks are relatively harmless, and unlike Claudio, he is quick to believe in Hero's innocence rather than her guilt. His wit and humor are never cruel and his criticism is never scathing. Even before his en-

trance Shakespeare prepares his audience by telling of his witty battles with
Beatrice, and Benedick does not disappoint. Every time he and Beatrice meet,
their clashing and yet similar personalities generate a sparkling display of
wit.

Benedick has more strength of character than Claudio, and he is the one
who suggests that Claudio fight back when he seems to have lost Hero to Don
Pedro. He is drawn as the cynic and professed hater of love who is certain
eventually to fall into that despised state. And when he does he contracts an
alliance which conforms to new and more liberal ideals of human behavior,
placing himself among those independent persons who extoll free, but not rash
choice. Thus Claudio, the conventional Elizabethan young man who marries
by arrangement, is contrasted unfavorably with Benedick who is a fine example
of the Renaissance gentleman as described (and idealized) in the courtesy books
of Italy and England. Rather than negotiating for a wife, Benedick finally
chooses Beatrice freely, preferring a virtuous and witty lady to one of tractability
and silence. But in order to reach this state he too needs education in love, and
Beatrice is one of the agents in this movement of spirit.

Like Benedick, Beatrice is intolerant of the faults of the opposite sex,
and in addition, asserts the equality, even the superiority of women. She will
not marry:

> Not till God make men of some other metal than earth. Would it not
> grieve a woman to be overmastered with a piece of valiant dust? to make an
> account of her life to a clod of wayward marl? No, uncle, I'll none. Adam's
> sons are my brethren, and truly I hold it a sin to match in my kindred.
> (II.i.51–56)

Beatrice's sentiments are found frequently in courtesy books which treat of
women's superiority. Heinrich Cornelius Agrippa (who wrote on both sides
of the woman question) claimed that the place of woman's creation, Paradise,
was inherently better than that of man.[57] Similarly, his follower, William
Bercher, maintained:

> . . . that yᵉ Begynnenge off woman / is ffar p̄fecter then of man by cawse
> Moses confessithe / that man was made of earthe / : and woman of ffleshe
> [:] and so moche as ffleshe is / more noble than earthe somoche is their
> beginnēge more excelent. / .[58]

Guazzo and others also comment that woman was made out of the side of man
to signify that she should not be trodden down, and should not be superior, but
instead treated as an equal, level with his heart.[59] And Beatrice certainly

agrees, insisting on her right of free choice in marriage.

She is the precise opposite of Hero, apparently an orphan, alone at the court, though under the protection of an uncle, and hence a young woman who must live by her wits. She also resembles earlier Shakespearean female characters like Kate in *The Taming of the Shrew* and the Merry Wives of Windsor in being dissatisfied with the social inferiority that conventions of the time demanded. Beatrice defies St. Paul's strictures in Ephesians 5 and insists upon her rights as a human person. By her very existence she demonstrates the superiority of the so-called "new woman" of the travellers' accounts over the silent, rather uninteresting, traditionally-educated Hero. To be sure, Beatrice possesses some of the more important moral virtues of the courtesy books: she is virtuous, wise, noble, and quick to right a wrong, beautiful, but by no means obedient or mild. Nothing is said of her riches or her ability in music, and therefore she does not meet Benedick's announced "requirements" for a wife. Even worse, from his point of view, she has the ill-repute of being too witty for her own good (II.i.18 ff.) and too proud to show affection (III.i.47–56). In fact, she uses her dazzling wit and brilliance in repartee as a means of hiding her heart. Guazzo's sober comment has some relevance here as a characterization of Beatrice:

> . . . where is least heart, is most tongue. And therefore silence in a woman is greatly commended; for it setteth her foorth muche, and maketh her thought to be verie wise.[60]

And Benedick obviously concurs in this judgment:

> O God, sir, here's a dish I love not. I cannot endure my Lady Tongue.
> (II.i.245–246)

He has good reason for this sentiment, because in nearly every one of their wit combats he is vanquished.

Like Kate in *The Taming of the Shrew* Beatrice wishes to assert her mastery and uphold her independence, but she uses the power of her intellect rather than ill temper. In this way she is also a development of the character of Portia, but with less sexual warmth and a more brittle wit. Even more important, she asserts herself as a female figure claiming power without benefit of disguise, the only major character of the mature comedies to present herself *in propria persona*. All the others spend at least some of the time disguised as men.[61]

Beatrice is most vocal in her refusal to consider marriage where she does

not love (II.i.45–48), but she is quite clearheaded about the dangers of rash
and sudden marriage:

> . . . For hear me, Hero: wooing, wedding, and repenting, is a Scotch jig,
> a measure, and a cinque-pace; the first suit is hot and hasty, like a Scotch
> jig (and full as fantastical); the wedding, mannerly modest, as a measure,
> full of state and ancientry; and then comes repentance and with his bad
> legs, falls into a cinque-pace faster and faster, till he sink into his grave.
> (II.i.63–69)

Shakespeare here inverts the *Quinze Joyes de Mariage* with additional irony,
by stating the situation from the woman's viewpoint. In her assertion of this
freedom, and in the exercise of her wit, Beatrice has often been compared with
the Lady Emilia Pia in Castiglione's *Book of the Courtier*, but she is even
more daring. There are similarities, to be sure, in that each is clever, rejoicing
in intellectual banter, but one must not forget that the Lady Emilia was automatically allowed more freedom by the fact of her marriage. In Castiglione's
day young unmarried women were automatically excluded from debates such
as those pictured in the court of Urbino. Such a salon was the province only of
married women. Another suggestion, by Barbara Lewalski, is that Benedick
and Beatrice follow Pietro Bembo's rules for rational lovers.[62] Perhaps so,
but the most notable thing about these two alleged haters of the opposite sex is
that they are both reacting against a combination of romantic posing and the
mercantilism of conventional marriages. They have allowed their knowledge
of the world and of human behavior to bring them perilously close to cyn-
icism and loss of faith in human nature. Like Claudio, they must be taught to
look beneath the exterior and see the reality of a faithful heart. They must
learn to allow desire to have some rein, though always tempered with reason.
Thus, in the course of the play they try various roles, even conforming to
some extent to the behavior of romantic lovers, sonnets and all, only to find
that for such rational lovers as they, love is not poetical, but rather an affection rooted in reciprocity, and refined by common sense. When they discover
that, they have become fit mates for each other.[63]

But these lovers whose god is their intellect and whose affection is hidden by barbed wit cannot admit love to heart (or liver) by any conventional
means, and hence they must be tricked into a recognition of affection, the one
for the other. Significantly, trickery is an important element in this play: Don
Pedro appears to trick Claudio; Don John tricks Claudio; the Friar, Leonato,
and Antonio combine with Beatrice and Benedick to trick Claudio; and finally,
the quarreling lovers are tricked into an engagement. Through this series of

tricks, the four main characters are forced to make a journey into their own hearts and there they find the truth about themselves, and perhaps other people. This pattern is, of course, less clear in the case of Hero, who remains a passive character throughout, and whose enlightenment is not shown. Claudio fails his first test in believing Pedro's treachery; he fails totally in the second test by doubting Hero, and passes only on the third attempt.

Benedick and Beatrice are tricked into self-examination when each is made aware of the alleged passion of the other, and their sufferings from *hereos*, the despairing disease of courtly love. This revelation instantly prompts each of the rational lovers to an intellectual re-evaluation of their past behavior: each reacts to a statement of personal faults and undertakes to reform. First, Benedick is appalled at the evil qualities attributed to him; he acknowledges his shortcomings, praises the virtues of the lady he had previously dispraised and vows to reciprocate her affection:

> . . . Happy are they that hear their detractions and can put them to mending. They say the lady is fair—'tis a truth, I can bear them witness; and virtuous—'tis so, I cannot reprove it; and wise, but for loving me—by my troth, it is no addition to her wit, nor no great argument of her folly, for I will be horribly in love with her. I may chance have some odd quirks and remnants of wit broken on me because I have railed so long against marriage; but doth not the appetite alter? A man loves the meat in his youth that he cannot endure in his age. Shall quips and sentences and these paper bullets of the brain awe a man from the career of his humor? No, the world must be peopled. . . .
>
> (II.iii.210–221)

And with this piece of concluding rationalization. Shakespeare is poking some sly wit at the traditional religious reasons for matrimony, beginning with the necessity of procreation. Now Benedick reveals a new gift for self-mockery rather than biting wit.

Similarly, Beatrice finds herself "condemned for pride and scorn" and determines to reform. Her spirits, described by Hero "as coy and wild / As haggards of the rock" (III.i.35–36), need to be curbed, and she recognizes the fact:

> And Benedick, love on; I will requite thee,
> Taming my wild heart to thy loving hand.
> If thou dost love, my kindness shall incite thee
> To bind our loves up in a holy band;
> For others say thou dost deserve, and I
> Believe it better than reportingly.
>
> (III.i.111–116)

She will renounce her own will for love of Benedick in a union in which each person respects the other. Certainly she has come a long way from her jocular listing of requirements for a husband:

> *Leonato*   Then half Signior Benedick's tongue in Count John's mouth,
> and half Count John's melancholy in Signior Benedick's face—
> *Beatrice*   With a good leg and a good foot, uncle, and money enough in
> his purse, such a man would win any woman in the world—if 'a
> could get her good will.
>
> (II.i.10–15)

Like Benedick, she now accepts without criticism the lover she has professed to despise.

The way to this safe haven of self-discovery is portrayed by Shakespeare in a merry spirit of mockery, this time at the expense of the romantic traditions of courtly love. As Benedick has previously claimed that Claudio was its victim, now the four plotters, Don Pedro, Leonato, Claudio, and Hero make use of the same tradition. "Methinks you are sadder," says Leonato, and the three gentlemen impute to Benedick the behavior discussed satirically by Cicero as quoted by Robert Burton:

> . . . Is this no small servitude for an enamorite to be every hour combing
> his head, stiffening his beard, perfuming his hair, washing his face with
> sweet waters, painting, curling, and not to come abroad but sprucely
> crowned, decked, and apparelled?[64]

But despite all this talk, Benedick's appearance, like that of Claudio, should not show any change when the play is staged in order to develop the visual irony. Similar behavior is also alleged of Beatrice—but her appearance should not alter appreciably:

> Then down upon her knees she falls, weeps, sobs, beats her heart, tears
> her hair, prays, curses—'O sweet Benedick! God give me patience!'
>
> (II.iii.137–139)

Even her possible suicide is hinted at. But the two lovers do not immediately fall into each other's arms. Further testing is yet to come, and it arises from the scene of Claudio's false accusation.

Beatrice, with her clever intuition, immediately perceives the possibility of a plot. She has had too long acquaintance with Hero to accept such a heinous allegation as truth, but she needs a champion, and naturally turns to Benedick. Here Shakespeare uses the conflict between competing codes of behavior—love and friendship. Beatrice imposes on Benedick a task fit for a romantic knight-errant: "Kill Claudio" (IV.i.285).

This scene is crucial in the history of Benedick's education into love, for it develops the idea of marriage as an exalted form of friendship more fully than in any earlier Shakespeare comedy. Whereas in the Sonnets the poet uses the language of love to celebrate friendship, here he does the reverse, using the language of friendship for love. When Beatrice offers much to the man who would revenge Hero's wrong, Benedick, who has already shown his decency in rejecting the accusation asks:

> Benedick   Is there any way to show such friendship?
> Beatrice   A very even way, but no such friend.
> (IV.i.260–261)

Tentatively, they move into talk of love, but after they have exchanged their vows of affection Beatrice, in imposing the task of vengeance upon Benedick is testing her lover, asking him to demonstrate total commitment to her and to justice, even if this means the sacrifice of a friendship. The obligations of love are superior to the claims of friendship:

> You dare easier be friends with me than fight with mine enemy.
> (IV.i.295–296)

Benedick's momentary hesitation calls forth a barrage of words from Beatrice insisting on the innocence of Hero, and bewailing her own femininity:

> O God, that I were a man! I would eat his heart in the market place.
> . . . .
> O that I were a man for his sake! or that I had any friend would be a man for my sake! But manhood is melted into cursies, valor into compliment, and men are only turned into tongue, and trim ones too. He is now as valiant as Hercules that only tells a lie, and swears it. I cannot be a man with wishing; therefore I will die a woman with grieving.
> (IV.i.302, 311–318)

Here Shakespeare piquantly exploits the original casting of the play with a boy actress, but at the same time he is expressing a surprisingly modern concept of marriage in terms of reciprocity, mutuality of interests, and friendship, as Beatrice finally persuades Benedick to take a leap of faith in her judgment, accept the task and follow the course of justice. He has believed in Hero's innocence and has said so, but the thought of action has never entered his head. Beatrice is, more the man than he, and now she has taught him to look beyond himself and his love problems and shown him that his new obligation to her requires him to right a wrong. Yet Benedick is also humoring her, because both these

lovers know that Hero is not dead, and a more sensible approach would certainly
be to find out the truth, rather than to undertake a duel. Benedick is now no
longer Signior Mountanto, not a man of mere words, but someone actively
committed to justice and love.

The two aspects of the play now come together. The triple challenges by
Leonato, Antonio, and finally Benedick, bring no repentance to the hearts of
Claudio or Don Pedro. They are satisfied, smugly so, in fact:

> *Pedro*   My heart is sorry for your daughter's death;
> But on mine honor she was charged with nothing
> But what was true, and very full of proof.
> (V.i.103–105)

As they see things, justice has been served, and Hero's death is fit punishment
for unchastity. Only with the revelation of her innocence does Claudio come
to an appreciation of the enormity of his action. For the first time in the play
he shows his potential for development as he proceeds "through repentance,
penance, and faith,"[65] to enlightenment. Hero, then, should now be perceived as the passive agent of Claudio's education in matters of the spirit.

Yet Claudio is not yet ready for the reward of love and he needs further
testing, like Benedick, to prove the truth of his moral improvement. Leonato
lays what is in effect a fairly heavy penalty on Claudio, since he has expressed
heartfelt sorrow for his action, but his final exculpatory comment indicates the
need for further penance:

> . . . yet sinned I not,
> But in mistaking.
> (V.i.261–262)

Now he must, by public confession of Hero's innocence in effect accuse himself of fault, and in an ironic inversion of the sonnet-writing traditionally expected of a romantic lover, he must write an epitaph on Hero's "grave." This
he does, and indicates the depth of his desire to make satisfaction, or restitution, insofar as that be possible, by vowing to go beyond Leonato's requirement, promising to make a yearly penitential pilgrimage to the lady's monument.

Finally, he must submit to an arranged marriage, and this is in effect an
act of faith similar to that which Beatrice had asked of Benedick. Claudio must
now trust Leonato, the man he has wronged, in order to gain an even richer
matrimonial prize. Leonato indeed twists the knife in the wound by insisting
that this lady, Hero's "cousin" is heir to the fortune of both him and his

brother, Antonio. He also insists, with apparent distrust, that Claudio go through with his blind bargain without seeing the lady beforehand. All these conditions Claudio agrees to, and then in his betrothal words to the masked Hero he shows a new humility, in sharp contrast to the words of his earlier espousal. This time he says "I am your husband if you like of me" (V.iv.59).

Claudio, then, is shown as a young man of potential who has advanced in virtue because of the virtue of a woman. So too has Benedick, whom Beatrice has shown that love does not arise from the sonnet writing he performs so lamentably, but in service. Claudio's spiritual development is even more marked, and clearly Shakespeare expects us to consider that he has now become a worthy husband for the gentle Hero.[66] It has often been objected that Hero is treated unfairly in being married to Claudio at the end of the play, an act that seems devoid of rationality. However, as Nadine Page properly points out, in Elizabethan law, she cannot marry any other man but Claudio. He has repudiated her, certainly, but with the disqualification of the evidence, the impediment of antenuptial unchastity has been removed and the original spousal thus continues in force. Hence, Claudio could not claim mistaken identity as an impediment on the discovery that he has betrothed himself once more to the same woman. In addition, had both of them decided to void the original contract, then Hero herself would not be a good matrimonial bargain. No matter how strong the protestations of the young man concerning Hero's innocence, who would believe him—or her, for that matter. What is more important than all these legalities is the moral development of Claudio. We, the audience, are expected to forgive him and rejoice in his marriage to Hero, whose patience and passive virtue have helped educate him.

Finally, the quarelling lovers come to the altar themselves. Benedick has proved his constancy and Beatrice her loyalty, but the last step of reciprocal humility is yet to come, and as before, a trick is required: the discovery of their mutual sonnets and the public revelation of their love. In their vows, in words of the present tense, they continue their ironic game: Benedick will "take thee for pity," while Beatrice quickwittedly answers in terms of their alleged *hereos*:

> I would not deny you; but by this good day, I yield upon great persuasion,
> and partly to save your life, for I was told you were in a consumption.
>
> (V.iv.93–96)

They understand the reality beneath the appearance and can mock romantic pretensions whose appearance and form count for more than truth, and hence they are rational enough to laugh at excessive passion. They have learned the art of detachment and the truth of commitment by means of their own testing. They are intellectuals and will work together in reciprocal equality; they know the nature of love and the necessity of reason, as Claudio has learned that excessive prudence must also be tempered with passion. Both sets of lovers have thus moved toward a middle ground, and into marriages which signify permanence and harmony. The conclusion with music and a dance indicate the harmonious correspondence with the cosmos that marriage is in terms of humankind.[67]

Throughout this play Shakespeare makes use of comparison and contrast, employing matrimonial law as plot device, and showing the shortcomings of restrictive social conventions and romantic transports. He demonstrates that true and tested love leads men and women to a union that is analagous to that of Christ and His Church. The movement of spirit that gives form to this play is not that of mystical neoplatonic union with the ultimate being, but rather the achievement of a reciprocal charity of human love which "seeketh not her own" and is not proud. The only persons unenlightened and unmoved in the course of the play are those to whom no love-relationship is vouchsafed, the clowns, and the villainous Don John, all of whom remain in a limbo-world, while Leonato, Antonio, and the lovers celebrate the knitting of souls and bodies in marriage.

The play thus concludes with the promise of satisfied sexuality, and the pivotal problem of the play, suspected fornication, is resolved in virtuous marriage, but only after the young men have been taught the truth of love by their women. The mutual acceptance of male and female sexuality will come with the consummation of the marriage. Each pair of lovers has tested society's norms and has finally reached an accommodation with them. The men have demonstrated potential for growth and change, and the happiness of both couples seems assured. The feminine world of love, marriage, and sparkling social discourse has triumphed over prudent mercantilism; the villainy of Don John has been temporarily vanquished, if only by chance, and rationality has triumphed over posing.

SECTION 3
All's Well That Ends Well—The Rights of Matrimony[68]

All's Well That Ends Well shares two things with *Much Ado About Nothing*: a singularly unlikeable masculine character and an emphasis on matrimonial law as central plot device. If ever a young man needed education in loveworthiness, it is Bertram, and for much of the play one wonders why Helena exercises such ingenuity in securing him as a mate. In fact the conclusion of the play can even leave doubts as to whether all does indeed end well with their marriage now consummated and ratified into permanent union.

The emphasis on matrimonial law and contracting also allies *All's Well* with that other problem play of the period (1602–04), *Measure for Measure*, with which it also shares the theme of human sexuality. The two are also transitional, experimental works, serious but not satirical plays, which show an imperfect conflation of cerebral material and comic form, forced into an uneasy alliance by ingenious use of legalistic means. *All's Well* represents a curious mixture of romantic and bourgeois comedy, folk-tale, matrimonial law, and some qualities of Christian morality, while *Measure for Measure* combines Italianate intrigue comedy with matrimonial law and Christianity to develop a quasi-theological case for Christian charity.

In some ways, perhaps because of their emphasis on strictly interpreted sexual *mores*, these two plays are today somewhat outmoded in an age where solutions to the difficulties of the principal characters are infinitely more simple, more direct, and certainly less conducive to guilt. The shock felt by Victorian critics (and others) over the bed-tricks is not shared by a modern audience, while Isabella's dilemma rarely strikes a responsive chord in either men or women, and the reaction to Helena's tricking Bertram into marriage and then its consummation is sometimes one of bemusement that she might even desire such a poor bargain.[69]

Both of these plays illustrate the strength of woman's love, and even more important, feminine sexuality in its wish for fulfillment through procreation, renewal, and human continuance. But in the context of the action these qualities and desires can legitimately be satisfied only within marriage. For this reason the plotting of these dramas depends on a knowledge of English matrimonial practice, a factor which has gone almost unnoticed in *All's Well That Ends Well*, though it forms a major part of *Measure for Measure* criticism.[70] Certainly W. W. Lawrence mentions it in his study; and G. K.

Hunter appends some thought-provoking annotations to the Arden edition. But in general, critics pay too much attention to the nature of the bed-trick and insufficient to the nature of matrimonial contracting as it is used to explain the actions of Bertram and Helena, to contribute to their characterization, and finally to unravel the confusion of Act V and reveal the underlying order and thematic significance of the play.

Helena from the first is quite clear concerning her desires and shows a full understanding of the difficulties facing her as she carefully works to achieve a marriage with Bertram. First she must bridge the gap of rank, for Bertram is of noble birth, while she is the orphaned and dowerless daughter of a mere physician, in Shakespeare's day considered little better than a tradesman. Her priceless asset, and one that is slowly revealed through her conduct, is her possession of that true nobility which arises from virtue. Lineage itself means little when each member of a family is expected to ratify gentle birth by good conduct. As G. K. Hunter puts it: "*shape, blood,* and *birthright* are what one inherits; *manners, virtue,* and *goodness* are what one achieves."[71]

She is also a character of redemptive force, the feminine center of the play, who looks backward to the manipulative heroines of the mature comedies and ahead to the young women of the late Romances. In fact this characteristic tempted G. Wilson Knight to date this play among the romances.[72] Robert Grams Hunter notes a mythic substructure with Helena related to the healer of the fisher king and then becoming the restorer of life to the dying worlds of France and Rossillion. His further suggestion that her Shakespearean name (instead of Giletta as in the source) is meant to recall St. Helena, the finder of the True Cross, also develops the resonance of a morality play with Helena as Grace and Bertram as unredeemed man.[73] The folklore background investigated by W. W. Lawrence additionally allies her to the "clever wench" tradition, and also helps to illuminate aspects of the bed-trick. But she also represents an inversion of another folklore heroine, patient Griselda who must prove herself worthy of her aristocratic husband. In Shakespeare the lady is the active educational force of the play.

Dramatically, the play also represents a response to prevailing English dramatic taste in its use of two themes commonly found in Citizen or Bourgeois Comedy: the prodigal son and "social mobility and opportunism."[74] Helena certainly represents the intelligent girl of low degree who manages to translate her dreams into actuality, with an admixture of the romantic heroine for whom love supplies the strength to conquer all obstacles.

Small wonder then, that with such density and multiplicity of resonance,

Helena is hard to categorize, while the play, because of its singular inclusiveness is sometimes considered "in some sort a failure."[75] Helena in her central role is awarded a multiplicity of tasks: (1) she must heal the king in order to achieve title to Bertram; (2) she must educate her aristocratic young husband to be her equal in virtue; (3) she must bring him to an understanding of his sexual role; (4) she must ensure the validity of her marriage by fulfillment of the conditions laid down by her husband; (5) she must bring him to a free and unforced consent to the consummated union through his learning the nature of love. Above all, Helena is a profoundly sexual being; no cold virgin she, but a virtuous flesh and blood woman whose aim in the play is to fulfill her function of feminine fertility by losing her virginity to someone who pleases her.[76] This aspect of her character is revealed early in the action through the frequently criticized exchange with Parolles:

> *Helena*   . . . Man is enemy to virginity; how may we barricado it
> against him?
> *Parolles* Keep him out.
> *Helena*   But he assails, and our virginity, though valiant, in the defense
> yet is weak. Unfold to us some warlike resistance.
> *Parolles* There is none. Man setting down before you will undermine
> you and blow you up.
> *Helena*   Bless our poor virginity from underminers and blowers-up! Is
> there no military policy how virgins might blow up men?
> *Parolles* Virginity being blown down, man will quicklier be blown up;
> Marry, in blowing him down again, with the breach yourselves
> made you lose your city. It is not politic in the commonwealth
> of nature to preserve virginity. Loss of virginity is rational
> increase, and there was never virgin got till virginity was first
> lost. . . .
>
>   (I.i.108–124)

This debate is by no means a blot on the fair fame of an innocent girl, nor is it gratuitous bawdy. It indicates the clever wit of a young woman who is able to discuss the war between the sexes in the same terms·as those of a military operation, another masculine *rite de passage*. At the same time it shows the intense physical desire which motivates Helena in her quest for possession of Bertram, something that was earlier masked in her religious metaphor of an "idolatrous fancy / [that] Must sanctify his relics" (I.i.93–94). Then she had less ambition, seeing Bertram as "a bright particular star"

>   . . . so far above me.
> In his bright radiance and collateral light
> Must I be comforted, not in his sphere.

> Th'ambition in my love thus plagues itself:
> The hind that would be mated by the lion
> Must die for love. . . .
>
> (I.i.83–88)

But after the interlude with Parolles she thinks differently and decides to take action to achieve fulfillment of her passion:

> . . . Who ever strove
> To show her merit that did miss her love?
> The king's disease—my project may deceive me,
> But my intents are fixed and will not leave me.
>
> (I.i.218–221)

This same tension between chastity and desire is developed in Helena's interview with the Countess, who herself still remembers the passion of her youth. In answer to the Countess's question, Helena reveals her love, but insists that she will not possess Bertram sexually until she deserves him, using the image of a "captious and untenible sieve" (I.iii.195) into which she pours the waters of love. Emblematically, the sieve is one of the attributes of chastity, and also of discernment, or testing. Cesare Ripa in his *Iconologia* illustrates this virtue as a vestal virgin to commemorate the account in Pliny (*Natural History*, Book 28, chapter 12) of Tuscia, or Tuccia, who proved herself innocent of the charge of infidelity by carrying water in a sieve.[77] Thus Helena is also speaking of testing, of discernment, of making herself worthy of Bertram, but her speech concludes with an outburst of controlled passion, when she begs the Countess's help after indicating the idolatry of her love:

> . . . but if yourself
> Whose agèd honor cites a virtuous youth,
> Did ever in so true a flame of liking,
> Wish chastely and love dearly, that your Dian
> Was both herself and Love, O, then give pity
> To her whose state is such that cannot choose
> But lend and give where she is sure to lose;
> That seeks not to find that her search implies,
> But riddle-like lives sweetly where she dies.
>
> (I.iii.202–210)

The chastity to which Helena aspires, however, is that of "married chastity," the sexual exclusivity of a virtuous wife. For this she will exercise love's usury, lending and giving without hope of return; she can but die of her love, when in fact she would prefer another sort of death, in sexual consummation.

Moved by this appeal, the Countess treats Helena as the daughter she has in effect always been to her, and now wishes she could literally become, in marriage to Bertram. She questions Helena, testing her to discern the quality of her love and the nature of her plans, leaving her with hope: "What I can help thee to, thou shalt not miss" (I.iii.249). Helena will now proceed to the court to attempt to cure the king and there in that "learning place," she will help bring Bertram to maturity and administer to him the education he so desperately needs.[78] In so doing she proves herself very much the "clever wench" in her interesting exercise of law and legal quibbles in gaining possession of her rightful husband.[79]

Matrimonial law thus becomes important for an understanding of Helena and her actions. This play is no exception to the rule enunciated earlier that in his depiction of the law of marriage Shakespeare essentially followed current practice in Elizabethan and Jacobean England where the view of Gratian was still held: a matrimonial contract effected *matrimonium initiatum* only, and physical consummation was necessary for *matrimonium ratum*, a marriage made quite indissoluble by sacramental symbolism. The bed-trick thus constitutes nothing that is intrinsically immoral, since its aim and successful outcome is to gain performance on a bond, and bring about the ratification of a perfectly legal contract. John C. Bean suggests that "What shocks us is not the bed-trick itself, or any subtle problem of ethics, but the collusion of the human and the mechanical."[80] To some extent, then, Helena's careful planning of an event that matters emotionally and erotically to her, seems too businesslike. But Shakespeare has long been accustomed to employing the language of business to love's usury. Beauty unspent is "unthrifty," worthless, because it leaves nothing of value to the world (Sonnet 4), which, as Benedick said "must be peopled." Marriage, and consequent loss of virginity, is an investment that yields an excellent return. In the words of Parolles:

> Out with't! Within ten year it will make itself ten, which is a goodly increase, and the principal itself not much worse. Away with't!
>
> (I.i. 142–144)

The capture of the immature, unwilling Bertram is the first task for Helena to fulfill. But before proceeding further, a few comments about this foolish and ambitious young man are essential because there are some extenuating circumstances which mitigate his actions and explain his apparently reprehensible behavior. One must allow him some very real justification for his opposition to the marriage the King of France forces upon him.[81] As the son of a deceased nobleman, Bertram is a royal ward, under the direct control, and even the gift of the monarch, who could assign him to the care of an appointed guardian who would manage his estates. One major duty of a guardian was to arrange a suitable marriage for a ward, but always subject to two limitations: equality of rank, and consentual freedom of the ward.

The original idea of wardship was actually very sensible, for it aimed at preserving the estates of a nobleman from mismanagement and misuse by dishonest staff, a foolish minor, or predatory relatives. In actual fact, however, it could substitute one kind of wastage for another, and wardships in England and elsewhere were often lucrative investments for nobleman. Joel Hurstfield says that King Henry VII made considerable profit out of this revivified institution. Similarly, Lord Burleigh, Queen Elizabeth's Master of the Wards, managed to arrange marriages for his wards which were profitable to him— and he was considered a conscientious officer. Even in the famous household of Sir Thomas More in the 1520s where wards were treated with kindness and their education and estates administered with care and consideration, the Lord Chancellor married his son to one of the wealthy wards in his care[82]

The King of France here violates the two major duties of guardianship: in effect he "sells" Bertram's marriage in payment for his own cure, marries him to a woman of inferior rank, and enforces his will through intimidation and threats sufficient to put fear of death into a strong man (*metus qui posset in virum constantem cadere*). In England "a ward who was threatened with disparagement [of rank through an unworthy marriage] . . . could appeal to the medieval centuries and to the law,"[83] according to Hurstfield, who offers Bertram's case in evidence, but is unable to find a relevant English lawsuit in protest against the situation.[84] The second matter, that of enforcement, is even more important because it violates the doctrine of "espresse and free consente of both partyes,"[85] and could render a marriage null and void *ab initio*, even if the union had been consummated.[86] However, to judge from the history of drama, enforced marriage was fairly common in England, with misery the frequent result. That Shakespeare intends this situation to be important is signified by the way in which he changed his source:

> The enforcement motif has been heightened . . . , and Bertram's neglect follows more dramatically from this motivation. . . . Perhaps we should today regard Bertram in the light of seventeenth-century attitudes which explained his behavior as a victim of a king's will unjustly imposed through the prerogatives of wardship.[87]

On her arrival at court to practise her healing function Helena hides the true nature of her errand, though she does use her Rossillion connection to gain audience with the king through the influence of Lafew. He leaves Helena with the king after a curious reference to himself as "Cressid's uncle" (II.i.97); and in a sense he is just that at some remove, by indirectly bringing Helena and Bertram together. Her curing by means of a secret recipe left by her father, as precious as "a triple eye," introduces a mythic, folkloric quality to Helena. She, a young virgin, is aided by beneficent powers in the performance of her therapeutic miracle. She is also a gambler, risking and hazarding her most precious possessions, honor and life, on the success of her venture. If she fails her punishment should be

> Tax of impudence,
> A strumpet's boldness, a divulgèd shame
> Traduced by odious ballads; my maiden's name
> Seared otherwise; nay, worse of worst, extended
> With vilest torture let my life be ended.
> (II.i.170–174)

Persuaded that she is indeed the vessel of "a blessed spirit" the king agrees to the cure, and in this manner Helena's own virtue is also tested.

In setting marriage as her price for success, she shows her clear understanding of her disadvantages of ignoble birth and poverty; this last is an addition to the Boccaccio source where Giletta was a wealthy heiress. Again, Helena speaks in terms of sexuality as she denies a wish to "propagate" her "low and humble name" with royalty. She refuses three out of four lords with such grace that even the experienced courtier Lafew fails to realize what she is doing, but when she comes to Bertram she offers herself with words of humility and total feminine submission:

> I dare not say I take you, but I give
> Me and my service, ever whilst I live,
> Into your guiding power.—This is the man.
> (II.iii.101–103)

Obviously this speech is a classic statement of a *de praesenti* spousal, but with the unusual variation in which the woman speaks first, adding a slight change dictated by humility in the first line. Here Helena's consciousness of role reversal in initiating the contracting, together with her hypersensitive awareness of the social gulf between her and Bertram, leads her to change the words slightly from "I *take* thee for my wife, or husband," though the intent and meaning remain the same.

The king, standing *in loco parentis*, promptly gives his blessing and consent to the match: "Why then, young Bertram, take her; she's thy wife" (II.ii. 104). The use of the word "wife" is noteworthy; although espousals did not confer all the rights of marriage, the titles "wife" and "husband" were frequently used for betrothed couples, even if they were well under the age for consummation of the union, canonical majority being considered fourteen for boys and twelve for girls. Bertram's reply is one that has on occasion incensed critics even though the young man is asking nothing more than the right to choose his own wife rather than having one forced upon him. With some justice, he fails to understand why he should pay the price for his guardian's cure:

> My wife, my liege? I shall beseech your highness,
> In such a business give me leave to use
> The help of mine own eyes.
>   (II.iii.105–107)

In desperation he looks for reasons to make the match unsuitable, beginning with difference in rank and fortune:

> I know her well;
> She had her breeding at my father's charge.
> A poor physician's daughter my wife? Disdain
> Rather corrupt me ever!
>   (II.iii.112–115)

The king promptly dismisses that possibility by offering to give Helena both title and money, pointing out that she already has the attributes of spiritual nobility. He rebukes Bertram for his false values in equating nobility with rank and wealth instead of virtue, claiming that Helena is more than fit to be the young man's bride:

> She is young, wise, fair;
> In these to nature she's immediate heir;
> And these breed honor. This is honor's scorn,
> Which challenges itself as honor's born
> And is not like the sire. Honors thrive,
> When rather from our acts we them derive
> Than our foregoers. . . .
> . . . .
> If thou canst like this creature as a maid,
> I can create the rest. Virtue and she
> Is her own dower; honor and wealth from me.
>   (II.iii.130–142)

Once again Shakespeare insists on virtue as the true nobility, and these words recall the Countess's farewell speech to her son, about whose stability she clearly had doubts:

> Be thou blessed, Bertram, and succeed they father
> In manners as in shape! Thy blood and virtue
> Contend for empire in thee, and thy goodness
> Share with thy birthright. . . .
> . . . .
> 'Tis an unseason'd courtier. Good my lord,
> Advise him.
>
> (I.i.57–67)

In this speech the Countess summarizes the internal action of the play. Manners, virtue, and goodness are qualities Helena possesses in abundance, but Bertram has not yet achieved them.

The reluctant bridegroom then seeks for another reason: "I cannot love her, nor will strive to do't" (II.iii.143), and to some extent his reaction is comprehensible. He knows Helena altogether too well, for she has been brought up like a sister to him, and he may never have thought of her as a sexual partner. Indeed, such a relationship might seem almost incestuous to him. In addition, he has just escaped from a house of mourning and the care of his mother at Rossillion; for the first time he is beginning to get a taste for pleasure and the freedom available to him at court. The last thing he needs is to be auctioned off as the husband of the king's savior. Also, Helena is too much like his own mother, and Bertram is currently trying to separate himself from the maternal calling of woman's love.[88] So here we have a double incest taboo.

Despite Helena's attempt to withdraw her offer and refuse her bargain, the king remains adamant, threatening the young man with punishment and loss of royal favor, asserting his prerogative as guardian to insist upon the union (II.iii.148–165). This threat brings Bertram to heel, and so with a very bad grace he speaks words of apparent acquiescence:

> Pardon, my gracious lord; for I submit
> My fancy to your eyes. When I consider
> What creation and dole of honor
> Flies where you bid it, I find that she, which late

Was in my nobler thoughts most base, is now
The praisèd of the king; who, so ennobled,
Is as 'twere born so.

(II.iii.166–172)

Bertram then takes the lady's hand, saying merely "I take her hand" (II.iii.175), an action the king obviously takes as an act of handfasting and outward sign of consent. No further words are exchanged, but they were not necessary for a binding contract, as Henry Swinburne notes:

> . . . albeit neither of the Parties express any words at all, but some *third* person recite the words of the Contract, willing them if they be content, to joyn their hands together, or to embrace each other; the Parties so doing, the Contract is of like Efficacy, as if they themselves had mutually expressed the words before recited by the Third Person.[89]

The king, in giving his blessing and consent as Bertram's guardian, takes the joining of hands as free and unforced consent on both sides, and the rest of the court act as witnesses. Neither nuptial kisses nor rings are exchanged, but the words of the king indicate that he considers a contract to have been made:

Good fortune and the favor of the king
Smile upon this contract, whose ceremony
Shall seem expedient on the now-born brief,
And be performed to-night. The solemn feast
Shall more attend upon the coming space,
Expecting absent friends. As thou lov'st her,
Thy love's to me religious; else, does err.

(II.iii.176–182)

Such a ceremony of spousing was, of course, followed by a religious ceremony *in facie ecclesiae*. Usually, in Elizabethan England, banns would have been called; but in many cases, including Shakespeare's own marriage, the banns were dispensed with. It was this ceremony *in facie ecclesiae*—and not the *sponsalia per verba de praesenti*—that actually conferred all the rights and physical privileges of matrimony.[90] William Harrington's statement to this effect was as true in Shakespeare's day as it had been in 1528.[91] If, however, the betrothed couple did consummate their contract before the church ceremony, the sin was generally considered venial rather than mortal, because of the existence of the contract.[92] Nevertheless, the Church would still insist upon the ceremony, and ecclesiastical penalties could be imposed.

The king thus proposes that the church ceremony be held that very evening, and that the wedding banquet, a purely social appendage, be postponed until a later date. Apparently the religious service takes place almost immediately, because later in the same scene Lafew enters with "Sirrah, your lord and master's married; there's news for you. You have a new mistress" (II.iii.257–258). Bertram also reinforces this evidence that public espousals have been ratified *in facie ecclesiae*:

> Bertram Although before the solemn priest I have sworn,
>   I will not bed her.
> Parolles What? what, sweetheart?
> Bertram O my Parolles, they have married me!
>   I'll to the Tuscan wars and never bed her.
>
>   (II.iii.263–267)

And so he departs for the wars to initiate himself into manhood, leaving Helena waiting to initiate herself into marriage. This action is usually taken as singularly reprehensible, but Bertram is, in fact, taking the only practical course open to him. The religiously ratified *de praesenti* matrimonial contract that he has just entered into is binding and almost indissoluble, but the important element of consummation is lacking. Should Bertram avoid cohabitation and refuse to consummate the marriage, then he would still have the possibility of escape on several grounds: (1) consent obtained by threats sufficient to arouse fear in a strong man; (2) consent obtained through respect for authority (*per metus reverentialis*); (3) mental reservation at the time of the ceremony;[93] (4) refusal to consummate the marriage indicated by a three-year absence from the province, or a two-year absence within the province.[94] Therefore, one may say that by refusing to go to bed with Helena, Bertram is doing the only sensible thing under the circumstances, because the act of consummation could be considered the outward sign of consent on both sides. He would then be condemned without legal recourse to indissoluble marriage with his unloved wife. It is interesting to note that Bertram can on occasion disobey the king, but only in his guardian's absence. In both the espousal scene of Act II and the concluding scene of Act V he is quite unable to protest satisfactorily when the king is present.

The central emphasis in the matrimonial affairs of the play now shifts from Bertram to Helena, and the remainder of the plot is concerned with what W. W. Lawrence called the theme of the "clever wench" or "the fulfilling of the task." In the manner of a truly obedient wife, Helena at first acquiesces in Bertram's desire to postpone consummation of the match. She then leaves the court to return to the only home she has ever known, Rossillion, where she is shown to have gained the consent of the Countess herself, who also stands *in loco parentis* to Helena: "It hath happened all as I would have had it, save that he comes not with her" (III.ii.1–2). At this time Shakespeare plays on the sympathies of his audience by even having the Countess comment disparagingly on the conduct of her own son and praise the virtues of Helena. All blame is now fastened on Bertram, and Helena is all-praised—and decidedly resourceful.

Bertram's letter to his mother is exactly what one would expect, and it is significant that this is the first time the young man has put a statement of his attitudes and proposed actions in writing:

> 'I have sent you a daughter-in-law; she hath recovered the king and undone me. I have wedded her, not bedded her; and sworn to make the "not" eternal. You shall hear I am run away; know it before the report come. If there be breadth enough in the world, I will hold a long distance. My duty is to you.'
>
> (III.ii.19–24)

This letter is Shakespeare's addition to his Boccaccio source and it serves two purposes: it could be excellent evidence for the annulment of the marriage, and it gains further sympathy for Helena when she reads Bertram's accompanying letter of conditions:

> 'When thou canst get the ring upon my finger which never shall come off, and show me a child begotten of thy body that I am father to, then call me husband; but in such a "then" I write a "never." '
>
> (III.ii.56–59)

Such conditions are of course typical of those in the "clever wench" genre of folktales so admirably described by Lawrence, but the letter can also be read as a conditional espousal added to the earlier, public, and unwilling one. It will be recalled that such conditions were not supposed to be impossible or to cause grave sin, and Bertram is saying nothing more than that he will refuse to accept the *title* of husband until he has *acted* as Helena's husband, consummated the marriage—which he has so far obstinately refused to do—and begotten a child on Helena. All that Helena does from that time is to find a way to fulfill Bertram's conditions, to obtain her conjugal rights, and to lose her virginity to her own "liking," a situation entirely different from that described in *Measure for Measure*. We now have the picture of a woman desperately in love who wants quite frankly to consummate her marriage and is prepared to go almost any lengths in order to do so.[95] Certainly the means she uses to obtain her end seem to arise rather too much from coincidence—but there Shakespeare was following his source. But his interpretation of this part of Boccaccio's tale is original, and one cannot fail to note how carefully Shakespeare makes the material fit English patterns of spousing. This is particularly important in examining the implications of Bertram's alleged sexual relations with Diana.

Helena now has a set of tasks which are both literal and psychological. On the literal level she must fulfill the stipulations of Bertram, and also ensure the validity of her marriage, and on the psychological she must educate him to appreciate her virtue and understand his own sexual role. Only then will he be able to give his free and unforced consent to the union. Helena, then is also undertaking a task analogous to the miraculous cure of the king—the psychological and moral cure of Bertram. Above all else, she needs to gain his love, and in order to do so she sets up situations which force him to confront himself and assess his actions with a new maturity.

In his flight from court to test himself at the wars, Bertram embarks on his journey toward maturity. He proves himself on the battlefield, and then tries to prove himself sexually by soliciting Diana. The careful intercutting of the Helena-Diana aspect of the plot with that of Parolles is important here, because in effect they echo each other. In the discomfiture of the coward he had taken to be courageous, Bertram discovers what Helena has always known about him: he looks only at the surface of things. Similarly, in the bedroom where Helena substitutes herself for Diana, he does not see the reality beneath the appearance.

This assignation is actually a brilliant piece of planning on Helena's part, because in addition to Bertram's desire to avoid an indissoluble matrimonial union, he may be afraid of failing in his first sexual encounter. Helena is too competent, too maternal, and intercourse with her also has the implications of an incestuous relationship with a "sister." Thus the episode with "Diana" is important because it brings Bertram to lose his virginity and prove himself sexually in the belief that he is following the traditional way of a soldier with a prostitute or chance acquaintance. Helena's insistence on secrecy and exchange of rings thus has significance over and above the fulfillment of Bertram's task: he now has the evidence that he need no longer fear impotence before Helena, while she has evidence of the consummation. Thus she initiates Bertram into sex, and later into love, by saving him from the apparent consequences of his lust. Only when he learns humility through self-knowledge will he be a fit husband for Helena and accept her willingly and *thankfully* as his wife.

In the last scene of Act V the entire court of France is mourning the supposed death of Helena, and in a situation reminiscent of *Much Ado About Nothing* a second match is proposed as a consolation prize for the young man who has learned the worth of his jilted lady too late:

> . . . she whom all men praised and whom myself
> Since I have lost, have loved, was in mine eye
> The dust that did offend it.
>
> (V.iii.53–55)

As with Claudio, these sentiments should be taken at their face value, and like him, Bertram has come to feel repentance for his action. He has also become more mature and less hasty since the revelation of Parolles's cowardice and pusillanimity has awakened him to his own lack of perception and faulty character judgment. That the audience is expected to forgive him and see him as greatly changed is shown by the fact that Lafew, who has been the moralist of the court, is pleased to allow the marriage of his daughter, Maudlin (whom we never see), to Bertram.

Thus, in the public spousal scene with the substitute lady, a scene which parallels the earlier one of II.iii, Bertram's behavior shows considerable alteration. Instead of protest there is deference and and obedience to his guardian's wishes (V.iii.36–37). The king expresses a desire for the match, and "The main consents are had" (V.iii.69). In other words the king and countess as guardian and parent of Bertram, Lafew as father to the young woman, and Bertram have all agreed, while Maudlin is reported as consenting to the match. Lafew then asks for the usual token, and Bertram naturally gives a ring from his finger—but it is the ring given him in bed by the supposed Diana, and both courtier and king recognize it as the royal gift to Helena, to be sent to the monarch if ever she were to need help.

Thus at the moment Bertram thinks himself safe from an unwanted wife and restored to the king's favor, his hopes are dashed. Unknown to him, Helena has more tests for her young husband; at first he fails, by concocting a self-serving lie that the ring was given him by a noble Florentine lady who refused its return. The king's suspicions are aroused to the extent of wondering whether the unwilling bridegroom might not have done away with his unwanted wife (V.iii.115–120). As Bertram tries desperately to squirm out of the situation he ironically states the truth that he "husbanded her in Florence." On top of these revelations, a letter arrives from Diana in which she claims that Bertram is now legally contracted to her:

'Upon his many protestations to marry me when his wife was dead, I blush to say it, he won me. Now is the Count Rossillion a widower, his vows are forfeited to me, and my honor's paid to him. He stole from Florence, taking no leave, and I follow him to his country for justice: grant it to me, O king! In you it best lies; otherwise a seducer flourishes, and a poor maid is undone. Diana Capilet.'

(V.iii.139–147)

Shakespeare has already prepared the audience for Bertram's discomfiture in the preceding act when he has Diana, at Helena's behest, propose an exchange of rings as her price for entertaining him:

When you have conquered my yet maiden bed,
Remain there but an hour, nor speak to me;
My reasons are most strong and you shall know them
When back again this ring shall be delivered.
And on your finger in the night I'll put
Another ring, that what in time proceeds
May token to the future our past deeds.
Adieu, till then; then fail not; you have won
A wife of me, though there my hope be done.

(IV.ii.57–65)

This riddling speech with the careful doubling of rings is original to Shakespeare, and G. K. Hunter appends the following perceptive comment:

The exchange of rings was part of the ceremony of betrothal. . . Since Diana claims Bertram as her husband in V.iii perhaps the exchange is thought of as having similar force here. . . .[96]

Diana's reference to "wife" is obviously meant to be Helena, but Bertram has already promised to marry Diana "When his wife's dead" (IV.ii.72).

What Diana describes in her statements is a conditional and secret spousal ratified by an exchange of rings. The fulfillment of the condition (i.e. the death of Helena, provided Bertram had not engineered it) would leave him secretly espoused to Diana. Consummation of such a relationship would ratify the contract, constituting a putative marriage, recognizable under law.[97]

At this point in the action Diana's role in Bertram's discomfiture is paramount, a fact which allows sympathy for Helena to accumulate, since she does not appear to be a relentless and predatory woman out to capture her man. As Harold Wilson says: "the controlling idea of the play that emerges is the conception of Helena's love as far stronger than Bertram's arrogance, a love which works unobtrusively and with humility toward an end that heaven favors."[98]

The great confrontation scene now ensues which serves to torture Bertram further, bring him to repentance, and indicate that by the end of the play he has in fact gained sufficient self-knowledge and maturity to comprehend the true nobility of Helena.[99]

On Diana's appearance Bertram is cornered; his accomplice in what he considered a mere soldier's flirtation has come to claim him. Most unchivalrously he attacks Diana's reputation, at which point the girl produces Bertram's ancestral ring as evidence both of the contract and his perfidy; lust is shown to have been more important than pride in his nobility. By now Bertram is completely crushed and can do little more than gibber wildly in an undignified attempt to cover himself, while Diana relentlessly exposes each lie. Bertram is finally forced to confess openly that he received the king's ring from "Diana," and listen while the foulmouthed braggart Parolles tells all. Diana's behavior here seems to be too importunate and unlikable, and critics since Johnson have objected to this part of the scene. It is important, nevertheless, because her stalling and her pert answers to the king forfeit any sympathy she might gain from either court or audience. Further, it is dramatically necessary that Bertram be given a very real scare. His shortcomings in preferring Diana to his lost wife, who loved him for himself, must be revealed. Bertram, now knowing himself for the fool he has been, can thus react positively when Helena, the *dea ex machina*, announces fulfillment of the conditions he had set her.

With the appearance of Helena, the now humbled young man rejoices. Some of his joy may also be dictated by the fact that she is undoubtedly saving him from the undesirable match in which he had believed himself trapped. The existing contract with Helena, though consummated by a trick, has now become binding, indissoluble matrimony; and it certainly outweighs any other contract into which Bertram might have entered. He has now been "doubly won" and his lines

> If she, my liege, can make me know this clearly,
> I'll love her dearly—ever, ever dearly
> (V.iii.312–313)

may bear the added meaning of gratitude towards his lady. Bertram can now compare the love and forgiveness of Helena with the almost shrewish insistence of Diana. He is still understandably confused, however, since he has only riddling words as a guide. This time he goes with relief into what he had formerly considered "loathsome bondage" with Helena, now apparently giving "free and unforced consent."[100]

Thus the play ends happily with a reconciliation scene, accomplishing that transition from sorrow to joy characteristic of Shakespearean comedy. Bertram, the immature young man of Act II, has discovered through his own experience the nature of love and marriage. Any fears he may have had concerning his own sexual potency are now dispelled through his inadvertent consummation of the match, and he has now become worthy of the resourceful, faithful, and forgiving Helena. In arranging this *dénouement* Shakespeare has also made skillful use of the intricacies of matrimonial law and Elizabethan wardship, material doubtless familiar to his audience, to point up motivations and explain the actions of some principal characters.

The prodigal son has returned home to receive the forgiveness of wife, mother, and king. Helena, the redemptive and erotic force of the play, has cured the king, reformed Bertram, and in her pregnancy she has returned fertility to the dying world of Rossillion to redeem it too.[101] Through their progeny the young couple are bringing new life to an old world, continuing the cycle of life, and the Countess's wishes are fulfilled. The play thus ends on a note of reconciliation with fruitful marriage and the same sense of openendedness that is characteristic of the last plays. The old, mourning world of Rossillion with its double deaths of fathers and the illness of the king has been transformed through the energetic and passionate actions of Helena. On a literal, legal level, she has manipulated the forces of law to gain her desires,[102] but on a deeper, more important level, she has taught her husband to know himself and brought him to a new moral, emotional, and sexual maturity. Harmony has been restored to Rossillion; the coming child is its seal, and as the play ends with its meeting of generations and celebration of the power of femininity, one looks ahead to a future in which Helena will become the great lady of Rossillion, personifying the tradition of love's virtue and its curative power.

CHAPTER II

Trouser Roles and the Teachers of Love's Truth

SECTION 1
Introduction

T he education of young men into love-worthiness is a pervasive theme of
Shakespeare's comedies, particularly those which utilize the device of
transvestism by which heroines lead their lovers to become their suitable sexual and emotional partners. Of the eight plays which deal primarily with courtship, half of them make use of disguised ladies to further this learning process:
The Two Gentlemen of Verona, The Merchant of Venice, As You Like It,
and *Twelfth Night*. Those which have women as teachers without resorting to
transvestism are, *Love's Labor's Lost* (where the educational process is left in-
complete), *All's Well That Ends Well*, and *Measure for Measure*, where legal-
isms and bed-trick substitutions are the prominent plot devices; and *Much
Ado About Nothing*, the only mature comedy in which the heroine achieves
the reformation of her lover in her own person—though one might consider
Beatrice's witty demeanor to be something of a mask, a disguise.

This suggestion also explains the emphasis on matrimonial law as plot
device in *Much Ado* and the two dark comedies. Separated by convention from
social equality with their lovers and hence unable to exert direct educational
influence on them, the women of these plays find the use of legalities necessary as one of the tools of moral instruction. As masculine disguise gains in
importance, reliance on matrimonial law as linch pin for action diminishes, so
that it becomes ancillary to the plot, useful to explain portions of and develop
character motivation. Of this group of ladies Portia, the one who spends the
least portion of the plot in male disguise, is the only female character to display legal knowledge and make use of contracts.

Of recent years, feminist scholarship has investigated anew the reasons for Shakespeare's employment of transvestite heroines in the comedies of the 1590s, a time when, as Linda Woodbridge notes, "female transvestism was out of fashion on London Streets."[1] The first and simplest answer is the fact of the boy actor, who would be more credible in doublet than farthingale. In addition, such disguising was often already in the Shakespearean source. Juliet Dusinberre suggests that the device has a greater social and philosophical importance for the dramatist, inviting him "to explore masculinity and femininity,"[2] in this way coming to a discovery of the nature of women when they are freed from customary constraints. Her most telling comment is that "A woman in disguise smokes out the male world, perceiving masculinity as a form of acting, the manner rather than the man."[3] Thus Shakespeare is perceived as saying something very specific about the nature of femininity; clothes are in themselves a form of disguise, and sexual behavior is independent of clothes, hence masculine disguise changes a woman character "only because it allows her to express a part of her nature which society suppresses."[4] Hugh M. Richmond, working from a psychological approach, thinks that Shakespeare may have been experimenting with the kind of situation later discussed by Jung when writing of "the creative possibilities of at least some bisexuality."[5]

But there is a paradox in women's adopting male disguise, as Paula S. Berggren has noted. In so doing they voluntarily doff their role of primary power, their procreative capacity and their strength in the world of love, which is the world of comedy. To a great extent in these plays masculine clothing is required because "the heroine needs to present herself in circumstances where a woman would be rebuffed or, more typically, subjected to injury.[6] Disguise also gives the women characters greater freedom to be with their men as social equals and as a consequence they can experience friendship, usually considered a masculine preserve.[7] This fact also explains the frequency of love-friendship debates in the "disguise plays." However, Shakespeare is no radical feminist and his cross-dressing ladies do not challenge the male world; when disguise has served its purpose all of these women quite happily turn to their next role, that of wives. And in all the marriage plays of Shakespeare the man is quite clearly perceived as *primus inter pares*; he has the educational function over his wife, except for that single exception, *The Merry Wives of Windsor*.

Shakespeare's women adopt male disguise only as a temporary expedient, and the womanly qualities persist underneath the clothes. A Rosalind can faint, Julia and Viola can weep; Portia alone seems comparatively comfortable in her masculine attire, but she can also utilize the law as a stalking horse. In summary, then, masculine role-playing for comedic heroines is useful for four main reasons: (1) the exigencies of casting; (2) a means for the women characters to gain a temporary freedom from convention; (3) a method of redefining relations between the sexes during the period of courtship; (4) the acquisition of additional credibility in the education of their menfolk. These heroines are the manipulators of the comedies of courtship and through their male images they remake their men, forcing them to re-evaluate their attitudes towards marriage and its conventions so that they perceive the relationship on which they are about to venture as one of mutuality and reciprocity. Shakespeare does not continue their history after the courtship and one does sometimes want to speculate about the future of these marriages, as John Fletcher did in *The Woman's Prize, or The Tamer Tamed* (1612), in which the widowed Petruchio recalls that his life with Kate was distinctly uneasy.

SECTION 2
The Two Gentlemen of Verona—Julia and Love's Loyalty

The Two Gentlemen of Verona, the first of these disguise plays, has, in the words of Anne Barton "the unenviable distinction of being the least loved and least regarded of Shakespeare's Comedies."[8] It is an imperfect fusion of plot, theme and character stitched together with omnipresent punning and parodic contrast, while the conclusion comes so suddenly that it almost defies logic. At the same time it is an anthology of Shakespearean comedy, almost a blueprint for his future work. It is also probably the first play in which he treats his major comedic theme: the process of courtship which ends in marriage.

This theme is made less clearly discernible because the action is muddied by the competing claims of the codes of love and friendship, which Shakespeare then burlesques through Launce, who shows more loyalty to his dog than Proteus and Valentine do to each other. Ironically, a female character, Silvia, the representative of love's passive fidelity, proves the truest devotee of *philia,* that ideal of friendship praised by classical writers and commentators who confined its exercise to men. In the way Silvia respects the rights of the jilted Julia she shows more sisterhood, friendship, if you will, than one might expect, given the social convention that women are in effect competing for men. In addition, this play also develops a hierarchy of love and lovers, something Shakespeare explores more fully in *As You Like It*. From lowest to highest the range is from the totally physical (Speed and his kitchen maid) to the celibate devotee of love, the ineffectual Sir Eglamour, but with emphasis on the attainable ideal of balance between reason and passion. Nonetheless, one does wonder whether the huddled and speedy *dénouement* indicates that the symmetrically paired lovers have in fact reached that plateau.

Julia is the most important and most fully developed character in this play and the first Shakespearean woman to adopt masculine disguise. She combines emotional involvement, critical detachment, and resourcefulness: "In displaying her feelings, she also displays a refreshing capacity for wry, satiric self-criticism."[9] She plays the game of love in exchanging comments on her catalogue of suitors, presenting a façade of reason to Lucetta in refusing Proteus's love letter, then tearing it, but when she is alone succumbing to her passion, reading and kissing the pieces and finally piling them up with a sly conceit:

> Thus will I fold them one upon another—
> Now kiss, embrace, contend, do what you will.
>   (I.ii.29–30)

Though Proteus and Julia have exchanged letters, their first joint scene is one of farewell, and it displays the practical side of Julia (II.ii). Instead of laments, of poetic conceits, letters lodged in bosoms and other romantic devices, she devises what is quite clearly a betrothal. Proteus promises to return as soon as he can; the two lovers exchange rings and "seal the bargain with a holy kiss" and handfast themselves "for my constancy" says Proteus with unconscious dramatic irony. This scene possesses the outward signs of a sixteenth-century betrothal in words of the future tense. This contract, though unwitnessed, would give the couple a quasi-legal claim on each other, and thus the actions of Proteus are even more inexcusable. The best one can say about him at the moment is that he is suffering from a severe case of love's inertia, or dotage. He is well aware of his plight, but unlike Julia, he lacks the intellectual flexibility to comprehend its risibility:

> Thou, Julia, thou has metamorphosed me,
> Made me neglect my studies, lose my time,
> War with good counsel, set the world at nought;
> Made wit with musing weak, heart sick with thought.
>   (I.i.66–69)

Clearly Proteus needs to learn the nature of love, and his very name, that of a shape shifter, indicates what will happen. Similarly, in his scoffing at love, the ironically named Valentine indicates that he is certain to experience love's pain.

Julia's decision to follow Proteus is another aspect of her practicality and resourcefulness, her decision to travel in male attire being dictated by pure pragmatism:

> . . . I would prevent
> The loose encounters of lascivious men.
> (II.vii.40–41)

She sets the pattern for later ladies who adopt men's clothing by being concerned about modesty:

> But tell me, wench, how will the world repute me
> For undertaking so unstaid a journey?
> I fear me it will make me scandalized.
> (II.vii.59–61)

She will wear whatever is fitting in masculine fashion, even to include a codpiece, but she will not do anything irrevocable, such as cutting her hair. Clearly she is not trying to prove anything about masculinity and femininity; she is concerned to protect her virtue, and when one considers how close Silvia comes to rape in the last scene, her precautions are indeed necessary. In following Proteus, then, Julia is demonstrating her loyalty, but when she discovers him false she takes service with him, patiently waiting for him to regain his senses, like the later Viola even wooing a rival for his sake.

The treachery of Proteus is in total contrast to the loyalty of Silvia who is a gentler, less witty Julia, and more concerned with social conventions. Masculine disguise is not for her, and so when she flees after the banished Valentine she chooses as the escort to guard her honor Sir Eglamour, one sworn to celibacy in memory of his dead love. Silvia has an important educational role in this play as she plays with her doting lover, Valentine, exploiting his love-blindness by making him write his own love-letter, in effect act as his own go-between, an ironic parallel to Speed's letter and what occurs later when Julia is sent to woo Silvia as Proteus's messenger.

The structure of the play now moves away from simple parallel development with the clowns acting as a kind of comic chorus. The two love affairs had appeared to be following the conventional pattern of love-sickness leading to betrothal, but three obstacles are suddenly placed in the way of Silvia and Valentine in the persons of her father, Sir Thurio, and Proteus. The theme of

the enforced marriage to an old man, a *miles gloriosus* with money, here signifies the intrusion of the world of mercantilism into the world of love—and
Valentine is too besotted to survive the concerted onslaughts of a false friend
and a hostile father.

From the time of her arrival in Milan, Julia controls the play, as exposi-
tor, commentator, servant, go-between, and above all else as educator.[10] At this
point she becomes the moral center of the action, and also the manipulator, for
she conveniently fails to return to Proteus the ring she had herself given the
faithless young man and which Silvia had refused as a gift. Here masculine
disguise is of great practical advantage to Julia in her dealings with both
Proteus and Silvia. As Sebastian, servant to her lover, she can chide him with
his infidelity to his lady, and with Silvia she can sing her own praises to gain
his pity. Her garb gives her both freedom of movement and speech, while her
role as servant is also useful because as go-between she must hear Silvia's
comments on Proteus's reprehensible conduct. Even in the serenade scene
(IV.ii) Julia's comments are those of sorrow, never of blame; her loyalty and
love remain total, as she tries to bring Proteus to a recognition of his fault.
Her words to both Proteus and Silvia are always aimed to evoke their pity for
the forsaken Julia; her harshest remark is to Silvia, "Poor gentlewoman, my
master wrongs her much" (IV.iv.159). In soliloquy however, the truth of her
femininity and affection are made clear. The woman's heart still beats beneath
the doublet as she laments her task as go-between and with some irony discusses the conflict of loyalties she faces:

> I am my master's true confirmed love,
> But cannot be true servant to my master
> Unless I prove false traitor to myself.
> Yet will I woo for him, but yet so coldly
> As, heaven it knows, I would not have him speed.
> (IV.iv.101–105)

Fortunately for her, Silvia's loyalty to Valentine makes such deliberate sub-
version unnecessary; but she does display a certain amount of competitive jealousy as she compares their relative beauties:

> What should it be that he respects in her
> But I can make respective in myself
> If this fond love were not a blinded god?
> Come shadow, come and take this shadow up,
> For 'tis thy rival. O thou senseless form,
> Thou shalt be worshipped, kissed, loved, and adored!

And, were there sense in his idolatry,
My substance should be statue in thy stead.
I'll use thee kindly for thy mistress' sake,
That used me so; or else, by Jove I vow
I should have scratched out your unseeing eyes
To make my master out of love with thee
(IV.iv. 192–203)

This speech also indicates both the depth of her hurt and an understanding of Proteus's behavior. In speaking of Love as blind Cupid she indicates her comprehension of Proteus's passion as that of irrational sensuality, for sighted Cupid indicates iconographically a rational love, while blindness illustrates the instability of amatory desires.[11] Her echo of Proteus's request for Silvia's picture, with its shadow and substance contrast re-emphasizes her earlier, cynical aside:

If 'twere a substance, you would, sure, deceive it.
And make it but a shadow, as I am.
(IV.ii. 126–127)

Julia's use of the aside also makes her to some extent a chorus character, a reference point for the audience, not only in this scene but also in the curious little scene with Proteus, Thurio, and her. She is acting as comic commentator, almost in the same manner as the clowns in the earlier part of the play, but the scene itself is merely a filler, meant to indicate the passage of time, in order to move the action from court to forest.

For the first time Shakespeare makes use of his "green world" and the revelatory journey to it, a place where order will be recreated and reality will be reorganized. Certainly this particular wood and its denizens partake more of the comic illogic of Gilbert and Sullivan's *Pirates of Penzance* than Elizabethan comedy,[12] and Valentine's last minute cavalry-style rescue seems almost parodic. Perhaps Shakespeare meant this scene to be funny, perhaps he rushed his conclusion, or perhaps as Leggatt suggests, the play lacks a solid center.[13] The only value that is affirmed is love, and even that is left undefined. Lovers there are aplenty, but which is the true love that is celebrated?

Certainly it is not the sighs, moans, and inertia of Proteus at the beginning of the play, for that has led him to falsehood and failure to pursue honor. Proteus's moral instability increases throughout the play. Like the later Romeo with Rosaline, he speedily falls out of love; but unlike Romeo, he commits further folly. There seem to be no limits to the perfidy of Proteus as he violates sworn vows of love, the priorities of friendship, resorts to treachery, and finally attempts rape. His kind of love offers nothing affirmative. The mercantile matrimonial approach of Sir Thurio can similarly be dismissed, while Proteus's heretical statement "In love / Who respects friend" (V.iv.53–54), followed by Valentine's equally outrageous:

> And that my may appear both plain and free,
> All that was mine in Silvia I give thee.
>
> (V.iv.82–83)

indicates that friendship too cannot be accepted as a value.

But Shakespeare may really intend parody here, and there are elements in the *dénouement* which support this possibility. To begin, Proteus's sudden conversion is astonishing, yet one should also recall that instant enlightenment could happen in drama, and the doctrine of humors believed that a sudden shock could restore the balance of an otherwise disorganized personality. Even Valentine's astonishing generosity, which led Quiller-Couch to expostulate "there are no gentlemen in Verona," can be read as parody of such famous friends as Titus and Gisippus, as recounted by Sir Thomas Elyot in *The Boke Named the Gouernour* (1531) and in the tale of Palamon and Arcite from Chaucer's *Knight's Tale*, dramatized at least in part by Shakespeare as *The Two Noble Kinsmen*. Such friends were prepared to give up the beloved woman to satisfy the wishes of a friend. One nagging question remains; what if Proteus had decided to accept Valentine's offer?

The answer is that Valentine has made Proteus an offer that he cannot accept, and it is not in Valentine's power to make, since he and Silvia are already betrothed—and Proteus knows it (II.iv.176–182), even though the specific details are unstated. Similarly, Proteus is betrothed to Julia (II.ii), and Silvia knows it, as her comments to the disguised lady indicate:

> *Julia*   Madam, he sends your ladyship this ring.
> *Silvia*   The more shame for him that he sends it to me,
> For I have heard him say a thousand times
> His Julia gave it him at his departure.
> Though his false finger have profaned the
>   ring,
> Mine shall not do his Julia so much wrong.
>
> (IV.iv.131–135)

Here Julia, who has kept possession of that ring, shows herself possessed of remarkable prescience of mind—and one may debate endlessly the reason for her swoon. Perhaps it was provoked by Valentine's offer, but her confusion does seem distinctly purposeful, and her diversionary tactics prevent Proteus from making an answer before she produces the ring which signifies their vows. At this moment Julia, after a very speedy recuperation, returns him the betrothal ring that Proteus had given her, not "the ring you sent to Silvia." The moment of revelation has arrived and Julia reveals herself:

> Behold her that gave aim to all thy oaths,
> And entertained 'em deeply in her heart.
> How oft hast thou with perjury cleft the root!
> O Proteus, let this habit make thee blush;
> Be thou ashamed that I have took upon me
> Such an immodest raiment, if shame ·live
> In a disguise of love.
> It is the lesser blot, modesty finds,
> Women to change their shapes than men their minds.
> (V.iv.102–110)

Julia now combines the swoon of a woman with the eloquence of a young man (for that is her outward appearance) in the sole speech of the play in which she upbraids her lover. She has disguised herself as a page, but he has disguised himself morally as a lover, when in fact he has been spiritually unfaithful. What else is noteworthy, is her apology for acting in an immodest manner in order to achieve her love; she is now dwindling into a wife, asking forgiveness for adopting her masculine attire.

Proteus, shocked out of his folly, looks rationally, with new eyes, on the lady who has loved him, served him as his page, and also educated him to see the nature of his misdeeds. He has learned what he must do, and discovered the value of the lady he had redpudiated, though in his penitence he does sound a trifle ungracious to Silvia. Valentine proves himself worthy of Silvia, challenges the foolish Sir Thurio, and with the consent of Silvia's father, is granted the possession of his love. Then, to conclude the reconciliation, Valentine asks and is granted pardon for his bandits.

At this moment one must see that if love is the center of this play, it must be the love of Julia and Silvia for their men. Julia demonstrates fidelity, resourcefulness, and grace under pressure; Silvia shows sympathy and understanding in a manner that transcends the literary approaches to the values of friendship. Julia has demonstrated the courage of an emotional commitment in risking her modesty in male attire, and Silvia's near rape indicates the common sense of her decision. But more important, Julia has made use of her temporary identity (for it is always a role to her) to educate Proteus, show him the wickedness of his behavior, and also to bring him to marriage. Both she and Silvia have taught or shamed their men into common sense by means of their own steadfastness, initiative, and even trickery. This is the moral center of the play: that marriage under the tutelage of such intelligent and faithful women who take risks for love will bring these immature poseurs to an appreciation of love's mutuality.

SECTION 3

The Merchant of Venice—Portia, the Friendly Adversary

The tone of *The Merchant of Venice* differs markedly from that of *The Two Gentlemen of Verona*. Whereas the early play is comically exaggerated, detached, at times broadly humorous, and in its conclusion hard to take seriously, the later one is infinitely more emotional, more erotic, drawing its audience into the action both through its near tragedy and basic romanticism. The true themes of this play have recently been blurred as a result of the Holocaust of the 1940s, and it has been made to bear the burden of interpretations which would not have occurred to a majority of Elizabethans. Shylock, in actuality the blocking figure of a romantic comedy, has taken control of the play as the ultimate spokesman for a victimized people, and the themes of friendship, love, and the nature of love's commitment are sometimes slighted. Stage history, particularly in the nineteenth century, began this trend, even to the extent of concluding the play with the trial scene, with Shylock stabbing himself on stage (Richard Mansfield, 1893). Henry Irving, in interpolating a scene in which Shylock, carrying a lantern, knocks on the door of his empty house achieved an extraordinary visual effect by echoing that famous Pre-Raphaelite painting, Christ, the Light of the World, "Behold, I stand at the door and knock."[14]
      Structurally the play is a romantic comedy with Shylock as a blocking figure, and an admixture of the folkloric in the matter of the three caskets. Throughout, the audience must suspend its disbelief and avoid raising such practical matters as Antonio's inexplicable failure to buy marine insurance (which was available at the time), or the nature of Portia's legal "cram course" which makes her an instant expert in contracts and permits a rescue almost comparable with that of *The Two Gentlemen of Verona*.

Love, then, is *the* important element of the play, and its treatment is a logical development from *The Two Gentlemen*. The central characters must again weigh the competing demands of love and friendship, with the resolution of the play coming only when Bassanio is brought to see where his first loyalties are due, and when Antonio recognizes that friendship has more than one dimension. This moral advance is made through the tutelage of Portia, partly in her masculine disguise, but more fully, in her own, feminine attire. She is the moral and educative center of the play as she brings both her lover and his friend to an apprehension of the truth of love and an ideal matrimonial relationship based on the ethical imperative of equity, "the spirit and habit of fairness, justness, and right dealing which would regulate the intercourse of men with men,—the rule of doing to all others as we desire them to do to us,"[15] and more than this, without counting the cost.

The first important emotional commitment to be treated in the play is that of friendship, and a number of critics have suggested that "the main action of the play is centered on the struggle between Portia and Antonio for Bassanio's love."[16] Hugh M. Richmond speaks of "The self-deceptions of emotional commitment not only in sexual but also in social and legal terms,"[17] while John Russell Brown speaks of the triumph of love's generosity and the amplitude of love's wealth which it demonstrates.[18] Leggatt neatly resolves the problem of divided affections by commenting "It is the capacity to love that matters, and love can extend itself beyond a single person,"[19] and this is one of the major lessons Portia teaches in a tripartite educational enterprise conducted both in male disguise and in her own person.

Antonio's deep melancholy opens the play; he must play a sad part in the world since he is faced with the imminent loss of Bassanio's friendship if the young man marries. He is discovering himself an outsider, but by the play's end will learn how to relinquish a friend and be reintegrated into a new society in which the claims of friendship coexist with matrimony. Bassanio seems rather inconsiderate of the consequences this new relationship will have for his friend as he answers Antonio's questions about the lady with an immediate request for another loan in addition to what he has already borrowed and squandered. Only when Antonio agrees to lend once more to him, out of the generosity of friendship, does Bassanio speak of the wealthy lady he wishes to woo. But already one can see an element of selfishness in this friendship; to be sure, Antonio's generosity is limitless, but that can also be another face of selfishness, of obligation, of possessiveness. Antonio's later action in sending a letter requesting Bassanio's presence at his death reinforces this doubt.

According to John 15:13 "Greater love hath no man than this, that a man lay down his life for his friends," and Antonio expects to do this, but at the same time he is not doing his good by stealth. He wants the satisfaction of Bassanio's presence, even though it can avail nothing, and in addition, his request (fortuitously or not) arrives just at the moment of Bassanio's espousal, so that Antonio forces Bassanio to choose the claim of friendship over that of marriage. Hence Antonio lacks true generosity in making the request, which is couched in unexpectedly mercantile terms:

> . . . my bond to the Jew is forfeit. And since in paying it, it is impossible
> I should live, all debts are cleared between you and I if I might but see you
> at my death. Notwithstanding, use your pleasure. If your love do not
> persuade you to come, let not my letter.
>
> (III.ii.317–321)

Mercantile images also pervade the early speeches of Bassanio, but they are not to be taken literally.[20] Certainly he begins by speaking of Portia as "a lady richly left" (I.i.161), but then she is immediately compared with "Cato's daughter, Brutus' Portia," one of the paradigms of classical wifely fidelity, who committed suicide rather than bear her husband's disgrace. The emphasis is on her virtues, her uniqueness, her moral value and spiritual worth; she is the golden fleece, "And many Jasons come in search of her" (I.i.172). This reference, with resonances of the fate of Medea, moves on to another business image:

> O my Antonio, had I but the means
> To hold a rival place with one of them,
> I have a mind presages me such thrift
> That I should questionless be fortunate.
>
> (I.i.173–176)

But this in not mere economics, but rather the "hazard" of an emotional investment, from which an intangible return of love will come, since Bassanio has already received "fair speechless messages from her eyes," and in order to capitalize upon them he must undertake a double mercantile journey to mend his spiritual and monetary fortunes. At this point Bassanio is emotionally committed to Portia's love, but he has not yet proved himself; as a prodigal spendthrift on the literal level, he could prove the same in love. He is an untried lover.

Untested, yes, but Bassanio is not an unworthy lover, as is made clear when the scene shifts to Belmont, a name which has religious resonances on the analogical level as the heavenly city, as Barbara Lewalski suggests.[21] However, on the literal level there may also be a punning anatomical reference to the fair mount of Venus, signifying here sexual fulfillment. And to judge from the specific sexuality of the last line of the play in which "Nerissa's ring" is a well-known bawdy pun, such a suggestion makes sense. Belmont is indeed a place where desires are satisfied, dreams are fulfilled, love's priorities are established, and the ultimate harmony of human existence is celebrated in marriage.

Matrimony and the matter of the three caskets are the central business of Belmont, and the mode of choice of course has its basis in folklore. In this hazard Portia's dead father reaches beyond the grave to ensure that his daughter is betrothed worthily. Portia quite obviously resents the curbs this illogical contest has placed on her, because it makes her an object, a prize, not a flesh and blood woman,[22] and has caused a swarm of unsuitable candidates to descend upon her. Portia and Nerissa discuss them all with derogatory and brittle wit until the maid reveals that the paternal stipulations have at least had some good effect, because all this motley crew have decided to desist, unless the rules are changed. But Portia will remain obedient to her father:

> If I live to be as old as Sibylla, I will die as chaste as Diana unless I be gained by the manner of my Father's will. . . .
>
> (I.ii.98–100)

But Nerissa introduces a new topic, Bassanio, and the reason for Portia's melancholy at the beginning of this scene is revealed: she is in love with him, and he is a worthier candidate than his mercantile remarks in Venice have shown him:

> *Nerissa* Do you remember, lady, in your father's time, a Venetian, a scholar and a soldier, that came hither in company of the Marquis of Montferrat?
> *Portia* Yes, yes, it was Bassanio—as I think, so was he called.
> *Nerissa* True, madam. He of all the men that ever my foolish eyes looked upon, was the best deserving a fair lady.
> *Portia* I remember him well, and I remember him worthy of thy praise.
>
> (I.ii.103–112)

Bassanio then, follows the professions of learning and arms, which Castiglione's courtier was recommended to undertake, and the fact of his travelling with a nobleman signifies him to be of good birth. Further, his visit came when Portia's father was alive, and one can legitimately suppose that they met, and this was the occasion of Portia's "fair speechless messages" of love for a "worthy" gentleman. These noble qualities are not demonstrated elsewhere in the play, but they must never be forgotten in the face of Bassanio's only real disadvantage—lack of money to support his gentility, and to attain Portia, whose instant recollection of his name (and subsequent hesitation) reveal her heart.

This scene also reveals the reflexive structure of the play; Venice resonates permanently against Belmont, the world of affairs with the world of love. Bassanio in Venice is emotionally committed to Belmont, but lacks the cash to get there, while the lady of Belmont has both the money and the means to satisfy him—if he will submit to the casket ordeal. The skilful progression of the casket scenes is a useful structural and expository device. As each scene progresses it increases suspense, reflects or comments on the actions in Venice, and reveals character through the choice of casket. The three metals are important in possessing revelatory qualities, acting as a kind of psychological litmus paper to expose the faults of each suitor as he goes to the *hazard*, a word that is repeatedly used in this world of love. Only those lovers who gamble away themselves, with complete commitment to their emotions, are the winners in this event.

Consequently it is no surprise that Morocco fails; he looks at the caskets for their intrinsic value. Leggatt suggests that his "mistake is to make a judgment about Portia: thinking of her in a literary, emblematic way,"[23] and thus he concludes with a clumsy compliment: "Never so rich a gem / Was set in worse than gold" (II.vii.53–54). He has taken the appearance for the truth, and is rewarded with a death's head, because attraction to the things of the world lead to the death of the spirit. Shylock's confusion of value "My daughter! My ducats! O my daughter!" in the succeeding scene is Venice's reflection of Morocco's shortcomings.

The Prince of Arragon has the narcissistic pride his name implies, revealing his almost total self-absorption in his answer to Portia's comment on those who come "to hazard for my worthless self." Though Portia may have said too much, it is lost on proud Arragon, who ought at least to have replied with a suitable compliment. He cannot give, cannot bend, and in choosing silver he assumes dessert, takes the motto literally and is awarded "The portrait of a blinking idiot" (II.ix.53). Here, following Ripa, it is tempting to suggest that in fact he is given a mirror, an iconographical symbol of pride,[24] perhaps decorated with a fool's cap. This suggestion makes good sense of the lines on the scroll:

'The fire seven times tried this;
Seven times tried that judgment is
That did never choose amiss.
Some there be that shadows kiss;
Such have but a shadow's bliss.
There be fools alive iwis,
Silvered o'er and so was this.'
(II.ix.66–69)

As Arragon departs, a breathless messenger announces the arrival of a Venetian, introducing him with stupendous praise and leading Nerissa to hope "Bassanio, Lord Love, if thy will it be!" (II.ix.100). This scene has resonances in Venice with proud Shylock's reactions to the prodigality of his daughter, and also in the announcement that Antonio's confidence has been misplaced and the bond is due. His misfortune becomes an ironic counterpoint to Bassanio's wooing.

With the arrival of Bassanio in Belmont, the erotic tone of the play becomes dominant; Portia obviously loves him, but wishes to have him wait before he chooses, so she may learn to know him better. She is confused, ruled by her emotions rather than her head, as she begs him to delay his hazard, breathlessly speaking in fits and starts, first almost revealing the truth about the caskets, and then withdrawing, almost confessing her affection until, "divided" by his eyes, she offers a vow of loving gift:

One half of me is yours, the other half yours—
Mine own I would say; but if mine, then yours,
And so all yours! O these naughty times
Puts bars between the owners and their rights.
And so, though yours, not yours. . . .
(III.i.16–19)

Totally distracted by her emotion, Portia here loses any advantage she might have exercised, and to cover herself she resorts to the witty badinage she has earlier used in speaking of and to her suitors. But this is only a pose, as her careful staging of a ritual of choice for Bassanio indicates. She calls for music, throughout Shakespeare's plays often associated with love, and particularly with marriage as the harmony of existence. She muses on the state of her heart in imagery of matrimony, and heroism, and sacrifice; as Hercules rescued Troy's daughter, so Bassanio may rescue her. For this lover Portia has done everything possible to offer him subliminal aid in his choice; the song's first three lines rhyme with *lead*, but even more important it warns against trusting appearance, since the eyes are not a reliable guide, leading here to a sensual delight.

One must of course be wary of overstating the hints Portia offers through this song, for that would detract from the character of Bassanio, who, truth to tell, is not at this moment a good economic risk, since he is living on capital borrowed from a friend, as the interfaced Venetian scenes continually recall. The song does plant some seeds of thought in Bassanio's heart as he muses on appearance and reality in the three worlds of law (business), religion, and beauty (love), concluding that since "outward shows" are a trap to catch the unwary, he will choose lead. The motivations of Bassanio in this decision are not developed much further, except in the comment that it "rather threaten'st than dost promise aught" (II.ii.105), but a further hint comes from the death knell of fancy in the song. Lead, the coffin metal, threatens by reminding humankind of its last end; it is the covering of all that is mortal, in this case the shadow, the portrait of Portia.[25] Thus, in choosing lead, Bassanio is hazarding his life, and paradoxically choosing "death" in a sexual sense, which will lead to fertile marriage and earthly immortality through progeny. Bassanio, by looking within himself with humility has been able to succeed where his more rational predecessors, Morocco and Arragon have failed.[26]

The words that both lovers speak here are supercharged with emotion, physical desire, and "excess." Portia fears a "surfeit" of joy, while Bassanio is rendered "Giddy in spirit" intoxicated with victory, after he kisses her. Both are in a state of sexual euphoria. Bassanio is the first to recover, as the two betroth themselves, each displaying humble generosity to the other:

> *Bassanio*   I come by note to give and to receive,
> Like one of two contending in a prize,
> . . . .
> So, thrice-fair lady, stand I even so
> As doubtful whether what I see be true,
> Until confirmed, signed, ratified by you.
> (III.ii.140–148)

The concluding lines may sound rather too legalistic, but in effect they constitute a freely made betrothal vow, and ask the same from Portia. Her deed of gift at first glance appears rather excessive in its submission, perhaps needlessly full of self-abnegation, as she calls herself

> . . . an unlessoned girl, unschooled, unpractised;
> Happy in this, she is not yet so old
> But she may learn; happier than this,
> She is not bred so dull but she can learn;
> Happiest of all, is that her gentle spirit
> Commits itself to yours to be directed,
> As from her lord, her governor, her king.
> Myself and what is mine to you and yours
> Is now converted. But now I was the lord
> Of this fair mansion, master of my servants
> Queen o'er myself; and even now, but now,
> This house, these servants, and this same myself
> Are yours, my lord's. I give them with this ring,
> Which when you part from, lose, or give away,
> Let it presage the ruin of your love
> And be my vantage to exclaim on you.
>   (III.ii.159–174)

Careful examination reveals a curious resemblance to the so-called submission speech of Kate in *The Taming of the Shrew*. Bassanio is to be "her lord, her governor, her king," and in so stating her obligations to Bassanio she implies the reciprocal duties of the ruler toward his subjects. He must never act tyrannically, and must treat them as a loving father treats the members of his family. Her next words show that even at this moment Portia has some knowledge of the laws of matrimonial contracting, as she willingly enters her new legal status as betrothed wife, a *femme couverte* whose legal personality is subsumed in that of her husband, who now controls her property.[27] In giving Bassanio the betrothal ring she seals the bargain, but she also imposes a specific condition—fidelity, a condition always imposed on the wife by the husband, not the other way around. Wives were expected to forgive their erring husbands, but Portia will insist on her bond.[28] Still dizzy with joy, Bassanio willingly accepts the bargain, not quite realizing all its implications. Portia has given everything that is material, for that is necessary, and in return Bassanio, in *submitting* to this bargain, takes an initial step in his education in the way of reciprocal marital love as a primary obligation:

> . . . But when this ring
> Parts from this finger, then parts life from hence;
> O then be bold to say Bassanio's dead!
>   (III.ii.183–185)

The bond is immediately tested with the news of Antonio's misfortunes;

Bassanio laments his part in them, but Portia instantly offers an eminently acceptable compromise, obviously accepting the obligations of Bassanio's friendship as compatible with and complementary to those of marriage. First she insists on the church ceremonial, but orders him to Venice before the consummation of their love in order to save Antonio by paying off the bond:

> For never shall you lie by Portia's side
> With an unquiet soul . . . .
> (III.ii.306–307)

By this action she quite frankly asserts her physical rights over Bassanio, and indicates the differentiation between the two bonds of love. She foresees no conflict of affections, and her decision to go to Venice is both to save Antonio and surprise her husband by her unexpected appearance. Instead she herself is surprised by Bassanio's misunderstanding of love's priorities.

That Portia did not expect to test Bassanio is indicated by her approach to the adoption of male disguise. Like Julia in *The Two Gentlemen of Verona* she does so for safety on her journey and also to ensure credibility as a legal expert when she appears in the appropriate robes. Her attitude toward her attire is humorous; the husbands upon seeing the disguised ladies "shall think we are accomplishèd / With that we lack" (III.iii.61-62), and Nerissa replies with another piece of merry bawdry "Why, shall we turn to men?" (III.iii.78). Portia's transvestism has the qualities of a game and it also shows a clear understanding of the faults of young men as she gleefully recounts the parodic way in which she will play her new role:

> . . . I'll hold thee any wager,
> When we are both accoutered like young men,
> I'll prove the prettier fellow of the two
> And wear my dagger with the braver grace,
> And speak between the change of man and boy
> With a reed voice, and turn two mincing steps
> Into a manly stride, and speak of frays
> Like a fine bragging youth, and tell quaint lies,
> How honorable ladies sought my love,
> Which I denying, they fell sick and died—
> I could not do withal! Then I'll repent,
> And wish, for all that, that I had not killed them.
> And twenty of these puny lies I'll tell,

> That men shall swear I have discontinued school
> Above a twelvemonth. I have within my mind
> A thousand raw tricks of these bragging Jacks,
> Which I will practice.
>
> (III.iii.62–78)

No lamentations about immodest behavior for this disguised lady! But we never see either Portia or Nerissa in their pages' dress, only in their professional robes, so that the game of the love-pursuit is not played. The original idea was obviously for the ladies to reveal their identities immediately upon the completion of the lawsuit, but the behavior of the young men makes that outcome impossible. Portia has delayed the consummation of her marriage once, and will do so again, not for lack of desire, but rather because of her common sense and rational conduct. After teaching Bassanio and Antonio the priorities of love she will lose her virginity in a true union of body and spirit, not mere sensuality. After the successful completion of her dual mission of saving Antonio from death, and defining the limits of friendship and love, she will now bind Bassanio more closely to her in gratitude. She understands the necessity of measure in love.

The marriage of Jessica and Lorenzo here acts as a foil to that of the lovers of Belmont. They are impulsive, romantic rule-breakers, lacking measure, and following the rule of blind Cupid. Jessica defies her father's will (albeit Shylock is never shown as a loving father), and she literally steals from him as she brings with her a casket of jewels to serve as her dowry. She too dresses in male attire, but is distressed at the immodesty of her action—a reaction that is explicable because of the Jewish prohibition against cross-dressing, which was often cited in conduct literature and was thus common knowledge in Shakespeare's day. She also changes her religion, but one must note that her conversion was necessary for a legal marriage to a Christian because otherwise the diriment impediment of *disparitas cultus*, forbidding marriage between an unbaptized and a baptized person would have abrogated and nullified the contract.

Her enterprise in eloping and hazarding everything for love may be considered admirable, but both she and Lorenzo lack reason and rule. Certainly Jessica shows the effects of freedom too long deferred in her prodigal expenditure of her father's goods, even giving her mother's ring in exchange for a monkey. These lovers have yet to learn measure in their love, and by V.i they are groping towards it as they discuss lovers who risked everything: Troilus, Thisbe, Dido, and Medea. But in each case the generous lover was betrayed,

and at the pinnacle of them comes Jessica, guilty of material theft, who doubts
Lorenzo, who did

> . . . swear he loved her well,
> Stealing her soul with many vows of faith,
> And ne'er a true one.
>   (V.i.19–21)

Such "unthrift love" needs ordering, and reason. This is the educative theme
of the famous "How sweet the moonlight sleeps upon this bank" (V.i.54–87)
exchange between Jessica and Lorenzo in which the young husband begins to
initiate his wife into the harmony of marriage. The sensuality with which
Gratiano and Salerio had discussed this marriage they were abetting in II.vi
has an echo in the "race of youthful and unhandled colts" tamed by music.
Jessica apprehends the power of harmony, and Lorenzo will teach her to
comprehend it. This is the office and duty of a husband, to educate his wife,
and these two lovers are shown as having the potential to develop their
relationship from passionate sensuality into the disciplined harmony of ideal
marriage which puts humanity in tune with the cosmos.

In Venice Portia plays a tripartite educational role, embracing all the
participants in the complaint of Shylock. Usually this section of the play is
seen as an unqualified victory for Portia, but in fact it is not so when evaluated
as an educational exercise in love's obligations for Shylock, Antonio, and
Bassanio. Certainly Portia is successful on a material level in procuring the
life of Antonio and gaining handsome compensation from Shylock, but she
does not succeed on the moral level.

Her most notable failure is with Shylock. Throughout the trial scenes
she has tried to educate him to practice mercy, one of the faces of Love as
defined by St. Paul, and recognize the moral imperative of equity, a quasi-legal
restatement of the Golden Rule. In both of these attempts she is notably unsuccessful, and Shylock is forced into submission, his heart remaining closed
to this virtue. His conversion to Christianity is forced upon him, he is fined,
and he leaves the courtroom "content," he says, but with no moral commitment to
love, and as he himself indicates, he cannot understand music, and therefore on a
symbolic level is not part of the harmony of human existence and is "fit for
treasons, stratagems, and spoils" (V.i.85). Once he loved Leah, his wife, but
that was long ago and nothing in his behavior throughout the play now indicates that he loves anything more than material goods. Nominally he has
been forced into a religion that promises salvation, but spiritually he remains

unmoved and unforgiving. Wrongs have been inflicted upon him, certainly, and his motivations are explicable, but he has made no moral advance and Portia has failed. Shylock may even begin his business again.[29]

Portia does not fail with either Antonio or Bassanio. She initiates the educational process while she is disguised as the lawyer, but it is not completed until all have returned to Belmont. She saves Antonio's life by means of an act of love—love for her husband in exerting herself for a friend she had never met, but to whom she feels some obligation because of his assistance in gaining her a husband. In that way she too may be construed as indebted to Antonio, and with her last-minute intervention she offers him a new life, whereas he had perhaps hoped to perform the ultimate act of friendship's love by dying for his friend. Now he must learn how to live in a world where his love for Bassanio cannot be exclusive.

Her next task is to teach both men the relative values of matrimonial love and masculine friendship. During the legal hearing Bassanio has shown himself governed by such an excess of emotions that he forgets the marriage vows so lately given:

> Antonio, I am married to a wife
> Which is as dear to me as life itself,
> But life itself, my wife, and all the world
> Are not with me esteemed above thy life.
> I would lose all, ay sacrifice them all
> Here to this devil, to deliver you.
>   (IV.i.280–285)

Portia's dry retort offers a mild rebuke to Bassanio:

> Your wife would give you little thanks for that
> If she were here to hear you make the offer.
>   (IV.i.286–287)

After Gratiano and Nerissa echo this exchange, the young men in so defacing their marriage bonds, earn the contempt even of Shylock, the enemy of joy. He understands the obligations of a contract which should supersede the bond of friendship, and Antonio in forcing Bassanio to choose, does not; neither do his companions.

Portia now puts Bassanio to the test, and Nerissa echoes it by testing Gratiano. She asks rewards, first gloves from Antonio: an amusing request since gloves were the only articles of clothing that chaste maidens and matrons could without blame receive from men. After Antonio complies, she then asks

Bassanio for his betrothal ring, which to his credit, the young man refuses. In the source, *Il Pecorone*, the ring was given at the first request, but Shakespeare has Bassanio pass the first test:

> Good sir, this ring was given me by my wife,
> And when she put it on she made me vow
> That I should never sell nor give nor lose it.
> (IV.i.439–441)

Portia attempts again to persuade him and departs. This initial refusal is important in indicating that Bassanio is well aware of the significance of the ring as the outward sign of matrimonial bonding; thus, when he sends it to her, in accordance with Antonio's request, he cannot fail to be aware that he has been disloyal to Portia by valuing the claims of friendship above those of marriage. Nerissa, in an unstaged scene, manages also to gain her husband's ring.

The final scene is certainly a parody of the trial in Venice. Bassanio is tried, along with Gratiano for non-performance on a bond. Actually Bassanio is in a difficult legal situation; he has defaulted on his bond, and violated an oath which was a condition of his betrothal. This espousal has been ratified in a church, but it is as yet unconsummated, and he might lose his lady should she wish to "exclaim" on him. To his credit, Bassanio does not lie, but pleads abjectly for forgiveness. However, the fact remains that Bassanio has indeed broken a sworn agreement, though at the urging of a friend. Portia promptly claims equality with her husband, denying the double standard; if he gives away her betrothal ring, then she is permitted to give away the ring and jewel of her chastity to whomever she pleases, and who is more entitled than the young doctor who already has her finger ring. If he can give away her property, the ring, then she is entitled to give away Bassanio's property, her body. This time it is Antonio's turn to save his friend; whereas before he had used his body as security for the bond with Shylock, now he places his "soul upon the forfeit," a bond which indicates the superiority of matrimony to the merely material. Earlier, Portia had not fully educated Shylock into love, simply outward compromise; here, she has brought Antonio to the discovery that friendship and love are not mutually exclusive so that he has now reached the truest understanding of love: unselfish renunciation of claims on the friend or beloved. Antonio can now become part of the charmed circle of lovers, in a new, more mature friendship.

In a reversal of the conclusion of *The Two Gentlemen of Verona*, Antonio in effect gives all that he owns in Bassanio to Portia, who has led them both to an understanding of love, marriage, and reconciliation. Gratiano and Nerissa have also been reconciled and now that the two young men have reached an understanding of themselves and their duties, they are ready for initiation into marriage, and it is no accident that the play ends with a bawdy joke. These women have tested their men, educated them, gained mastery over them by means of their wit and wisdom; but most importantly, they have forgiven them, and these two marriages begin on a basis of mutuality and reciprocity.[30]

SECTION 4
As You Like It—Rosalind as Love's Organizer

I n As You Like It, Shakespeare creates his most openly manipulative comic heroine, and in Rosalind the woman of power stage-manages almost the entire play.[31] Without her, there would be scarcely any action at the center which, as Anne Barton comments, is unusually still, with "a flurry of events" at the beginning and end.[32] The two major lovers meet in Act I and the remainder of the play is concerned with getting them to the altar. But they arrive there only after Orlando has been educated into an acceptance of Rosalind's clear-eyed view of love in which sexuality is an important component, and romantic idealism falls before the realities of joyously human imperfection.[33] Her character also represents a development and advance on Shakespeare's earlier educative ladies. She has the wit of Beatrice without her brittleness, the frank acceptance of feminine sexuality demonstrated by Portia, but unlike her she is given the opportunity to play the gleeful game of parody that Portia only talks about.

She differs from her immediate predecessor in another important way. In the course of educating Orlando she uses what might be termed extraneous sociological material. In The Merchant of Venice matters of law, contracts, bonds, and equity give form to the totality of the play's action, for Portia translates those same materials and interrogative techniques from the legal court-room of Venice to the mock courtroom of moonlit Belmont. Rosalind, how-ever, draws heavily on the kind of material found in conduct books, love debates, anti-feminist propaganda, moral tracts, and even the Colloquies of Erasmus as she leads Orlando on the pathway to a happy marriage. Like Portia she is an excellent teacher, but instead of cat and mouse tactics Rosalind employs direct, witty debate confrontation; she never makes Orlando squirm with any serious sense of guilt, but slowly brings him to the realization that he will happily scrap all romantic idealism for possession of his very human lady, if she will have him.

Part of Rosalind's extraordinary appeal arises from the manner in which Shakespeare exploits the androgynous possibilities of transvestism.[34] Continually, one looks at both Rosalind and the action from several viewpoints simultaneously, in the same manner as one observes the *Las Meniñas* of Velasquez at the Prado, where by the use of external mirrors one participates differently in the picture, beholding the grouping from the viewpoint of both artist and king. Teiresias-like, Rosalind has a double understanding of the faults and virtues of both sexes, and as she enters more and more fully into her masculine role she demonstrates her sympathy with the longings, satisfactions, and torments of man and woman, while at the same time she maintains a rational detachment which lends her the skill to criticize without malice in each of her sexual roles. This bifurcation of understanding also gives further humanity to her treatment of the suffering Orlando and similarly makes her more harsh with Phebe, the only sexual withholder of the play. In this way she combines the stereotypically assigned virtues of masculine rationality and feminine sympathy in one person.

While in disguise, her chief comedic devices are those of parody, burlesque. As an enemy of women she outdoes the excesses of antifeminists, but as a woman *in* love, she feels the pangs of lovelonging. She will be bolder than any young braggadocio, yet she faints when she hears of Orlando's hurt. Like the later Helena of *All's Well* she intrigues to gain the man she wants for a husband, but where Helena began her chase by employing the masculine office of healing, Rosalind uses the feminine weapon of words, using her masculine disguise as a means of acquiring that direct, egalitarian, masculine approach to her lover that would otherwise be socially impossible for a modest young woman. Always, of course, even in the highest reaches of witty repartee, the audience is kept aware of her true femininity, her longing for Orlando, yet her desire is to be accepted on her own terms as a human lover, not an ideal to be worshipped. Additionally, one must not forget that in Shakespeare's day a further layer of disguise existed because Rosalind's part was played by a boy actor, a complication exploited further when Phebe falls in love with Rosalind. One is tempted to see a series of mirrors reflecting opposites receding into infinity.[35]

The world of *As You Like It* represents in the Forest of Arden the ultimate "green world" of Shakespearean comedy, as well as the device of the revelatory journey. All the characters who come to the wood are in flight, in exile from their true place, their roots, and each one finds in the forest during the play an individual solution to problems of spiritual, sexual, political, or personal identity. Thus the action of *As You Like It* is primarily internal, consisting as it does of a journey into the heart of self. Almost from the beginning Rosalind possesses this self-knowledge, and her task is to lead the remaining characters of the play to it. But the green world is also important in having a tonic effect on characters to whom Rosalind's educational efforts are not directed. In fact Arden as a place elicits multiple descriptions from those who enter it for the first time that are almost comparable with the island of changing perceptions in *The Tempest*. It is a place where moral lessons are learned and characters develop into understanding. It is no ideal pastoral woodland with permanent summer, moonlight, and ageless shepherds and shepherdesses. Instead it is peopled with genuine Warwickshire rustics, shepherds whose animals are cut during the shearing of their odoriferous pelts, and an unwashed goatherd with a lummox lover, a place where landlords threaten eviction for nonpayment of rent, and life is made physically uncomfortable by the passage of the seasons which no amount of moralizing rhetoric can overcome. Shakespeare takes care not to romanticize the pastoral life, doing just the opposite, in fact, and making fun of those conventional approaches that do so. Killing of animals takes place in Arden, female infidelity is possible, and danger is present, sometimes from confusingly panclimatic fauna, which may have more psychological than biological significance.[36] In this way Shakespeare avoids cloying sentimentality. He puts contemporary people into the ideal world of literary stereotype and shows them that it is illusory; they then work themselves out of illusion into a new interpretation of themselves and the realities of daily existence. All who surrender themselves to the curative power of this quasi-magical forest are changed; Touchstone, the sensual man does not alter, while Jaques, an *isolato* like Shylock, has no place in a resocialized world. Since he does not wish to change, he willingly removes himself from those courtiers whose lives have been changed by coming to know themselves.

Though Rosalind controls the play, the first scene introduces the male characters of Oliver and his brother, Orlando. As Nancy Hayles notes, theirs is a world of competition, a masculine world, whereas the feminine milieu of Celia and Rosalind is one of cooperation, of mutual support.[37] Orlando is portrayed in the uncomfortable role of Tudor younger brother, whose

> . . . birth and bringing up, will not suffer him to descend to the meanes
> to get wealth: but he stands at the mercy of the World, and which is
> worse, of his brother. . . . Nature hath furnisht him with a little more
> wit upon compassion; for it is like to be his best revenue. . . .[38]

Penniless, since Oliver's hostility has refused him the small bequest of a
thousand crowns from his late father, Orlando also lacks education:

> . . . My father charged you in his will to give me good education: you
> have trained me like a peasant, obscuring and hiding from me all gentle-
> manlike qualities.
>
> (I.i.61–64)

Nonetheless, as the jealously competitive Oliver recognizes:

> . . . he's gentle, never schooled and yet learned, full of noble device, of
> all sorts enchantingly beloved; and indeed so much in the heart of the
> world, and especially of my own people, who best know him, that I am
> altogether misprised. . . .
>
> (I.i.153–157)

He is a natural gentleman, despite his disadvantages, for

> . . . gentle race, besides other good effects, maketh a man ashamed to
> degenerate from the vertue and valour of his ancestours. Yea and gentry
> is to be honored for this respect, that for the most part the better lineage
> we come of, the better behaviour wee are of. . . .[39]

Only once does Orlando momentarily lapse from civility, when he approaches
the banished duke with drawn sword (II.vii.88–106), though his violence
arises from charity to Adam, the old servant. Orlando, then, is a young
gentleman with unrealized potential.

Rosalind's situation is analogous to Orlando's and her subordinate presence on sufferance at the ducal court is the result of that same masculine
competitiveness that has kept Orlando in an inferior position. Fortunately,
Rosalind is saved from the same frustrations as Orlando by the generous support of her cousin, Celia, who offers to forgo her own inheritance for
Rosalind's sake. Duke Frederick tries unsuccessfully to introduce competition into their relationship, to refashion it on a male model, in his attempt to
arouse Celia's jealousy:

> Thou art a fool. She robs thee of thy name.
> And thou wilt show more bright and seem more
>   virtuous
> When she is gone. . . .
>
> (I.iii.76–78)

The two young women are complementary characters, each gifted with rationality, practicality, and satiric insight, as well as emotion, capable of verbally
skewering each other when either commits faults against reason, love, or gender. Throughout the play Celia acts as the female constant, a control figure,
the voice of femininity, tempering Rosalind's sometimes giddy delight in the
freedom of her masculine role, reminding her of her own identity and acting as
audience while her cousin performs.[40] Until Celia awakens to love she acts as
comic and rational commentator on feminine sexuality and Rosalind's erotic
desire.

The worlds of masculinity and femininity collide in "the wrestling match
between Charles and Orlando, . . . a formalized and ritualistic expression of
male rivalry."[41] Looked at from a societal viewpoint wrestling was not considered fit employment for the nobly born, and, as Touchstone points out:

> . . . It is the first time that ever I heard breaking of ribs was sport
> for ladies.
>
> (I.ii.123–125)

This incident, as well as bringing the two unfortunate lovers face to face, thus
also serves to underline the corruption, the illegitimacy, of the court of Duke
Frederick. Rosalind appears to have fallen in love with Orlando at first sight,
even before he actually undertakes the wrestling match, as her attempts to
dissuade him, at the Duke's request, show, while Celia's comments become
echoes of Rosalind's. Leggatt suggests that "she seems impressed by
Orlando's simple dignity in his misfortunes, and it may well be that between
them there is not just arbitrary love but sympathy and fellow feeling."[42] After
the completion of the match and Orlando's undiplomatic confrontation with
Duke Frederick has revealed his legitimate pride of family, Rosalind is clearly in
love. She demonstrates initiative by making the first overture in her gift of a
chain, while Orlando is tongue-tied, even when she turns back and offers him
another chance to speak:

> Sir, you have wrestled well, and overthrown
> More than your enemies.
>
> (I.ii.235–236)

But Orlando cannot speak to *her*, only to *himself*; he cannot speak to a woman.
At this moment, Bertrand Evans's comment that he is here "a sturdy booby,"
seems justified,[43] but in extenuation one must recall his culturally deprived
background. He has the natural gifts of virtue, but as yet lacks maturity and
smoothness of manners, as his earlier outburst has shown. At the same time,

he is the conventionally romantic young man struck dumb by love.

Rosalind is in little better case, surprised into near silence by love "for my child's father" (I.iii.12), as she tells Celia, in a frank expression of procreative feminine sexuality. Instantly Celia adopts her role of rational raillery, as she had done earlier (I.ii.24), when Rosalind's choice of love as a debate topic reveals her as ripe for romance. At the same time this earlier exchange has also indicated her dissatisfaction with Fortune's gifts to women, "gifts of the world" (I.ii.39), which can be read as a chafing at the societal restrictions on femininity.

Consequently Rosalind's decision to adopt male attire after her banishment may arise from this desire for freedom as well as a wish to ensure her safety: "Beauty provoketh thieves sooner than gold" (I.iii.106). After all, the later decision to take Touchstone with them theoretically removes the necessity of Rosalind's disguise. Her words accompanying her decision to adopt masculine dress are similar to those of Portia, for she too sees her new role as something of a parodic game (I.iii.110–118); the appearance of valor in men is often taken for the real thing. Even at this moment, desperately in love and banished from court, she can still summon comic detachment and observation to her aid as she chooses a name suited to her transvestism—Ganymede, the gods' cupbearer.

As she becomes accustomed to the freedoms of masculinity and its permissible liberty of tongue and movement, Rosalind grows into her masculine role, learning to control it, and playing it with considerable delight. But first she learns its responsibilities as she enters the Forest of Arden:

> I could find in my heart to disgrace my man's apparel and cry like a woman; but
> I must comfort the weaker vessel, as doublet and hose ought to show itself
> courageous to petticoat. Therefore, courage, good Aliena.
>
> (II.iv.4–8)

Later she discovers its disadvantages, particularly when Phebe falls in love with her, but more immediately, when she is caught in disguise at the moment of Orlando's entry into the forest: "Alas the day! what shall I do with my doublet and hose" (III.ii.208–209). Until that moment she had been reacting to this unknown lover on multiple levels. She responds to the abysmal quality of his verses as witty literary critic, as a rejected lover, like Silvius, and also as a woman deeply in love and filled with erotic desire. In speaking to the Fool she is a saucy courtier, but to Celia she reveals her womanly feelings—her outward appearance at odds with her heart:

> . . . Dost thou think, though I am caparisoned like a man, I have a doublet and hose in my disposition? One inch of delay more is a South Sea of discovery. I prithee tell me who is it quickly, and speak apace. I would thou couldst stammer, that thou mightst pour this concealed man out of thy mouth as wine comes out of a narrow-mouthed bottle; either too much or none at all. I prithee take the cork out of thy mouth that I may drink thy tidings.
>
> *Celia*   So you may put a man in your belly.
>
> (III.ii.185–194)

This unexpectedly bawdy exchange reveals both Celia's clear understanding and the erotic desires of Rosalind whose breathless questioning and lovesick comments indicate imprisonment in her disguise. She wants to have the advantages of both sexes; as a woman, "When I think, I must speak" (III.ii.237–238), she tells Celia, but as a man she can engage in badinage on a plane of equality with Orlando.

Her role playing allows the tongue-tied Orlando to speak unselfconsciously, as Rosalind picks up the tone of his exchange with Jaques. The young man relates quickly to this androgynous character whose masculine appearance and manner attract his intelligence and test his wit, while her feminine qualities subliminally engage his emotions. At this moment Rosalind perceives the advantages of male disguise which enables her to transcend the recommended norms of female social behavior. Silence, obedience, and passivity are not virtues she cherishes. She revels in the egalitarian relationship that outwardly masculine appearance allows her with Orlando and she uses it to bring her lover to the understanding that true, lasting love is not a romantic, literary ideal, but is based on accepting the humanity of the beloved.

This humanity also includes a healthy recognition of physical sexuality, and the play is filled with frequently overlooked sexual innuendo, bawdy by-play, and erotic desire, all held in skilful balance. The witty spokesman for sensuality is the fool, Touchstone, an important name, for it signifies his function in the play. As Celia is the female constant, the heart-whole rational commentator on feminine sexuality for much of the play, then the fool represents the lowest common denominator of the masculine constant—unadulterated sensuality. Whichever love affair is discussed, or whatever the level of sexuality in an exchange, Touchstone manages to reduce it to anatomical "country matters," burlesquing the poetic Silvius with references to "cods" (II.iv.48), and parodying Orlando's weak poem into the final bawdry of "love's prick" (III.ii.107). The exchange with Corin on courtly manners also has its references to prostitution ("grease of a mutton" [III.ii.53]), sexuality ("good piece of flesh" [III.ii.63]), and animal copulation treated in terms applicable to human matrimony (III.ii.74–81). Even at the end of the play, with all the lovers in couples, like animals entering the ark, Touchstone brings Audrey along with a characteristic *double entendre*:

> . . . I press in here sir, amongst the rest of the country copulatives, to swear and to forswear, according as marriage binds and blood breaks. . . .
>
> (V.iv.52–54)

Touchstone's continual sexual jesting has an important function in freeing the remaining lovers for other matters, in the same way that the Nurse in *Romeo and Juliet* releases the young people for more poetic passion. Here the lovers can engage in intellectual rather than sexual banter, because that exists like the ground bass of an orchestral work, to underpin other, more glittering dialogue. The fool's marriage, as he himself well knows, is undertaken strictly for lust; *remedium concupiscensis* is the sole reason. Sir Oliver Martext would have done as well as a real priest, "so wedlock would be nibbling" (III.iii.72) and he could later leave his wife. In Touchstone, bawdry is triumphant, sexuality rules his life, and his match with Audrey represents the lowest level on the scale of four that culminates in the marriage of Rosalind and Orlando. Touchstone, the sensual man, marries Audrey, the keeper of goats—a stereotype of sexual potency—who wishes to "be a woman of the world" (V.iii.4), which in the sense of prostitute is indeed an inadvertent "dishonest desire."

Rosalind and Orlando are both seeking to attain their honest desires, and through their love debates they test each other, with Rosalind educating Orlando into a balanced perception of marriage. Throughout this process she engages in an openly adversarial approach of masculine competetiveness in what is basically a literary conflict: Petrarchan idealism encounters antifeminism. But in order to espouse (and of course parody) the misogynistic approach and continue the debate on an egalitarian level, Rosalind adopts another disguise, this time an intellectual one, drawing her material from the vast array of literature on "the woman question." That this additional mask is essential is shown in her opening meeting with Orlando in the forest. She is so unnerved at meeting Orlando face to face that she forgets her resolve to speak to him "like a saucy lackey" (III.ii.282) and lamely asks a trivial, incongruous question:

> *Rosalind*   I pray you, what is't o'clock?
> *Orlando*   You should ask me, what time o'day. There's no clock in the forest.

> *Rosalind*   Then there's no true lover in the forest, else sighing every
> minute and groaning every hour would detect the lazy foot of
> Time as well as a clock.
>
> (III.iii.286–291)

By her second speech Rosalind has recovered something of her composure,
but in so doing she has resorted to a literary commonplace. Orlando picks up
the debate and moves to discuss time, and Rosalind, on safe ground, apparently, offers to define those for whom time ambles, trots, gallops, and stands still.
However, she gives away her own longing almost immediately, beginning with
the word "marry" and continuing throughout with subliminal sexuality, using
the example of horse and rider:

> Marry, he trots hard with a young maid between the contract of her
> marriage and the day it is solemnized. If the interim be but a se'nnight.
> Time's pace is so hard that it seems the length of seven year.
>
> (III.ii.299–302)

Here one can see a possible Freudian association with the symbol of the horse.
She is more successful with the rest of her definitions, but is again caught off
balance when Orlando, intrigued, asks her a personal question:

> *Orlando*   Where dwell you, pretty youth?
> *Rosalind*   With this shepherdess, my sister; here in the skirts of the
> forest, like fringe upon a petticoat.
> *Orlando*   Are you native of this place?
> *Rosalind*   As the cony that you see dwell where she is kindled.
>
> (III.ii.317–322)

Rosalind's similes here are distinctively feminine, and certainly not what one
would expect from a young man. Again recovering herself, Rosalind starts to
take control by turning to the game of antifeminism, now exploiting her androgynous appearance, while using the words of a fictitious uncle

> . . . I thank God I am not a woman, to be touched with so many giddy
> offenses as he hath generally taxed their whole sex withal.
>
> (III.ii.329–331)

By refusing to list these faults at Orlando's request,

> No, I will not cast away my physic but on those that are sick.
>
> (III.ii.338–339)

Rosalind has both gained the upper hand and signified her curative purpose, as
she laughs at "that fancy-monger" poetaster engaged "in deifying the name of
Rosalind," clearly evidence of a severe case of *hereos*. On Orlando's so identi-

fying himself, Rosalind is in full cry, hunting down the absurdities of literary passion, countering them with comparably absurd antifeminist charges. She is at her wittiest when she is engaged in parody, hiding behind a stalking horse erected out of words; this and later confrontations with Orlando are thus a development of the love-debates of medieval and Renaissance writers. By use of this form and frequent employment of the commonplaces of conduct books she manages to maintain her identity as Ganymede, but her intellect does not always control her emotions, and her wit can turn serious when that happens.

Here, however, she is in control and ready to show Orlando what love is. She refuses to believe that he is the lover he claims to be, since he shows none of the signs of a true Petrarchan lover:

> A lean cheek, which you have not; a blue eye and sunken, which you have not; an unquestionable spirit, which you have not; a beard neglected, which you have not; but I pardon you for that, for simply your having in beard is a younger brother's revenue. Then your hose should be ungartered, your bonnet unbanded, your sleeve unbuttoned, your shoe untied, and everything about you demonstrating a careless desolation. But you are no such man: you are rather point-device in your accoustrements, as loving yourself than seeming the lover of any other.
>
> (III.ii.352–362)[44]

However, the tension between her two roles surfaces even here, and once again she nearly gives herself away by revealing knowledge of Orlando's identity as a younger brother, but this revelation is masked in the plethora of details describing the "Amorist,"[45] and Orlando is so far in love that he fails to perceive it. Rosalind then experiments further with him, in effect giving comfort by suggesting that women "give the lie to their consciences" (III.ii.368) by loving, but keeping silent—as of course, she herself is doing. So far Rosalind has been using a dual response to Orlando, employing her two roles. She does this even in her attack:

> Love is merely a madness, and I tell you, deserves as well a dark house and a whip as madmen do; and the reason why they are not so punished and cured is that the lunacy is so ordinary that the whippers are in love too. Yet I profess curing it by counsel.
>
> (III.ii.376–380)

From this time on Rosalind will undertake the cure of love, and this duality of responses continues as subtext—for neither really wishes to be cured—while Rosalind adds an extra element of impersonation to her already complex role-playing, as she recounts her success in dealing with a fictitious case of love:

. . . He was to imagine me his love, his mistress; and I set him every day to woo me. At which time would I, being but a moonish youth, grieve, be effeminate, changeable, longing and liking, proud, fantastical, apish, shallow, inconstant, full of tears, full of smiles; for every passion something and for no passion truly anything, as boys and women are for the most part cattle of this color; would now like him, now loathe him; then entertain him, then forswear him; now weep for him, then spit at him; that I drave my suitor from his mad humor of love to a living humor of madness, which was, to forswear the full stream of the world and to live in a nook, merely monastic. And thus I cured him; and this way will I take upon me to wash your liver as clean as a sound sheep's heart, that there shall not be one spot of love in't.

(III.ii.382–397)

Even here, Rosalind reminds us of her true identity, in her aside referring specifically to women, and she also ironically points up the "madness" of celibacy, "merely monastic." Her approach is to play out the role of erotically experienced enemy of love, who knows full well what women are:

> This sexe is fraile, spitefull, and giuen to reuenge: and therefore men are to vse the greater prudence in the gouerning and managing of them.[46]

On occasion too, such sentiments were expressed by women, as witness the words of the Lady Hecatonphila blaming women who show

> . . . ouer-much inconstancie, pride, wilfulnes, disdaine, and such like, which prooues more to our owne harme, then theirs we seeke to hurt.
>
> . . . .
>
> There are some of vs women, who deeme themeselues neuer satisfied with pride, furie, and scornfulnesse, which makes but a bad agreement among vs: for where disdain is entertained, contempt of all kindnesse is the more increased, and it is pittie a true Louer should haue such a reward for his labour.[47]

This kind of comment furnishes a basis of familiar material to which a Shakespearean audience could relate in appreciating the literary tactics of this *remedium amoris*: which Rosalind is practising.

But "the whippers are in love too," and when Orlando fails to arrive, Rosalind drops her masculine pose and in a role reversal she becomes the helpess lover with Celia playing the curative scoffer. She claims that this young, heart-whole man Orlando, is a deceiver, a betrayer, whose "kisses are Judas's own children" (III.iv.8), but Rosalind counters by comparing them with "holy bread" (III.iv.13), the sacrament instituted just before Christ's betrayal. She is totally committed:

But what talk we of fathers when there is such a man as Orlando?
(III.iv.34–35)

Celia again tries to laugh her out of her melancholy, using the same tactics that Rosalind has used with Orlando, emphasizing the normality of the young man—no ideal lover he:

> O, that's a brave man; he writes brave verses, speaks brave words, swears brave oaths, and breaks them bravely, quite traverse, athwart the heart of his lover, as a puisny tilter, that spurs his horse but on one side, breaks his staff like a noble goose. But all's brave that youth mounts and folly guides.
>
> (III.iv.36–41)

Rosalind also needs to be educated in love, to accept her own lover for what he is, not her own ideal, and Celia's merry attacks on Orlando foreshadow what will happen to her when she too is struck by love. Celia's speeches opposing this commitment are completely different from Rosalind's, and have little of the conventionally literary about them. She seems less sophisticated, but yet in some ways more original than her cousin, with a healthy appreciation of human sexuality, as her sometimes bawdy remarks indicate.

    This skilful alternation of scenes gives motivation for Rosalind's harsh treatment of the shepherdess Phebe, the one sexual withholder of the play, as she trifles with Silvius's faithful heart. This lady, in a parody of pastoral wooing, tortures her lover for mere enjoyment and is too self-centered to see her faults. Rosalind, in the throes of her own love-melancholy, equates herself with Silvius, as she has done from her entry into the forest, and now she makes use of her disguise once more, this time to upbraid a woman. To be sure, Phebe would never have listened to Rosalind in her woman's clothes, and Silvius would not have welcomed female intervention, especially in her criticism of his longsuffering behavior:

> 'Tis not her glass, but you, that flatters her,
> And out of you she sees herself more proper
> Than any of her lineaments can show her.
> But mistress, know yourself. Down on your knees,
> And thank heaven, fasting, for a good man's love;
> For I must tell you friendly in your ear,
> Sell when you can, you are not for all markets.
> Cry the man mercy, take his offer;
> Foul is most foul, being foul to be a scoffer;
> So take her to thee, shepherd. Fare you well.
>
> (III.v.54–63)

Rosalind's love-sickness is smoothly masked by wit when Orlando does finally arrive; tardiness in a mere game is not important to him, but Rosalind is playing seriously and surprises him with the vigor of her attack, proving him once again no true lover. Now she attacks the entire institution of romantic love:

> . . . Men have died from time to time, and worms have eaten them, but not for love.
>
> (IV.i.96–98)

As before, her examples are those of literature and legend, in Troilus and Hero. But then, having forced him to defend his lady, "Virtue is no horn-maker, and my Rosalind is virtuous" (IV.i.57–58), she turns unexpectedly serious by suggesting that they go through a spousal ceremony with Celia as priest. In so doing they follow the words of the *Book of Common Prayer* and contract *sponsalia per verba de praesenti*. Rosalind fully understands what she is doing, and this is signified by her insistence that the correct tense be used: not "I will," as Orlando begins, but "I take thee, Rosalind, for wife" (IV.i.124). Momentarily, she twits him about his "commission" to do this, since he has not yet asked his lady's consent:

> . . . but I do take thee, Orlando, for my husband. There's a girl goes before the priest, and certainly a woman's thought runs before her actions.
>
> (IV.i.125–128)

The word "but" is important here as indicating her capitulation and it is the equivalent of Orlando's "I can live no longer by thinking" in the next act (V.ii.48). Beneath the merriment of this mock-espousal there is considerable seriousness, for she is fully vowing herself to Orlando, binding herself to him in her own person, while Orlando wishes that he were speaking these words to the lady of his heart, rather than Ganymede. The impediment of *error personae* would prevent this ceremonial from being legally binding, but in fact the consent of the lovers does indeed contain the elements of voluntary and unforced vows that the church required,[48] something the audience doubtless understood.

Once again, Rosalind has momentarily dropped her gamesome mask, revealing her true thoughts, but instantly she recovers and takes shelter behind her literary, intellectual disguise, parodying the allegations of the books of behavior:

. . . men are April when they woo, December when they wed. Maids are May when they are maids, but the sky changes when they are wives. I will be more jealous of thee than a Barbary cock-pigeon over his hen, more clamorous than a parrot against rain, more newfangled than an ape, more giddy in my desires than a monkey.

(IV.i.134–139)

In the complexity of her roles as ardent young woman, cynical young man, and literary parodist Rosalind fulminates like the antifeminist Edward Gosynhill:

> And whyles, the woyng time doth last.
> I mean with them, that maydens be
> Lothe to displease, loue sure and fast
> Are what ye wyll, and spede may ye
> Fewe or none, for the most partye
> Gentlye entreatyd, deny you can
> With her tables, to entre your man.
>
> . . . .
>
> Wed them ones, and then a dewe
> Fare well all truste and houswyfrye.[49]

And as if these "joys" of marriage are not a sufficient deterrent:

> I will weep for nothing, like Diana in the fountain, and I will do that when you are disposed to be merry; I will laugh like a hyen, and that when thou art inclined to sleep.
>
> (I.i.140–143)

In thus escalating her catalogue of wifely abuses of matrimonial privilege, Rosalind fastens on one of the cardinal rules for a woman's place in marriage, as enunciated by Erasmus:

> . . . As a mirror, if it's a good one, always gives back the image of the person looking at it, so should a wife reflect her husband's mood, not being gay when he's sad, or merry when he's upset. But whenever he was more upset than usual, I'd either soothe him with pleasant conversation or defer to his anger in silence until he cooled off and an opportunity came to correct or advise him. I'd do the same if he came home tipsy; at the time I'd say nothing except what was agreeable; I'd just coax him to bed.
>
> . . . .
>
> . . . Husbands have much to endure from . . . [wives'] habits as well. On occasion, however—in a serious matter, when something important's at stake—it's right for a wife to reprove her husband; trivial matters are better winked at.[50]

Finally, Rosalind brings up the ultimate fear of the married man—cuckoldry, alleging the insatiability of women, and the inability of the husband to control his wife:

> . . . You shall never take her without her answer unless you take her without her tongue. O, that woman that cannot make her fault her husband's occasion, let her never nurse her child herself, for she will breed it like a fool.
>
> (IV.i.157–161)

As Orlando momentarily suspends the game Rosalind once more tells the truth about her love: "Alas, dear love, I cannot lack thee two hours" (IV.i.163), but again recovers herself in an explosion of wit, extracting a promise of punctuality from her lover, as he departs. Now that the two women are alone, Celia adopts the role of woman's defender, castigating her cousin in very frank language:

> You have simply misused our sex in your love-prate. We must have your doublet and hose plucked over your head, and show the world what the bird hath done to her own nest.
>
> (IV.i.185–188)

As before, she is the voice of common sense to her cousin who oscillates between masculine masquing and feminine feeling, with emotions currently in the ascendant.

Shakespeare, ever in careful control of his material in this play, here avoids sentimentality by undercutting love's fidelity with Jaques' parodic praise of cuckoldry (IV.ii.13–18), and following it with another burlesquing episode. Phebe's letter of love, delivered by Silvius, offers an echo of Orlando's unsuccessful romantic poems and also his "cure." Faithful love will remain constant, as Silvius demonstrates, while the more Rosalind/Ganymede rails, the more Phebe will pursue her passion. Once again Rosalind takes on the role of educator as she plans to support the cause of Silvius, the "tame snake," and bring Phebe to accept a lover who has demonstrated fidelity comparable to Orlando's.

The passage of time, and the unpunctuality of Orlando, eventually reveal the truth of their femininity to both Rosalind and Celia, through another message bearer, Oliver, who reveals Orlando's advance in virtue. He has proved himself faithful in love, and virtuous in forgiveness in saving his wicked brother from certain and deserved death. This disinterested action leads Oliver to confess and repent his own fault as he tells his tale. The first result of this account is Rosalind's swoon; her intellect, no longer able to control the emotional, psychological strain of her masculine disguise, has taught her that she cannot live without Orlando, whose potential for unselfish affection (revealed earlier by his treatment of Adam) has now been fully demonstrated by his risking his life for a professed enemy who had sought his life.

Two scenes later, the effect of this incident on Celia is shown, as Oliver asks his brother's consent to their marriage, underlining the depth of his repentance in offering restitution; he will give all his worldly goods to Orlando. The sudden affection of Oliver and Celia has often been criticized as mere dramatic convenience, but Shakespeare has prepared for it throughout the action. Celia has long been a scoffer at Rosalind's passion, but her earthy imagery and frank acceptance of feminine sexuality offer a contradictory subtext. Like Rosalind, she has needed to meet a handsome, eligible young man, and her immediate passion for the reformed Oliver parallels that of her cousin for Orlando. There is also a further similarity, for in planning to renounce his inheritance, Oliver, like the earlier Orlando, is now a poor man. Thus both cousins have fallen in love with the persons, not the possessions of their lovers. Immediate marriage is what Oliver and Celia desire—no Neoplatonic ladder of love for them, as Rosalind well understands in her comic account:

> . . . your brother and my sister no sooner met but they looked; no sooner looked but they loved; no sooner loved but they sighed; no sooner sighed but they asked one another the reason; no sooner knew the reason but they sought the remedy; and in these degrees have they made a pair of stairs to marriage, which they will climb incontinent or else be incontinent before marriage: they are in the very wrath of love, and they will together; clubs cannot part them.
>
> (V.ii.31–39)

This is the catalytic event. Orlando's cure has worked in the way Rosalind has planned; his love is no longer a literary passion, and for the first time he commits himself to a wish for marriage, envying Oliver "in having what he wishes for" (V.ii.45). The game of love no longer satisfies him and he wants to possess his very human Rosalind with all her faults and virtues. He loves a woman, not an idealized image, while Rosalind loves the man she has tested and educated into admitting the sexual desire they both share—as her *double entendre* indicates:

> *Rosalind*   Why then, to-morrow I cannot serve your turn for Rosalind?
> *Orlando*   I can live no longer by thinking.
>
> (V.ii.46–48)

In her role as stage manager and manipulative figure, even magician, Rosalind orchestrates herself and Orlando, Silvius and Phebe into a laudatory litany of love. Paeans of praise speedily turn to practical, legal business, as (still disguised) she gains the *de futuro* consents of both her father and Orlando. But with Silvius and Phebe she arranges an espousal not seen before in Shakespearean comedy, a *conditional espousal*, an exchange of vows which would create an indissoluble union on fulfilment of the condition, in this case Phebe's refusal to marry Ganymede/Rosalind.[51]

Of all the lovers, only one pair appears without the machinations of Rosalind. Touchstone and Audrey's unexpected arrival underlines the second major reason for marriage, *remedium concupiscensis*, and emphasizes its essential sexuality. Structurally, this incident, with its literary parody of the rules of dueling, serves to allow Rosalind time to change into feminine attire. Hymen, appearing by magic, celebrates the primary purpose for marriage in both Anglican and Roman canon law—procreation. The third reason for marriage, companionship, is never mentioned, only implied in Jaques' evaluation of all the marriages. The important element of this scene is the emphasis on fertility and procreation which Shakespeare had displayed in *A Midsummer Night's Dream* and which looks ahead to the dynastic conclusions of the last plays. But not all these marriages seem destined for success, as Jaques points out. Orlando and Rosalind display the perfection of passion and mutuality; Oliver and Celia will need further development in the second quality, while Silvius and Phebe need to develop the first. Last come Touchstone and Audrey, whose match is the common metal that tests the true gold of the ideal relationship, of Orlando and Rosalind. The concluding action of the play also celebrates matrimonial harmony in its use of the symbolic dance, but the last line recalls the audience to the recognition of sexuality as Duke Senior gives his blessing:

> Proceed, proceed. We'll begin these rites,
> As we do trust they'll end, in true delights.
> (V.iv.191–192)

As You Like It thus explores both masculine and feminine sexuality. Through her disguise Rosalind plays both erotic roles and comes to understand that the love-relationship is one of reciprocity, tolerance, and mutuality, teaching her lover in the process. She is the *primum mobile* of the play's cosmos, and like Portia in the courtroom of Venice, she uses her disguise to initiate direct, confrontational, adversarial attacks, but unlike her predecessor, she carries the game further, revealing her identity only when Orlando's education has been completed. Her complexity of roles and attitudes gives her an appeal for both the men and women of the audience through her ironic detachment and virtuosic qualities, not found in other transvestite heroines. She controls the central action of the play, the movement of spirit, through her disguise, and though her appearance is androgynous, her temper is not. Always, she remains feminine, and Shakespeare never allows his beholders to forget it. She gladly relinquishes her male disguise, despite the social freedom it confers. For her it was merely a role, assumed first for safety and continued for educational reasons. Her literary and antifeminist mask is doffed just as easily, for it is no longer needed now that love's satisfaction is near, and identities (both literal and spiritual) are revealed. She has examined both gender roles and happily chooses that of wife.

The spiritual journey to the heart of self, which is the real agenda in the curative Forest of Arden has now been completed. Reconciliations have been accomplished, and those courtiers and couples who have been tested and changed by the green world are now ready to put their new knowledge to use in the outside world of affairs. Only the melancholy Jaques and the repentant Duke Frederick remain as additions to the original population of Arden.

Fittingly, in view of her cardinal role as teacher in this merry school for lovers, Rosalind, now in feminine clothing, is given the traditionally masculine task of reciting the epilogue. Even here, as she *conjures* applause from both men and women by appealing to their mutual affection for each other, Shakespeare exploits disguise again, drawing piquant attention to the fact that the role is still being played by a boy, a dimension that is now lost in modern performance. Thus, even here, Rosalind emphasizes her power of understanding the thoughts and hearts of man and woman, the mutuality of matrimony, and the interdependence of the genders. Rosalind alone of all the comedic women has quite this dualism of spirit allied to an intellectual skill tempered with affection and tried in adversity. She brings reconciliation, respect, and tolerance to the competitive masculine world of two generations—the dukes and the young men. Through her, the feminine values of cooperation and mutual support triumph with the aid of a disguise which allows her a freedom of witty expression and a credibility of comment often denied the woman of Shakespeare's day.

SECTION 5

Twelfth Night—Viola, the Exemplum of Patience

With *Twelfth Night* we come to Shakespeare's final romantic comedy containing his longest and most subtly complex trouser role, together with the last lesson in what can be called his comedic school for refashioning the art of love.[52] The title of the play, with its resonances of Epiphany and the Feast of Fools, also indicates the end of that merry season of misrule, and can also signify Shakespeare's farewell to this particular comic genre. As the merrymakers of this season return to a workaday, serious world, so too the author turns to dark comedy and tragedy. The subtitle, "What You Will," can also be variously interpreted. It can mean nothing more than romantic flummery, a bagatelle, and the New Arden editors deny serious implications to both parts of the title.[53] But it can also mean "what you desire," [54] and that may well be a happy ending, with reconciliations and marriages. Another possibility exists, by analogy with the "Will" sonnets (Nos 135–136), which leads to a consideration of the confusions of sexuality which pervade the play and are finally resolved in the promise of sexual satisfaction in matrimony.[55]

Reprise and farewell are also important elements of *Twelfth Night*, for here Shakespeare redeploys and revises an astonishing number of devices and characters from the earlier comedies. The identical twins of *The Comedy of Errors* are now twins of different sexes; the closed world of *Much Ado About Nothing* is developed into the two carefully differentiated houses of melancholy ruled by Orsino and Olivia.[56] Shylock, the *isolato*, the enemy of joy, reappears as the narcissistic Malvolio, who is also ejected unrepentant from the stage.[57] Friendship is subsidiary here, but it is touched on in Sebastian and Antonio. Olivia, the grieving and wilful heiress, is Portia without the disguise; Toby is another Falstaff, and of course Viola is the final comedic development of the earlier transvestite heroines, Julia of *The Two Gentlemen of Verona* in particular.

The theme of the play is as before, the education of lovers so that they finally achieve in marriage a balanced relationship of intellectual judgment, mutuality, and sexual union.[58] At the same time, as Anne Barton notes, the play stands in an analogous position to *The Tempest* with its return from the sea, its heavy dependence on music, and its heroine, Viola, who differs greatly from her witty, openly manipulative predecessors, Portia and Rosalind.[59]

Here "in her strange passivity, her insistence upon enduring events rather than creating them,"[60] she looks ahead to the young women of the romances, though she lacks their mysterious quality of what might be called "salvation." They call forth the goodness of humanity and bring other characters to a fuller understanding of themselves in particular and human behavior in general. Here, however, this enlightenment is not fully achieved, particularly among the downstairs denizens.

The basic structure of this complex play is that of division, both of character and milieu. Viola and Sebastian, the twins, are divided from each other; Orsino and Olivia are similarly divided from their true selves because of their excessive emotionalism. The action of the play, the, leads to their integration, their discovery of wholeness, their psychological health in marriage. This separation is underscored by the completely different atmosphere of the two houses of the action, Orsino's being shadowy, populated with characterless attendants, while Olivia's is more free-wheeling, filled with very recognizable eccentrics. Individual characters can move from place to place and into incongruous environments, so that different worlds, social classes, plot and subplot interpenetrate at all levels.[61] The tonal quality of the play is also complex and varied, with its use of resonantal parody, of contrast and different levels of comedy from the wit of comedy of manners, through quasi-Jonsonian satire to the boisterous low comedy of Toby and his ilk.[62]

Overall, however, *Twelfth Night* leaves its audience with a sense of finality, a feeling that a world of release, of merriment, a place where time is beneficent, not destructive, has vanished. Thus, Feste's concluding song is far more than the "nonsense song" some critics have believed it to be,[63] and closer to the ages of man tradition of Jaques in *As You Like It*.[64] Also, in its phallic reference to "A foolish thing," it recalls the basic sexuality of the action, looking back on past joys and ahead to the realities of existence. Dame Ngaio Marsh (better known for her detective novels than her distinguished stage productions) once staged this conclusion with singular understanding of its atmosphere. Having finished his song, Feste laid down his lute, crumbled a rose over it, and stole, emptyhanded, away—perhaps back to the theatrical world of wish-fulfillment, while the theatregoers must pass out into the wintry weather of both life and the elements.[65]

"This is Illyria, Lady" (I.ii.2), identifies the strange land of the play,[66] so far known to the audience as the home of two melancholy folk, Orsino and Olivia. It also introduces two themes, the return from the sea and the revelatory journey. Thrown suddenly upon her own resources Viola is forced to work out her own destiny, and this is finally brought about by the return of her divided self in the person of Sebastian, from the sea. In the meantime, Viola must take some action, and she decides like her predecessors, to adopt masculine disguise; however, because her motivation is not discussed at length, it is sometimes considered suspect because of her comment

> Orsino! I have heard my father name him.
> He was a bachelor then.
>
> (I.ii.28–29)

Samuel Johnson, followed by later critics, consequently dubbed her an "excellent schemer,"[67] and indeed her action does at first seem questionable since she originally expressed a wish to serve the lady Olivia, whose mournful situation parallels her own in the loss of a brother

> . . . for whose dear love,
> They say, she hath abjured the sight
> And company of men.
>
> (I.ii.38–40)

The precise interpretation of these lines can afford a clue. C. J. Sisson, emphasizing the word "company" and associating it with courtship, concluded that they referred specifically to Orsino,[68] but if one defines "men" as humankind in general, then Olivia is indeed planning to live a cloistral existence. Thus, Viola can be cleared of the charge of scheming, since she could not serve "that lady." The closest Viola can come to her feminine *alter ego* is to serve Orsino, the lady's lover, and for safety's sake she chooses to adopt the appearance of her masculine complement, her twin brother, Sebastian. Then she will wait and see what will happen: "What else may hap, to time I will commit" (I.ii.60).

After this scene she spends the entire play as Cesario, never resuming her feminine garb, even when her task of educating Orsino in love is finished. Once donned, her physical disguise is never removed, though the audience sees behind her psychological mask as she laments the problems attendant on her new identity. Unlike Portia and Rosalind who enjoy the societal freedom conferred by disguise and who control affairs through their masculine appearance, Viola in her numerous asides and soliloquies laments the alienation that her disguise has inflicted on her. This insecurity in her new role arises from the fact that she is totally alone throughout the play; she has no Nerissa, Celia, or even Silvia to offer her any comfort, and thus she can never put aside her mask (or her male attire) to gain some respite from the tension of the part she plays. Consequently she must enlist the audience's sympathy by means of direct address.

Thus Viola is imprisoned by her role which frees both Orsino and Olivia to speak frankly to her, but forces her into silence, into passivity. Rosalind *uses* time by anticipating and organizing its effects, but Viola *submits* to time as her difficulties and complications increase, operating negatively by withdrawing from action:

> O Time, thou must untangle this, not I;
> It is too big a knot for me t'untie.
> (II.ii.39–40)

The Time in which Viola places her trust is beneficent, not human *tempus* which implies physical decay, but rather the "ever-flowing, vivifying dynamism" of the new conception of "another aspect of Time—its continuity and practical infiniteness, . . . [not] Time's transitoriness."[69] This then is cyclic Time, the time that brings forth truth through the invocation of the benign metaphysical entities of fortune and nature as well.[70] In effect, Viola *invests* her trust in Time hoping to gain a return, a happy outcome, a disentangling of confusion, a new order to replace what was destroyed by shipwreck. This is Time as an affirmative principle, not the time that wastes, the *tempus* of the "bending sickle," which Feste's melancholy song recounts, the payment of humanity's debt to mortality. Thus, Viola's apparent inaction is really a delegation of activity to a metaphysical conception, a faith in the ultimate goodness of the universe.

Her passivity also possesses another, archetypal quality which arises from her twinning. Whereas Portia, and more particularly Rosalind, take pleasure in their control of disguise because they can both discover and exercise traditionally masculine roles and qualities normally forbidden them by society, Viola cannot do so. Experiment with the disguise/game of masculinity is all but impossible for her, and the answer is to be found in the androgynous myth of Plato's *Symposium* where, in the days before the giants Otys and Ephialtes threatened the supremacy of Zeus,

> The sexes were not two, as they are now, but originally three in number; there was man, woman, and the union of the two, having a name corresponding to the double nature, which had once a real existence, but is now lost, and the word 'androgynous' is only preserved as a term of reproach.[71]

As punishment, Zeus punished humankind by dividing the androgyne into two parts which forever seek their lost counterparts:

And when one of them meets with his other half, the actual half of himself, whether he be a lover of youth or a lover of another sort, the pair are lost in amazement of love and friendship and intimacy, and one will not be out of the other's sight, . . . even for a moment.[72]

This is Viola's situation in the loss of a brother, her twin. She has lost the masculine part of herself, as Sebastian has lost his lifelong feminine counterpart, and hence the two are helplessly divided, separated from the psychic complementarity and subliminal communication that modern psychology has verified as existing between twins, even of different sexes. Their relationship is one of fraternal emotion, for neither has yet been sexually awakened, but here Shakespeare in this play comes nearer than usual for him to the titillating exploitation of a potential incest-motif. This search for a lost masculine principle in her life can also explain how Viola's original desire to serve Olivia (whose grief she equates with her own) is easily transferred to serve Orsino, a representative of the masculine companionship she has lost. She can *play* the external aspects of the male role well enough, because she has seen it in her twin, but she remains totally feminine, continually conscious of what she lacks—a penis and all that its possession implies in terms of valor and enterprise. "A little thing would make me tell them how much I lack of a man!" (III.iv.282–283)[73] Her continual recognition of this "lack" explains why she takes no joy in her role, and why she remains the most female, least aggressive, most introspective, and most complex of Shakespeare's transvestite heroines.

When Viola goes to Orsino's house in her disguise she considers herself as having renounced sexuality, rather than taking on a masculine identity: "Thou shalt present me as an eunuch to him" (I.ii.155–156), she says to the Captain. Unlike Portia and Rosalind, she makes no affirmative comments about her masculine appearance, and in dressing herself as Sebastian she "unsexes" herself in a manner totally opposed to that of the later Lady Macbeth, embarking on a journey into a limboland of asexuality. But, as the action of the play frequently demonstrates, Viola is not an expert in long-range planning, because she responds to events rather than initiating them, and thus miscalculates. The first evidence of this is the unexpected sexual tension she encounters in her new role.

Orsino instantly responds psychologically to her feminine qualities, while she is instantly awakened sexually and psychologically to a masculinity she has not discovered before. As a result she wishes within three days to be his wife, while he spends the rest of the play learning to respond sexually to her. At the beginning of the play, as Leggatt suggests, Orsino is "a character in search of an attitude, full of emotion but with no satisfactory outlet for emotion, nothing around which to shape it."[74] With Viola's arrival he discovers such a focus as he responds, unknowing of the consequences, to her femininity:

> . . . Diana's lip
> Is not more smooth and rubious; thy small pipe
> Is as the maiden's organ, shrill and sound,
> And all is semblative a woman's part.
>
> (I.iv.31–33)

But she is compared with Diana, not Venus, because Orsino is committed to adoration of a nonexistent ideal, personified for him by Olivia.

She responds to Viola also, in a reversal of the situation. She reacts psychologically and sexually to the appearance of Cesario's masculinity, which is demonstrated by the verbal wit that the disguised lady employs in their scenes together, and which is absent from her scenes with Orsino. In addition, Viola's feminine attributes, particularly her emotional empathy with the bereaved Olivia, render her even more attractive. Then when Sebastian appears, Olivia instantly responds to the totality of his maleness, while he rediscovers the feminine principle he had lost in the "death" of his twin, but this time he too is sexually awakened to a redefinition of the relationship by marriage.

Throughout the play Viola is the catalytic figure as she discovers her own sexuality in her relationship to Orsino, and through her androgynous appearance and passive indirection she is the agent through which Orsino, Olivia, and Sebastian discover their sexual identities and define their commitments to each other. In short, she is another example of the Shakespearean comic heroine who teaches other characters to alter their perceptions of love. But before this result is achieved, Viola undergoes greater psychological and physical suffering than any of her predecessors, including even Julia in *The Two Gentlemen of Verona*, whose predicament is sometimes parallel. This is the reason that audiences and critics usually admire Portia and Rosalind, but react emotionally to Viola.

At first Viola's disguise works to her advantage. With the barriers of sex obliterated, Orsino is freed to offer her his confidences:

> Thou know'st no less but all. I have unclasped
> To thee the book even of my secret soul.
>
> (I.iv.12–13)

On her side Viola has fallen immediately in love, as her first words delivered in disguise to Valentine, an attendant, indicate:

> You either fear his humor or my negligence, that you call in question the continuance of his love. Is he inconstant, sir, in his affections?
>
> (I.iv.4–6)

With almost equal celerity, Viola discovers that her disguise, which at first seemed to offer security and then access to the man she has come so quickly to love, has concomitant liabilities. She who almost instantly thought of marriage to Orsino, quickly finds herself powerless, trapped and imprisoned in her dual role of young man and loyal servant. Unhesitatingly she opts for patience, persistence, secrecy, and service to her beloved, virtues which recall those of the traditional courtly lover. Regretfully she proceeds to the wooing of Olivia:

> . . . Yet a barful strife!
> Whoe'er I woo, myself would be his wife.
>
> (I.iv.40–41)

Orsino has been right in his assessment of Olivia, perceiving that she has not yet been sexually awakened:

> O, she that hath a heart of that fine frame
> To pay this debt of love but to a brother,
> How will she love when the rich golden shaft
> Hath killed the flock of all affections else
> That live in her; when liver, brain, and heart,
> These sovereign thrones, are all supplied and filled,
> Her sweet perfections, with one self king.
>
> (I.i.34–40)

She is now introduced as an independent, witty young woman with a mind of her own, the chatelaine of a remarkably populous house where revelry and eccentricity coexist, even thrive, in the face of grief. Her character is, however, a trifle inconsistent, because in age she is apparently meant to be somewhat younger than the twins, since Shakespeare never violates the decorum of age in marriage. However, she is authoritative, much more aggressive than Viola, and well able to control unruly servants, relatives, and friends, personality traits that derive from her original, the wealthy young widow, Julina, in the source tale of *Apolonius and Silla*.[75]

These qualities have importance for Viola's first messenger scene (I.v) which is developed by means of role-playing, parody, and variation of emotional response. The scene echoes and reverses the preceding one between Orsino and Viola, master and servant (I.iv), with communication facilitated and confidences frankly exchanged through the aegis of Viola's disguise. The mourning lady has repeatedly refused Orsino's suit, yet Viola gains entrance, not so much because of her importunate stubbornness, but rather because of Malvolio's provocative description:

> [He is] Not yet old enough for a man nor young enough for a boy; as a squash is before 'tis a peascod or a codling when 'tis almost an apple. 'Tis with him in standing water, between boy and man. He is very well-favored and he speaks very shrewishly. One would think his mother's milk were scarce out of him.
>
> (I.v.150–155)

The unexpected bawdry of Malvolio's choice of words ("peascod," "codling," and association with the apple of temptation), together with an overall impression of an attractive, androgynous personality, decides Olivia to interview this young man, who sounds more like a plaything than a threat, an innocent source of entertainment for a young woman for whom grief is beginning to pall. Some respite from her cloistral existence is indeed welcome.

This scene with Olivia demonstrates Viola's most complex role-playing to date. She presents herself with parodic exaggeration as a saucy, witty lackey, delivering volleys of praise befitting her part of romantic wooer: "Most radiant, exquisite, and unmatchable beauty" (I.i.162); then she immediately undercuts her speech as she refers to it with comic detachment as a mere artifact, written and delivered to order, not from the heart:

> . . . I would be loath to cast away my speech; For, besides that it is excellently well penned, I have taken great pains to con it. Good beauties, let me sustain no scorn. I am very comptible, even to the least sinister usage.
>
> (I.v.165–168)

Continually she insists on her role-playing, using it as defense: "That question's out of my part" (I.v.170), and "I am not that I play" (I.v.176). Here we can observe some of the same "layering" as in *As You Like It*, which later in the scene develops another level when Viola plays the role of an idealized Orsino to Olivia's hardheartedness, while simultaneously revealing her own tactics in gaining his love—patient fidelity. However, Viola's last words in this quoted speech also indicate her acute sensitivity, the ease with which she can lose control of the parts she is playing.

After further exchange of wit Viola returns to the wooing, asking impudently to behold the veiled lady's face, at which vision she betrays a very feminine jealousy when confronted with her competitor, a fine piece of Shakespearean exploitation of "discrepant awareness." "Excellently done, if God did all" (I.v.223), nettles Olivia, unprepared for such a response from a servant, a go-between.[76] Viola now recovers herself as she praises the lady, exhorting her to matrimony, using the philoprogenitive argument of the sonnets. Olivia now replies in parody of the blazon poem, only to call forth a rebuke from Viola who is playing her role as Orsino's advocate at the cost of her own peace of mind. She does not wish her beloved to be hurt by this proud lady, and in her service to him she seeks to gain his love.

The interaction between the two ladies becomes more complicated as they start to speak at cross purposes. "Wooe not by Embassadour," Alexander Niccholes had warned, with considerable perspicacity.[77] Viola tries to teach Olivia how to love, while pleading the case of Orsino, but that only increases Olivia's passion for "Cesario." At the same time, Olivia's high praise of the Duke's very considerable virtues intensifies Viola's love-longing. The scene is now tripartite: Viola wooes for Orsino, but wishes him for herself; Olivia wooes Viola, whose lack of response increases her affection for a "dream," one which will eventually come true in the person of Sebastian.

The famous "willow cabin" speech in which Viola proclaims her fidelity to Orsino wins Olivia, and it is also a fine piece of romantic poetry. However, no one in the play fully follows this formula, certainly not Viola, who becomes the pattern of patient service, waiting for time to bring truth to light. Olivia is now sexually awakened by this eloquent stranger:

> You might do much. What is your parentage?
> (I.v.263)

Here one can see both desire and reason in conflict, while Viola's reply once more indicates role-playing:

> Above my fortunes, yet my state is well.
> I am a gentleman.
> (I.v.263)

This reply gives Olivia further hope, and she casts caution to the wind as she undiplomatically attempts to press money on Cesario, and then sends him a ring, a compromising gift which usually indicated betrothal.

Viola's reaction is one of perplexity, confusion, and sorrow. She and Olivia are two of a kind. Their "waxen hearts" have received the stamp of love's false coinage: Orsino, who seems unattainable, and Viola/Cesario who is impossible. Viola here perceives their mutual plight with bifurcated vision: as a woman she understands the ease with which men can deceive by false exterior, and most "masculinely" she perceives "the plasticity of Olivia's female nature."[78] Simultaneously she experiences and understands the pangs of unsatisfiable love felt by herself, Orsino, and Olivia. Clearly, then, her disguise has been a "wickedness" since it has prevented full communication with Orsino, but has allowed him to confide in her. Paradoxically, and to Viola's chagrin, it has done the same thing for her and Olivia; the deaths of brothers are forgotten in matters of wooing. But on a level that Viola does not yet know, her disguise has been an agent in her own sexual awakening, as well as that of Olivia, and for the remainder of the play she will, by her submission to the good offices of time, bring *both* Orsino and Olivia to the achievement of their desires. Far from serving "as a gallery for victims of quaint sexual neuroses,"[79] the action of *Twelfth Night* details a journey into marriage and an acceptance of the mutuality and interdependence of masculinity and feminity within that relationship. Each of the characters learns to understand and accept individual sexuality and gender identity.

Viola's "cure" of Orsino is accomplished indirectly, and in a manner far different from the cure of *As You Like It*, where Rosalind added another element of role-playing. Here, Viola's disguise has removed Orsino from the shackles of romantic idealization of woman, facilitating communication, even criticism, as they debate on love. Orsino begins as master to his servant, offering advice, but then with unexpected insight he notes of men:

> Our fancies are more giddy and unfirm,
> More longing, wavering, sooner lost and worn,
> Than women's are.
>
> (II.iv.32–34)

This indicates some self-knowledge, some potential for Orsino's development into suitable marriage material for Viola. He repeats the usual rule that a woman should "take an elder than herself," adapting to her husband and becoming used to his ways. But the relationship should not be one of master and slave, "So sways she level in her husband's heart" (II.iv.30).[80] At this moment, however, his commitment to such mutuality is overshadowed by his limitless romantic passion for Olivia, which will not accept refusal:

> There is no woman's sides
> Can bide the beating of so strong a passion
> As love doth give my heart; no woman's heart

So big to hold so much; they lack retention.
Alas their love may be called appetite,
No motion of the liver but the palate,
That suffers surfeit, cloyment, and revolt;
But mine is all as hungry as the sea
And can digest as much. Make no compare
Between that love a woman can bear me
And that I owe Olivia.
                              (II.iv.92–102)

Clearly his current understanding of love is still totally narcissistic, as he insists on the alleged sexual insatiability of woman, and the all-devouring quality of his own passion—which will eventually be satisfied by Viola, a gift from the sea. She, by her very presence on stage here offers visual evidence that Orsino has much to learn about love. Hence her revelatory speech on the fidelity and silence of woman's love is a first step in his education as she tells him the truth about herself, which her disguise frees her to do, by using the tale of a mythical sister as a mask. She almost reveals herself as she controls this portion of the scene, transcending gender roles and forcing Orsino to listen. But this "Unstaid and skittish" lover is still so enwrapt in his own passion that hearing, he does not understand. Viola realizes this, as she reaches the end of her speech of love, exemplified by the fate of her "sister":

        . . . She never told her love,
        But let concealment, like a worm i'th'bud,
        Feed on her damask cheek. She pin'd in thought;
        And, with a green and yellow melancholy,
        She sat like Patience on a monument,
        Smiling at grief. Was this not love indeed?
        We men may say more, swear more; but indeed
        Our shows are more than will; for still we prove
        Much in our vows, but little in our love.
                              (II.iv.109–117)

This evokes Orsino's pity, and in her riddling reply to his request for information concerning the young woman's fate Viola comes perilously close to telling all:

        I am all the daughters of my father's house,
        And all the brothers too, and yet I know not.
        Sir, shall I to the lady.
                              (II.iv.119–121)

Quickly she changes the subject, and Orsino orders her to continue the wooing of Olivia. He is not yet aware of the fidelity and patience of woman's love. However, there is a hidden irony in this exchange which is manifested only at the end of the play. Viola does not pine away with any green and yellow melancholy, because she works behind the scenes, impressing Orsino with continued protestations of love which Shakespeare, with admirable dramatic economy, does not stage. Orsino and Viola are not seen together again until the last scene of play, when the Duke, realizing Viola's true gender identity, comes to recognize that Viola's love for him is that of a woman, not the loyalty of a servant. Now he recalls:

> Boy, thou hast said to me a thousand times
> Thou never should'st love woman like to me.
> (V.i.259–260)

Orsino's addressing her as "boy," is indicative of his surprise, but Viola is now freed from the constraints of disguise and can speak openly of the constancy and love she has shown and will continue to owe Orsino. Time has aided Viola and her indirection has helped bring the truth of her affections to light.

Olivia, however, operates quite differently from Viola, because she takes immediate action, whereas Viola is a user of words and it is by them, as well as service, that she succeeds in gaining Orsino. Through words Viola gains access to Olivia, and her skill in repartee wins the heart of the lady. By III.i, as Viola courts her in formulaic words, "Most excellent accomplished lady, the heavens / rain odors on you" (III.i.82–83), Olivia is direct, wooing the disguised Viola without concern for her honor. As before, in her scene with Orsino (II.iv), Viola is forced on the defensive, but here she is playing the role of hardhearted lover listening to the hopeless suit of a woman whose situation is parallel to her own. But even though she is playing a part, and continually insists on that fact, Viola is shown as reacting to Olivia's situation as a fellow-victim:

> By innocence I swear, and by my youth,
> I have one heart, one bosom, and one truth,
> And that no woman has; nor never none
> Shall mistress be of it, save I alone.
> (III.i.154–157)

Now, in the farcical center of the play, almost all aspects of the plot collide with and interpenetrate each other, with the marriage of Olivia as the focal point. Malvolio, the ambitious steward,[81] becomes a grotesque parody of the narcissistic Orsino, and the butt of unsuccessful attempts at reformation. At the same time Shakespeare further exploits the problems Viola faces in her disguise. Her duel with Andrew, the gull and unsuccessful suitor of Olivia, becomes an hilarious parody of that masculine *rite de passage*—physical prowess and skill in arms. Viola's weapons are the passive feminine ones of words, while Andrew has absolutely no weapons, intellectual, martial, or even physical, since he appears to be literally a eunuch, ironically a role Viola adopted at the beginning of the play. Masculine appearance and dress do not imply the existence of masculinity. This duel, apart from its comic quality, has great structural importance, for it reveals that Sebastian lives, that he is a man worthy of Antonio's friendship (III.iv), that he is valorous (IV.i), and that he is indistinguishable from his sister. This physical similarity then becomes the major comic device which leads to the final revelation, and Shakespeare exploits it to a grand total of eight confusions. Agreed, this does seem improbable, but in Illyria, and on the stage, when revelry and rapid action supersede rationality, the situation is more acceptable than in the study.

Submitting oneself to the logic of farce, in this case the indistinguishability of twins of different sexes (and of course begging the question), Olivia's "rescue" of Sebastian from Sir Toby can be accepted. Even Sebastian's sudden love for Olivia can also be explained by recalling the *Symposium* and its belief that when those lovers destined for each other meet, their affections are totally and irrevocably engaged. Olivia had fallen in love with the shadow, the dream, of Sebastian in the disguised Viola, and now she meets the reality. Shakespeare takes some pains to defuse criticism of this love in two ways. First he interpolates a scene in which Malvolio asserts his sanity in the face of the Fool's determined gulling, and then (IV.i) he brings Sebastian to a similar assertion of sanity, of reality, in the face of inexplicable events. One scene underlines the other. Second, he has Olivia rush the dazed young man to exchange solemn vows of love before a priest following the ritual of espousal:

> A contract of eternal bond of love,
> Confirmed by mutual joinder of your hands,
> Attested by the holy close of lips,
> Strength'ned by interchangement of your rings;
> And all the ceremony of this compact
> Sealed in my function, by my testimony.
> (V.i.150–155)

This report gives Shakespeare's most complete report of a witnessed religious espousal, but whether in terms of present or future tense is not quite clear, though Olivia's earlier words "Plight me the full assurance of your faith" (IV.iii.26), indicates the former. As before, in *As You Like It*, the absolute legality of this contract is doubtful, given the obvious impediment of *error personae*, but free and unforced consent is surely there. The serious nature of the contract does, however, lend credibility to the situation.

By now, those of literal mind must question Viola's curious failure to follow up on her discovery that Sebastian lives (III.iv) and her continuance of what is now obviously an unnecessary masquerade, particularly when Orsino threatens her with death, believing her to have been unfaithful in her relations with Olivia. Structurally, this situation is the culmination of Viola's problems with disguise, but is also the ultimate test of her fidelity and Orsino's commitment to his servant. Viola will die "a thousand deaths" for him as she goes

> After him I love
> More than I love these eyes, more than my life,
> More, by all mores, than e'er I shall love wife.
> If I do feign, you witnesses above
> Punish my life for tainting of my love.
>   (V.i.128–132)

In her outward appearance she does indeed feign, but not in her heart.

With the deliberately parodic recognition scene between Viola and Sebastian the twins are again united, but paradoxically separated through their sexual awakening and discovery of a new, mature affection. ". . . Nature to her bias" drew Olivia to Sebastian, both "maid and man," so that they will initiate each other into full sexual union. He is now ready to affirm his vows with his own body. Orsino now looks again at Viola and his affections undergo complete transference to her, remembering her vows of love and service, perceiving also that his own affection for this young "man" was in fact that of man for woman. He too has found his sexual counterpart and plights his troth to her; "Give me thy hand" (V.i.265). But he is still intellectually confused, for old habits die hard, and he continues to address the disguised Viola as Cesario, but he happily looks forward to their new relationship:

> . . . when in other habits thou art seen,
> Orsino's mistress and his fancy's queen.
>   (V.i.376–377)

These final words of the play indicate Orsino's advance in an understanding of love and its patient, lasting commitment. Theirs is a love which has grown slowly, been tested in service, and has now developed into mutuality.

The events of this play of confusion, revelry, and psycho-sexual development are not subject to the rules of daily existence. The action of this comedy really shows the objective manifestation of masculine and feminine sexuality, each character seeking fulfillment in a member of the opposite gender, a destined counterpart.[82] The twins, exemplifying femininity and masculinity are restored to their psychic complementarity when they find each other. But they have also undergone changes in discovering love's sexuality and seek an additional, different relationship in marriage to Orsino and Olivia, both of whom have been led to an understanding of themselves and refined into love by Viola, who has taught by example and patient sympathy, because she has briefly experienced something of the nature of both sexes. Nonetheless, the actual nature of the marriage relationship is never discussed on an intellectual level in this play, unlike *The Merchant of Venice* and *As You Like It*; here the lovers discuss the quality of emotional experience, and in entering into marriage they trust their hearts and physical desires rather than reason. When they leave the stage empty, except for Feste, they have decided to seize the moment.

For this reason the songs of Feste have importance throughout the play, with their insistence on the passage of time, of death, and the transitory nature of human life. Revelry, the time of youth, of folly, is short-lived, and though the journey of this play has ended in marriage, "in lovers meeting," the reality that life, as imaged in the action, will also pass away is continually emphasized in the songs. For this reason it is fitting that this comedy, the last of Shakespeare's romantic comedies, should end in solitary fashion on a note of sadness, nostalgia for past revelry, for lost youth, leaving the audience with a sense of melancholy, of evanescence, and a recognition that "youth's a stuff will not endure."

Part Two

THE WAY OF WIFELY BEHAVIOR

CHAPTER III

Society's Conventions and
The Comedy of Errors

W ith their particularly notable gallery of enterprising young women the
quintessential Shakespearean comedies are devoted to the single theme
of successful courtship that ends in marriage. This new relationship, achieved
after many vicissitudes, based on love, mutual respect, and egalitarianism
appears bound for long and happy success. But the marriages depicted in
comedy, tragedy, romance, and poem display noteworthy difficulties. It is not, as
Rosalind jokingly suggested that "the sky changes when . . . [women] are
wives," but because the characters are in conflict with a rigid system of convention, of attitudes toward matrimony which inhibit the merriment of the earlier
comedies because they place women under more limitations than men.

Thus, throughout what may be called "the marriage group" of the
Shakespearean comic canon, there are only two plays devoted entirely to matrimony, *The Taming of the Shrew* and *The Merry Wives of Windsor*. To be sure,

there are matrimonial subplots in *The Comedy of Errors* and *A Midsummer Night's Dream*, and all four plays develop the same theme: spirited, rebellious, or witty women who chafe against the bit, attempt to exert independence, and finally reach an accommodation with their social situation. They seek the relationship that was promised at the end of the courtship comedies, challenging husbandly tyranny and denying the double standard. The sexual fidelity of both husbands and wives is insisted upon, particularly in that highly moral comedy, *The Merry Wives of Windsor* which, according to Leggatt, deals with adultery in a manner "amusing, judicious, and humane."[1]

The age, however, was less tolerant, and since it considered woman morally "the weaker vessel," even denying independent legal status to married women, feminine adultery could not long remain a laughing matter. Masculine honor is a fragile thing when it is confronted with the violation of a husband's property rights to the exclusive possession of his wife's body. Adultery, even suspicion of it, becomes an unforgivable sin in both the tragedies and romances, with vengeance exacted, whether through the murder of Desdemona, the attempted murder of Imogen, or the supposed death of Hermione. All these women are assumed guilty on hearsay evidence, either convicted without trial or against the logic and truth of their testimony. Even Lucrece, the unwilling victim of rape, believes herself required to commit suicide in order to preserve the honor of her husband and family.[2]

In the romances, the patient long-suffering virtue of the women aids in achieving the happy ending, and the educative value function of their endurance on those around them is stressed. Like their earlier tragic wifely counterparts, however, their roles develop into passivity, even if they have shown momentary rebellion or even enterprise, like Lady Macbeth (never, of course, accused of adultery), and Desdemona, whose early courage contributes to her destruction. The solutions in the romances offer a return to the educative approach of the comedies. Imogen, as many critics have noted, is a development of the character of Viola in her use of masculine disguise and the patience of her submission to Time, which brings truth to light. Similarly, Hermione trusts to Time, while the education of Leontes is given to a feminine teacher, Paulina, the portrait of retributive Charity, who brings him to repentance.

In short, the comedic marriages challenge and reinterpret the conventions of Elizabethan and Jacobean marriage; the tragedies (and *Lucrece*) submit to them, and the romances offer a fusion of the two approaches. Time tries truth, but the wit, anger, and even the shrewishness of the early comedic wives, become long-suffering patience, even passivity, the so-called proper conduct for women, among the wronged ladies of tragedies and romances. The center of power has moved from the unmarried young girls of the courtship comedies to husbands in the marriage plays where the most successful attack against masculine tyranny is that of the *Merry Wives*, and the best mutual accommodation is in *The Taming of the Shrew*.

These plays concentrate on human relationships rather than serving to educate the beholder in the intricacies of law or societal *mores*. Nonetheless, the code of behavior that was preached, if not totally observed, and often enshrined in statute, exists as a foundation, a bedrock for the action of these plays. These Elizabethan and Jacobean matrimonial conventions were, of course, based on the total submission of wife to husband. Only with widowhood did a woman gain total independence. T. E., in *The Lawes Resolutions of Womens Rights* (London, 1632), makes this point precisely:

> Why mourne you so, you that be widowes? Consider how long you have beene in subiection vnder the predominance of parents, of your husbands, now you be free in libertie, & free *proprii iuris* at your owne Law.[3]

Chaste, Silent, & Obedient,[4] the ideal young Elizabethan woman was expected to mould herself to her husband's wishes. Her upbringing had quite specifically been aimed to fashion a virtuous malleable helpmeet for the ideal gentleman. She would have been at least functionally literate if she were a member of the bourgeoisie, and might even have received a classical education if she belonged to the upper class, but even then, her reading would have been closely supervised so that her virtue would be preserved from contact with lascivious works.

In marriage, as she moved from one form of masculine domination to another, she was expected to continue the practice of the maidenly virtues she had learned, while also undertaking a new set of duties:

> 1. To giue honor, reuerence, and respect to her husband, as to her master and lord. . . . 2. To giue obedience in all things just and lawfull, applying and accommodating her selfe to the manners and humours of her husband, like a true looking-glasse. . . . 3. Seruice, as to prouide either by her selfe or some other his viands, to wash his feet. 4. To keepe the house. . . . 5. To be silent, and not to speak but with her husband, or by her husband. . . . 6. To employ her time in the practice and study of huswiferie, which is the most commodious and honorable science and occupation of a woman.[5]

As a housewife she is instructed in the care and feeding of her children and in the manner of overseeing her servants. She should not treat them too leniently, but consider them recalcitrant children, rebuking them, and rearing them in the ways of service. Her chief task is to preserve and keep what her husband has obtained in the outside world of "foreign" affairs. Her best model, however, was the biblical good wife of Proverbs 23:13–27:

> She seeketh wool, and flax, and worketh willingly with her hands. She is like the merchant's ships; she bringeth her food from afar. She riseth while it is yet night and giveth meat to her household, and a portion to her maidens. . . . . She girdeth her loins with strength and streng- theneth her arms. She perceiveth that her merchandise *is* good: her candle goeth not out by night. She layeth her hands to the spindle, and her hands hold the distaff . . . . Strength and honour are her clothing, and she shall rejoice in time to come. She openeth her mouth with wisdom; and in her tongue *is* the law of kindness. She looketh well to the ways of her house- hold, and eateth not the bread of idleness.

Such a paragon of activity would obviously have little time for polite classical learning, or the reading of romances, let alone active wantonness. But an even more important biblical legacy for wives and moralistic writers was St. Paul in Ephesians 5:22–25, where he counsels:

> Wives, submit yourselves unto your husbands, as unto the Lord. For the husband is the head of the wife, even as Christ is head of the church: and he is the saviour of the body. Therefore as the church is subject unto Christ, so let the wives *be* to their husbands in every thing.

This sentiment is expressed *ad nauseam* throughout English conduct litera- ture, and received religious endorsement from its inclusion in the marriage ceremony of the *Book of Common Prayer*. Thus, a wife should have no thoughts, opinions, or interests other than those of her husband and must study "to bee silent, obedient, peaceable, patient, studious to appease his cho- ler, if he be angrie, painful and diligent in looking to her businesse."[6] Shakespeare's wives usually have difficulty with this kind of self-abnegation.

One may well ask whether marriage required any duties at all of the husband, who appears in marriage to have gained an unpaid servant. They are given occasional admonitions, though their duties are less onerous, especially since they are predicated on their position as monarch of the household, ex- ercising sway over "the weaker vessel." Pierre Charron codifies husbandly duties neatly into five rules:

> 1. to instruct his wife with mildnesse in all things that belong vnto her duty, her honor, and good, whereof shee is capable. 2. to nourish her, whether she brought dowry with her or no. 3. to cloath her. 4. to lie with

her. 5. to loue and defend her; the two extremities are base and vitious, to hold her vnder like a seruant, to make her mistresse by subiecting him-selfe vnto her.[7]

Woman's submission in matrimony extended also to her legal rights in *propria persona* because her legal personality was merged with that of her hus-band. As a *femme couverte* she was *in potestate mariti*, not permitted to hold property in her own right, or to exercise control over the "money, plate, ieuelles, cattaile, and generally all moueables" she had brought with her into marriage.[8] They became the property of her husband to sell or bequeath as he wished. Land, however, was a different case. If the wife brought land with her into the marriage, or later inherited it, she was not permitted to administer it, but "that lande descendeth to her eldest sonne, or is diuided among her daughters. Also the manner is, that the lande which the wife bringeth to the mariage or purchaseth afterwardes, the husbande cannot sell or alienate the same, no not with her consent."[9] But if a child were born to the couple and was heard once to cry, then the husband was entitled to the usufruct of his wife's lands in the event that she died first. As Sir Thomas Smith puts it, "that is called the courtisie of Englande."[10] However, this policy was disadvantageous to the woman who obtained a legal separation *a mensa et thoro* (from bed and board) from her husband—divorce not being permitted. Since the marriage was still legally in existence, the *husband* controlled his wife's property during his life-time and she was entitled to nothing. For this reason very few separations were granted on the petition of the wife, since her husband retained a legal claim on any money, whether wages or inheritance, that she might receive.[11]

In the matter of inheritance, women had very few rights, since the property of a father went entirely to the eldest son or else was divided equally among the daughters. Therefore the custom of entailing property on the nearest male relative was instituted as a means of preserving the entity of an estate. Smith insists, in an amusingly sexist manner that women

> . . . for the most part . . . can handle their husbandes so well and so doulcely, and specially when their husbands be sicke: that when the lawe giueth them nothing, their husbandes at their death of their good will giue them all.[12]

Fortunately, in "London and other great cities" women were better treated. The goods of a deceased husband were divided into three parts, one third for his burial, another third for the wife, and the final third for the children.[13]

In the married state, then, woman was perpetually subordinate, "*quodammodo* an infant," as T. E. notes.[14] Consequently she was liable to his physical discipline, and it was not until the reign of Charles II that English women received legal protection against any beating they might receive from their husbands.[15] Until that time a married woman's only legal recourse was an appeal to the ecclesiastical courts, which had jurisdiction over matrimonial causes.[16] T. E. prefers the direct approach, suggesting that the woman retaliate with blows upon the wife-beater, if she dare, but he also limits the husband's heavy hand, saying that it should only be raised for "lawfull and reasonable correction."[17] There were other, more outspoken opponents of physical force, and William Heale in 1609 took issue with William Gager, the Oxford divine who objected to feminine cross-dressing and supported the right of a husband to beat his wife. Heale particularly attacks the legal differentiation between husbands and wives, especially in regard to that double standard which allows to a husband conduct (or rather misconduct) for which a woman would be deprived of her dower rights.[18]

After a recital of these legal disabilities, it is hard to believe that English women, particularly married women, were considered to possess a freedom of conduct unique in Western Europe. Shakespeare, however, obviously understood the problems encountered by women as a result of their required subordination in marriage and in *The Comedy of Errors* he bases the subplot on some of them. At the same time he establishes his own pattern for marriage comedies. A matrimonial relationship is challenged by an independent woman (perhaps a shrew); problems ensue, with adultery sometimes alleged; and finally a resolution is reached. The woman usually accommodates her outward conduct to that of the man, but in also asserting her love, she shows such freedom of spirit that roles and attitudes are redefined in a marriage that is evolving towards mutuality and companionship. The husband is no longer foolish or tyrannous, the wife no longer shrewish, and the laws of fidelity and chastity are upheld.

That Shakespeare intended the subplot of *The Comedy of Errors* to be more than mere contrast or farcical padding is obvious from the fact that he changed the venue of his Plautine source from Epidamnum to Ephesus, famous for sorcerers, but more important here because St. Paul addressed his famous epistle on wifely submission to its inhabitants.[19] This biblical resonance is increased by the deliberate patterning of the debate between Adriana and her sister Luciana after the "Conjugium," one of the colloquies of Erasmus which Shakespeare may well have studied in school. In Erasmus, Xantippe is the archetypal shrew and Eulalia, the wife who speaks well of matrimony. She preaches that the wife should be the looking glass of her husband, reflecting his every mood, ministering to his every whim, and above all, showing forbearance, even if the husband takes a mistress. As an example she tells of a noblewoman whose husband took a peasant girl for his love, and she, as patient wife, took care to send the girl a comfortable bed, furnishings, and the husband's favorite food. As a result he was overcome with remorse and returned to live lovingly with his wife.[20]

Shakespeare's matrimonial debate begins with the entry of Adriana, complaining about her husband's lateness for dinner, while her unmarried sister, Luciana—giver of light—counsels her to display the patience proper to a wife. Adriana, however, will not be appeased and asks a very simple question, "Why should their liberty than ours be more?" (II.i.10) To this, Luciana offers a Pauline argument of submission, using analogies from the animal world, where females are always subject to male domination:

> Men, more divine, the master of all these,
> Lords of the wide world, and wild wat'ry seas,
> Indued with intellectual sense and souls,
> Of more pre-eminence than fish or fowls,
> Are masters to their females, and their lords:
> Then let your will attend on their accords.
>   (II.i.20–25)

Here, because Shakespeare has made his apologist for matrimony an unmarried woman rather than the wife in Erasmus, Adriana offers a very sensible reply:

> . . . thou that hast no unkind mate to grieve thee,
> With urging helpless patience wouldst relieve me;
> But if thou live to see like right bereft,
> This fool-begged patience in thee will be left.
>   (II.i.38–41)

Despite this legitimate objection to Luciana as educator, Adriana's violence against her servant, railing against her husband, and immediate conclusion that his tardiness is due to his having taken a mistress signify her as a shrew. However, even at this early point in the play, Shakespeare takes pains to indicate that she is more than the conventional English shrew, for she has affection for her husband:

> . . . My decayèd fair
> A sunny look of his would soon repair.
>   (II.i.98–99)

But she is also at fault for being too possessive, wishing to limit masculine liberty as her own is circumscribed, as she demonstrates in her later use of clinging, grasping, smothering images when she speaks to Antipholus of Syracuse, mistaking him for her husband:

> Come, I will fasten on this sleeve of thine:
> Thou art an elm, my husband, I a vine,
> Whose weakness married to thy stronger state
> Makes me with thy strength communicate.
> If aught possess thee from me, it is dross,
> Usurping ivy, brier or idle moss;
> Who all for want of pruning, with intrusion
> Infect thy sap and live on thy confusion.
>
> (II.ii.172–179)

Ironically she here also shows some of that self-deprecation that antifeminist writers employ against women:"*Mulier est hominis confusio*," said Chaucer's Chauntecleere.

Throughout the entire play Adriana is continually given an emotional dimension beyond that of the traditional shrew, the one-dimensional figure of farcical fun who needs to be beaten into submission. As a result there is a conflict of tone in this play; the rollicking horseplay of the mistaken identities does not meld with the matrimonial subplot, where Luciana's total submission and Adriana's ultimate assertion of love and fidelity look ahead to later plays, not back into farce.[21] Luciana, despite her apparent gentle pliability, also comes across as distinctly coldblooded in her suggestion to Antipholus of Syracuse (mistaken for his brother) that he dissemble, appear to love Adriana while seeking enjoyment elsewhere. She apparently accepts the double standard and has no qualms about suggesting that he married Adriana for money rather than affection:

> If you did wed my sister for her wealth,
> Then for her wealth's sake use her with more kindness:
> Or if you like elsewhere, do it by stealth;
> Muffle your false love with some show of blindness:
>
> . . . .
>
> Look sweet, speak fair, become disloyalty;
> Apparel vice like virtue's harbinger;
> Bear a fair presence, though your heart be tainted;
> Teach sin the holy carriage of a saint;
> Be secret-false: what need she be acquainted?
> What simple thief brags of his own attaint?
>
> . . . .
>
> Alas, poor women! make us but believe,

Being compact of credit, that you love us;
Though other have the arm, show us the sleeve;
We in your motion turn, and you may move us.
                    (III.ii.5–24)

This code of behavior leaves a nasty taste with the audience; the mettlesome
wife has a legitimate complaint, and with feminine friends such as Luciana an
enemy is superfluous.

The fact that Antipholus of Syracuse instantly falls in love with Luciana
indicates the acceptance of masculine superiority as the cornerstone of
marriage as far as he is concerned. Ironically, Luciana finds herself the victim
of her own words, as she believes her own brother-in-law to be attempting
seduction in reply to her suggestion of deceit. Adriana's reaction to this news
is at first as angry and full of invective as one would expect from the archetypal
shrew, while the formerly patient lady adds fuel to her sister's rage. Erasmus
and his counsels of patience are being subverted here. But then Adriana reveals
a softer, tender, forgiving aspect of her personality and her unconditional love:

Ah, but I think him better than I say,
And yet would herein others' eyes were worse.
Far from her nest the lapwing cries away;
My heart prays for him, though my tongue do curse.
                    (IV.i.25–28)

These lines offer ironic contrast to the double vengeance that Antipholus of
Ephesus plans to take on his wife. Instantly believing her guilty of adultery when
he cannot enter his house, he resorts to the prostitute Adriana had berated him
about, and then will beat his spouse for the fault he has himself committed.

From this time on the emphasis is on Adriana's love for her errant husband,
but she is not totally cowed. When he confronts her with his accusations she
defends herself; but she sends money to pay his alleged debt, without asking questions, and believing him mad, she will pay anything for a cure. Above all, she
wishes for his return, willingly accepting the Abbess's "strong reproof" for her
behavior in reprehending her husband:

In bed he slept not for my urging it;
At board, he fed not for my urging it;
Alone, it was the subject of my theme;
In company I often glanced it.
Still did I tell him it was vile and bad.
                    (V.i.63–67)

Luciana, however, instantly defends her sister, pointing out that Adriana's behavior was justified under the circumstances. The two ladies have changed places, and Adriana has become the paragon of wifely patience. She insists on the sanctity of the marriage bond and refuses to allow the Abbess to perform a cure on her husband, even petitioning the Duke to obtain redress. Adriana has seen her husband in a state of undisciplined behavior, and like the later Kate in *The Taming of the Shrew*, she sees the mirror of her own behavior and consequently is now eager to reach an accommodation, a reconciliation with the man she realizes that she indeed loves.

The discovery that the reprehending Abbess is Adriana's mother-in-law is more than a stock joke; it is also an ironic and amusing reference to the Erasmian colloquy. There Xantippe is brought to accept her wifely duties and practice patience only when Eulalia forces her to the realization that both her stepmother and her mother-in-law would be most gratified to see the couple separate. Thus in Erasmus, the redefinition of the wife's role comes from an external influence, whereas in *The Comedy of Errors* it represents an internal development. Even in this early comedy Shakespeare is treating the shrew with some humanity, allowing her motivation for her frustrations in the limitations imposed on women in marriage. Both Adriana and Luciana have developed in the course of the play—something unusual in a farce—and both have learned something of the *realpolitik* of marriage, the necessity of tolerance and understanding in both wives and husbands. Obviously Adriana is expected to forgive her husband for his infidelity, and Shakespeare has taken pains to give him motivation (albeit mistaken) for his action, while Antipholus of Syracuse will marry his lady, Luciana, and Egeon and Emilia (formerly the Abbess) are reunited. At the conclusion of the play Adriana has certainly not gained the mastery, though she does now have something with which to upbraid her husband, while he does not. What is important is that her shrewishness has been revealed as a reaction to the frustration of those deprived of legitimate liberty; in the words of battling Gwenthian in *Patient Grissil*, "'Tis not fid that poor womens be kept always under." Adriana has shown her mettle and now accepts her wifely duties with love, a situation that Shakespeare treats more fully in *The Taming of the Shrew*.[22]

In *The Comedy of Errors* the matrimonial subplot obviously has serious import, as its religious resonances indicate, and even more notable is the portrait of the astonishingly modern Adriana, kicking against the goad, but never actually offered physical violence. Whereas the shrews of earlier plays were beaten into submission, Adriana is brought to understand that marriage is an institution that evolves, as it does in this play, through love, into mutuality.

CHAPTER IV

The Manning of the Haggard:
or *The Taming of the Shrew*

T *he Taming of the Shrew* is, in George Hibbard's phrase, "a play about marriage in Elizabethan England,"[1] and also a unique example in the Shakespearean comic canon because of its concern with the behavior of husband and wife after the marriage ceremony. At the same time it also offers a distinctly subversive approach to an antifeminist genre, that of the wifebeating farce. In this play Shakespeare has skillfully remolded his material to portray an atypical Elizabethan attitude towards marriage through the development of a matrimonial relationship in which mutuality, trust, and love are guiding forces.

Shakespeare's method at this early stage of his career makes use of the familiar device of contrast. He takes the three most frequent matrimonial situations of Elizabethan England, and indeed any time and place: a marriage arranged by parents for economic gain, marriage to a widow for her money, and a marriage of compatibility and equality. This last, the marriage of Kate and Petruchio, at first seems to be one based on economics, but by the end of the play it is shown to be the model for the others, and indeed the only one that is for more than "two months victuall'd." The play then is Shakespeare's reinterpretation of that traditionally male-oriented view of marriage which requires the molding of a wife, by force if necessary, into total submission to her husband.[2] In *The Taming of the Shrew*, however, the action shows the failure of what would then have been considered "proper" marriages and the boisterous success of the relationship of equality between the sexes personified by Kate and Petruchio.

The imagery and method of the taming need exploration as contributing to the development of this theme, and they represent an amalgam of two approaches, those of falconry and the conduct books of Elizabethan England.[3] Petruchio follows the principles and uses the imagery of hawk-taming while following the letter of the conservative English conduct books, but subverting their repressive intent. The principles of the conduct books and the legal position of women in Elizabethan England are developed along with the methods of training and skill by which one subdues a hunting bird, and the result is a completely different view of the "oeconomie" of matrimony.

Shakespeare here shows women as independent entities. They are not mere chattels, but individual human beings with wit, intelligence, and psychological needs. He exploits the never-ending war between the sexes, but without bitterness. He humanizes it to make it a clash of equal personalities, raising it to a level of intellectual subtlety. Thus Petruchio in *The Taming of the Shrew* is not the wife-beating Mr. Noah of the mystery plays. Shakespeare demythologizes what M. C. Bradbrook identifies as "the oldest and indeed the only native comic rôle for women,"[4] so that Katherine is closer to what has sometimes been called the "new woman" of the Renaissance, a woman of wit, independence, business acumen, and humor.[5]

Petruchio wants this "new" kind of wife rather than the conventional Elizabethan servitor. Certainly his wife will have a position of legal inferiority, but for him marriage is also a compatible partnership. He may be *primus inter pares*, but his wife must not be simpering, coy, and humble. He wants a woman of wit and spirit and sees beneath Kate's apparent shrewishness to the warm, highspirited woman who has consciously or unconsciously adopted shrewish behavior out of sheer frustration—a reaction against the strictures laid on her by a repressive society and a father guilty of favoritism.[6]

Petruchio rejoices in Kate's alleged faults. She will be a haggard worth the taming, a good hawk for his hand:

> I am as peremptory as she proud-minded,
> And where two raging fires meet together
> They do consume the thing that feeds their fury.
> Though little fire grows great with little wind,
> Yet extreme gusts will blow out fire and all.
> So I to her, and she yields to me,
> For I am rough and woo not like a babe.
> (II.i.131–137)

And further, he is a fit husband for her:

> For I am he am born to tame you, Kate,
> And bring you from a wild Kate to a Kate

Conformable as other household Kates.
(II.i.278–280)

Thus at the very beginning of the play, Petruchio sees the esential similarity between the two of them. He willingly undertakes the task of taming in full knowledge of its challenging difficulty, as a falconer brings a difficult hawk to submission. Consequently, the imagery of much of the play indicates a perception of the matrimonial state as similar to the compact between falcon and keeper. The falcon must be taught obedience to her master, but at the same time her wild and soaring nature must be preserved. This is a cardinal principle of hawk-taming. The bird must retain her hunting instinct; otherwise she is useless. But she must be taught to exercise her wild nature on command, to hunt under the government of her keeper/master.[7] Accordingly, the hawking passage of IV.i.175ff. is extremely important, as also is the image of Bianca as a "proud, disdainful haggard" (IV.ii.39). Hortensio cannot remain with a woman who will be "ranging" abroad to cast "wand'ring eyes on every stale" (III.i.88). This last word has several allied meanings: in falconry it is the decoy of dead prey used in the training of a bird, in general Elizabethan parlance it means allurements, and also common prostitute. Thus, in equating Bianca with an inferior bird that will turn aside from suitable live prey, Hortensio is also accusing her of unbridled desire, immediate physical satisfaction, uncontrolled by reason. In addition, this comment also gives a clue to the existence of shrewishness beneath the appearance of conformity, which will only be revealed in Bianca in the last act of the play. Hortensio, then will look for what he thinks easier game—the Widow. But Petruchio operates differently from the moneyminded Hortensio and the swooning romantic Lucentio. He has the patience to tame his wild bird without breaking her spirit, perceiving the advantages that will accrue to him in training a good hunting hawk, while Hortensio will marry a wealthy widow, only to find himself discomfited, and Lucentio will find himself married to a shrew, Petruchio will preserve Kate's witty and independent nature so that in partnership they may hunt down pretension and falsehood in others.

Thus the hawking imagery carries more weight than the mere suggestion that wives and falcons are more tractable when half starved. Its real value lies in emphasizing the fact that the taming of the wild, mature falcon aims at achieving mutual respect between bird and keeper. As a result of this battle of wills, the bird learns her function and purpose, and the keeper learns that he must continually work to preserve the bird's obedience. Kate and Petruchio develop similar attitudes toward each other, and implicit in this image is that of marriage as a partnership, neither party in full control of the other, yet each owing something to the other: respect and consideration on the part of the man, and obedience and respect on the part of the woman. As the falconer never asks the impossible of his bird, as he cherishes, feeds, and keeps it, not attempting irrevocably to alter its nature,[8] so too should a husband behave toward his wife, taking care never to lose her friendship. And, to carry the analogy with falconry further, the keeper must expect his bird to be moody and un-predictable, and he must never relax his vigilance, for he can never be sure that he is in complete control of his hawk.[9] Finally, the compact between master and falcon is basically a voluntary commitment. When it soars, waiting for its prey, the bird is capable of flying away free, and only the kindness of the keeper and the consequent gratitude or indebtedness of the bird can keep it under control.[10] So too with Kate and Petruchio.

This falcon metaphor is a most fitting one for Kate. She is a haggard, "an excellent good bird . . .the most excellent . . . of all other Falcons . . . endowed with beautie and excellencie."[11] She is a wild adult bird in full plumage, a long-winged hawk already accustomed to field hunting, soaring high and swooping down after her chosen quarry. She know how to prey on lesser creatures such as Bianca. But with such temperamental birds, as indeed with all falcons, "Art must supply the restraints of kind, by cunning."[12] The tamer must "vse her gently, and be patient with hir at the first,"[13] so that the falcon will discover that gentleness and obedience on her side will beget kind treatment from her keeper.

Petruchio instinctively knows how to "man" his haggard as he combines conduct-book rules with those of hawk-taming. His approach is that of a true falconer: "when by cunning and subteltie you haue beguiled and taken [your falcons]; and how by skill and art euer after to order and gouerne [them] changing (by your wit and watchful diligence) their naturall timeritie and wildnes into loue and gentlenes."[14] He first hears of Kate as an ideal match for any sensible young man: she is wealthy, young, beautiful, and well-bred, though "intolerable curst" (I.ii.87). But to the man who has stated his desire to marry for wealth, money is all important (l. 91). As M. C. Bradbrook notes, "Money is always to the fore in tales about shrews,"[15] and hence this attribute of Petruchio may be taken as a stereotype. Kate and Petruchio, however, are variations on the stock situations and stock characters, and here the "suppose" theme comes into play. As Petruchio *appears* to be the conventional shrew-tamer, so Kate, an intelligent, mettlesome young woman, victimized by her social role and Baptista's favoritism for Bianca, *appears* to be the conventional shrew to be tamed by beating. As C. C. Seronsy says:

> . . . in the shrew plot the supposition represents a deeper more conscious
> attempt to make real and establish beyond cavil what everyone else fails to
> see. The distinction is one between outer circumstance and inner convic-
> tion, a kind of triumph of mind or personality over a world of stubborn
> "fact" not quite so real as had been supposed.[16]

Thus Petruchio teaches Kate a new role by means of subtlety, opposing rage
with rage, and wooing by opposition, all the while assuming in the young
woman qualities which she does indeed possess: "patience, good sense, a
capacity for humor, and finally obedience, all of which she comes gradually to
manifest in a spirit chastened but not subdued."[17]

Petruchio follows the mannerly Elizabethan approach to marriage by asking the lady's father for permission to woo his daughter. But he is also a very
shrewd young man who sizes up Baptista astutely. In his most businesslike
manner he gives Baptista a resumé of his financial situation—his father is
dead and he himself is sole heir. Then without hedging he asks,

> Then tell me, if I get your daughter's love,
> What dowry shall I have with her to wife?
> (II.i.118-119)

Baptista names his figure: twenty thousand crowns in cash and half his lands
after his decease. It is a good offer, and despite Baptista's obvious desire to be
rid of Kate, Petruchio does not haggle for a larger sum. Instead he offers his
part of the bargain, the jointure:

> And, for that dowry, I'll assure her of
> Her widowhood, be it that she survive me,
> In all my lands and leases whatsoever.
> Let specialties be therefore drawn between us,
> That covenants may be kept on either hand.
> (II.i.123–127)

All this is eminently businesslike, not merely materialistic, and it follows the
traditional approach to marriage in Elizabethan England among both the
mercantile and upper classes. The Elizabethan father might not always have
worried about the compatibility of the pair, but he did want to be sure that his
daughter would be left well provided for as a widow. Perhaps she might be
able to use her jointure to remarry and improve her social position.

Thus the financial arrangements for Kate's marriage are concluded, with
Baptista relieved to get his older daughter off his hands on any terms. The

younger one is a more tempting match as far as he is concerned, and hence he has bargained with her hand in order to gain assistance from Bianca's suitors to marry off the undesirable girl who is his older daughter. Then he will, in effect, sell Bianca's marriage to the highest bidder, regardless of his suitability as a husband. Baptista does, however, take one wise precaution in warning Petruchio indirectly of Kate's temper (II.i.62–63, 139), a sensible move, since the impediment of "certain conditions unknown" could allow Petruchio to break the contract before marriage.

Petruchio now brings to bear on Kate all his cunning, subtlety, skill, and art. At first he has seemed merely an ambitious fortune hunter come "to wive it wealthily in Padua" (I.ii.73), but his combative instinct is aroused by what he hears about "Kate the curst":

> Now, by the world, it is a lusty wench.
> I love her ten times more than e'er I did.
> O, how I long to have some chat with her!
> (II.i.160–163)

His self-confidence is also such that he has no fear of verbal battles (I.ii.195–207). As soon as he meets Kate he treats her with affability and consideration, disarming her by addressing to her those words of praise and love that men have usually employed to her sister. Hence he lauds her mildness and silence (II.i.191–192), and the more she rages the more he compliments her:

> . . . I find you passing gentle.
> 'Twas told me you were rough and coy and sullen,
> And now I find report a very liar,
> For thou art pleasant, gamesome, passing courteous,
> But slow in speech, yet sweet as spring-time flowers.
> Thou canst not frown, thou canst not look askance,
> Nor bite the lip as angry wenches will,
> Nor hast thou pleasure to be cross in talk.
> But thou with mildness entertain'st thy wooers,
> With gentle conference, soft and affable.
> (II.i.244–253)

Here is the portrait of the ideal lady of the conduct books, in words that seem more applicable to Bianca than to Kate. However, this approach is in truth that of a good falconer, for "kinde dealing with her, does draw her loue to you."[18] Further, this scene is tied together by explicit and implicit images of hawking. Kate is metaphorically a *kite*, a falcon not normally used for hunting because of its poverty of nature and habit of feeding on small reptiles, insects, sickly prey, or offal.[19] In fact this is the only kind of prey Kate has known up to this time—Bianca and a rather poor lot of wooers. Kate picks up the reference when she calls Petruchio a buzzard (II.i.208) a hawk even less valued than a kite and never used in hawking because it is "deficient in speed and in pluck."[20] Then she compounds the insult by suggesting that Petruchio is too "craven" or cowardly to be a fit mate for her (II.i.230).

Kate retaliates superbly in this scene; but it is not the first time she has used hawking terms, for she has earlier asked if her father intends to make her a "stale," a lure made of dead prey, among these mates or wooers, with additional witty punning elements indicating laughingstock and harlot (I.i. 57–58). In this comment she has also summed up her postion *vis à vis* Bianca: she is the despised lure and Bianca the desired game of the wooers. Petruchio then carries his hunting imagery further by including Diana, the chase goddess (II.i.260–263), and announcing his taming policy, with more puns on kites, cates, and cats (II.i.278–280). In taking on the office of falconer he is "persuading . . . [his falcon] to live quietly among men,"[21] and learn a new role in concert with her keeper.

So far Petruchio has proved himself a good tamer. He has begun the process with kindness; the more Kate has railed, the more he has complimented her, applying to her all the virtues of an ideal lady. His subtlety, however, is further demonstrated because he has apparently seen that Kate is not merely shrewish for its own sake,[22] and indeed as Hibbard suggests, "What we have here is a woman whose dignity as a woman has been outraged, and who in retaliation has allowed the assertion of her pride to get out of hand in a violently unfeminine manner."[23] In fact her shrewishness seems more like a "common human response to the situation"[24] she finds herself in. Her father considers her an encumbrance who must be married off whether she will or not (I.i. 48–54) so that he can bargain with Bianca's hand (II.i.328–400). Bianca, weepy, dishonest, and mealymouthed, is her father's favorite (II.i.31–36), while Kate, the girl with legitimate pride, receives little more than abuse (II.i.26). Kate's difficulty lies in her astute intelligence and impatience with stupidity which make her despise the meek conformity of Bianca and rebel against the limitations that Elizabethan society place upon women:

> I see a woman may be made a fool,
> If she had not a spirit to resist.
> (III.ii.216–217)

A glance at Bianca's wooers should suffice to show their manifest unsuitability and Kate's good taste. Gremio is an old man, virtually decrepit, and obviously incapable of satisfying the sexual needs of a young woman.[25] Hortensio is strictly out for money, and like many Elizabethan young men, he opts for a rich widow who will bring her fortune with her for his use, only to find a stock situation fraught with disaster—the young man married to a rich wife.[26] Even Lucentio, the most eligible of the three, is a conventional romantic who has to be pushed into the practical step of clandestine marriage. Kate is forced by such circumstances to the self-defensive stand of shrewishness to discourage such suitors.

Why, then, does she accept Petruchio? The answer is to be found in the wooing scene of II.i. where Petruchio demonstrates a wit equal to her own. Her violence and intelligence do not frighten him away but rather inspire him to new heights of witty and mildly obscene badinage. For perhaps the first time, each engages in a combat of wit with a member of the opposite sex who possesses equal intelligence, flexibility of repartee, and vigor. Kate for the first time has had a prospective husband praise her for her virtues, and her suitor is a handsome man with economic as well as physical advantages. She clearly recognizes the advantages of this eminently eligible suitor, and as Petruchio holds her close to him to immobilize her hands, Kate is sexually awakened for the first time. At this moment her shrewish mask slips a trifle.

The boisterous wooing ends with Petruchio's unsupported assertion that "we have 'greed so well together / That upon Sunday is the wedding day" (II.i.299–300). Kate is swept off her feet. Baptista joyfully accepts Petruchio's words as truth, despite Kate's *pro forma* protests, and with evident relief he unites the two in a public spousal ceremony, joining their hands in token of "free and unforced consent" before Bianca's salivating lovers, who willingly act as witnesses. The bargain is then sealed with the spousal kiss: "And kiss me, Kate, 'we will be married o' Sunday'" (II.i.326). Kate and Petruchio are now, by virtue of this espousal in words of the future tense, man and wife in name, but not yet in bed. A church ceremony is still canonically required, but they are almost indissolubly knit together.[27]

An understanding of this situation is essential in order to understand the horror of Petruchio's late arrival at the wedding. Shakespeare shows a Kate very much afraid of being deserted at church by her madcap lover, and indeed, her current experience with men would lead her to expect that Petruchio has merely been making fun of her. But even worse, if Petruchio were not to arrive, she might have to remain unmarried. Her espousals have been performed publicly, and she is indeed "mad Petruchio's wife, / If it would please him come and marry her!" (III.ii.19–20) Further, his failure to appear to claim his bride, though grounds for dissolution of contract,[28] could also irrevocably ruin her reputation and make her unmarriageable. She could be thought "damaged goods"—Petruchio must have known something detrimental about her morals if he refused her—and hence she would be unfit for marriage elsewhere. Kate could thus be condemned to a life of frustrated spinsterhood. Here one must again emphasize that Petruchio is a very attractive and handsome man of wit and spirit. He represents escape from an intolerable home situation and also offers a sexual suitability which makes him much more desirable than the whole pack of Bianca's wooers. No wonder then that when he does arrive she goes with him to church no matter what he is wearing. Indeed she really has no option.

This is another step in the taming process in that Petruchio makes Kate grateful to him for having come at all. However, he also shows an honest and sincere view of the married state, and even some self-knowledge in hinting that appearance can belie reality:

> To me she's married, not unto my clothes.
> Could I repair what she will wear in me.
> As I can change these poor accoutrements,
> 'Twere well for Kate and better for myself.
>
> (III.ii.113-116)

Then, from the reported wedding scene one may see that Petruchio has continued the taming process by showing himself as violent and unpredictable as the shrew he has married. He turns the whole marriage ceremony topsy-turvy, horrifying the starchy wedding guests and terrifying Kate. She, however, is so glad he has come that she does and says nothing.

After the wedding Petruchio, the falconer, asserts his authority over Kate, the falcon he has captured. She must go with her husband wherever her keeper wishes, since she now belongs to him. As early as this moment (III.ii) Petruchio indicates the nature of his taming process: he will woo her by opposition, denying her wishes while claiming what is in fact the truth—that his motivation is his great love and care for her well-being. Thus she cannot bring any of her customary weapons to bear. When begged to stay for the wedding feast, Petruchio pretends fear of armed attack; he draws his sword and swears to defend himself and his wife against all comers. Kate, of course, can say and do nothing. Her attempts at pleading have failed, and defiance has led to a recital of her legal position as a wife:

> She is my goods, my chattels; she is my house,
> My household stuff, my field, my barn,
> My horse, my ox, my ass, my anything;
> And here she stands, touch her whoever dare.
>   (III.ii.226–229)

In short, she is his property, and consequently she must go with him and submit her will to his.

The postmarital taming now begins in earnest with its combination of the principles of falconry and the recommendations of conduct books on the rights and duties of the married. Petruchio shows himself well equipped to employ both these modes of instruction, and ironically the result is a wife of spirit, wit, and comic intelligence who will lead him a merry chase, offering the charms of intellectual equality tempered with love and outward submission. This is a compact between falcon and keeper, two mutually interdependent personalities working together as they hunt through life.

Petruchio follows up his initial advantage at the wedding feast during the return to his house. On the way he beats his servants for their incompetence, and for the alleged reason that they have discommoded his wife. Thus he forces Kate to intercede for someone other than herself. But he has also performed his first duty as a husband by looking after his wife's comfort.[29] Of course he has at the same time managed to frighten Kate by acting in a manner as unbridled as her own, thus showing her the mirror of her own conduct. But although Petruchio may beat his servants, he never raises his hand to his wife, however much she provokes him. Here he follows a double precept. The first is from the conduct books, advising a husband not to "offer her any iniury, either in deed or word, but [to] honor and make much of her. For the Husband that honoureth his wife honoureth himselfe."[30] Second, he is attempting to gain the friendship and affection of his wild haggard by caring for her comfort, speaking gently and lovingly to her, but still showing his authority.

Next, Petruchio calls for food, and though he and Kate are both hungry, he rejects it because it is too well done, maintaining, in acordance with good Renaissance medicine, that overroasted meat would add to the choleric condition of them both.[31] Here he is performing another husbandly duty in caring for his wife's bodily welfare, but at the same time he is taking one of the first steps in bringing his falcon to "reclayme":

> Yf ye wyll reclayme your hawke ye must depart one meele in thre meeles vnto the tyme that she woll come to reclayme. And when she woll com to reclayme: encreece her meele euery daye better and better. And or she

come to the reclame make her that she soore not. For though she be wel
reclamed it maye happe that she woll soore soo hyghe in to the ayre that ye
shall neyther se nor fynde her.[32]

Then Petruchio takes Kate to bed where, as his servant tells us, he
begins the wedding night by "making a sermon of continency to her"
(IV.i.170–173). Here he may be considered as officially delivering his wife
a monitory address: that is, he is performing the important husbandly duty of
caring for her moral well-being, for woman is "the weaker vessel" (1 Peter
3:7). But though he has chosen not to assert his marital rights, he has decided
that he will not permit her to sleep, and now he specifically allies his plan of
campaign to the taming of a hawk:

> My falcon now is sharp and passing empty,
> And till she stoop she must not be full-gorg'd,
> For then she never looks upon her lure.
> Another way I have to man my haggard,
> To make her come and know her keeper's call:
> That is to watch her, as we watch these kites
> That bate and beat and will not be obedient.
> She eat no meat to-day, nor none shall eat;
> Last night she slept not, nor to-night she shall not.
> As with the meat, some undeservèd fault
> I'll find about the making of the bed,
> And here I'll fling the pillow, there the bolster,
> This way the coverlet, another way the sheets.
> Ay, and amid this hurly I intend
> That all is done in reverend care of her.
> And in conclusion she shall watch all night,
> And if she chance to nod I'll rail and brawl
> And with the clamor keep her still awake.
> This is a way to kill a wife with kindness,
> And thus I'll curb her mad and headstrong humor.
> He that knows better how to tame a shrew,
> Now let him speak; 'tis charity to show.
>
> (IV.i.177-198)

Petruchio's words require careful examination. He gives here a very
precise account of the method of taming a falcon, bringing her to reclaim, or
calling her back to her keeper after she has soared. In refusing meat to his
haggard, Petruchio is attempting to enforce obedience by showing her that she
will be fed only at the good disposition of her keeper, and as a reward for her
own kindness and good behavior. She will be "full-gorg'd" only when she has

learned what she should do—look upon her lure and return to her husband's fist, or to her perch.[33] This is good falconry, as is the denial of sleep. This method of gaining obedience, though cruel, is one that lays equal demands on both bird and keeper. As long as the bird is "watched," an average of three nights, so long does the keeper have to go without sleep, suffering the same hardships as his falcon, until she stops her bating, or flying off the perch, and beating her wings in an endeavor to escape her leg restraints, or jesses.[34] The keeper must, throughout this time, also bring the bird to love and trust him by speaking soothingly to her, making her understand what she must do, not through fear, but through friendship and mutual endurance. Petruchio must first break his haggard of her kitish tricks of flying disobediently at inferior game and refusing the lure.[35] Thus he starts his reign by trying to "curb her mad and headstrong humor." The word "curb" is the operative one here. Petruchio is too good a falconer to *break* his haggard's spirit; he will teach her to control her wildness so that she will attack prey, but will be discriminating and not merely soar after any game she sees. He will civilize his falcon and make her able to live comfortably among men; but her hunting instinct must be preserved. In other words, Kate must be taught to control her pointless rages and direct her anger and aggression against legitimate quarry.

In pursuit of these ends, Petruchio uses both kindness and authority. In his rages he mirrors Kate's behavior, ironically inverting the precepts of conduct books, but through his actions he prevents his wife from complaining, since her welfare is ostensibly his main consideration. Thus Kate sees her irrational anger directed toward others and kindness shown to herself, a situation that reinforces Petruchio's authority through her fear that such rage might be directed against her, should she fail to fulfill her husband's wishes. At the same time, too, Kate is brought to see the futile folly of continual anger, for no amount of fury will make Petruchio change his mind, once he has decided that a course of action is for her own good. To her chagrin Kate gets the point:

> And that which spites me more than all these wants,
> He does it under name of perfect love,
> As who should say, if I should sleep or eat,
> 'Twere deadly sickness or else present death.
> (IV.iii.11–14)

But then Petruchio offers food to his half-starved wife, food which, like a good falconer, he has prepared himself. He alone knows with the utmost precision the requirements of his captive falcon.[36] And again the bird must reciprocate. Kate must "offer thanks" by means of her good behavior, otherwise she will not be fed.

So far Petruchio has used the precepts of falconry, but he has also fulfilled three of the duties expected of an Elizabethan husband: he has instructed his wife for her own moral good; he has nourished her with carefully selected food, and presumably he has lain with her. Now he comes to perform another husbandly duty: he must clothe her suitably, and for that purpose he brings clothiers to the house (IV.iii.59–165). Then he harasses both tailor and haberdasher because their wares are unsuitable. They have even brought a loose-bodied gown—fit only for a loose woman, and conventionally the gown of an Elizabethan harlot. Kate, still the headstrong haggard, protests against her keeper's actions; but instead of new clothes, she receives another homily, this time on the honesty of mean apparel (IV.iii. 166–180). As Petruchio had said before the wedding, inward worth is of more importance than outward show (III.ii.113–116); he has already proved this, too, by seeing beneath Kate's shrewish exterior and recognizing her possibilities.

After having gained some show of obedience from Kate, Petruchio, while on the road to Padua, experiments in flying his haggard a short distance after game (IV.v). He demands Kate's agreement with outrageous statements concerning the time of day, and again that the moon rather than the sun is shining. This time Kate does not "bate and beat" but follows Hortensio's suggestion and performs as her keeper demands—with some verbal exasperation at her inability to resist, knowing that the only way to get what she wants, a trip to Padua, is to agree with her husband/keeper. Petruchio "flies" her again at Vincentio, and this time she indeed proves herself a fine game bird when she carries the joke even further than her keeper expects (IV.v.27–48). Her grotesquely fulsome compliments to the "young, budding virgin" are a brilliantly created piece of farce, extending the impossible premise to supremely logical conclusions. Then, when Petruchio tests her again by asking her to admit her error, she notifies him that she is "tamed" by cooperating with him in his trick. Her error has arisen because of her "mistaking eyes, / That have been so bedazzled with the sun" (IV.v.44–45). All she need do is indicate by a question in her voice her mischievous doubt as to which, sun or moon, is shining.[37] Now Kate has outsmarted Petruchio, but her method shows her advancement in civilized subtlety by her use of the private joke they share.

Kate has now shown herself a worthy haggard, a good hunting companion for Petruchio. She can engage in witty badinage without compromising her inner independence of spirit and initiative. If Petruchio makes fun of her, she will enjoy the joke and reply in kind; thus she serves notices that he must keep his wits about him if he is to continue to control his haggard. She can now cooperate with her husband, and hence the taming process is almost completed. The bird has flown after game and has returned to her keeper's fist as commanded. But Kate's farcical initiative indicates that, though curbed, her witty and comic spirit has not been broken. She has discovered the art of playing, and has learned that "If she bends a little she and her husband can also entertain themselves gloriously at the expense of others."[38]

Petruchio will now reward his haggard with a kiss, but here the modest matron demurs. She must be coaxed, and at the same time she is gaining her indirect revenge. Since Petruchio wishes her to play the part of the perfect conduct-book wife in public, she will play it to the letter and avoid open displays c f affection. As Guazzo points out: "I cannot like of those which will be stil dalying with their wives before others: for they doe therby set other mens teeth on edge and make their wives less shamefast and modest."[39] Petruchio threatens to return home if his haggard refuses to perform his will, but this time Kate offers him a term of endearment to signify a love-truce: "Now pray thee, love, stay" (V.i.136).

Finally, in the banquet wager, Kate is given her real test in flying at a quarry. Even here Petruchio has followed a good falconer's rule, for he has not flown his hawk far on the first occasion, on the road to Padua. Now Kate has a chance at better game—Bianca and the Widow. That Katherine is still a hunting falcon of great spirit is obvious from the beginning of V.ii, where she objects to the Widow's "very mean meaning." At this point Kate's feathers are so ruffled that she is in a hunting mood, in good flying condition. With the departure of all the women, Petruchio wagers with the other husbands, noting (ironically, perhaps) that he will lay odds twenty times greater on his wife than on his hawk or hound.

Kate, moreover, is out for vengeance, and she receives a very sweet reward from her husband for her part in the wager when she is told to herd the recalcitrant wives back to the banqueting hall. She has detested Bianca's slyly obedient approach in the past, and now she will bring upon her and the Widow the same kind of opprobrium formerly visited upon her because of her own allegedly shrewish behavior. The keeper and his bird are thus working together in their hunt after pretension; and Petruchio, the good falconer, allows Kate another reward when he permits her in effect to feed upon her quarry by giving the two women a homily on wifely behavior. Such a reward will keep the affection of the falcon so that she can be permitted longer flights at liberty.

Kate's set speech on wifely duties (V.ii.140–184) has frequently been misunderstood and often misplayed. Sometimes it is performed too obsequiously, and sometimes too ironically, with a too broad wink at the end, but more frequently it has been completely misread. What it celebrates is a mutual agreement, a bargain in terms of separation of powers.[40] The husband is legally the head of the wife as her lord, keeper, king, and governor, but he also has duties. He must provide for his family, and as prince in his own household, he should rule its members with justice and loving kindness rather than cruelty and injustice. In return, the wife too has duties, basically those of "love, fair looks, and true obedience" (l. 158). She owes her husband the same "duty as the subject owes the prince" (l. 160). She must submit to his "honest will" (l. 163), and not rebel against his resonable demands. This situation seems to indicate a mutuality of aims and a tolerance of personal differences.

The key words of the speech are "true obedience" and "honest will." Neither of these concepts of behavior indicates force or tyranny, but rather mutual respect, trust, tolerance, and understanding. Women's physical weakness should indicate to them the nature of the weapons they should use. For herself, Kate no longer acts with the violence born of frustration. She can govern her passions and will use softness, humor, subtlety—perhaps exploiting her physical weakness in order to act in loving partnership with her husband. Now that she has found a suitable mate, she no longer needs to act the part of a shrew. In public she will be the epitome of obedience, the embodiment of the model wife, according to the moralistic principles of conduct books. She has now shown love, honor, and reverence; she has obeyed Petruchio's commands (reserving to herself the right to think some of them ridiculous); she has been silent unless spoken to; and now in offering to place her hands below her husband's foot, she makes a statement and a gesture of ultimate humility. But the key words here are "if he please" (l.183). Kate knows her man, and Petruchio knows better than to accept. He has no need to exact total submission from such a woman as Kate. He is too secure in his own personal identity. Instead he refuses the proffered hand beneath his foot, bends down and sweeps her to her feet with a merrily possessive, "Why, there's a wench! Come on, and kiss me, Kate" (l.185). As on the road to Padua, the falcon is rewarded for hunting down her prey, and both bird and keeper rejoice in the success of their mutual joke at the expense of the rest of the company. The wager has been won. Petruchio has received another dowry, and the two hunters can laugh together. Kate and Petruchio instinctively understand each other; one madcap sense of humor has found its like, and each has come to respect the other's verve, vigor, and human personality. Each can now play the game of human relationships to the everlasting joy and amusement of the other. Whatever else one may say of this marriage, it will surely never be dull.

As a result of Petruchio's regime Kate is tamed, but only insofar as developing an appreciation of the *realpolitik* of matrimonial relationships under the tutelage of her keeper, who has been careful "not to reduce unduly the courage, activity, and other qualities necessary in a good hunting falcon." [41] She is now the wife of a man who respects and rejoices in her integrity of spirit and independence. She and her husband are allies against the rest of the world in hunting down "supposes" or pretension. She pays lip service to the conduct-book wifely precepts, but her frame of reference is different. As her husband's ally and partner, she does not need to be completely silent and submissive; her spirit is as volatile as ever, but she has learned to temper it publicly for policy and love. Kate and Petruchio have shown by their actions the superiority of their alliance in mutuality over the other marriages conceived according to rule. Thus they make fun of romantic idealism, fortune hunting, and the strictures of a repressive society. Further, through the careful equation of the taming of a wife with the "reclaiming" of a haggard, Shakespeare has conveyed the ideal matrimonial situation. Both keeper and falcon, husband and wife, have their own areas of superiority, but when both work together at a given hunting task they are incomparable. Each needs the other, and each recognizes the necessity of love and obedience on the part of the one, and consideration and trust on the part of the other. Each has duties and both have rights. The keeper has the right to "true obedience," but a good falconer will never require unreasonable performance from his haggard. Similarly, the falcon has the right to expect consideration, respect, and reward for good hunting and good deportment.

Thus Shakespeare has shown a surprisingly modern attitude toward marriage and a new approach to the taming of a wife, not by physical force, but by subtlety, art, reason, and love. The advice, then, is that of the homilies in its most ideal sense: "honest natures will sooner be retained to doe their duety, rather by gentle wordes, then by stripes." [42] Woman is not merely the weaker vessel, to be borne with. She has her own role to play, and that is what Kate learns. The hunting falcon must do without total liberty and work in concert with her keeper, who draws her to him with love, trust, and rewards, not with blows. In a similar way Kate and Petruchio achieve an ideal partnership, and by allying it to the imagery of falconry, Shakespeare has conveyed the subtlety and delicacy of this matrimonial relationship.[43] Kate's soaring spirit is not destroyed by her husband, and Petruchio is no bitter fortune-hunting tyrant. These two allies have reached a civilized and rational appreciation of their respective roles, and thus happiness in the mutuality of their partnership must surely follow.

After *The Taming of the Shrew* Shakespeare's next comic treatment of marriage is found in the fairyland subplot of *A Midsummer Night's Dream*, which Jeanne Addison Roberts sees as foreshadowing the "marital chaos" of later plays, the tragedies in particular. One last full-dress comic treatment of this theme remains—*The Merry Wives of Windsor*—in Roberts's words, "a true domestic comedy of marriage—the problems of achieving it and the perils of maintaining it."[44] This is indeed the case and the play provides a gallery of matrimonial enemies personified: Falstaff is lust, Ford is jealousy, the Pages both represent aspects of greed and social climbing, and Slender, together with Falstaff, exemplifies stupidity. All these adversaries are defeated; love triumphs in this comedy of adultery and the audience is presumably expected to enjoy the farcial, if vicious, defeat of Falstaff, and the discomfiture of Ford and the Pages.[45] Marriage, trust, and love are affirmed, and folly is punished, but the emphasis on jealousy and cuckoldry leads Shakespeare thereafter away from matrimonial conduct as a subject for comic exploitation and into investigation of its tragic import.

CHAPTER V

The Indiscretions of Desdemona[1]

O *thello* is curiously allied to Shakespeare's mature romantic comedies, and even to *The Taming of the Shrew*, because of its theme of love and marriage, traditionally the province of comedy rather than tragedy. But in this play, to quote Susan Snyder, "Shakespeare subjects the comic assumptions about the love union, nature, and reason to a radical reassessment."[2] In so doing he also inverts both traditional stereotypes and form. The black man, the Renaissance symbol of evil, becomes a basically noble and heroic figure who engages audience sympathies, despite the fact that at the end of the play he is a murderer who then commits suicide. Similarly, the mistaken cuckold, the jealous husband, and the January–May marriage belong in the farcical world of *The Merry Wives of Windsor* rather than in an Italianate play of tragic revenge. The overall structure, with its links to the *commedia dell'arte*, offers incidents of overhearing and mistaking, stock figures like the prostitute and confidant, together with the more limited domestic and socio-sexual world of comedy rather than the cosmic universe of tragedy. Comic themes, forms and values are reinterpreted, turned topsy-turvy, so that in the words of Carol Thomas Neely:

> The play is a terrifying completion of the comedies. In them, realism and romanticism, lust and love, desire and illusion, love and friendship, cuckoldry and marriage, masculinity and femininity are held in precarious balance. . . . In *Othello*, the men's murderous fancies are untouched by the women's affection, wit, and shrewishness. The play ends as it began, in a world of men—political, loveless, undomesticated.[3]

But what causes this tragic outcome? Why does the noble Moor of Act I degenerate into the vengeful Moor of Act V? Why does the efficient military commander become the dupe of his ancient? It is not enough to dismiss Iago

135

as Satanic, though in the final scene Othello momentarily suggests that equation (V.ii.266–287). Iago is basically a skillful opportunist who turns situations to his own account; chance aids him so well that one almost begins to believe in the possibility of a hostile First Mover, but devil-worship appears nowhere in the play.

As a primary device of villainy, Iago uses deliberate misconstruction of the action of others, operating on the principle that falsehoods repeated frequently will eventually discredit truth. In other words, some mud is bound to stick. But in order to do this, Iago needs evidence, and in one of his soliloquies he takes the audience into his confidence and reveals the tactics he will use to discredit Desdemona:

> So will I turn her virtue into pitch,
> And of her own virtues make the net
> That shall enmesh them all.
> (II.iii.343–345)

He will therefore deliberately misinterpret the motivations for Desdemona's actions from womanly virtues of love, sympathy, kindheartedness, and fidelity in friendship into the vice of insatiable lust, a common antifeminist allegation. We have here the paradox of goodness—that innate moral decency and humanity can be misconstrued. Desdemona tries to be truly human in a world that is inhuman and this is what raises the play of *Othello* above the constraints of domestic tragedy and places it in a universal context.

The character and actions of Desdemona therefore need to be analyzed in an attempt to explain the paradox that goodness can be used as the instrument of destruction. The extraordinary innocence of Desdemona has frequently been praised, and Bradley extolls her sweetness, submission, and pathos, though Neely does suggest that "The source of her sainthood seems a passivity verging to catatonia."[4] And recently one critic has questioned the generally accepted truths about her character, suggesting that she may even have something of the witch, as well as Griselda, in her.[5] But negative responses to Desdemona are not new. Georges Bonnard suggested that both major characters are guilty, Desdemona of being "a rebellious child," and Othello of a "lack of wisdom in his love."[6] John W. Draper was at least evenhanded in his blame, saying that "Probably Desdemona never really understood Othello, nor he her."[7] Irene Dash, on the other hand, sees Desdemona's tragedy as that "of a woman, of women, pummeled into shape by the conventions that bind."[8] At the commencement of the action she is seen as capable of defying custom by marrying both outside her race and without parental consent. Like Kate, she too is tamed, but her spirit is destroyed by "a slow wearing away of the resistance, a slow imposition of patterns,"[9] a sad commentary on marriage. H. B. Charlton makes substantially the same point when he comments lyrically, "Love of such an ideal kind as that of Desdemona and Othello needs time and occasion to habituate itself to temporal and corporal domesticity."[10] Clearly, up to the time of her marriage Desdemona has demonstrated self-confidence and enterprise, qualities that are praised in this century but run counter to the traditional Elizabethan code of feminine conduct.

That Shakespeare means us to assess Desdemona's conduct against the paragons of submission portrayed in such diverse places as homilies, broadside ballads and conduct books is made clear in II.i.147–159, where Iago gives his interpretation of this ideal and Desdemona laughingly rejects it. Carroll Camden, working with this speech and exploring its analogues, concludes that Desdemona is portrayed as an exemplary matron,[11] but Bonnard claims that Shakespeare "wanted to convey to the audience that her terrible fate was not totally undeserved."[12] This judgment is both simplistic and harsh, indicating that Desdemona's conduct is reprehensible, whereas her chief fault is the same as her husband's—loving "not wisely but too well." She follows her heart rather than her head in marrying Othello, and then tries to continue the relationship as a loving partner in a hierarchical society, a military encampment where obedience to senior officers is mandatory, orders are enforced, and wives must know their place. As Dash points out, the marriage of Emilia and Iago indicates the accommodations wives are required to make.[13] In having Iago state the ideals to which Desdemona does not conform, Shakespeare furnishes a reference point for his audience which would make the motivation for Othello's later fury more explicit to the playgoer of the seventeenth century than the twentieth-century counterpart who is more likely to be aware "that women are the victims of a marriage system in whose origin they had no voice and a double standard concerning chastity in which they were never consulted."[14] Desdemona herself is also vulnerable on other grounds; she has led a sheltered life in the house of a permissive and adoring father and is innocent of the wickedness of the world outside. She is a loyal, loving, free spirit whose inexperience and decency blind her to the possibility that her motives might appear questionable and her actions capable of misconstruction. Iago, however, sees all too clearly how he can attack such virtue.

To support this offensive Shakespeare has Iago draw his ammunition from the so-called rules governing feminine behavior. Undoubtedly Jacobean life was not lived completely by the rules and precepts of conduct books, but the code existed and could always be invoked, despite the relative freedom of women in England, an exception to the rest of Europe, where they were often strictly sequestered. Travelers to England frequently commented on this apparent freedom, and the comments of Jacob Rathgeb made in 1592 were equally applicable to the early seventeenth century. According to him

> The women have much more liberty than perhaps in any other place; they also know well how to make use of it, for they go dressed out in exceedingly fine clothes, and give all their attention to their ruffs and stuffs . . . [15]

Nonetheless, women possessed few legal rights, even in England, and it was generally accepted that the code of conduct laid down in most courtesy books, especially those with a Continental origin, represented a substantially correct picture of ideal female behavior and a fair approximation of woman's lot in Europe. Courtesy books thus formed a convenient codification of correct behavior in sixteenth- and seventeenth-century England, especially among the upwardly mobile bourgeoisie.[16]

This English conduct literature was, as is well known, far removed from the philosophical courtliness of Italy, being instead a solidly practical genre concerned with virtuous living and with a heavy emphasis on feminine chastity—largely for property considerations. An unchaste woman lost her value on the marriage market; and if already married, she might corrupt the pure line of descent by insinuating a bastard into it.[17] Consequently a young virgin was counseled to live before her marriage in an utterly chaste manner. The frequent reprinting of Juan Luis Vives's *The Instruction of a Christian Woman* bears witness to the continuation of this strict school. Even after the English Reformation, Vives remained a major spokesman, insisting that a young woman should leave all matrimonial arrangements to her parents:

> . . . which loue her as wellas [*sic*] as her selfe doth. And lette her thynke that her father and mother will prouyde no lesse diligently for her, than she wolde for her selfe: but moche better, by the reason they haue more expery-ence and wysedome.[18]

Similarly, the maiden should remain completely silent during such negotiations, and she should not in any way indicate a desire for marriage. She should also avoid any behavior which might compromise her honor. For instance, she ought never to speak with a man, unless an older woman were present. Even social gatherings might be a dangerous occasion of sin, and Vives castigates a

. . . mad and a frantike opinion, which bothe maydens and wyues haue . . . that thynke it is expedient for maydes, that are come to lauful age of mari- age, to be sene ofte abrode amonge people, goodly and pykedly arayed, and to kepe company and communication with men, to be eloquent in speche, and counnyng in daunsyng and syngyng.[19]

As we have seen, maidens were warned most strenuously against undertaking marriage for love, because affection without the concomitant advantages of reason and financial ability is bound to be short-lived.[20] As a natural corollary to this advice, conduct writers insisted upon the necessity of parental consent before a marriage should take place. The Canon Law of the Church of Eng- land agreed with this proposition and the *Constitutions and Canons Ecclesi- astical* of 1604 insist on it in Canon 100:

No children vnder the age of one and twentie yeeres complete, shall con- tract themselves, or marrie without the consent of their Parents, or of their Guardians and Gouernours, if their Parents be deceased.[21]

Further agreement with the attitudes of conduct writers may be found in other documents stating official church policy. The Church of England objected to secret marriages and insisted on the calling of banns. William Harrington's pronouncement of 1528 remained valid law:

. . . In specyally y[t] nother matrymony nor spousage oughte to be made but in honest places and afore honest wytnes. And that they do not solem- pnysate matrimony afore y[t] banes be thre tymes asked: for they do they be a cursed with many other thynges consernyng y[e] sacramēt of matrymony whiche be declared at large afore. . . .[22]

The Church of England gave its official sanction to this view in Canon LXII of the *Constitutions* of 1604:

. . . Bannes of Matrimonie . . . [must be] first published three seuerall Sundaies or Holy dayes in the time of diuine Seruice in the Parish Churches and Chappels where the saide parties dwel.[23]

Licenses to marry without banns were to be granted only under special con- ditions.[24]

After marriage, the ideal wife of the conduct books was not supposed to have any further freedom than before, though doubtless English women did go abroad unescorted. Her duties were manifold and generally followed those of Proverbs 23:13–27. The books were often even more specific than the Bible, and Guillaume de la Perrière, for example, gives an admirable summary of the conduct desired, though not always found, in an Elizabethan or Jacobean wife: (1) she should take care of all domestic business, and look after the household; (2) she should not allow any person to come into the house without the express consent of her husband; (3) she should oversee all household expenses; (4) she should not dress too richly, for that is the forerunner of adultery; (5) she should take no interest in foreign affairs; (6) she should wholly obey her husband, even in those things that concern business and outdoors; (7) she should account the conditions of her husband to be the laws of her life, and if bad, she must patiently bear them; (8) she should love, esteem, and honor him in adversity, as well as in prosperity.[25]

The similarity between this long list of wifely duties and Iago's account of the perfect wife is surely deliberate:

> She that was ever fair, and never proud;
> Had tongue at will, and yet was never loud;
> Never lacked gold, and yet went never gay;
> Fled from her wish, and yet said 'Now I may';
> She that, being ang'red, her revenge being nigh,
> Bade her wrong stay, and her displeasure fly;
> She that in wisdom never was so frail
> To change the cod's head for the salmon's tail;
> She that could think, and ne'er disclose her mind;
> See suitors following, and not look behind;
> She was a wight (if ever such wight were)—
> . . . . . .
> To suckle fools and chronicle small beer.
> (II.i.147–159)

The overt purpose of this speech is to entertain Desdemona and also to reply to her request for praise of "a deserving woman indeed—one that in the authority of her merit did justly put on the vouch of very malice itself"[26] (II.i.144–147), possibly her own image of herself. Iago's reply becomes quite eloquent as he lists the attributes which were "perhaps taken seriously by some men in search of wives";[27] but then at the penultimate line he pauses to deliver a *coup de grace* to the whole ideal; in Neely's words, "his verses extravagantly praise the virtuous woman, the better to be able to diminish her."[28]

The tone of this scene is hence very important. It is one of sophisticated badinage and merry courtly repartee, but Iago contributes an undertone of contempt which gives the incident the serious weight of menace and foreboding. He seems in fact to accept the traditional antifeminist views he proposes ostensibly for Desdemona's entertainment: women are hussies, sexually insatiable, untrustworthy, and the ideal woman he has described probably cannot

exist—certainly not in the world. Even Michael Cassio, whose respect for
Desdemona is clearly shown, agrees with the cynical Iago when Desdemona
asks him for refutation:

> He speaks home, madam. You may relish him more in the soldier than in
> the scholar.
>
> (II.i.164–165)

This unexpected support of Iago's derogatory remarks serves two important functions. First, in giving approval to antifeminist allegations, it
prepares the way for Iago's open attacks on Desdemona's virtue. Second, in
following the cynically lyrical account of the ideal "wight," it emphasizes the
virtues ostensibly desired in a paragon of connubial virtue. Iago's "dream-
woman" would be a lady of beauty and pecuniary substance, sober in dress and
mien, humble in respect of her own wishes, forgiving and tolerant of masculine
peccadilloes, wise, virtuous, and circumspect. The demeanor of Emilia toward
Iago indicates that to a great extent she fulfills this ideal. The place of such a
lady was that suggested by the Church Fathers, the Book of Proverbs, the
Homily on Matrimony, conduct books in general, and Iago in particular—she
should remain sequestered in her house bringing up her children. Such a
suggestion is clearly a deliberate attack on the very existence of Desdemona,
the conversation in which she has just taken part, and on her liberated mode of
life.

Now if Desdemona is later to be considered the perfect wife, as some
critics have suggested, she would be expected to possess these characteristics
and practice these virtues. However, in the first part of the play, she is shown
as flouting strictures on maidenly modesty, marrying clandestinely for love,
and after her marriage continuing to act in a singularly liberated manner. It is
only in the last two acts, when actually all is lost, that she develops an almost
catatonic submission. Romantic pro-Desdemona critics look only at the
pathetic victim, not the independent, indeed rather stubborn, young woman
who follows the dictates of her own generous heart rather than the societally
imposed strictures imposed by conduct books and insecure men. The result is
that her continued independence and her defiance of accepted norms of
behavior give Iago material which he can deliberately misconstrue, misinterpret,
and manufacture into "evidence" with which to deceive Othello, a warrior
whose earlier relations with women seem to have taken place in the brothel
rather than in the sophisticated society of Venice. An audience familiar with
the portrait of the ideal lady would be able to understand quite clearly how and

why Othello is tortured into accepting Iago's skillful innuendoes and allegations as truth.

As a maiden, Desdemona seems at first to be the mild-mannered, silent
virgin depicted by the conduct books. Brabantio initially calls her

> A maiden never bold;
> Of spirit so still and quiet that her motion
> Blushed at herself; . . .
>
> (I.iii.94–96)

She also seems to perform her household duties with efficiency, if not alacrity,
because Othello remarks

> But still the house-affairs would draw her thence;
> Which ever as she could with haste dispatch,
> She'ld come again, and with a greedy ear
> Devour up my discourse: . . .
>
> (I.iii.147–150)

Nevertheless, she takes an unexpected and perhaps unmaidenly interest in
Othello's accounts of his adventures and hardships. She also speaks alone
with her father's visitor,[29] an invited guest, to be sure, but her action is still
indiscreet, especially since it is she who speaks first of love to Othello,
although her declaration is veiled:

> She wished she had not heard it; yet she wished
> That Heaven had made her such a man. She thanked me,
> And bade me, if I had a friend that loved her,
> I should but teach him how to tell my story,
> And that would woo her. Upon this hint I spake.
>
> (I.iii.162–166)

Desdemona is shown here as well able to make use of her unusual personal
freedom, explicable only by her apparent position as the chatelaine of
Brabantio's household. Nevertheless, the situation would have been highly
irregular in Venice, where girls of good family were closely watched and even
married women were little better off. Coryat notes with a certain wonderment
that

> . . . The Gentlemen do euen coope vp their wives alwaies within the
> walles of their houses for feare of these inconueniences [assaults on their
> chastity] as much as if there were no Cortezans at all in City. . . .[30]

The conduct of a young lady in the courtesy books is also a far cry from
that of Desdemona in her matrimonial arrangements. She marries against the

precepts of both courtesy books and canon law, without consulting her father. Iago notes the unnaturalness of this act in the first scene:

> Your daughter, if you have not given her leave,
> I say again, hath made a gross revolt.
> (I.i.134–135)

The two are married, but Shakespeare obviously makes it a secret and irregular ceremony without banns; he does not rehearse it, however, probably because it is irrelevant to the main argument of the play, which concerns the marriage itself. We are told that Desdemona went to her marriage

> . . . with no worse nor better guard
> But with a knave of common hire, a gondolier,
> (I.i.123–124)[31]

and Othello admits his abduction of the willing lady with great dignity before the Venetian Senate:

> That I have ta'en away this old man's daughter,
> It is most true; I have married her.
> The very head and front of my offending
> Hath this extent, no more. . .
> (I.iii.78–81)

Nevertheless, in terms of Venetian practice and Elizabethan precepts, the behavior of the lady is unfilial and unnatural indeed, while the occurrence is made even worse because of the obvious unsuitability of Othello, the much older Moorish soldier, her father's friend, as a husband.[32] It would therefore seem that audience reaction to the situation would be one of shock, perhaps similar to Brabantio's

> Look to her, Moor, if thou hast eyes to see!
> She has deceived her father, and may thee.
> (I.iii.292–293)

One error may be earnest of more to come. Desdemona here has followed her passion rather than her reason, falling in love with the alien hero of a thousand romantic exploits, and contracting a match which both the world of Venice and the Elizabethan audience could not fail to recognize as unnatural.[33] So far, Desdemona is not the ideal young lady of precept, and the audience could automatically expect nothing but disaster of such a match, not only because of the young woman's rashness, but also because of the the January–May relationship of the couple.[34]

The independence and self-confidence notable in Desdemona the maiden are also demonstrated in her behavior as a married woman. Certainly she possesses some of the gifts of the Renaissance courtly lady as drawn by Castiglione, and Othello rejoices in them:

> . . . 'Tis not to make me jealous
> To say my wife is fair, feeds well, loves
>   company,
> Is free of speech, sings, plays, and dances;
> Where virtue is, these are more virtuous.
>   (III.iii.183–186)

She also possesses other virtues to be found in the courtesy-book description of the perfect wife. Nothing can be said of her as mistress of her household because, except for a few statements in Act I and in her relations with Emilia, she is not shown in such a situation. She undoubtedly loves, esteems, and honors Othello, and she does put up with her husband's unpredictable changes of mood with the almost saintly longsuffering of a Griselda. Still, she is wanting in other matters: she entertains Cassio without Othello's permission; she takes an interest in "forraine" affairs, business outside her household;[35] and she does not wholly obey her husband. She likewise lacks two further virtues listed by Iago: humility in respect of her own wishes, and circumspection in behavior. Certainly she has the gifts of natural virtue, but they are not enough, because, as was said of Ceasar's wife, "*A woman must not onely bee free from the fault but also from all suspition thereof.*"[36] And it is on the evidence of her misinterpreted actions that Desemona is convicted at the tribunal of Othello's justice.

Shakespeare shows this situation as really arising from the impulsive and sympathetic nature of Desdemona which leads to her questionable behavior. She is by no means a frightened little girl, but a warm, vital, passionate, strong-willed, though rather inexperienced young woman. As a result, she spontaneously espouses the cause of Cassio, who comes to visit without Othello's knowledge, and in fact while he is suffering under the displeasure of the Moor. In thus seeing Cassio privately, and without her husband's consent, Desdemona unthinkingly lays herself open to the charge of wantonness, especially since she appears to entertain him in a manner too free to be consistent with virtue. Iago takes the fullest advantage of this situation; and after helping to arrange this first clandestine, though innocent, meeting (II.iii.366–370), he sows suspicion in Othello's mind (III.iii.35ff.).

The shrewdness and skill with which Iago is made to arouse Othello's distrust are most remarkable. The Ensign continually plays upon Othello's lack of courtly knowledge. He is shown throughout the play as deliberately misconstruing Desdemona's every action; and if one keeps in mind the courtesy-book precepts of wifely conduct, it must be admitted that Desdemona inadvertently gives cause for suspicion.

Throughout his plotting, Iago adopts the solicitous pose of a man who wishes to save his friend and superior officer from all unnecessary pain; and when he and Othello first come upon Desdemona and Cassio, Iago attracts Othello's attention with a half-smothered exclamation. "Ha! I like not that" (III.iii.35), which he speedily retracts when questioned. But then he claims that Cassio should not have left so "guilty-like," and at this utterly inopportune moment Desdemona begins her pleading for Cassio's reinstatement. Here, as on other occasions throughout the play, Shakespeare has Desdemona assess the situation incorrectly. She presses for a decision when Othello is not minded to give one. Thus she may be said to offend against another canon of wifely conduct. As the lady Eulalia of Erasmus and Snawsel says:

> . . . it beseemes an honest wife to frame her selfe to her husbands affection, and not to be merry, when he is melancholy, not iocond when he is sad, much lesse fliere when hee is angry. And if at any time he were stird, I would either pacifie him with gentle speech, or giue way to his wrath, til it were somewhat allayed; or else I would keepe silence, til there were fit time for cleering my selfe, or aduising him with reuerence and discretion.[37]

Desdemona is not yet ready for this kind of wifely submission; she is a new bride, accustomed to unusual freedom, who is continuing the tactics of courtship into matrimony, totally confident that she can wheedle her husband and bend him to her will as she has in the past. Thus she assures Cassio that success is certain, planning the use of loving persuasion, but her approach can also be misconstrued as shrewish:

> . . . My lord shall never rest;
> I'll watch him tame, and talk him out of patience;
> His bed shall seem a school, his board a shrift;
> I'll intermingle everything he does
> With Cassio's suit . . .
>
> (III.iii.22–26)

Once more the conduct writers rebuke this practice, la Primaudaye maintaining that a good wife must always attend

> . . . to that which sitteth neerest hir husbands heart, that is, to hir behau-
> iour, manners and conversation, taking order that these things be not
> heard, troublesome, or irksome to hir husband euerie day, but such as
> please him agree with his conditions. For the troublesome conuersation of a
> Wife that alwaies iarreth, in the end maketh even hir honest behauiour
> odious. . . .[38]

Likewise, both conduct books and common sense recommend that differences between husband and wife not be taken to bed, although the "boulster lecture" seems to have been a commonly recognized wifely weapon.[39]

Desdemona's very interest in the Cassio case may also be interpreted as a wifely fault in her—and naturally Iago seizes upon it. She is taking an interest in happenings occurring outside the limits of her household, and which therefore ought not to concern her, but should be the sole prerogative of her husband. She is also shown failing to obey her husband in all things, even in matters outside the domestic sphere, by refusing to drop the subject of Cassio. Thus she so enrages her husband with harping on the lieutenant's disgrace that her joy on hearing the news of Othello's impending return to Venice and his replacement in Cyprus by Cassio (IV.i.231) further increases her husband's suspicions. Certainly Desdemona is not designed as an intentionally disobedient wife, but as a woman with a strong will. She refuses to be fobbed off with excuses; and although she bows to Othello's demand that she leave him alone for a few minutes, she returns to the problem (III.iv.50), unknowingly choosing an inopportune time. Yet she can later be extraordinarily obedient and the mirror of wifely humility when she is publicly struck and humiliated (IV.i.233).[40]

Shakespeare makes Iago fan Othello's suspicions by the use of another common belief. He asks whether Cassio had been privy to the Moor's wooing of Desdemona (III.iii.94ff.), and on hearing that the lieutenant had frequently acted as a go-between, he makes the ambiguous statement, "Indeed!" Now as is well known, the use of a third party in a wooing is conventionally expected to end in the acceptance of the agent rather than the principal, and consequently the courtesy books warn men, "Wooe not by Embassadour," advising married men further, "Make not thy friend too familiar with thy wife."[41] Shakespeare's audience presumably would have understood the implications of Iago's questioning and again would be able to comprehend the reason for Othello's increased rage.

Another weapon still remains to Iago: the lascivious reputation of Venetian women in the early seventeenth century. He carefully repeats to Othello the customary aspersions against their virtue, implying that Desdemona is a typical example:

> I know our country disposition well:
> In Venice they do let God see the pranks
> They dare not show their husbands. Their best conscience
> Is not to leave't undone, but to keep't unknown.
>   (III.iii.201–204)

Despite the strictness with which women of good family were generally kept, travelers had often brought home to England reports of the alleged looseness of Venetian women, whose dress was considered by Coryat to be "a great incentiue & fomentation of luxurious desires."[42] In general, Europe's ill opinion of the morals of Venice seems to have arisen from the fact that alone among the peoples of Europe, the Venetians permitted licensed prostitution:

> . . . For they thinke that the chastity of their wives would be the sooner assaulted, and so consequently they would be *capricornified*, (which of all the indignities in the world the Venetian cannot patiently endure) were it not for these places of euacuation.[43]

And again we are told that "the name of a Cortezan of Venice is famoused over all Christendome."[44] Shakespeare's audience was well aware of this evil repute and therefore they could understand Othello's horror at the rehearsal of the commonplace, especially since it is made clear that Othello is not experienced in the ways of Venetian society. The reason for his increased revulsion is even more easily understood when one remembers that Oriental races were thought to hold great store by the chastity of their wives, since both a man's honor and virility were impugned if his wife were unfaithful.[45] Here Shakespeare faces a difficult task because the Elizabethans regarded the cuckold as an object of mirth and derision; but in this play, the situation is tranformed through Shakespeare's delineation of the tortures of Othello's disbelief and doubt.

That Iago's allegations of frequent immorality among Venetian women remain festering in Othello's mind is clearly shown from the Moor's concluding speech in the "brothel" scene of IV.ii:

> I took you for that cunning whore of Venice
> That married with Othello—[*calling*] You, mistress,
> That have the office opposite to Saint Peter
> And keep the gate of hell!
>   *Enter Emilia.*   You, you, ay, you!
> We have done our course; there's money for your pains:
> I pray you turn the key, and keep our counsel.
>   (IV.ii.89–94)

Othello here betrays a very intimate understanding of the etiquette of the brothel, something which clearly indicates the kind of experience he has previously had with women. It also helps to give Othello further motivation. As a soldier he has not had the opportunity to meet with women of social and courtly grace, like Desdemona. To him she has seemed an ideal creature, perhaps scarcely a sexual object, [46] yet Iago has proved to him that she is no better than all those women he has previously used to satisfy his lust.

Iago's arguments throughout have been skillfully used on this assumption, as he discusses the unnaturalness of Desdemona's conduct noted by Brabantio in the first act:

> For I'll refer me to all things of sense,
> If she in chains of magic were not bound,
> Whether a maid so tender, fair, and happy,
> So opposite to marriage that she shunned
> The wealthy curlèd darlings of our nation,
> Would ever have, t'incur a general mock,
> Run from her guardage to the sooty bosom
> Of such a thing as thou—to fear, not to delight.
>   (I.ii.64–71)

Iago never allows this doubt to leave Othello's mind as he skillfully restates it with the further insinuation that Desdemona might now see the folly of her impulsive, indeed unnatural, action. Even more damaging to the psyche of a valiant commander is the suggestion that she, who may well have married him to satisfy her own physical "will" or lust may now find him, the older and alien man, sexually deficient:

> Ay, there's the point (to be bold with you)
> Not to affect many proposed matches
> Of her own clime, complexion, and degree
> Whereto we see in all things nature tends—
> Foh! one may smell in such a will most rank,
> Foul disproportions, thoughts unnatural—
> But, pardon me—I do not in position
> Distinctly speak of her; though I may fear
> Her will, recoiling to her better judgment,
> May fall to match you with her country forms,
> And happily repent.
>   (III.iii.228–238)

This implication is the more appalling to Othello because Iago has used it in reference to an earlier suggestion arising from a piece of real evidence:[47]

Iago   She did deceive her father, marrying you.
                And when she seemed to shake and fear your looks
                She loved them most.
Othello   And so she did.
Iago   Why, go to, then!
                She, that, so young, could give out such a seeming
                To seel her father's eyes up close as oak—
                He thought 'twas witchcraft—but I am much to blame.
                I humbly do beseech you of your pardon
                For too much loving you.

                                        (III.iii.206–213)

This inflammatory pity offered by a subordinate also recalls Brabantio's last words of angry prophecy[48] and adds to all the earlier specific examples of independent and even shrewish behavior which Desdemona has demonstrated. Such examples, together with poisonous insinuations of misconduct, based as they are on misinterpretations of the innocent actions of a woman who appears to see herself as her husband's partner rather than a mere subordinate, lead Othello to suspect his wife of duplicitous cunning. But not only does Shakespeare make Iago attack Desdemona's actions through misconstruction, but also through Othello's pride in winning such a desirable matrimonial prize. At the same time, the deliberate use of conduct-book material would clarify to the audience the way that a skillful liar like Iago could manipulate the openminded and socially inexperienced Othello who tortures himself with doubt, tries not to believe, and acts only after receiving what he takes as "ocular proof" in the scene where Cassio and Iago discuss Bianca (IV.i.92–166).

At this point one must consider whether the suggestion that Desdemona contributes in any way to her tragedy forfeits the audience's sympathy for her.[49] Shakespeare tries to prevent this by emphasizing her beauty, charm, submission, and eagerness to please her husband throughout the last two acts, going far beyond a mere portrait of the ideal wife. Irene Dash's suggestion that he shows "the decline of a woman from a single, self-confident person to an uncertain, married woman still attempting to understand her role"[50] helps to explain Desdemona's mild reaction to public rebuke, humiliation, and violence (IV.i). At the same time it underlines the horror of her situation, particularly in the next scene of private humiliation in her own home, where Othello treats her like a whore. Psychologically beaten into near catatonia, she is unable to rouse herself to any action, except the pathetic one of calling for her wedding sheets, presumably thinking of them as a symbol of her consummated love and married chastity. The very transparency of her virtue blinds her to the possible implications of some of her previous actions as she discusses the possibility of having offended Othello, trying too late to placate rather than cross him. She looks at her own conduct, vainly seeking to find the "ignorant sin" which might have caused his accusations of whoredom. All unknowingly, she hits on the truth and at that moment she is indeed more than that model of wifely patience and humility praised in the courtesy books as she accepts the blame for own conduct:

> 'Tis meet I should be used so, very meet.
> How have I been behaved, that he might stick
> The small'st opinion on my least misuse?
> (IV.ii.107–109)

And again, with a masterly stroke of dramatic irony, Shakespeare has her rehearse the very sins of which Iago has indirectly accused her, while begging the villainous Ensign for his assistance:

> . . . Here I kneel:
> If e'er my will did trespass 'gainst his love
> Either in discourse of thought or actual deed,
> Or that mine eyes, mine ears, or any sense
> Delighted them in any other form,
> Or that I do not yet, and ever did,
> And ever will (though he do shake me off
> To beggarly divorcement) love him dearly,
> Comfort forswear me! Unkindness may do much;
> And his unkindness may defeat my life,
> But never taint my love. . . .
> (IV.ii.151–161)

The irony of the tragedy continues into IV.iii. where Desdemona identifies with the willow song sung by the dying and forsaken maid, Barbary, a strange name reminiscent of Othello's own origins. Barbary's fate Desdemona takes as foreshadowing her own; but then she makes an astonishingly apposite error "Let nobody blame him, his scorn I approve," by which "she twists the words of the ancient song so as to apply them to her own tragic situation."[51] This is the way of acceptance, of endurance, of the conduct praised in Erasmus's Eulalia, in Griselda, and above all in "the virtuous and godly Susanna" who did not speak in her own defense, allowing her innocence to speak for her. This is the recommendation of the conduct books, and Desdemona here follows it. However, she did indeed have another choice, one which she herself states in the last lines of her rewritten willow song:

'I called my love false love; but what said he then?
Sing willow, willow, willow:
If I court moe women, you'll couch with moe men.'
(IV.iii.53–55)

This gives the pragmatic and worldly-wise Emilia a chance to discuss woman's only weapon—retaliation in kind, the one thing that men fear.[52] However, such is Desdemona's steadfast love that she chooses acceptance, a nonaction that leads directly to her own death when her frenzied protestations of innocence are ended by her ambiguous and ill-chosen words on hearing of Cassio's supposed death: "Alas! he is betrayed, and I undone!" (V.ii.76). Again Othello misunderstands Desdemona. His suspicions are kindled into greater certainty, and he inflicts the penalty of Moorish justice, killing an adulteress "to redeem her from degradation."[53] Even in her last moments, Desdemona's actions are open to misinterpretation to a mind already poisoned. Othello must not, of course, be considered blameless, but there are extenuating circumstances, something that Desdemona herself appears to understand as she perjures herself on her deathbed, risking eternity in a final act of love to save her husband. When asked by Emilia to disclose the name of her murderer, she accepts the blame herself and refuses:

Nobody—I myself. Farewell.
Commend me to my kind lord. O, farewell!
(V.ii.125–126)

These are the words that finally lead Othello to a comprehension of the nature and quality of his action and appreciation of the worth of what he has lost. The pathetic nature of Desdemona's fate is further reinforced by the compounding of misunderstanding, the more so since Iago's skillful attack is made largely with ammunition supplied unknowingly by the victim.

By examining the character of Desdemona through concentration on this single area of feminine behavior, one can perceive more clearly the way in which Shakespeare has managed to elucidate and give immediacy to the tragedy that overtakes the principal character. Shakespeare is making use of popular opinions and ideas to explain both the character of Desdemona and Othello's misinterpretations to his audience. Certainly, if one keeps in mind the precepts of the courtesy books, Desdemona is at fault in her wifely conduct and innocently supplies the evidence that leads to her own death through her assertion of her own independence. And certainly Othello's suspicions are at least explicable. Yet the "gross revolt" and matrimonial inadvertences of

Desdemona are all but forgotten in the light of the last act, so that the audience remembers only the death of someone beautiful, innocent, good, and above all, steadfast and forgiving. If, however, we recognize Desdemona's partial responsibility for the tragic action of the play, our sympathy for and understanding of Othello are thereby increased, so that his behavior becomes at least comprehensible. His actions thus gain further dramatic impact, as also does the death of the virtuous Desdemona who through love found the courage to disobey the conventions of feminine behavior only to become their physical and psychological victim.

Part Three

WOMEN WITHOUT POWER

CHAPTER VI

The Siege of Lucrece

The Rape of Lucrece has often been criticized because of its static quality, its digressions, and the relentless loquacity of its central character. The poem is therefore dismissed as an ambitious, yet flawed work of inordinate length, with Lucrece herself perceived as no heroine for today. Yet there is a rationale to the structure, and its discovery also leads to interpretation of the action. The key to both structure and interpretation can be found in Shakespeare's use of military language and military law as metaphorical and structural device.

The equation of sex and war is extremely ancient and by no means unusual. The association of the phallus with swords, falchions, or firearms can be
discovered with ease in literature at all levels from *Romeo and Juliet* to the
drill sergeant's lowly ditty quoted by Susan Brownmiller:

> This is my weapon, this is my gun,
> This is for business, this is for fun.[1]

Similarly the language used to describe rape has military connotations,
whether in the term "assault" found on the police blotter, or the siege of the
castle of virtue, which often appears in *The Faerie Queene*. Even today "the
battle of the sexes" continues unabated, with theories of recent psychologists
and feminists indicating that sexuality is at the center of a permanent kind of
civil war. Thus it should be no surprise to find Shakespeare using military
language and imagery in sexual matters.

The *Rape of Lucrece*, the "graver labour" that succeeded the erotic
epyllion of *Venus and Adonis* develops a variation on this military theme
which goes beyond the often-discussed equation of Lucrece's ravishment and
the fall of Troy. The rape itself and Lucrece's lamentations both illustrate
Shakespeare's clear understanding of the rules of land warfare which provide
the basic structure of the poem. These rules of land warfare are found in what
are called "the customary laws of war," which predate both the Hague and
Geneva Conventions of 1907 and 1949 respectively, and have their origins in
such diverse places as Deuteronomy and the Roman military writer, Vegetius.
Perhaps one of the more precise modern definitions of these "laws of war" is to
be found in a fairly recent United States Army document:

> As a result of centuries of warfare between various nations, unwritten
> laws and rules governing the conduct of war developed. These unwritten
> laws are known as the customary law of war. The customary law of war is
> finally based on the lessons of history, which have shown that the purpose
> and result of these rules is to allow the military force to accomplish its
> mission without causing unneccesary suffering or destruction. The
> general purpose of these rules is to limit the suffering to military targets
> and to provide humane treatment for all persons who are taken out of the
> fight.[2]

Such comments may at first sound more applicable to *Henry V* than *Lucrece*,
but there is one most relevant aspect of the customary law of land warfare
which had slightly different, and even more detailed rules—siege warfare:

From the legal point of view, there were two methods by which a town or fortress could be taken. It could be taken by assault, either by escalade or ambush, that is, stormed after its defenses had been breached by cannon or siege engines. Or it could be surrendered by *appointment* or treaty.[3]

Each method had its own rules, though both sets of ordinances could be used in a single siege as it progressed through the usual three stages: "the reduction of the suburbs, of the town itself, and of the citadel."[4]

The usual medieval and Renaissance approach was to send a herald or similar messenger to the captain of the garrison, asking him to surrender the town on suitable terms, which varied to suit the situation. If the treaty terms were refused, and if the city refused to open its gates to the besiegers, then the plenipotentiary would announce that there would be no further negotiations and the town, when captured would be put to the sack, when freebooting, pillage, rape, and even murder, were permitted as legitimate vengeance.[5] This is the "havoc" spoken of in *King John* (II.i.357), *Julius Caesar* (III.i.273), and *Coriolanus* (III.i.273 *sic*). Today, "the pillage of a town or place, even when taken by assault is prohibited" by Article 28 of the annex to Hague Convention No. IV.[6] But customary law, as Marlowe's Tamburlaine well knew, required a signal which indicated that the hour of mercy had passed. In ancient warfare it was the onslaught of the battering ram against the wall of the city, and later, with the invention of gunpowder, it was the firing of the first cannon shot. Alberico Gentili notes that "the battering ram was called the exterminator; because when it was brought up it was a sign that the town was to be utterly destroyed."[7] These rules also have a biblical precedent in Deuteronomy 20:10–14. In the King James translation:

> When thou comest nigh unto a city to fight against it, then proclaim peace unto it. And it shall be, if it make thee answer of peace and open unto thee, then it shall be that all people that is found therein shall be tributaries unto thee, and they shall serve thee. And if it will make no peace with thee, but will make war against thee, then thou shalt besiege it. And when the Lord thy God hath delivered it into thine hands, thou shalt smite every male thereof with the edge of the sword. But the women, and the little ones, and the cattle, and all that is in the city, even with the spoil thereof, shalt thou take unto thyself.

Henry V himself observed this rule of severity at the siege of Caen in 1417. Titus Livius, as quoted by Holinshed, noted that Caen had refused to make composition and hence the assault was renewed. After the capture of the town, its defenders were executed or fined, while Henry "distributed to euerie man, according to his desert, the spoile and gaine gotten in the town, chéeflie bicause at the assault they had shewed good proofe of their manhood and valiant courages."[8]

Hebrew siege law, however, had one peculiar characteristic, as is noted by Hugo Grotius and other writers on military law. One part of the city was left unsurrounded to allow inhabitants to come forth to surrender and be pardoned by the leader of the investing force. This, however, did not meet with general acceptance in the customary law of war, probably because captains of garrisons could take advantage of this situation by driving out numerous inhabitants from a starving town for the sole purpose of embarrassing the besiegers into feeding them and thus prolonging the siege. Henry V himself, though a model of chivalry on most occasions, found himself in this predicament at Rouen in 1418 when as Holinshed records:

> A great number of poor sillie creatures were put out at the gates, which were by the Englishmen that kept the trenchès beaten and driuen back againe to the same gates, which they found closed and shut against them. And so they laie between the wals of the citie and the trenches of the enemies, still crieing for helpe and releefe, for lacke whereof great numbers of them dailie died.
>
> Howbeit, king Henrie mooued with pitie, vpon Christmasse daie in the honor of Christes Natiuitie, refreshed all the poore people with vittels, to their great comfort and his high praise.[9]

And that the conduct of Henry indeed warranted this "high praise" is borne out by the fact that in his mercy he went beyond even the current provisions of the Hague and Geneva Conventions. The United States Army Field Manual, *The Law of Land Warfare*, specifically notes that

> Subject to the foregoing exceptions [wounded, ministers of religion, and medical personnel] there is no rule of law which compels the commander of an investing force to permit noncombatants to leave a besieged locality. It is within the discretion of the besieging commander whether he will permit noncombatants to leave and under what conditions. Thus, if a commander of a besieged place expels the inhabitants in order to lessen the logistical burden he has to bear, it is lawful, though an extreme measure, to drive them back so as to hasten the surrender.[10]

But as always, the law is more complex than it might at first appear. Obviously the severity of punishment inflicted by successful besiegers is mitigated by the speedy surrender of the city. Yet what about the duties of the garrison assigned to hold a fortress against a siege? Balthasar Ayala, Judge

Advocate General of the Spanish forces in the low Countries in the reign of Elizabeth, says unequivocally that "failure to hold a fortress, or the surrender of a camp to the enemy, is punishable under the *Lex Julia* about treason."[11] He further notes that the Spanish forces are particularly strict about observing this rule. He does, however, admit that in some cases of necessity a city may surrender: if it is ungarrisoned, because the king has failed to provide the means of defense, and also if resistance would mean "absolutely certain death to the hurt rather than to the profit of the State."[12] More specifically, Edward Davies in *The Art of War and Englands Traynings* (1619) says:

> . . . .respect is to be had, which must be holden as a Maxime, that where the place may be defended by assault without batterie, that at least one assault is to be abidden, and mo to be aspected if that be possible: and if it can suffer batterie, they must abide at least a volee of Canons: and if the place be so weake that it cannot sustaine, neither the one nor the other, and that it be so far distant from succours: to yeeld doth merit neither punishment of the Prince, nor of the enemie: But otherwise being of force able to sustaine the enemies furie, and cowardly or traiterously to deliuer the same merites death of the one and the other.[13]

This rule is therefore analogous to the diriment impediment to matrimony in canon law by which such force is exerted to compel matrimony as would strike fear into the heart of a strong man (*metus qui posset in virum constantem cadere*). Here the touchstone of behavior is when "it is like a man of valour would have done so."[14] This situation may also be termed the necessity and doctrine of adequate defense.

One other possibility remained to the beleaguered city: truce, the *lex deditionis*, as some writers call it. By this means an arrangement could be made to suspend both siege and defensive operations to await the arrival of adequate relief, at which point hostilities would recommence. In the meantime, the forces of each side must remain in place and neither repair of fortifications, nor strengthening of assault engines could be undertaken. If, after the expiration of the given period, no relief arrived, then the city was to be surrendered to the besiegers.[15]

But all these "laws" failed fully to solve the basic problem of the city's captain of the garrison. Either surrender or resistance damned him: "If he surrendered, he acted treasonably by his former lord, in obeying his capital adversary. If he held out, he might be condemning the men in his charge, not to mention the unfortunate townsfolk, to death and destruction."[16] The honor of the monarch as proprietor, and that of the captain as the defender of that honor, were both injured by the surrender of a city, and a surrendering captain could be found guilty of treason.[17] Hence Ralph Grey of Werke was degraded from knighthood in 1464 after being found guilty on the double charge of failing to offer an adequate defence of Bamborough Castle and then accepting command of the same castle from the opposing forces (those of Margaret of Anjou).[18]

The basic problem, then, was the indefinable border between adequate defense which would satisfy the requirements of loyalty to a lord, and obstinate defense, which would increase the severity of the punishment inflicted on the city by enraged besiegers. Alberico Gentili notes that such acts of vengeance did occur, despite their illegality,[19] while Grotius follows Cicero (*De Officiis*, xi.35): "You must both be merciful to those whom you have had to overcome by force, and accept the surrender of those who lay down their arms and take refuge in the good faith of generals, even though the battering-ram hath already battered the wall."[20] "Obstinate defence," then, ought not to be treated by the victors as a punishable offense. Needless to say, it frequently was so punished, and one need only recall Henry V's manifestly illegal hanging of the unfortunate trumpeter of Meaux in 1422, because the king considered that he had blown his horn in a singularly insulting manner during the course of that long and very difficult siege.[21] Such, then are the general and customary rules of siege warfare, but as M. H. Keen sensibly notes it was to be distinguished from Fluellen's "law of arms":

> . . . when we speak of the law of arms as an international law, we must guard against thinking of it as a law governing the conduct of warring nations. It was not this: it was a law governing the conduct of men who fought to settle by arms quarrels which were made in private, and whose importance may be judged by the social status of the principals involved. In this context, rules, which seem to us cruel and inhuman, could appear just and natural, for nothing was more just than the punishment of contumacy.[22].

Perhaps, then, even the poor trumpeter was guilty of a crime against the honor of Henry V.

Now an understanding of the laws of siege warfare has considerable relevance to an understanding of Shakespeare's *Rape of Lucrece*, largely because the entire poem is constructed around an orchestration of siege metaphors which go far beyond the frequently discussed equation of the ravished wife with the betrayed and ravaged city of Troy. Shakespeare seems deliberately to have chosen to treat his theme by following out the rubric of siege, assault, defense, and surrender, together with a kind of arraignment in which the captain of the garrison explains to his superior the circumstances of surrender in order to avoid a charge of treason. By studying the poem in this way, one can also gain a deeper understanding of the motivations and suicide of Lucrece, the mirror of chastity.

As Nancy Cotton Pearse has pointed out, the tale of Lucrece was "enormously popular during the Middle Ages and the Renaissance,"[23] and her example was frequently quoted to English women for their emulation, though not literally, of course, since suicide was antithetical to Christian teaching, a problem that Augustine in *The City of God* attempted to solve in the following analysis of Lucrece's act:

> Her killing of herself . . . was due to the weakness of shame, not to the high value she set on chastity. . . . Since she could not display her pure conscience to the world she thought she must exhibit her punishment before men's eyes as proof of her state of mind. She blushed at the thought of being regarded as an accomplice in the act if she were to bear with patience what another had inflicted on her in violence.[24]

William Tyndale, in *The Obedyence of a Chrysten Man* (1561) continues to express this view, and even less temperately than Augustine as he castigates Lucrece's pride:

> She sought her own glory in her chastite and not gods. When she had lost her chastyte, then she counted her selfe most abhominable in the sight of al men, and for very payne and thought which she had, not y^t she hath displeased god by y^t she had lost here honour, slew herself. Loke how great her glory and reoiycing therin, and moch despised she them that wer otherwise, and pytied them not, which pryde god more abhorreth then the whoredome of anye whor.[25]

Geoffrey Chaucer, in *The Legend of Good Women*, however, had seen her as a martyr; so poet overcame theologian and thus she remained. As Pearse notes, her tale becomes "the basic story of the chaste woman who commits suicide after being raped by a tyrant."[26] But as usual, Shakespeare made additions to his sources, most particularly in the digressions which, except possibly for the one concerning Troy, are seen by the New Arden editor, F. T. Prince, as "consistently" weakening the poem. [27] The addition of Lucrece's careful equation of her fate with this fallen city of Troy, taken by treachery is, however, exceedingly important for the purpose of this study. To be sure, the generality of modern readers will probably agree with Prince, and they may be forgiven if they find themselves overwhelmed and even bored by Lucrece's digressive

verbosity. However, her loquacity is not only essential to her character but
also to the overall structure of the poem. As Juliet Dusinberre observes,
women's "sphere of action is words rather than deeds,"[28] and for women words
give "the illusion of action."[29] This is the only way in which Lucrece can offer
an adequate defense of her virtuous personal city, that keep of good conduct
whose defense has been entrusted to her as its captain in the absence of its
lawful owner, her husband, Collatine.

Shakespeare uses the imagery of siege warfare both implicitly and explicitly throughout his poem, and his audience would be expected to observe
this fact. After all, one must remember that sieges and siege warfare had
become fairly familiar things to Elizabethans as a result of their intervention
in the Low Countries which was primarily conducted by a series of notable
sieges such as Antwerp, Flushing, Smerwick, and Ostend, which also had
reverberations in drama. Indeed in *All's Well That Ends Well* (1602-03) in the
much discussed exchange between Helena and Parolles on virginity
(I.i.108–121), Shakespeare specifically employs the military language of
siege warfare as sexual metaphor, trading on its familiarity as a commonplace. By 1612, John Fletcher in his "sequel" to *The Taming of the Shrew*,
entitled *The Woman's Prize: Or the Tamer Tamed*, stages an hilarious siege of
the bridal chamber with very specific reference to the siege of Ostend.[30]

In *Lucrece*, like Spenser in *The Faerie Queene* (I.vi.5; III.x.10),
Shakespeare employs the basic vocabulary and occurrences of siege warfare
always with deliberate sexual connotations, and in none of the plays is the
incidence of military language used figuratively quite so pervasive. Thus
rape, siege, and warfare come together linguistically and structurally in
Lucrece, and it is this reworking of the classic tale on the structure of military
law that is unique to Shakespeare.

The inciting action of the poem itself involves the siege of the city of
Ardea, as in all the sources, but Shakespeare concerns himself very little with
that, beginning the action of his tragic poetic psychodrama *in medias res*. His
Sextus Tarquinius is to be shown in his assault upon the city of Lucrece's
chastity, and then Shakespeare will be concerned with the consequences of
this masculine "victory." Hence all the earlier material concerning the wager
and the visit to Lucrece by Collatine and Tarquin are placed in the Argument.
Almost from the very beginning of the poem, military language is employed,
with the image of a castle:

Honor and beauty in the owner's arms,

Are weakly fortress'd from a world of harms.
(ll.27–28)

And again, Beauty and Virtue offer warfare on the battlefield of Lucrece's countenance (ll. 50–70). Then, as Tarquin meditates upon his forthcoming treachery, he evaluated his action as a "siege that hath engirt" the marriage of Collatine (l. 221).

Now, as we have seen, a city may be captured by famine, by assault, and by composition or treaty. And to all of these must be added treachery or stratagem, the latter an ill-defined term to this day, as *The Law of Land Warfare* points out: "Ruses of war are legitimate so long as they do not involve treachery or perfidy on the part of the belligerent resorting to them. They are, however, forbidden if they contravene any generally accepted rule."[31] Tarquin, however, has indeed acted treacherously, even this early in the poem, by misusing the ancient laws of hospitality for his own nefarious purposes, a situation that reminds one instantly of Paris's violation of Menelaus's hospitality in carrying off Helen. That Tarquin fully understands the nature and quality of his act is also clear from his preliminary debates with himself when he openly admits, again in military terms, that passion, whose blood-red banner he follows, is the captain of his soul. Then, as he approaches the bedchamber of Lucrece, overcoming the obstacles of locks, of winds, and of nocturnal animals, he is in effect passing over the defensive outworks, the suburbs of Lucrece's fortified city. The only injury Tarquin sustains on this journey is being pricked by a needle that Lucrece left embedded in a glove she had been mending. This combination of passive wounding and domestic detail emphasizes the physical weakness of Lucrece. Domestic virtue cannot prevail against phallic power.

In looking upon Lucrece as a chaste city, something she herself does in comparing Troy's fall with her own rape, one must not fail to examine the importance of her matrimonial status.[32] As Tarquin himself says, "She is not her own"(l. 241), for she is the property of Collatine, a situation equally Renaissance as Roman. She is therefore a citadel of honor that is both physically her own and the legal property of her husband, her lord and master, her captain, Collatine. And in his absence she is expected to preserve herself, both as her husband's property and as the embodiment of their mutual honor, from assault and defilement. One must not also forget that in England as a wife's legal personality was submerged in that of her husband, so too was her honor; therefore she must safeguard her reputation from all harm lest she should also dishonor him. Her honor, left in her keeping is, however, "weakly fortress'd" because of her inferior physical strength as well as her popularly supposed spiritual weakness, and here one should remember that religious and moral writers in Shakespeare's day usually followed St. Paul in stigmatizing woman as "the weaker vessel." Lucrece, then, has been left by Collatine to guard her chastity, meaning here her marital sexual exclusivity, from all harm. She is thus the garrison captain of her physical and moral city, and as Collatine's appointed deputy, she must defend herself against all hostile assaults.

As Tarquin enters Lucrece's bedchamber, his eyes, conventionally the harbingers of affection and Neoplatonic love, the least harmful of the senses, commit high treason, and give the "watchword" to his hand to draw the curtain that hides her nakedness. Another protective outwork, the bed curtain and the cover of darkness, has fallen to the treachery of lust. As Tarquin gazes upon her, Shakespeare describes the beauty of Lucrece, carefully choosing his epithets and emblems to emphasize her virtues: she is "a virtuous monument" (l. 341); her coverlet is green, the canonical color of faith; she is white as a daisy, the flower of innocence, while her eyes are marigolds to signify grief at the absence of her husband. But then Shakespeare takes the traditional Petrarchan image of Lucrece's breasts as "a pair of maiden worlds unconquered" (l. 408) and speaks of Tarquin's Alexander-like ambition to find new fields of combat and to act like a "foul usurper" to "heave the fair owner" out of her city, by destroying the integrity of her matrimonial oath to Collatine.[33] Every detail of Lucrece's innocent and unprotected person increases the strength of Tarquin's erotic passions which eventually "mutiny" against the eye, which reflects the soul or the inner virtue of mankind.

At this point Shakespeare turns to military language as he describes with considerable accuracy the havoc that ensues when a city is put to the sack: slaves fight for pillage, death and rapine are permitted, and then Tarquin commences his physical assault. His heart is the military drumbeat which gives the alarm; he gives passions, here compared to horses (a traditional symbol of lustful sensuality), the order to charge, to assault the innocent fortress of Lucrece. His hand then advances in an escalade of the turrets of her breasts. The assault of the beleaguered city is now clearly under way! Lucrece is "fearfully beset" as Tarquin's hand remains on her bosom as a battering ram against the ivory wall of her modesty. With this action, in accordance with the rules of siege warfare, the assault is announced, the defensive outworks of the town have been reduced, the "exterminator" has been brought up, and the time for mercy seems to be past. Lucrece's heart, the frightened citizen of her bodily city, beats so fearfully that it increases Tarquin's lustful excitement, and he can hardly wait to make a breach in her wall of chastity and enter her body.

But rather than use mere assault, Tarquin tries first to take this city by means of composition, and so his tongue, like a trumpet, sounds a parley. This, as we have seen, was the first move in an attempt to gain a city without resort to the more expensive and slower method of assault. Certainly, as Pierino Belli points out, defenders of cities should avoid talking to the enemy, "for as common saying has it, 'the castle that parleys is half surrendered'."[34] However, Lucrece has no option but to "parley" in order to discover the reason for Tarquin's unauthorized presence in her bedroom. So, following still the rules of siege, Tarquin announces his intent—his hand, the battering ram, still against the wall of her bosom. He will "scale / Thy never-conquerèd fort" (ll. 480–481), and violate the very citadel of her being. However, he endeavors to implicate her in the crime by claiming that her beauty is the cause of his desire, an argument that Shakespeare gave to Richard III in his wooing of Anne Neville. He tries to get his weaker adversary to yield to him, to open the gates of her city, rather than force him to make a breach, to rape her. Tarquin then offers threats against Lucrece, a common method during a truce parley as a means of reaching a composition with the defending garrison. His horrifying statement that he will first rape her, then kill her, and lastly place the murdered body of a "worthless slave" in her bed is ultimately shocking to Lucrece. In Tarquin's proposed explanation, it would signify that she had descended to whoredom, to the base gratification of her lustful desires—and what is worse, Lucrece seems to consider that others in Rome, even including her husband, would believe her guilty of such an obscene act, since women are weaker vessels and more prone to sins of lust, according to popular antifeminism.

Since the loss of her personal honor would also include the loss of her husband's honor, and her guilt would also taint her children, Lucrece must in some way defend herself, because otherwise she has acted traitorously to her lord in failing to offer an adequate defense of his castle, his chaste property. Like a captain left in command of the garrison of a beleaguered city, she "is bound to make good defence by virtue of the office assigned . . . [and] is not excused because of accident that befalls unless . . . [she] demonstrates . . . freedom from blame."[35] Indeed, a defense should be conducted even at the expense of the captain's life—unless such an act would cause damage to the state.

Thus Lucrece is faced with an almost impossible dilemma: if she submits to Tarquin, she has failed to offer an adequate defense and has surrendered Collatine's city traitorously. If she holds out against this sexual assault, she will lose her honor and her life so that she will be unable later to defend herself against accusations of adulterous treason against her husband's honor. Like Caesar's wife, an *exemplum* so frequently quoted in English conduct books, a woman must not only be free of the fault itself, but from all appearance of it as well. Lucrece, then, may have to submit for the good of the "state," for the reputation of her marriage. Nonetheless, a defense is essential, and Lucrece must attempt to fight back, to prevent Tarquin's assault, and preserve her honor. But, as Shakespeare points out, she must plead "in a wilderness where are no laws" (1. 544).

Pleading, then, is the basis of Lucrece's defense, and her weapon is the feminine one of words, the only thing with which she can mount opposition to an assault on her virtuous citadel. Language and logic, then, are the only forces she can muster, and this is the reason for her relentless torrent of argumentative rhetoric and later of carefully organized lament. Thus her verbal volleys are not mere posing, rhetorical flatulence, indicative of feminine hysteria, not to be taken seriously, or simply boring. They are a skillful defense against Tarquin's preliminary attempts to force a surrender by treaty. When understood in this manner, they develop a new sense of immediacy; and Lucrece's rhetoric develops something of the cut and thrust of a duel, a *combat à l'outrance*. She marshals her logical forces well, and in this "wilderness where are no laws" she points out to Tarquin the written and unwritten laws that he has violated, beginning with a careful introduction in which she reminds him of obligations due to the gods, to the law of knightly behavior (anachronistic, to be sure), to gentility, friendship, and pity, the "holy human law" (1. 571), vows of humanity, and all the powers of heaven and earth. In other words, she pleads by all the known laws governing human conduct.

She then proceeds to specific argument: Tarquin has violated the laws of hospitality and friendship (ll. 575–583), but then she must (like every woman victim in a similar situation) try to elicit pity from her merciless raptor (ll. 575–595). Her defense turns more subtle as she proceeds to another approach—the dishonorable results of his action, together with the dishonor accruing to his office and his reputation. All these things are marshaled to remind him of his totally forgotten obligation. Skillfully she moves from the merely political duties of royal office to the necessity of moral rule—where reason should control passion. Her entire argument, therefore, is based on five different kinds of legal and quasi-legal imperatives: knighthood and gentility, the obligations of office, the laws of morality, "holy human law," and the "common troth," matrimonial law, a subsidiary aspect. All of these are used in an attempt to turn Tarquin aside, but her argument as defense reaches its high point when she works up to the honor of Tarquin as monarch whose conduct, instead of being a good example to his subjects, will instead be an incitement to evil. Here, of course, one must remember the view of such writers as Sir Thomas Elyot in *The Boke Named the Gouernour* and Erasmus in *The Education of a Christian Prince*, both of whom taught the necessity of an upright moral life for a ruler. Shrewdly, she works on the notion of virtuous government, turning to the disordered moral state of Tarquin, whose lustful passions control his reason, "the exil'd majesty" (l. 640) who should be repealed from banishment to resume his proper role as governor. Her pleading has now moved from the duties of externally recognized law to the internal self-directed moral government of Tarquin, and it is clear that she has to some extent reached him, for he now turns upon her in a violent assault, an escalade, upon her chastity.

Once again the subliminal imagery of a city taken by assault and put to the sack is found, in this "forcèd league" which brings the "further strife" of psychodrama to both parties. Lucrece's "pure Chastity" is wantonly pillaged, and Tarquin can only feel remorse for his act of violent lust. Shakespeare develops this act of rape with singular delicacy and lack of prurience, trusting largely to the value of suggestion, and able now to trust to understatement after having so carefully prepared for the violent incident with his metaphors of siege and defense. He is little concerned with describing the physical fact of the rape, but rather with the psychological motivations and the consequences of this assault on the moral integrity of a single human being.

But siege imagery does not cease with the rape, since Tarquin is shown as having in effect lost his spiritual integrity. His soul is seen as a ruined temple manned with troops of cares, and her "consecrated wall" has been battered and breached by her rebellious subjects, the senses. Already he feels guilt. Thus in departing from Lucrece's room, Tarquin is in effect responsible for a double assault and spoliation: first of the chaste bodily city of Lucrece, and second of the fair temple of his soul where, by committing one of the capital sins, he has laid waste his own immortality. Once again, there is an image of treachery, in that the rebellious senses have gained their victory with "foul insurrection." Tarquin bears within himself the spiritual disgust of his action and the horror of his own guilty mind to haunt him. He has been responsible for the sack of his immortal temple, the central citadel of his being. Lucrece, however, has suffered the rape of her body only, and the rest of the psychodrama is devoted to establishing the fact that her immortal citadel, her soul, remains pure, because she did not willingly submit. She has conducted an adequate defense of her virtue, her husband's honor left in her care. Her reason has never submitted to give consent to the act; and thus while her mortal chaste city has been violated, her central keep, her citadel of virtue, has remained defended to the last.

Left alone, Lucrece again has recourse to her only weapon—words, as she launches into a series of plaints, fearing discovery of her ravishment, and then apostrophizing Night, the bringer of all evil.[36] Her sense of guilt is most exquisitely sensitive at this point, and for the moment even the purity of her poetic imagery suffers in her curious reference to the sign of "leaping houses," "the weary noontime prick" of the clock (l. 781). Such words seem more compatible with a Mercutio (*ROM*, II.iv.107) than a Lucrece, but they may well indicate her feeling of inner degradation. All she can currently perceive is that her "married chastity" has been violated, and that she is automatically taken to be guilty of "loathsome trespass" (l. 812), coupled in infamy forever with her ravisher. Further ages will sing "How Tarquin wronged me, I Collatine" (l. 819). As we have seen, and Coppélia Kahn has well illustrated, both Renaissance and Roman matrimonial custom would consider this act dishonorable to both husband and wife. However, a return to the rules of siege can add further resonance to a statement that seems needlessly harsh to modern readers. Did Lucrece offer an adequate defense against the threats and falchion-wielding force of Tarquin, or was her failure to hold her fortress an act of treason to the honor of her lord? And, it should be recalled, such a surrender was then considered a capital offense, punishable under the *Lex Julia*,[37] justifiable only if the city's king had denied it suitable means of defense.

Lucrece's initial reaction, then, is to treat her situation in its harshest manner in terms of the legal concepts which dictated English matrimonial relationships. But she soon begins to attempt a justification as she points out that the mutual honor of both herself and Collatine was lost only after "strong assault" (l. 835), and also by treachery, since Tarquin had gained entrance to her house by violation of the laws of hospitality, laws which she had observed in the manner of an honest wife. Denial of hospitality to a superior in rank would constitute an act of dishonor to both Collatine and the Roman throne. The rest of Lucrece's fatal night is given over to complaints against Treachery, Opportunity, and finally, Time. With that, she turns from mere lamentation to curses, and then, her preliminary anguish spent, she looks back at the impotence of her "helpless smoke of words" (l. 1027) and turns to a discussion of suicide, the only action which seems fitting for her case.

She now looks at herself with a somewhat different eye as she bitterly reassesses her weakness in the face of Tarquin's physical and mental threats. She does not believe that she offered an adequate defense of chastity. This sentiment would seem to stand behind the lines:

> But when I feared I was a loyal wife.
> So am I now—O no that cannot be:
> Of that true type hath Tarquin rifled me.
>
> (ll. 1048–1050)

She vacillates between protesting her innocence and wondering whether indeed she may have been to some extent a guilty accomplice. This ambivalence also colors the lines

> This bastard graff shall never come to growth:
> He shall not boast who did thy stock pollute
> That thou art the doting father of his fruit.
>
> (ll. 1062-1064)

Now in Shakespeare's day it was believed that pregnancy resulted from a rape only if the woman contributed in some measure to the act by even a moment of consent, be it only a second of fleeting physical pleasure, which, it was believed, was in effect a consent.[38] Thus, an illegitimate child might inherit property from a putative father, and *The Lawes Resolutions* . . . (1632) expatiates on this possibility as a major motivation in the uncompromising insistence on the preservation of matrimonial chastity.

Lucrece then turns to further discussion of her suicide, debating its legality in Christian rather than Roman terms. She debates the question first in the image of a pine tree whose heart is automatically destroyed when the bark is "pilled away" (l. 1169). But again she returns to the image of a pillaged city, strangely reminiscent of the earlier description of Tarquin's guilty soul:

> Her house is sacked, her quiet interrupted,
> Her mansion battered by the enemy;
> Her sacred temple spotted, spoiled, corrupted,
> Grossly engirt with daring infamy.
> Then let it not be called impiety
> If in this blemished fort I make some hole
> Through which I may convey this troubled soul.
>
> (ll. 1169–1176)

Her soul cannot live pure in a bodily city that has been sacked, battered, corrupted; hence another assault, this time by her own hand, to breach the wall to release her pure soul cannot be called impiety. In other words, if the ruins of a city are left standing, they sometimes offer greater military disadvantage and dishonor to the state than their complete destruction. Only by her own death does Lucrece believe that she can achieve vindication—for a city ought also to be defended even to the death of a garrison captain if service to the state requires it.

However, Lucrece must have publicity, but she does more than merely stage-manage "her death to maximize its social effectiveness for this purpose." [39] She must first report to her husband, her superior officer, her city's master, concerning the nature and quality of her defense; whatever his judgment, she believes now that she did attempt to mount an adequate defense of his city, but it was overcome by treachery and her own lack of physical strength. But with her death, her heart conquered by her hand, both spirit and body will be victorious in defeating the stain of both rape and slander. Again Lucrece has resorted to military imagery.

Momentarily the narrator of the tale steps in with a moral judgment of his own, requesting understanding and pity for women in such a state. Shakespeare is at least understanding of feminine faults and frailties. Women are open fields, open books, wax tablets on which men harshly imprint their image, and their faults, only to blame the women when these blemishes are plain to see.

Lucrece's next digression is that of Troy, which F. T. Prince thinks has a certain degree of success, but Douglas Bush dismisses in Lucrece's own statement as a "smoke of words." [40] To some extent this description of an as yet unidentified painting serves the dramatic function of "filler," a short scene or speech interpolated to cover the passage of time. Here, however, it is also a paradigm of the action of the poem, pulling together central concepts of rape, treachery, siege, and the helplessness of women in a world of masculine power. But the emphasis of Lucrece is at first unexpected. She merely mentions Helen's rape as the inciting action of the destruction of Troy, and certainly, despite the obvious parallel, she never identifies with her, for, as Shakespeare's later *Troilus and Cressida* indicates, Helen was perceived in the English Renaissance as a willing strumpet.

The Roman matron instead concerns herseelf with the destructive consequences of the rape, and her account of assault preparation carries one back to the assault on her personal city, to her own frantic, though weak defense.

Shakespeare is exceedingly precise in his description of the beleaguered city of Troy, and his account has the usual anachronisms of pioneers mining to blow up the outworks of the ancient city, the kind of illustration that is found in Lydgate's *Troy Book* (1513). He also includes the typical Renaissance emphasis on the brute strength of Ajax and the sly and reprehensible stratagems of Ulysses, while Nestor becomes a noble monarch whose words have the power of moral suasion. Slowly, Lucrece makes of this painting a true *pictura loquens;* and finally she finds one woman whose sorrow is like hers in Hecuba, the wife who has lost husband and children—all that is precious to her—and can do nothing but mourn. She, like Lucrece, is the victim of masculine drive for power. With that identification of herself with Hecuba as the figure of sorrowing femininity, Lucrece turns to Helen as the willing accomplice in an act of lust, performed in violation of the laws of hospitality. Lust is thus the cause of that disaster which ruined proud Troy and all her inhabitants.

But then Lucrece turns to the third important theme of this painting which operates as an expository device to tie up the various themes and images of this poem—the theme of deceit. Like the handsome Sinon who was extended hospitality by the Trojans, only to work for their destruction, so too did Tarquin. Lucrece now very specifically equates herself with the ravaged city of Troy, destroyed by the recipient of an act of hospitality. So, taking the painted likeness of Sinon as the surrogate for the real Tarquin, Lucrece attacks the image in an act which is as ineffectual as her "helpless smoke of words." But the analogy remains important: each of these traitors, operating behind a handsome and friendly vizard, has used stratagems to destroy a city, and their calculated deceits violate laws of honor, hospitality, chivalry, and even war itself.

Thus, far from being a digression, the Troy section should be perceived as organic to the poem which in effect should now be seen as consisting of several different sieges: first, the siege of Lucrece's physical and spiritual fortress; second, the psychomachic siege in which Tarquin's senses batter down the walls of his soul's sacred temple; and third, the siege of Troy. Only one important thing now remains to discuss here: the citadel of Lucrece's soul and whether or not it has suffered defilement.

Throughout her scene with Collatine and the lords as they return from the siege encampment at Ardea, this is Lucrece's primary concern—to defend her moral integrity and also justify to her husband her forced surrender to Tarquin. Collatine is appalled at the sight of his too-much-changed wife who tells him what has happened. Even then, the narrator resorts to military imagery to begin this revelation, as Lucrece raises sufficient fire through her sighs to "discharge one word of woe" (ll. 1604–1605). The overall tone of this opening part of her account seems strange to modern readers, for she is almost apologetic over an occurrence she could not prevent, something that she makes quite clear by recounting the facts which forced her submission. At first she might almost seem to be accepting some guilt for her rape, but once again, one must look at the situation not only from the viewpoint of English matrimonial law and practice, but also from that of the rules of siege.

Lucrece is, in effect, justifying herself to Collatine, the master of her city. She, his garrison captain, has been forced by means of assault, treachery, and threats which would put the fear of death even into a valiant man, to yield her chaste fortress to the enemy. She needs now to indicate that this city was not yielded treasonously to the enemy, that she had made a proper defense, given the forces at her command, and that she had indeed endured assault. Nonetheless, the loss of a city redounds to the dishonor of both its owner and its captain, and thus both Collatine and Lucrece are injured, even though Lucrece was the victim of superior force. In effect she is facing a court of inquiry concerning the loss of her fair city, and she once again uses her verbal feminine weapons, slowly revealing the facts of the case, beginning with the statement that "Her honor is ta'en prisoner by the foe" (l. 1608), building through the fact of her enforcement by means of threats, and finally coming to the most important assertion of all "Immaculate and spotless is my mind; / That was not forced" (ll. 1656–1657). In other words, though part of the city has been yielded, it is only the physical person that has been violated. The keep, the citadel of Collatine's city, Lucrece's personal virtue, remains inviolate. Indeed, with touching legality, Lucrece disclaims all "accessary yieldings" (l. 1658), indicating that she felt no pleasure in the act and hence is in herself not guilty. She is the victim rather than a participant, and hence, though technically guilty of having yielded a castle to an enemy, she has managed to preserve her spiritual virtue, her moral keep.

So far Lucrece has avoided naming her ravisher, and it is only when Collatine is overwhelmed with grief that she begs him to seek vengeance in terms of the obligations of knightly chivalry. Now she pleads again before this court of military honor, asking the assembled lords to decide whether the pure intent of her mind is sufficient to negate the loss of her physical city. Instantly the men, sitting as a kind of tribunal, acquit her of all charges: "Her body's stain her mind untainted clears" (l. 1710). However, Lucrece obstinately sees herself as offering an undesirable legal precedent to other women who might in the future yield more quickly than she and fail to offer sufficient resistance. Therefore in order to prevent herself from becoming an evil *exemplum* for future generations, she chooses to kill herself. Shakespeare thus makes her die for the reputation of womankind even more than for the preservation of Collatine's honor.[41]

The result of her suicide is a purely Shakespearean moral paradigm which clearly indicates the duality of body and spirit. The Elizabethans certainly did know the Aristotelian belief that corrupted blood was black and pure blood red,[42] and Shakespeare, by adding this to the conclusion of the poem manages to express something of the ambivalence of Augustine in *The City of God* concerning Lucrece. Geoffrey Fenton in his translation of Matteo Bandello's tragical history of Julya of Gazuolo found the answer to a similar question in a split decision. Julya drowned herself after being raped in order to preserve her reputation; she was then praised for her honor but burial in consecrated ground was denied her because she was a suicide.[43] A similar ambivalence is present in the image of Lucrece's body with blood pouring from its wounds, and bereft of both life and spirit, lying "like a late-sack'd island . . . / Bare and unpeopled in this fearful blood" (ll. 1740–1741). But part of her blood shows dark because it has been corrupted, and the "wat'ry rigoll" everlastingly weeps for Lucrece's bodily defilement. However, the red blood becomes the banner of a martyr, as Brutus uses her "chaste blood" as a means to rouse the Romans against the Tarquins. In this way the fate of Lucrece is similar to that of most of the women in Shakespeare's history plays: she is a sacrifice for the benefit of man's drive for power. The full morality of her suicide is not discussed: the result of it, the overthrow of tyranny, being so admirable. Thus Lucrece can be safely honored, and she can be praised for her valor, both in defending her honor, and in taking herself off the earth when her presence might cause embarrassment. Similarly, the assembled lords engage in a chivalric knightly quest to avenge her violation and in so doing they vindicate her defense against the assault of Tarquin.

Lucrece is thus a banner of brightness, an *exemplum* of fidelity, the epitome of a woman defender of her citadel of chastity, and the spiritual focal point of a republican revolution. Once again it is made clear that women have no strength in themselves, only that which derives from masculine power and honor. They can be symbols of revolution, but they do not lead one, and what actions they can take are essentially negative, like that of suicide.

Thus it may be seen that Lucrece's extraordinary loquacity and rhetorical skill are not merely hysterical utterances or weak self-indulgence. They are instead attempts to mount a defence against siege, treachery, and assault before the rape. After the rape, they serve a double purpose: first as a means of reaching a *rapprochement* with the situation, and second as a part of a defense against a possible charge of treason—for yielding the city of her body too soon, for violating the marriage vow by failing to withstand either the "exterminator," the battering ram of a weapon that brings death, or the "volee of canons" required of a more strongly fortified place. The "plaints" within *The Rape of Lucrece* are now revealed as contributions to the overall structure of the poem, rather than overwrought, self-conscious, and digressive. "Roman Lucrece" is a staunch defender of her chaste city, of her marriage, of the honor of her family, and of womanhood. Yet women, as is so very frequent in English Renaissance literature, are powerless except insofar as they can exert moral suasion; and when that is taken away as the result of her rape, Lucrece has little choice except to commit suicide to avoid creating an undesirable precedent. Rather than accepting Augustine's accusation that Lucrece's pride was the primary motivation for her suicide, Shakespeare portrays her as a defeated soldier whose "occupation's gone" and whose moral purpose has been destroyed in the "havoc" wrought upon the holy city of her body.

CHAPTER VII

A "Smoke of Words"—
Three Historical Ladies[1]

F *atti maschii, parole femine,* deeds are for men, words for women, the motto of the state of Maryland, has more significance than the merely misogynistic if it is taken figuratively to mean deeds are for the powerful, words for the powerless. In both meanings it describes the world of Shakespeare's English history plays which denies power to women, however hard they may try to exercise it. Indeed, in the second tetralogy, they are little more than "the recreation of the warrior," to quote Nietzsche. The history plays portray the relative roles of men and women as separate, men being identified with the active, fighting principle, and women relegated to the stereotypical role of passive, nurturing, docile femininity.[2] Lacking power as they do, women, as Juliet Dusinberre says, "are painfully aware that their only weapon is words,"[3] and the only men in the history plays who reach similar heights of loquacity, even eloquence, are those who either lack or have lost power.

Three of Shakespeare's historical feminine characters, Margaret of Anjou, Constance of Brittany, and Katherine of Aragon, offer interesting variations on this theme of deeds and words, and their characters exemplify the problems of women on the historical stage. All three are wives and mothers, and each emphasizes a different aspect of woman's roles in marriage: Margaret the termagant, Constance, the widowed mother of a beloved son, and Katherine the faithful and wronged wife. They also represent woman in her three allowed states of life, maid, wife, and widow, since Margaret by her presence in all the plays of the first tetralogy comprehends all these roles. All these women also have one common attribute: they are given to delivering long speeches in moments of crisis when in effect they must "arm themselves (to assume a male prerogative) with words."[4] Margaret is the most confrontational in her use of words, and because of her long tenure on the stage, she is also the most varied in her approaches. Constance, on the other hand, is almost entirely responsorial, while Katherine communicates a redemptive quality through her quiet, simple eloquence.

These differences are to some extent the result of chronological composition, with Margaret the first, Constance coming from that transitional play, *King John*, and Katherine from that disputed play, *Henry VIII*, which is closer to the final Shakespearean romances in its tone and theme. Ultimately, each of these women is a victim of the masculine drive to power, possessing no political strength in her own right. Whenever a woman does attempt to exercise power in the history plays she is judged by the other characters, and perhaps even Shakespeare himself, to be sexually insatiable, morally aberrant, and even more important, a violator of that order of nature which, according to such writers as John Knox, required the subjugation of women to masculine dominance. A successful woman ruler such as Elizabeth I was handily explained away by portraying her as a modern Deborah, specifically raised up by God for His own purposes which are incomprehensible to humanity.

Margaret of Anjou, the first important wife and mother of the history plays introduces several themes which are endemic to the genre: she represents the important equation of successful royal family life with political peace;[5] she introduces the theme of the disastrous foreign marriage which always causes political disturbance in England; and finally in herself she embodies the chaos that ensues when the traditional "specialty of rule has been neglected," when the members rebel against belly and the "great toe of the assembly" attempts to rule.

Margaret, then, is that violation of nature, a masculine woman, though one can argue that she was to some extent forced to aim for power, given the pathological reluctance (and incapacity) of Henry VI to rule for himself. She is the Amazonian woman who, as David Bevington so well points out, seduces men from their proper duties, largely by her sexual attraction.[6] Holinshed, following Fabyan, notes this combination of qualities: "This ladie excelled all other as well in beautie and fauour, as in wit and policie, and was of stomach and courage more like to a man than a woman."[7]

That the audience is expected to perceive Margaret pejoratively is indicated from the deliberate coincidence of her first appearance with the capture of Joan of Arc, so that she "is explicitly the successor to Joan as *femme fatale.*"[8] Joan, who has exercised masculine prerogatives throughout the play has just been shown as diabolically possessed, and the numerous lewd puns on *Pucelle* and *Pussell* throughout the play, indicate not only English chauvinism, but also the sexual insatiability and moral aberrance that male characters allege against such a woman. Joan herself seems to corroborate these allegations when "the holy maid" claims that she is with child in order to save herself from execution. Thus Joan's masculine proclivities and later her alleged immorality resonate through the scenes of Margaret's enchantment of Suffolk and her capture of the heart of Henry VI. Certainly, as Dash suggests, this beautiful maiden fears rape, the frequent fate of female prisoners; when Suffolk captures her, he instantly wants to appropriate her as a sexual prize, and propositions her.[9] Suffolk is totally seduced by her beauty when he perceives it in person, and so too is Henry VI when he perceives it through the eloquent description of Suffolk. Margaret makes no move toward either of them, but the alternating scene structure subliminally evokes the suggestion that she is an enchantress and a beguiling snare. As for her acceptance of Suffolk's plan to have her wed Henry, she has no choice (if her father consents) because she is but a matrimonial pawn—her status as Suffolk's pawn is not as yet quite clear to her. By the end of the play Margaret's marriage to Henry has already sown discord among English nobles, a discord that is echoed in Suffolk's decision to cuckold the king.

At her meeting with Henry (*2 H VI*, I.i), Margaret offers a conventional speech of submission, but despite her few words, she immediately gives a hint of her desire for power. Not yet crowned, and married as yet by proxy, the union still unconsummated, she replies to the nobles' greeting with the royal pronoun, "we." By I.iii she is using Suffolk as a confidant and a means to destroy her feminine arch-rival, Eleanor of Gloucester. Her arrogance also surfaces in her contemptuous destruction of a people's petition and dismissal of its bearers as "base cullions." The implication that Margaret is unfaithful to Henry is quite clear; by the third act of *2 Henry VI* she and Suffolk are governing quite openly, and Hall corroborates the "lasciuious souereigntie which the Quene with her minions and vnprofitable counsailes daily toke and vsurped."[10] This disaster in the marriage bed is clearly meant as a correspondence to the chaos that besets England in the Wars of the Roses. In *3 Henry VI*, King Edward IV specifically lays the blame for this civil war on Margaret's reversal of the traditional role of wife, and her attempt to exercise power unilaterally:

> For what hath broached this tumult but thy pride?
> Hadst thou been meek, our title still had slept,

And we, in pity of the gentle king,
Had slipped our claim until another age.
(2 H VI, II.ii.159–162)

And to a considerable extent the Chronicles agree, expecially Hall, though he
grudgingly admits that Margaret

> . . . was a woman of a great witte, and yet of no greater witte then of haute
> stomacke, desirous of glory, and couetous of honor, and of reason,
> pollicye, counsaill, and other giftes and talents of nature belongyng to a
> man, full and flowing: of fitte and wiliness she lacked nothyng, nor of
> diligence, studie and businesse, she was not vnexperte: but yet she had a
> poynt of a very woman: for often tyme when she was vehemēt and fully
> bent on a matter, she was sodainly like a wethercocke, mutable and
> turnyng.[11]

Shakespeare, however, takes no such antifeminist attitude, and rather
than depicting an hysterical Margaret he shows her as a shrewd manipulator.
This is particularly well illustrated in 2 *Henry VI* when Henry laments the
death of Gloucester, berating Suffolk as the bearer of bad news. Earlier,
Henry had unpacked his heart with words when he had found himself powerless to prevent Gloucester's arrest (III.i.198–222). Now, equally powerless
to prevent his uncle's murder, Henry resorts to words but in Margaret he
meets more than his match. She is more skilled than he in this feminine
weapon and speedily turns aside his legitimate wrath with skillful speech, first
by anticipating Henry's possible accusation of her complicity in the murder.
Daringly, she confronts him with the truth of her guilt, forcing him to absolve
her:

> What so I know the world may deem of me?
> For it is known we were but hollow friends.
> It may be judged I made the duke away;
> So shall my name with slander's tongue be wounded
> And princes' courts filled with my reproach.
> This get I by his death. Ay me unhappy,
> To be a queen, and crowned with infamy!
> (2 H VI, III.ii.65–71)

Then she attacks his grief by assuming the role of miserable, deserted, and unloved wife, even exploiting her relationship with Suffolk:

> How often have I tempted Suffolk's tongue
> (The agent of thy foul inconstancy)
> To sit and witch me as Ascanius did

> When he to madding Dido would unfold
> His father's acts commenced in burning Troy!
> Am I not witched like her? or thou not false like him?
> Ay, me, I can no more. Die, Margaret!
> For Henry weeps that thou dost live so long.
>   (2 *H VI*, III.ii.114–121)

This reference to Ascanius, who in the *Aeneid* was Cupid in disguise, coupled with Suffolk's comparison of himself with Paris seeking Helen at the end of *1 Henry VI*, clearly indicates the relationship between the two.

Curiously, Shakespeare does not exploit one aspect of the Suffolk affair as much as the Chronicles which hint at the possible bastardy of young Prince Edward:

> . . . whose mother susteyned not a little slaunder and obloquye of the commō people, saiying that the kyng was not able to get a chyld, and that this was not his sonne, with many slanderous woordes, to the quenes dishonor.[12]

To his credit, Holinshed does remark of this allegation, "muche part perchance vntrulie."[13] Perhaps, having already used the theme of Margaret's infidelity quite fully, he decided that this last allegation might constitute overkill, especially in view of the long Ovidian farewell of the lovers (III.ii) and the scene in which Margaret laments over the head of Suffolk, in an iconographical echo of Salome over the head of John the Baptist.

Shakespeare now develops another side of her character, a mother enraged by the irresponsible disinheritance of her son by a weakling spouse. Powerless to prevent this action taken without her knowledge or consent, Margaret has only the weapons of words and threats:

> Had I been there, which am a silly woman,
> The soldiers would have tossed me on their pikes
> Before I would have granted to that act.
> But thou preferr'st thy life before thine honor;
> And seeing thou dost, I here divorce myself
> Both from thy table, Henry, and thy bed
> Until that act of parliament be repealed
> Whereby my son is disinherited.
>   (3 *H VI*, I.i.243–250)

Clearly Margaret is violating once again the order of the sexes in marriage and politics, by asserting her authority over her lord and master, the king, refusing to allow him to speak, and then separating herself from him in the very words of canonical marital separation, *a mensa et thoro*. Finally, she attempts to subvert his authority in the political sphere by leading the royal army. She must take the action herself now, since Suffolk is dead, but what she does not realize is that the only power she, and any other woman in the historical plays, actually has, comes from the fact of her marriage to a man of position. Pillow talk, or the "bolster lecture" is the only way for women to exercise influence in this male-dominated world.

Margaret, like the other mothers discussed here, is never shown in a domestic situation with her child.[14] Instead she sees him as a future king, and her aim is to ensure his birthright. Nevertheless she obviously has some affection for the boy, which is displayed when she upbraids Henry for his pusillanimity:

> Hath he deserved to lose his birthright thus?
> Hadst thou but loved him half so well as I,
> Or felt that pain that I did for him once,
> Or nourished him as I did with my blood,
> Thou wouldst have left thy dearest heart-blood there
> Rather than have made that savage duke thine heir
> And disinherited thine only son.
>
> (*3 H VI*, I.i.220–225)

From this time on, Margaret becomes a monster, and her cruelty is continually shown as a violation of the stereotypical attributes of femininity.[15] Shakespeare increases the horror of her transformation by departing from his sources and making Margaret both present at and a participant in the death of York. In her taunting of him she goes much further than the later Lady Macbeth in unsexing herself, attempting to become more masculine than a man, exulting in the death of the youngest Yorkist son, Rutland, and developing a coronation ritual for his doomed father in an ironic and frighteningly detailed parody of the Crucifixion: a molehill becomes his Golgotha, a handkerchief soaked in the blood of "pretty Rutland," the veil of Veronica, and a paper crown the crown of thorns. She seems now to have stripped herself of all conventional womanliness, all sympathetic feeling, devising with cold intellectuality both physical and psychological torture that transcends gender.

York, now himself a helpless prisoner, rages with words, trying to defeat Margaret with the weapons of the powerless, showing his horror at this termagant in a series of insults: "She-wolf of France," "False French woman," "Amazonian trull," "Tiger's heart wrapped in a woman's hide!" Her beauty is but small, and she lacks government:

> Women are soft, mild, pitiful, and flexible;
> Thou stern, obdurate, flinty, rough, remorseless.
> (*3 H VI*, I.iv.141–142)

After this, Shakespeare overgoes his sources, by having her stab York as he lies dying—an act which signifies her almost total rejection of humankindness, and demonstrates a cruelty impossible even for Lady Macbeth. Role reversal is now almost total in *3 Henry VI*, with Margaret the "better capteine than the king, . . . a manly woman, vsyng to rule and not to be ruled."[16] Henry, bereft of power, is left to lament on his molehill, while Margaret does battle. Again, words are the weapons of the weak, and some of Henry's animadversions on the theme of time prefigure those of the imprisoned Richard II.

By the end of the trilogy Margaret has come full circle, from young captive beauty to exultant and terrible conqueror, to pathetic, though guilty, victim, captive once again after the murder of her son, Edward, whom Shakespeare economically develops as a true son of his intelligent and determined mother. Her lament over his body echoes that of York in Act I of *3 Henry VI* and also points ahead to her role as mourning Nemesis in *Richard III*. At the same time it is an outpouring both of her maternal feelings and frustrated ambition. She, more fit to rule than the king, must behold his worthier successor wantonly murdered:

> Butchers and villians, bloody cannibals,
> How sweet a plant have you untimely cropped.
> You have no children, butchers; if you had,
> The thought of them would have stirred up remorse;
> But if you ever chance to have a child,
> Look in his death to have him so cut off
> As, deathsmen, you have rid this sweet young prince.
> (*3 H VI*, V.v.61–67)

This is the kind of utterance that distinguishes her character in *Richard III* when words are the only "military" forces she can marshal. But they too are dangerous, as the future King Richard III well understands, when he threatens to execute her: "What, should she live to fill the world with words?" (V.v.43)

This is her role in *Richard III* where Shakespeare has unhistorically resurrected this wrangling woman who had long ago been ransomed home to France.[17] She is a needling, railing, lamenting, cursing woman in whom are embodied past, present, and future as she chants her continual litanies of past crimes and sorrows (recalled with editorial suppression of her own guilt) and prophesies the fates of her enemies. Through her curses the play is held together, with the motifs of vengeance, crime, and punishment never out of sight or hearing. She is no longer a great beauty, and fallen from power she is both victim and Nemesis, the equivalent of the Senecan furies. But in actual fact she, like the other women of the play, is impotent, except for her power over words. The three widows, Margaret, the Duchess of York, and Elizabeth, are deprived of their identities with the death of those husbands through whom they held power, and now words are their only weapons. Under Margaret's tutelage they briefly unite in cursing, making common cause against their mutual enemy, Richard,[18] but Margaret takes a perverse joy in their shared suffering. She has refused to make peace with God or humankind; she has learned no charity, no resignation, and feels no guilt for her crimes. Her frustrated energy remains, but it has all gone into exultant vengeance, into the world of words, curses which can strike fear even into the heart of Richard III.

Unlike Margaret, Constance of Brittany in *King John* is portrayed almost entirely in a maternal role. To be sure she does have some ambition as well, since she wishes to advance the claim of her son, Arthur, to the throne of England, but despite the allegations of some chroniclers,[19] Shakespeare's only suggestion that she might be seeking power for herself is put into the mouth of an enemy and is therefore suspect. Elinor of Aquitaine, on the other hand, is the ruthless executor of power whenever she can get the chance, through her identity as mother to King John. This play, then, is a battle of mothers, and in it the character of Margaret is in effect split into two parts, each defined by possibilities of power. Elinor is rational, intelligent, politic, succinct in speech, while Constance, lacking power, lets her emotions gush forth in the only ways possible for a woman victim—lamentation and railing.

The actions of the two women indicate the same contrast. Constance, young, beautiful, and witty, appeals to the sympathies of King Philip and the Dauphin in the hope that they will aid her, an unprotected widow, and her son, a pathetic child who in Shakespeare appears to be about ten years old, although historically he was sixteen, quite old enough in those precocious days to have begun a career as a warrior. A gentler character than Elinor, she looks ahead with fear to war, hoping to avoid it if possible, while Elinor, with typical directness, courts battle and embarks unhesitatingly for France. She is the complete pragmatist, as is well shown when she convinces the Bastard Faulconbridge that it is better to be the baseborn son of Coeur de Lion than the true-begotten son of a petty nobleman. Once again Shakespeare has hinted at the sexual aberrance or insatiability of a woman of power; by contrast, Constance, the powerless one, believes in matrimonial fidelity.

The confrontation of these two opposed mothers of royal sons in the presence of the assembled adversaries outside Angiers (II.i) is a skillful piece of character delineation and dramatic exposition. Nonetheless, their exchange of insults is curiously bloodless and rather obvious, being mainly attacks on the other's virtue. Elinor speaks first and Constance *responds*—a pattern that will continue throughout the play. In her reply she, the weaker and more stereotypically feminine character, loses any advantage she might have gained when she becomes emotional in rising to Elinor's bait:

> My boy a bastard! By my soul I think
> His father never was so true begot:
> It cannot be and if thou wert his mother.
> (II.i.129–131)

Elinor, obviously more in command of herself and the situation, seizes the opportunity to impugn Constance's maternal feelings: "There's a good mother, boy, that blots thy father" (II.i.132). Constance is now placed permanently on the defensive, forced to respond to and react against the remarks of others rather than initiating verbal conflict. Consequently, in this responsorial mode she adopts what is to become a distinguishing rhetorical device in which she is rivaled only by the deposed Richard II. She picks up a word introduced by others and rings changes upon it. This is the technique of the powerless, and Shakespeare builds his entirely original portrait of Constance upon it. There is very little in the chronicle sources concerning her, and nothing mentions this verbal technique. Similarly, she plays a very small role in *The Troublesome Raigne of King John*, so she is very specifically and idiosyncratically created by Shakespeare for this play.

One problem with Constance's devotion to this single rhetorical device is that her continual and artistic perorations on the words of others can raise doubts about her sincerity; excessive art can indicate detachment rather than intense emotional commitment. She picks up Elinor's "Come to thy grandam, child" and worries it to death with ridiculing baby talk:

> Do, child, go to it grandam, child;
> Give grandam kingdom, and it grandam will
> Give it a plum, a cherry, and a fig.
> There's good grandam.
>
> (II.i.160–163)

Even Arthur objects to this, and Elinor picks up on his shame, rebuking Constance for having made him weep. Instantly the nettled mother responds, summarizing her earlier replies:

> Now shame upon you whe'r she does or no!
> His grandam's wrongs, and not his mother's shames,
> Draws those heaven-moving pearls from his poor eyes,
> Which heaven shall take in nature of a fee.
> Ay, with these crystal beads shall heaven be bribed
> To do him justice and revenge on you.
>
> (II.i.168–172)

So engrossed in means does she become, that she almost loses sight of her end, playing relentlessly on Elinor's reference to "A will that bars the title of thy son," insultingly suggesting that Richard I's will was devised by her enemy:

> Ay, what doubts that? A will! A wicked will;
> A woman's will; a cankered woman's will!
>
> (II.i.194)

Respite from Constance's rage and verbal pyrotechnics comes only with a trumpet call that sounds a parley.

Thus, almost from the beginning of the play Shakespeare defines his distinction between the powerful and the powerless. Elinor, her character identified by her relationship to John, who holds the crown by possession if not by right, is secure, while Constance, mother of Arthur who represents right without possession, has no man to define her as a political entity. Her only armies are regiments of words, her only weapons volleys of verbosity. Nonetheless both kings, John and Philip, fear the fury of her invective and vainly hope that suitable honors heaped upon Arthur in lieu of the throne will "In some measure satisfy her? That we may stop her exclamation" (II.i.567–568). Blanche alone understands that Constance speaks from "her need," and this is significant, because the princess herself lacks power, for she too is but a matrimonial pawn in the world of men.

Nothing can satisfy Constance, and Shakespeare develops a thirty-line response in *The Troublesome Raigne* into 130 lines of self-pitying speeches which oppose the match of Blanche and Lewis of France (III.i). She continually advances her state as unprotected widow (another Shakespearean variation, for the historical lady was at that time married to a third husband),[20] portraying herself quite correctly as a victim of political expediency, and concluding this section in a dramatic manner. She seats herself on the ground as the queen of sorrows, an image that prefigures the powerless Richard II. From this time on, Constance becomes a permanent figure of lamentation, waging a war of words against all who have wronged her, and developing a ritual of cursing. But although she is the sincere mouthpiece of conscience, the enemy of political necessity, she cannot change things[21] and inadvertently turns her hearers against her, wearying them with the intellectual artistry of her rhetoric:[22]

> When law can do no right,
> Let it be lawful that the law bar no wrong.
> Law cannot give my child his kingdom here,
> For he that holds the kingdom holds the law;
> Therefore, since law itself is perfect wrong,
> How can the law forbid my tongue to curse?
> (III.i.185–190)

With the capture and death of Arthur,[23] Constance's maternal grief and lamentation have full rein as she improvises on the theme of death as paradox: "amiable, lovely death," "Oderiferous stench!" "Sound rottenness!" "Misery's love," continually asserting the logic of her grief by the careful rhetoric she uses as a means of clinging to her sanity. Whatever her enemies may say, Constance is not mad; her carefully contrived figures serve as a displacement of her grief, which finally wells out in the heartfelt lines which speak of her son as a human being, not a future king:

> . . . therefore never never
> Must I behold my pretty Arthur more.
> (III.iv.88–89)

The floodgates of maternal emotion are now opened, yet even here Constance in her feminine powerlessness responds to the words of others. Her reply to the suggestion of King Philip, "You are as fond of grief as of your child" (III.iv.92) is a speech that has at times been criticized for excess, and certainly Philip's comment undercuts it, so that the carefully developed conceit almost appears insincere:

> Grief fills the room up of my absent child,
> Lies in his bed, walks up and down with me,
> Puts on his pretty looks, repeats his words.
> Remembers me of all his gracious parts,
> Stuffs out his vacant garments with his form.
> Then have I reason to be fond of grief.
>   (III.iv.93–98)

Self-conscious and overwrought, perhaps, but the speech serves an important purpose to illustrate the dramatic function and characterization of Constance. "She never comes to terms with political realities and inevitabilities. . . . Her outcries and lamentations are the ultimate expression of rage and helplessness against the kind of behavior which characterizes political life."[24] She responds to the realities of power with her only weapon, words, and they are but breath, gone in an instant without the power to enforce change; but words are all the defense that such women as Constance, the victims of power-seeking men, possess. *Parole femine*, indeed!

After *King John*, women have no real place in the Second Tetralogy of Shakespeare's English history plays, not even the much-admired Katherine of France who is, after all, simply a pawn in the international marital chess game. Only with his last historical play, *Henry VIII* does Shakespeare (though probably in collaboration) do real justice to an historical lady, this time a faithful wife.[25] Again she is a victim, and again she achieves her force through the woman's weapon, her command of words. Katherine of Aragon is the quintessential victim of the history plays, a woman who is "sold" into a political marriage. Like Margaret of Anjou she is also a foreign-born queen, but not one who wittingly or willingly brings destruction to England, though the theme of the disastrous marriage in the Henry VI plays is resurrected. The play of *Henry VIII*, however, really belongs among the romances of the last Shakespearean phase rather than the earlier tetralogies, and indeed, Katherine seems to be an historical royal counterpart of Hermione, the strong, faithful, loving wife, the victim of her husband's suspicion and the eloquent pleader of her own case in *The Winter's Tale*.[26]

Henry VIII also touches on other themes treated in the earlier history plays. In addition to the unfortunate marriage, one finds the break with Rome in both *King John* and the romance *Cymbeline*, together with aspects of the misunderstood wife found in the latter. Katherine, however, brings an added, redemptive dimension to the histories, which is drawn from the women of the last plays. She is not the hostile confrontational character like Margaret of

Anjou, nor the responsorial rhetorician like Constance; instead she is an active force for good, a figure of virtue, and a sacrifice, a necessary one, for the glory that will be Elizabeth I. Above all, her tragedy is developed in personal, human terms, which transcend politics, and emphasize her postion as noble, loyal wife.[27]

Her opening speeches establish her humanitarian function as she pleads with Henry for remission of unjust taxation, speaking with skill and intelligence as an advocate of the common people (I.ii). She can also turn on Wolsey with dignified anger and ironic respect, "My learned lord cardinal, / Deliver all with charity" (ll. 142–143), and she displays genuine humility before her sovereign lord, her king and husband, while answering his questions concerning Wolsey's arrogant tyranny. She advises him to take immediate action to rectify injustice (I.ii.65–67); but when the monarch agrees, Wolsey indicates to his secretary in an aside that he himself will take the credit. Katherine also shows herself a regal helpmeet in counselling consideration for Buckingham, correctly perceiving that the evidence against him is suspect. This time Henry is not to be swayed, and through her pleading she has incurred the enmity of Wolsey, for she understands his ambition and his greed. The Cardinal is now eager for her destruction. Katherine thus becomes the victim of Wolsey's desire for power, and almost secondarily, of Henry VIII's desire for a son and heir. But for both men she becomes an obstacle that must be removed.

The trial of Katherine is the main confrontation scene of the play, and in it Shakespeare stays very close to his Holinshed source, portraying the queen arguing her case with dignity, honor, and restraint, while she controls her own deep sorrow.[28] Like Hermione at her trial, she refers to her lineage, expressing love and reverence for her husband, especially in her office as wife, "a true and humble wife" (II.iv.21), ". . . blest / With many children by you" (II.iv.34–35). Above all, she emphasizes her own honesty, her chastity in marriage, her fervent pursuit of her wifely duty, and her firm belief in the legality of their union. However, she is not lacking in spirit as she openly and eloquently accuses Wolsey of hostility toward her:

> . . . I do believe
> (Induced by potent circumstances) that
> You are mine enemy; and make my challenge
> You shall not be my judge. For it is you
> Have blown this coal betwixt my lord and me—
> Which God's dew quench! Therefore I say again
> I utterly abhor you, yea from my soul
> Refuse you for my judge, whom yet once more

> I hold my most malicious foe and think not
> At all a friend to truth.
>
> (II.iv.73–82)

Here and elsewhere throughout her ordeal, Katherine maintains her courageous composure, never falling into self-conscious volubility like Constance, and always putting her case with clarity, honesty, and eloquent understatement. Her deportment is dignified, and gently defiant as she departs from the chamber, refusing to continue before a court whose legality she refuses to accept.

The central aspects of the play are Katherine as wife, and the validity of her marriage in view of her earlier marriage to Arthur, Henry's older brother.[29] Henry presents himself as regretfully troubled in conscience over this matter, but Shakespeare has skillfully undermined this position through the scene of his meeting with Anne Bullen (I.iv) and the comments of the walking gentlemen and the nobles (II.ii). Thus the attitude of the audience is controlled so as to evoke its sympathy for Katherine, the paragon of women, the epitome of all the wifely virtues praised in the generality of Tudor marriage manuals. It is for those qualities that Henry praises her, observing her departure with an endearment:

> Go thy ways, Kate.
> That man i'th'world who shall report he has
> A better wife, let him in naught be trusted
> For speaking false in that. Thou art alone,
> (If thy rare qualities, sweet gentleness
> Thy meekness saint-like, wife-like government,
> Obeying in commanding, and thy parts
> Sovereign and pious else, could speak thee out)
> The queen of earthly queens. She's noble born,
> And like her true nobility she has
> Carried herself towards me.
>
> (II.iv.131–141)

How sincerely one should take this praise is not the question here; what is important is that these words, historically correct as they are, give added emphasis to Katherine's perfection as royal helpmeet. However, even her dedication to virtue is insufficient to save her from being cast aside, from becoming a victim like Margaret, the termagant wife. But Katherine is innocent of any crime, and as the voice of conscience against political expediency, she has some of the quality of Constance, at the same time displaying the intellectual dignity, spiritual strength, and persuasive tongue of the ladies of the romances. In short, she gains the moral victory over her enemy, Wolsey.

Nowhere is her righteous pride and faith in herself better illustrated than when Cardinals Wolsey and Campeius visit her (III.i) in an attempt to persuade her to compromise. They intrude upon a domestic scene, and Holinshed speaks of her receiving them "with a skeine of white thred about hir necke,"[30] and here one should recall that spinning and weaving were often cited in conduct books as wifely activities illustrative of honesty and virtue. She defends herself courageously, showing no fear of publicity; with a disarming femininity she asks to be addressed in English,[31] but at the same time reminds them that she has lived long in England and once again asserts her innocence:

> O, good my lord, no Latin!
> I am not such a truant since my coming
> As not to know the language I have lived in.
> A strange tongue makes my cause more strange, suspicious.
> Pray speak in English. Here are some will thank you,
> If you speak truth, for their poor mistress' sake.
> Believe me, she has had much wrong, Lord cardinal,
> The willing'st sin I ever yet committed
> May be absolved in English.
>
> (III.i.42–50)

This gentle humility soon turns to eloquent anger at the suggestion that she forgo her rights in law and sue to the king for kindness and consideration. As always, she stands on her dignity, status, and virtue as a wife, noting her chastity, love, total devotion, and lastly—"a great patience." Her defiance is both dignified and unshakable as she refuses the proposition (III.i.139–142); but then the sense of her wrongs overwhelms her and she speaks most movingly in an emotional speech, for which she later begs pardon (with what must be a touch of irony) as an "unmannerly" outburst:

> Would I had never trod this English earth,
> Or felt the flatteries that grow upon it!
> Ye have angels' faces, but heaven knows your hearts.
> What will become of me now, wretched lady?
> I am the most unhappy woman living.
> Alas, poor wenches, where are now your fortunes?
> Shipwracked upon a kingdom where no pity,
> No friends, no hope, no kindred weep for me,
> Almost no grave allowed me. Like the lily
> That once was mistress of the field and flourished,
> I'll hang my head and perish.
>
> (III.i.143–153)

This lament with its *ubi sunt* approach bears a superficial resemblance to Margaret's self-pitying speech with which she manipulates her husband (*2HVI*, III.ii.73–120); but Katherine's directness, her image of the lily, the symbol of chastity, and above all her care for her servants reveal a woman of larger spirit than Margaret who embroiders her speech with figures and concludes with classical references.

Katherine remains the embodiment of nobility, fidelity, and grace under pressure as she dismisses the churchmen, carefully staying within the limits of *noblesse* and traditional womanly behavior, barbing her words with quiet irony, yet always expressing true affection for Henry:

> Do what ye will, my lords; and pray forgive me;
> If I have used myself unmannerly,
> You know I am a woman, lacking wit
> To make a seemly answer to such persons.
> Pray do my service to his majesty,
> He has my heart yet, and shall have my prayers
> While I shall have my life. Come reverend fathers,
> Bestow your counsels on me. She now begs
> That little thought, when she set footing here,
> She should have bought her dignities so dear.
> (III.i.175–184)

With skillful use of contrast, Shakespeare moves to Wolsey's assessment of Anne Bullen as a "spleeny Lutheran," little dreaming that his own fall is imminent. Then, with his own eloquent farewell, and departure from the action "naked to mine enemies," Wolsey underscores the fact that words are indeed the weapon of the powerless. All his pomp and circumstance is transferred to the brilliant coronation of the pregnant Anne, in shocking contrast to Katherine in her spartan surroundings at Kimbolton, where she learns of Wolsey's death.

This entirely invented scene indicates a remarkable objectivity in dealing with Queen Katherine, who is a distinctively human character, not a cold saint. She shows some charity to her old enemy (who historically had been dead over six years), but still harbors resentment as she states his crimes with very human rancor. However, she is largeminded and humble enough to take to heart the rebuke of her usher, Griffith, who details some of Wolsey's good qualities, especially his services to education. She herself would wish for "no other herald" than Griffith who could so bring her to honor an enemy and teach her forgiveness. Then, as in the other plays of Shakespeare's final phase, a theophany ensues which indicates her fitness for heaven, giving attributes of sanctity to the final woman victim of the English history plays, a loyal wife whose behavior almost transcends humanity. However, with excellent psychological insight, Shakespeare gives Katherine an acerbic retort to a messenger who so far forgets himself as not to use her royal style and title, calling her "your grace":

> You are a saucy fellow!
> Deserve we no more reverence?
> (IV.ii.900–901)

The royal plural is carefully chosen to underscore her point. Her final speeches further convey her charity and readiness for death, but she is not so committed to the afterlife as to forget practical charity as she arranges legacies for her loyal servants.

Then, for the first time in the play, Katherine is revealed as a loving mother as well as wife in expressing her concern for the future of Mary, the daughter who never appears in the play, begging Henry to care for

> The model of our chaste loves, his young daughter—
> The dews of heaven fall thick in blessing on her—
> Beseeching him to give her virtuous breeding—
> She is young and of a noble modest nature;
> I hope she will deserve well—and a little
> To love her for her mother's sake, that loved him,
> Heaven knows how dearly.
> (IV.ii.132–138)

Her gracious self-control remains with her to the last as she emphasizes the legality of her marriage by asking for "maiden flowers" on her grave to signify her "married chastity." She holds steadfastly to recognition of her rightful status as "A queen, and daughter to a king" (IV.ii.172); then adept in the use of symbols to the last, she details her funeral rites in order of their virtuous importance to her as wife, queen, lady of royal birth.

In this last portrait of an historical lady, Shakespeare develops a character of greater courage and endurance than any other in this genre, but whatever her virtues, she is still a feminine figure powerless before the masculine drive for political and dynastic power. To be sure, her real enemy, Wolsey, is also destroyed, but the fact remains that in these plays no woman succeeds in exercising political power in her own right; she can do so only through a man who confers his identity upon her in marriage. Even the conclusion of the play, with its emphasis on Elizabeth rather than Anne Bullen, indicates some kind of divine justice which suspends the usual rules.

Nonetheless, while this play raises questions about the viability of women in political life, it ends on a hopeful note, largely because of the character of Katherine, which is developed through the brilliance of her use of language. Where Margaret and Constance become confrontational or merely voluble in their weakness, sometimes descending to pointless hunting of the word, Katherine alone achieves a totality of eloquence and simplicity of language that bespeaks honesty. Thus Katherine, who in the theophany is shown a heavenly crown, achieves a spiritual victory; she has gone beyond any thought of revenge or self-pity and in her death she becomes a sacrifice for the future of a greater England than she herself could envisage. With Katherine, words are more than merely the weapon of the weak; they have developed such soul force as to have the strength of redemption. *In principio erat Verbum*, said St. John: "In the beginning was the Word, and when that Word was made flesh," redemption ensued. Hence it is no accident that the last act of the play is concerned with the consolidation of the new religion and the future female monarch who would confirm it. Thus the play of *Henry VIII* looks ahead to a glorious era under the rule of Elizabeth I, the Virgin Queen, a modern Deborah.[32] But Katherine is not forgotten, as the epilogue of the play clearly states with its emphasis on "The merciful construction of good women / For such a one we showed 'em." Clearly, this refers to Katherine whose death now becomes a redemptive sacrifice through which a woman ruler will be successful in exercising power in her own person.

Part Four

MEN WHO LOSE POWER

CHAPTER VIII

The Degradation of Richard II
—An Inquiry into the Ritual Backgrounds[1]

S hakespeare's *Richard II* has long been noted for its preoccupation with
pageantry, ritual, and symbolic action. In particular, the invented scene
in which Richard solemnly uncrowns himself in a reverse coronation has been
the focus of considerable discussion. In 1889, Walter Pater wondered about
the source of this ceremony and noted that there is in the Roman Pontifical
"no rite of 'degradation' [for a king] such as that by which an offending priest
or bishop may be deprived. . . . It is as if Shakespeare had in mind some such
inverted rite, like those old ecclesiastical or military ones, by which human
hardness, or human justice, adds the last touch of unkindness to the executions of its sentences."[2] Pater's point is most telling, but in Shakespeare's
day the "old" rites of which he speaks were distinctly current; far from having
fallen into desuetude, they were either still being practiced, or had been pub-

licly performed within the forty years preceding the composition of Shakespeare's history plays. In addition, accounts of chivalric, military, and ecclesiastical degradations were readily available to Shakespeare and his contemporaries. These are the rituals on which, I believe, Shakespeare was able to draw as a frame of reference for the "inverted rite" of Richard II's discoronation.

I

Certainly Shakespeare knew cases of knightly degradation, as he shows in *1 Henry VI*, where Talbot tears the Garter from the leg of Sir John Fastolfe after his alleged cowardice at the battle of Patay, with the recommendation that he "Be quite degraded, like a hedge-born swain / That doth presume to boast of gentle blood" (IV.i.43–44). This historical fact is recounted in Monstrelet, Hall, and Holinshed, with the comment that "afterward by meanes of freends, and apparant causes of good excuse, the same [George and Garter] were to him againe deliuered against the mind of the lord Talbot."[3]

Degradation from even such a distinguished order of knighthood as that of the Garter was less rare than one might suppose. During the period 1459–1599 no fewer than ten formal degradations are listed in Shaw's *Knights of England*.[4] These, incidentally, are in addition to the many knights who were beheaded without the formality of ceremonial degradation. Not all Garter knights formally degraded were executed, and indeed five of them were later readmitted to the Order. Such degradations seem usually to have been based more on political considerations than on those of honor and chivalry, as a glance at the particulars of the restorees will indicate: Jasper Tudor, deposed 1461 and restored by Henry VII; Thomas Howard, 13th Earl of Surrey, degraded 1485 and restored 1490; Thomas Howard, 10th Duke of Norfolk, degraded 1546–47, restored 1553; William Parr, 1st Marquess of Northampton, degraded 1553, restored 1559; Sir William Paget, 1st Lord Paget de Beaudesert, degraded 1552, restored 1553.[5]

Chivalry, always interested in the subtleties of ceremonial, had very carefully designed gradations of disgrace, some of which could, at the request of the monarch, be dispensed with because of the past valor of the knight himself or past services done by members of his family. The complete form of knightly degrading was, however, most solemn, and indeed chilling in its logic, as is evidenced by William Segar, Norroy King of Arms and later Garter King. In

The Booke of Honor and Armes (1590), a work Shakespeare may possibly have used, since it appeared some years before the writing of *Richard II*, Segar gives an account of the ritual supposedly used to degrade a knight in or about the year 1020, the alleged period of Tristram and Lancelot. There is no evidence to show that this ceremonial was ever used in its entirety, but it does seem to constitute an archetype for almost all chivalric gradations. Part of its interest arises from its fusion of the three institutions of chivalry, arms, and religion, but even more from the inverted baptismal rite which helps illuminate Richard II's curious remark concerning his "usurp'd" baptismal name (IV.i.255–257):

If any Knight had in that time been corrupted with monie by his Princes enemie, or committed any other notable fault against loyaltie and honor, the other Knights forthwith made humble suite vnto the King that he might bee punished. Which request being granted, they apprehended the offender, and caused him to bee armed from head to foote, in such sort as if he should go to the field. Which done, they led him vp to an high stage made in a Church for that purpose, where [there] were thirteene Priestes saying those praiers ordinarily vsed at Burials, as though that Knight had lien dead at their feete. At the end of euerie Psalme they took from him one peece of his Armour. First, *they tooke off his Helmet as that which defended his traiterous eyes*, then *his Gauntlet on the right side as that which couered a corrupt hand:* then the *Gauntlet of the left hand, as from a member consenting.* And so by peecemeale dispoyled him of all his Armes, as well offensiue as defensiue, which one after another were throwne to the ground: and at the instant when euery part of Armour was cast downe, the King of Armes first, and after him all the other Herehaults cried aloud, *saying: This is the Helmet of a disloyall and miscreant Knight.* Then was brought thether a Bason of gold or siluer full of warme water: which being holden vp, the Herehaults with a loud voyce, sayd: *What is the Knights name?* The Purseuants answered that which in truth was his name. Then the King of Armes sayd. *That is not true, for he is a miscreant and false traitor, and such a one as hath broken the ordinance of Knighthood.* Thereunto answered the Chaplins. *Let vs giue him his right name.* Then spake the Trompets. *What shal be done with him?* To which words the King answered: *Let him bee with dishonor and shame banished my kingdome, as a vile and infamous man that hath done offence against the honor of Knighthood.* When the King had so said, the King of Armes and other Herehaults caste the warme water on the disgraded Knights face (as though he were new baptized) saying: *Hencefoorth thou shalt be called by thy right name, Traitor.* Then the King together with twelue other Knights put vpon them mourning garments declaring sorowe: and coming vnto the Knight disgraded put him down the stage, not by the staiers he mounted vp, when he was made Knight but threwe him downe tyed to a rope. Then with great ignomie he was brought to the Altar, and there laied groueling on the ground, an ouer him was read a Psalme full of curses.[6]

Degradation from the Order of the Garter follows the general pattern of this ritual, and John Stow's account of the degradation of Edward, Duke of Buckingham, in 1521 is notably extensive. Here the insult of degradation was leveled primarily at the duke's reputation and not his person, since he was not physically present at the ceremony, having been beheaded some three weeks earlier:

And now followeth the publication of the disgrading of the said *Edward* late Duke of Buckingham knight and companion of the most noble order of Saint *George* . . . in the quire of windsore college, [Garter King] standing on the high pase on the dexe, all the other officers of armes about him, there being also present the L. Marques Dorcet, knight of the same order, then being the kings deputy for the feast, the Earl of Essex, the earle of Wilshire, the earle of Kent, Sir *Thomas Louel*, and the lord *le Ware*, knights of the said order, with other great audience assembled there on the eight of June, the thirteene yeere of *Henry* the eight, the yeere of Christ 1521.

Be it knowen vnto all men, that whereas *Edward* late D. of Buckingham knight, and companion of the noble order of Saint *George*, named the Garter, hath lately doon and committed high treason against the King our soueraigne lord, and soueraigne of the said order of the garter in compassing and imagining the destruction of the most noble person of our said soueraign lord the king, contrary to his othe and due allegeance, and for the which high treason the said *Edward* hath been indicted, arraigned, conuicted, and attainted, and for the which detestable offence and high treason, the said *Edward* hath deserued to be disgraded of the said noble order, and expelled out of the saide company, and not worthy that his armes, ensignes, & hatchments should remaine among other of the noble ensignes of other noble, vertuous, and approoued knights of the said noble order, nor haue the benefites of the said noble order: wherefore our said soueraigne lorde the King, soueraigne of the said noble order of Saint *George* named the Garter, by the aduise of the other knights of the said noble order, for his offences, and committing of the said high treason, willeth and commandeth that the said *Edward* Duke of Buckingham to be disgraded of the said noble order, and his armes, ensignes and hachments cleerely expelled, and put down from among the armes, ensignes and hachments of the other noble knights of the said order, to the intent, that all other noble men thereby may take ensample hereafter, not to commit any such heinous and detestable treason and offences, as God forbid they should.

God saue the King.
It is to be remembered that Sommerset herault was in the roode loft
behind the hachments of the said Duke *Edward*: and when *Garter* spake
these words, *Expelled and put from the armes*, then the said Sommerset
violently cast downe into the quire, his creast, his banner, and sword. And
when the publication was all doone, the officers of armes, spurned the said
hachment with their feete, out of the quire into the body of the church,
first the sword, and then the banner, and then was the creast spurned out of
the said quire through the church out at the west doore, & so to the bridge,
where it was spurned ouer into the ditch. And thus was the said *Edward*
late duke of Buckingham fully disgraded of the order of Saint *George*
named the Garter.[7]

This same form of degradation, with a few minor variations, was repeated
in 1569 for Thomas Percy, Earl of Northumberland.[8] Queen Elizabeth, however, did show some clemency in the case of Robert Devereux, Earl of Essex,
who was not formally degraded, and whose banner was permitted to remain
above his stall, his achievements only being cast down.[9] In a similar case of
1603–04, James I allowed some mercy to Henry, Lord Cobham, convicted of
treason for complicity in the Bye Plot of 1603: "After the King of Arms had
thrown down and, in the presence of many onlookers, stamped on Cobham's
achievements, he kicked them only as far as the door of the Chapel and no
further; for James, out of regard for Cobham's nobility, had expressly forbidden the achievements to be cast into the common ditch."[10] The knight's
name was also officially removed from the roster of knights so that none of
his achievements would be preserved; one act of dishonor nullified all previous noble deeds.[11] Similarly, Richard II tries to remove himself and his
achievements from human memory (IV.i.213).

The continuing combination of the three estates of religion, chivalry, and
arms is indicated in Ashmole's 1672 statement of the points of reproach warrant-
ing knightly degradation:

> *Heresie*, Treason, or *flying from Battel*: We also find that *Prodigality* was
> made a fourth Point, where a Knight had so wasted his *Estate*, that he was
> not able to support his *Honor*. And the not being a *Gentleman of Blood*,
> both by Father and Mother, was the pretence, for devesting *William*
> Lord *Paget*, an.6 E.6. [MS. penes E.W.G., fol. 153] But *Fellony*
> comes not . . . among the *Reproaches* there reckoned up, and so it was
> adjusted in a *Chapter* held the 6. of *July an.*14. *Jac. R.* in the case of
> *Robert* Earl of *Sommerset*, then lately condemned for that Fact; whereup-
> on his *Hatchments* were not removed.[12]

The most serious of these causes were treason and offenses against the code of chivalry or against other knights. In the case of the Garter, of course, since the king himself was a member, treason was automatically included on a double basis: the breaking of an oath of loyalty to the monarch as liege-lord, and also to the king as fellow-knight, since members of the Garter were expressly forbidden to fight each other. Thus "a companion of a chivalrous order, though he might without dishonour take the part of his sovereign against the head of the order, must release a fellow member without ransom if he took him in war."[13] But in fighting for one's own monarch against the head of a knightly order, the member was supposed to render up the insignia of his knighthood.[14]

One particularly famous example of degradation for the double offense of treason to a liege-lord and violation of the laws of chivalry is recorded for a member of the Order of the Bath. Even though the incident occurred in 1464, the fate of Ralph Grey of Werke was still being rehearsed in 1614. The accusation was that he had both turned against his liege-lord and violated the laws of siege warfare when, having failed to offer a reasonable and adequate defense of Bamborough Castle, he yielded it to Margaret of Anjou and then accepted the post of captain of the garrison after she had "stuffed it with Scottes."[15] The Marshal Court, with John Tiptoft, Earl of Worcester, High Constable of England, sitting on the case at Doncaster, issued the following preamble to the judgment:

> Sir *Ralph Grey*, for thy treason, the king had ordained that thou shouldest haue had thy spurs striken off by the hard heeles by the hand of the master cooke, who is ready to do as was promised thee, at the time that he tooke off thy spurs, and said to thee as is accustomed: That and thou be not true to the soueraigne lord, he shall smite off thy spurs with his knife hard by the heeles; and so shewed him the master cooke redy to doo his office with his weapon and his knife. Moreouer Sir *Ralph Grey* the king had ordeyned, here thou maiest see, the kinges of armes, and heralds, and thine own proper coate of armes, which they should teare off thy body, and so shouldst thou as well be degraded of thy worship, nobles, and armes, as of thy order of knighthood. Also here is another coate of thine armes reuersed, the which thou shouldest haue worne on thy body, going to thy deathwards, for that belongeth to thee after the law: notwithstanding, the disgrading of knighthood, and of thine armes, and nobles, the king pardoneth that, for thy noble predecessors.[16]

Thus Grey escaped the final infamy of having his arms reversed as he was drawn to the place of execution, where "his body was shortēd, by the lēgth of his hed, and . . . thus was he rewarded for his doble deceipt and manifest periurie."[17] In 1497 James Touchet, 7th Earl of Audley, was less fortunate, for he was "drawen from Newgate to the Towre hil in a cote of his owne armes peinted vpon paper, reuersed and al to torne."[18] The depth of such disgrace was apparently still current knowledge in 1634 when John Ford, in *Perkin Warbeck*, recalls the event:

> . . . Let false Audley
> Be drawn upon an hurdle from the Newgate
> To Tower Hill in his own coat of arms,
> Painted on paper, with the arms reversed,
> Defaced and torn; there let him lose his head.
>   (III.i.94–98)[19]

One other aspect of chivalric degradation, clearly foreshadowing the dis-coronation procedure of Richard II's invented ceremony, is that of unclothing the knight in the reverse order of his investiture. Segar notes this ritual in his archetypal account, but the most frequently cited instance of its performance seems to be that of Sir Andrew Harclay (or Herkeley), knight, and Earl of Carlisle, after his treason committed against Edward III at the Battle of Beighland. The incident occurred in 1322, but chroniclers and chivalric writers continued to see in Harclay an *exemplum* like Ralph Grey, and Stow gives a lengthy and precise description of the ceremonial:

> About the feast of the purification of our Lady, Andrey de Herkeley late made Earle of Carlile, vnder couer of peace fayned that he would marrie Robert Bruse his sister. Whervpon the king reputing him a tray-tour, caused him to be taken by his trusty friend Sir Anthony de Lucie, who sent him in yrons straight to London, where he was iudged before sir Anthony de Lucy in this manner: he was ledde to the barre as an earle woorthily apparelled, wyth his sword girt about him, hosed, booted, and spurred, &c. vnto whom sir Anthony spake in this manner: Sir Andrew (quoth he) the king, for thy valiant seruice hath doone thee great honor, and made thee earle of Carlile, since which time, thou, as a traitour to thy Lorde the king; leddest his people that should haue holp him at the battell of Beighland, a way by the countrey of Copland, and through the earle-dome of Lancaster, by which meanes, our Lord the king was discomfited there of the Scots, through thy treason and falsenesse, whereas if thou haddest come betimes, he had the victory: and this treason thou com-mittedst, for the great summe of golde and siluer that thou receiuedst from James Dowglasse, a Scot, the kings enemy. Our Lord the king will therefore, that the order of knighthode, by the which thou receiuedst all thine honour and worship vpon thy bodie, bee brought to nought, and thy state vndone, that other knights of lower degree, may after thee beware, and take example hereafter truely to serue.

Then commaunded hee to hewe his Spurres from his heeles, then to break his Sworde ouer his head which the king had giuen him, to keepe and defend his land therewith, when he made him Earle. After this, hee let vnclothe him of his furred Tabard, and of his Hoode, of his coate-of-armes, and also of his girdle: and when this was doone, sir Anthonie sayde vnto him. Andrew (quoth hee) nowe arte thou no Knight but a knaue, and for thy treason, the King will that thou shalt be hanged and drawne, and thine head smitten off from thy bodie; thy bowelles taken out of thy body and burned before thee . . . and thy head to be set vpon London bridge . . . and thy foure quarters shall be sent vnto foure good townes of England, that all other may beware by thee.[20]

In addition to these indignities, Segar notes that "euerie peece of his Armour was brused, beaten, and cast aside."[21] Sir Andrew's case was a most celebrated one despite its antiquity, and references to it appear in almost all the major chronicle sources of Shakespeare's time.

II

Another form of degradation with analogies to Richard II's uncrowning is found not within the ranks of chivalric orders, but in military service, professional, volunteer, or conscripted. In a sense it was more international in application since it was not subject to the statutes of specific orders of knighthood, but to the "law of arms," an unwritten system known throughout Western Europe as concerning "the Roman people" and founded upon the Roman Catholic Church's Canon Law and the *Corpus juris civilis*. The law of arms was thus founded upon the *Ius gentium*, that human extension of the *Ius naturale* which covered all mankind, and it was concerned with the conduct of all military persons and operations.[22] English military law substantially followed European practice, as can be verified by reference to the sections on military discipline and punishment in Pierino Belli (1563), Balthazar Ayala (1582), and Alberico Gentili (1612).[23] The relative lack of such works by Englishmen can be attributed to the fact that England had no legally constituted permanent standing army until 1645. Hence the usual method of dealing with military discipline and punishment was to issue specific ordinances to cover individual campaigns and expeditions. This *ad hoc* method was used for the issuance of orders for the setting up of muster rolls to raise a military force for a specific purpose. A Royal Proclamation was issued; and when the danger was past or the expedition completed, additional proclamations were issued to regulate the speedy disbanding of units and to order the immediate return of demobilized persons to their homes. Penalties were imposed on wanderers who failed to return promptly to their place of enlistment.

In general, however, *re militari*, loosely translated as "military affairs," but actually meaning affairs of chivalry, were dealt with in England by the High Court of Chivalry, composed of the Earl Marshal of England and the Lord High Constable sitting together. This is what is meant by the English term "marshal law," unfortunately often spelled "martial law" and consequently confused with the idea of military rule by an army over a conquered or rebellious populace. The jurisdiction of the High Court of Chivalry, both in peace and war, as defined by 13 Richard II. st. 1.c.2, covers "cognisance of contracts touching deeds of arms and of war out of the realm, and also of things that touch [arms or] war within the realm, which cannot be determined nor discussed by the common law, with other usages and customs to the same matters pertaining, which other constables heretofore have duly and reasonably used in their time."[24] The High Court of Chivalry still exists, although rather an anachronism; as recently as 1954 it sat to decide a case of unwarranted display of the arms of the Manchester Corporation by a movie theater.[25] Nowadays, however, the court is concerned exclusively with matters of armorial bearings and assertions of nobility, any power over the law of arms and the army having been superseded in 1689 by the First Mutiny Act.

Contrary to the belief of some legal scholars, the High Court of Chivalry was not designed to deal with the specifics of military discipline over individuals. "Its records . . . do not include a single case relating to 'the offences and miscarriages of soldiers contrary to the laws and rules of the army'. There is nothing of desertion or mutiny or any other offence within the jurisdiction of the modern court martial."[26] Jurisdiction over military punishment rested on Articles of War, which in 1625 "seem to have been issued by the King on the Advice of a Council of War. . . . Authority was given 'to any three or more commissioners to call a Marshal Court, and sit in Commission to hear, judge, and determine, any fact done by soldiers; but to have no power to put to death till they have advertised the *General* that shall have *authority of life and death for such troops as he shall command*."[27] In other words, this was the "summary court," a court-martial in modern parlance, as opposed to the judicial institution of the High Court of Chivalry which exercised power over honor and arms, and over "the wrongs done by gentlemen."[28] This function of the High Court of Chivalry has some bearing on the opening scene of *Richard II* in which Bolingbroke, of the blood royal, accuses another gentleman, Thomas

Mowbray, Duke of Norfolk, of treason.[29]

Shakespeare seems to have been familiar with the rules of war and of military discipline, as a few examples will indicate. Henry V's order to the English at Agincourt to kill all their prisoners is not in itself a violation of the law of arms. Chroniclers and modern commentators are sometimes puzzled over whether Henry's motivation was revenge for the attack on the baggage train, traditionally considered a noncombatant unit, or fear of renewed attack by the French, as Shakespeare perhaps suggests (IV.vi.36–37). In either case, he could be justified by the rubric of the laws of war. Both Gentili and Ayala give sanction to such an act if there is danger that the prisoners might revolt, or that their number might endanger the capturing army. In Shakespeare's own lifetime, the massacre of the Spanish garrison at Smerwick was a famous such example, and one which Edmund Spenser approved.[30] Shakespeare seems, however, to emphasize Fluellen's explanation, but the fact remains that Henry was justified on the grounds of strategy. Similarly, in executing Bardolph for stealing a "pax" Henry is merely implementing the usual military punishment for unauthorized pillage. However, when Iago speaks of "when he's old, cashiered," he speaks merely of dismissal from the service when the soldier was no longer needed, as opposed to formal cashiering with infamy. Though the latter meaning is recorded in the OED in 1599, I have not found an account of the ceremonial in Shakespeare's day, though I have little doubt that it occurred.[31]

Formal cashiering with infamy consisted of "degradation from the rank of soldier and a gentleman: the execution of this sentence is attended with many ignominious circumstances, more terrible to a man of feeling than death itself."[32] The general form of this ritual, made so familiar by films that it is now common knowledge, consists of bringing the officer publicly to the head of his regiment, where his commission is solemnly cancelled, his sword, if any, is broken over his head, his decorations, buttons, and insignia are all ripped off, and he is turned out of line. By 1745 the provost-marshal's servant assisted the departure of the degraded officer by "giving him a kick on the posteriors."[33] The similarity of this ritual to the ceremonial for a knight like Harclay is obvious. Degradation rituals following this general pattern apparently existed in the seventeenth century for private soldiers. In the reign of Charles I they could be degraded to the nonrank of pioneers, or scavengers, the lowest and most despised members of the army. Degradatory punishments could also be meted out to entire regiments in case of refusal to fight, or flight in the face of an enemy. If the officers were found at fault, they were banished; if the soldiers were to blame, decimatory execution was practiced, and the remainder of the regiment forced to "serve for Pioners and Scavengers till a worthy exploit take off that blot."[34] This interesting extension of chivalric ritual and responsibility to the other ranks is also reinforced by the pronouncement of *An Abridgement of English Military Discipline* (1686): "Before a Soldier be punished for any infamous Crime, he is to be publicly Degraded from his Arms [weapons], and his coat stript over his ears."[35]

Military degradation thus represents a development of the old code of arms and chivalry, but its relevance to *Richard II* consists more particularly in the application of the laws of arms and the High Court of Chivalry to the judicial combat between Bolingbroke and Mowbray. There is some doubt as to whether this case did indeed fall under the jurisdiction of the High Court of Chivalry because Mowbray, as Earl Marshal of England at that time, was unable to sit on his own case in "marshal law."[36] However, since both lords appealed their dispute to the king, they followed perfectly legal procedure, because the monarch was the court of last resort in appeals from the High Court of Chivalry.[37]

Throughout the entire matter of the judicial duel in *Richard II* Shakespeare follows the ritual reproduced in his chronicle sources, but he takes as reason for combat the alleged involvement of Mowbray in the death of Thomas of Woodstock instead of the cause more frequently assigned by the chroniclers: Bolingbroke's critical remarks on the conduct of Richard II, which Mowbray allegedly relayed in a garbled manner to suggest treasonable motives on the part of Bolingbroke. Shakespeare also makes use of the law of judicial combat to indicate the difference between Richard II and Henry IV in terms of their demonstrated ability to control rebellious subjects. Of course the king had the power to take the quarrel "into his [own] hand and make peace betweene the parties without longer fight. . . . For the quarrell resting in the Kings hand, might not be renued, or any violence offered without prejudice vnto the Kings honor."[38] But whereas Richard II hesitates, and permits the matter to go to the lists at Coventry before intervening, Henry IV insists that the dispute of IV.i "rest under gage" until he, the king himself, can decide the outcome.

Actually, in England, the formal judicial *combat à l'outrance* was relatively rare, a total of only seven being recorded in books of arms covering the period from Canute to Elizabeth. However, Bracton claims that the accused had the right to choose between trial by jury and the judicial duel, "defending himself by his body," but this decision carried additional risk:

If the appellee is vanquished he will suffer capital punishment with dis-
herison and the loss of all his goods, as for a felony of any kind. If the
appellor is vanquished let him be committed to gaol to be punished as a
false accuser (but he will lose neither life nor members, though according
to the laws he would be liable to the talionic penalty if he failed in his
proof) and let the appellee withdraw quit of the appeal, unless the justices
cause him to be held because of some other suspicion or charge.[39]

Richard's settlement of the combat, however, is degrading to both of the
participants. Without allowing satisfaction "in honor," he in effect assumes
both parties to be guilty, but Mowbray more blameworthy than Bolingbroke.
Perhaps, by implying Richard's complicity in Woodstock's murder, Shakespeare is showing Richard as not merely capricious, but wishing to avoid an
even harsher penalty than Bracton suggests:

If the appeal was one of treason, the vanquished party, whether he was the
appellant or the defendant, was disarmed in the lists and drawn behind a
horse in the charge of the Marshal to the place of execution, where he was
beheaded or hanged. In the case of any other crime the indignity of being
drawn behind a horse was spared, and if the appeal related only to a 'deed
or action of arms,' the only penalty was being disarmed and put out of the
lists. The same result followed a confession of the charge.[40]

Yet Richard later compounds his injustice in distraining the property of
Bolingbroke after the death of John of Gaunt, because this action implies the
guilt of one of the participants in a judicial duel. Further, not even the High
Court of Chivalry had the right to distrain the lands and tenements of even a
convicted person; only his body and goods could be forfeit.[41] Richard has thus
degraded Bolingbroke to the situation of an "attainted person" whose lands,
name, and person are forfeit. It is an interesting byway of history that by
statute of 1 Henry IV.c.14 the new monarch forbade the High Court of Chivalry to interfere in any similar case of judicial combat.

III

So far the chief similarities notable between chivalric and military degradation have been those of symbolic unclothing, and reduction in each case to
the lowest possible status, that of knave or pioneer: "Nowe arte thou no
Knight, but a knaue," as was said to Sir Andrew Harclay. As such, both
degraded knights and soldiers lost any privileged position they might have in law

to be tried by their peers, be it a court of knights or a summary court, and
instead became liable to the penalties of the civil law. This also happened in
the third mode of degrading with which we must be concerned: that of ecclesiastical degradation. The ritual for this, developed by Pope Boniface VIII
(1294–1303) by analogy with the military ceremony which dates back to
Roman times, was applied—and technically still can be—to clerics of all
ranks. It constitutes "the canonical penal expulsion from the clerical state,"[42]
and it renders the cleric liable to the punishments of the secular arm by removing from him his "Benefit of clergy" in exactly the same way as a degraded
knight lost the protection of his order and his right to judgment by his chivalric peers.

Ecclesiastical degradation seems to have been a ceremonial which occurred almost as frequently in the sixteenth century as degradation from the
Garter. But since religion was literally a burning question, none of the degraded clerics mentioned in Foxe's *Actes and Monumentes* could be reinstated,
except posthumously. In 1400, during the reign of Henry IV, William Saw-
tre (or Hawtree), a priest of Wales, was solemnly degraded; in 1525, John
Castellane, an Augustinian friar of Metz, was similarly treated; and during the
reign of Queen Mary, six formal degradations took place which Foxe reports
in varying detail. In 1554, Bishop Hooper was degraded in Newgate Prison,
and the next year Rowland Taylor, Robert Farrar, Bishop of St. David's,
Nicholas Ridley, and Hugh Latimer were all similarly treated.[43] Most notable
of all, Thomas Cranmer, Archbishop of Canterbury, was solemnly and publicly degraded in Christ Church, Oxford, on February 14, 1556 and burned on
March 21 of the same year.[44] His repudiation of his earlier recantations and
Foxe's account of the ceremonial way in which the aged archbishop punished
his offending right hand by burning it first is almost as famous as Latimer's
"candle."[45]

The archetypal importance of this degradation for Shakespeare is hard to
estimate, but Foxe makes it the definitive account of ecclesiastical degradation
in England, treating it with the respect worthy of its subject. The public
humiliation and the execution of the man who had been the primate of all England, and who was more than any other cleric responsible for the liturgy of the
Church of England, must have struck fear into the hearts of Englishmen. Further, in terms of Shakespeare's possible familiarity with this occurrence, one
should remember the probability of additional interest in Stratford owing to
its geographical proximity to Oxford on the main highway from London. At
the time of Shakespeare's birth, not quite nine years had elapsed since Cran-

mer's martyrdom and the burning of the other Oxford martyrs, so that one may even postulate a local eyewitness. But above all, as a recent biographer of Cranmer has pointed out, in 1560 Queen Elizabeth had "sanctioned a propaganda campaign which identified Cranmer and his fellows as Martyrs,"[46] and as a result Archbishop Parker in 1572 had published a chapter on Cranmer in his *De Antiquitate Britannicae Ecclesiae*. Further, the discovery of new information, together with the recollections of Ralph Morice, Cranmer's secretary, had brought Foxe himself to a substantial revision of his original account.[47] Cranmer's candle was indeed burning bright. A further analogical importance for the Cranmer material with reference to Richard II lies in their comparable positions in ecclesiastical and monarchical martyrology. By the end of the sixteenth century, Richard had become a somewhat sacrificial figure, "a prince the most vn-thankfullie vsed of his subiects,"[48] as Holinshed puts it, a martyr to the cause of English monarchy which had reached its divinely directed triumph in Tudor rule. Cranmer, by a similar process, had triumphed over the very human weakness of his recantations, together with the hostility of Roman Catholic writers, to achieve a propaganda victory. He was now considered the premier martyr to the cause of the English Church, and his memory was constantly kept alive through his work in *The Book of Common Prayer*. As Richard was the monarchical martyr of England, so Cranmer was the highest ranking martyr to the cause of God's English Church, that other prop of Tudor power.[49]

In the ritual reproduced by Foxe, the cleric is dressed in the robes and attributes of his priestly and ecclesiastical office and powers. All these are ceremonially stripped from him, starting with the highest and ending with the innermost garments. The order of divesture for an archbishop is as follows: pall, mitre, book of the Gospels, episcopal ring, and crozier are removed; the chrism on fingers and head is ceremonially scraped off with a piece of glass; and finally the episcopal shoes are removed. Degradation from the priesthood now ensues, reversing the order of conferral of all major and minor orders, each external attribute being stripped away: (1) *Priesthood*: the chalice is seized, the canonical fingers are scraped to signify removal of the holy oils, and the chasuble and stole are removed; (2) *Deaconship*: the book of the Gospels, dalmatic, and stole are taken; (3) *Subdeaconship*: the book of the Epistles and Acts, the tunic, maniple, amice, containers of water and wine, empty chalice, paten, cincture, and alb are seized. Similarly, the subject is deprived of the minor orders of "bennet and collet" (acolyte), exorcist, reader, and sexton, by removal of candle, book of conjurations, book of holy legends, and keys. Lastly, the hair of the head is closely clipped to signify ceremonial obliteration of the first tonsure.[50] At this point the cleric, having lost his benefit of clergy, is reduced to the status of layman, and as such is delivered to the secular arm of the law "with an earnest entreaty that the life of the victim be spared."[51] To be sure, this last exhortation was sometimes omitted, and Foxe does not mention it in Cranmer's case, but it was a moot point whether such an omission might not constitute an irregularity.[52] The unfrocked cleric is not, of course, totally deprived of "the essential quality" of his priestly functions, which are conferred forever, but his exercise of those functions, though valid, is unlawful.[53]

The parallels with such knightly degradation ceremonies as those of Sir Andrew Harclay and the Segar archetype are very clear. As Harclay was now but a knave, so Edmund Bonner, Bishop of London, remarked scoffingly to Cranmer, who was now dressed in a poor thin garment barely enough to cover his nakedness: "Nowe are you no Lord any more: and so when soeuer he spake to the people of him . . . euer he vsed this terme: This gentleman heere. &c."[54] But throughout Cranmer's degradation, Foxe also implicitly develops a correspondence between Cranmer and Christ as victims, with the archbishop also betrayed by a false friend and follower and treated contumeliously by a high priest. This kind of parallel is on the whole a commonplace derived from the homilies, from biblical exegesis, and from religious literature in general, for Judas had become the type of friend-betrayer, as Christ was the type of the gentle, blameless, and forgiving victim, and Pilate had become the epitome of the false judge. All these correspondences are developed by Richard II at his discoronation.

Foxe draws attention to the difference between the two clerics who came to Oxford for the specific purpose of degrading Cranmer in an unusually dramatic way. Edmund Bonner, Bishop of London, seems to have thoroughly enjoyed the situation, but William Thirlby, Bishop of Ely, was apparently ambivalent, for he had resided for some time with Cranmer at Lambeth, where he had been treated less like a chaplain than a brother: "Which bymatter of the sayd Doctour Thirlby, I thought here to recite, not so much to rebrayd the man with the voyce of vnthankefulnes, as chiefly and onely for this, to admonishe him of olde benefites receiued whereby he may better remember hys olde benefactor, and so to fauour the cause and quarrell of hym whom he was so singularly bounden vnto."[55] Thirlby, then, is the false friend, and Cranmer the forgiving Christ. Thirlby even offered to become a suitor to the Queen and King for Cranmer, and "so protested his great loue & friendship that had been betweene them, hartily weeping. . . . [H]e earnestly affirmed that if it hadde not bene the King [Philip of Spain] and Queenes cōmandement, whom he could not deny, els no wordly cōmoditye should haue made him to haue done it, concluding that to be one of the sorowfull things that euer hapned vnto him. The Archb. gently seeming to cōfort him sayd, he was very well content withal."[56] Later, however, Cranmer showed himself more human and less forgiving: "Yea, . . . he myght haue vsed a great deale more frendship towarde me, & neuer haue bene the worse thought on, for I haue wel deserued it."[57] Bonner, on the other hand, seems to have behaved in a rude and arrogant manner to his erstwhile superior: " . . . the Bish. scraped the tops of hys fingers where he had bene anoynted, wherein B. Boner behaued himself as roughly and vnmanerly as the other Bishop was to him soft and gentle."[58]

Cranmer also raised a point of singular importance. Who has the authority to degrade a superior? Pope Celestine V had solved the problem at his abdication in 1294 by manufacturing his own ritual, divesting himself, and turning himself over to the electors as the only person capable of removing him from the pontificate.[59] The Bishop of Carlisle asks the same question in *Richard II*. Who can judge a king? Thus Richard, like Pope Celestine, must depose himself. In the case of Cranmer, we are told, the bishops did appeal to a higher authority, albeit one not recognized by their victim: " . . . when they came to take of hys Pall (which is a solemne vesture of an Archb.) then sayde he: which of you hathe a Pall to take off my Pall? whych imported as much as they being his inferiours coulde not disgrade him. Whereunto one of them said in y[t] . . . being the Popes delegates they might take his Pal, & so they did."[60]

Foxe then recounts how Cranmer was taken to prison in a poor gown and, but for the charity of an unnamed man of Gloucester who brought him his original gown and arranged for him to eat, would have suffered even further. Finally Foxe retells the story of Cranmer's heroic death. After six signed recantations, the Archbishop finally defied his enemies, denied his former declarations, refused the proffered comfort of a Spanish friar, and rushed headlong toward the flames that would bring him to eternity. Then, as the fire was kindled, he held his right hand into it as punishment for having written the documents of his fear.

Whether or not Shakespeare had actually read Foxe on this subject is difficult to determine, but I tend to think that even at this early date he was familiar with Foxe's work; Geoffrey Bullough thinks he may have read it in connection with the writing of *1 Henry VI*.[61] Holinshed's sketchy account of

Cranmer's martyrdom, a mere forty lines, comes from Foxe, and Shakespeare could have been led back to the original from the marginal note and thus have found the complete account of Cranmer's degradation. But he would have found even more as well: in particular the entire *Forma degradationis* drawn from the Roman pontifical together with the Latin text of the "Commission sent from the Pope with the sentence diffinitiue to proceed against the reuerend Archb. of Cant. Thomas Cranmer."[62] In the 1583 edition, and succeeding ones, this *Forma degradationis* is in an unusually noteworthy position, "The Appendix of such Notes and Matters as either haue bene in this History omitted or newly inserted"; further, it is schematically reproduced in a larger typeface than the remainder of the work.[63] The index to the 1583 edition also includes specific references to the degradation of Cranmer and of those other clerics mentioned earlier.

One cannot, unfortunately, assert that Shakespeare was specifically influenced by this account of Cranmer's fate, but it certainly represents the archetypal account for England of ecclesiastical degradation. It displays quite clearly the similarities to be found among the three rituals of degradation so far discussed: chivalric, military, and religious. Not only is the stripping of symbolic accoutrements of importance, but also the reduction of the legal personality of the individuals so treated. They are all now considered mere common men, unworthy of the judgment of their erstwhile peers and liable to the punishments of the secular arm of the law. What Shakespeare has done in *Richard II* is to have taken up the commonplaces of such rituals and combined them into an invented rite suitable for the solemnity of a king's abdication. One must recall, in considering the history of those monarchs and leaders who have been expelled from their positions of rule, or who have renounced them more or less voluntarily, that no formal ritual for such a transfer of power exists. One would hardly enshrine the format of a *coup d'état* in a quasi-religious document; even today the deliberate compilation of any formal deposition ceremony might be construed as dangerous.

IV

Shakespeare's ritual, however, underlines both the solemnity and the pathos of the occasion. It is also, as Kantorowicz suggests, a symbolic stripping of Richard, so that he takes off the trappings of office, crown, sceptre, and the royal pomp of his official body to reveal himself the possessor of nothing more than his corporeal mortal nature. The king is therefore a man, like the rest of humankind, and as such is subject to the law of the land without supervenient royal power. Thus, as a man, Richard is subject to the pains and penalties of his humanity and must suffer and die. The ritual stripping away of the outward trappings of kingship indicates the manner in which Richard takes off his political "body," that of the king who never dies, to become the victim who always dies.[64] In this situation Christological parallels are explicitly called to bear witness.

But what do the chronicles say? Might not they provide specific details which could have developed the totality of Shakespeare's ritual approach? To some extent the answer is affirmative, but only in the matter of a few details. Of all the chronicles, Hall alone gives a ceremonial account of the abdication. He speaks of Bolingbroke's causing

> . . . a great assemble to be apointed at the towre of London, where kyng Richard appareled in vesture and robe royall the diademe on his head, and the scepter in his hand came personally before the congregacion and said these wordes in effecte. I Rychard kyng of England . . . confesse and say before you my lordes and other oure subiectes, that by the hole space of .xxii. yere in the which I haue obteined and possessed the rule and regiment of this famous realme of Englande . . . [I] haue omitted and not executed my royall office and bounden dutie accordyng as I oughte to haue done in ministering iustice and prefermēt of the commonwealth. . . . And to the intent that it shall be lefull to you to electe and chose my cosyn germayne, Henry Duke of Lancastre, a man mete for a realme, and a prince apt for a kingdom to your kyng and souereigne lorde: I of myne owne mere mocion and frewyll do put and depose my selfe out of all royall dignitie, prehemynence & souereigntie, and resygne the possession. . . . And then with a lamentable voyce and a sorowfull countenaunce, delyuered his scepter and crowne to the duke of Lancastre, requiryng euery persone seuerally to graunt and consent that he might lyue a priuate and solitary lyfe.[65]

Holinshed, on the other hand, says nothing about Richard's clothing on this occasion; similarly, there is no sign of Hall's "great assemble," since Richard merely reads aloud in the Tower the instrument of abdication. He does, however, provide us with one ritual moment, in describing Richard as taking "a ringe of gold from his finger being his signet, and put[ting] it upon the said dukes finger."[66]

No other chronicler develops the aspect of ritual, but there is a curious French treatment of the correspondences between Richard II and Christ with Henry IV as Pilate. The idea of Pilate as the type of false judge is obviously a commonplace, but the application to Henry's treatment of Richard II is new. As rendered in a fifteenth-century text of Jean Créton's *Histoire du Roy d'Angleterre Richard II* in translation, the equation is made most specific:

> Then spoke Duke Henry quite aloud to the commons of the said city. "Fair Sirs, behold your king! consider what you will do with him!" And they made answer with a loud voice, "We will have him taken to Westminster." And so he deliuered him unto them. At this hour did he remind me of Pilate, which caused our Lord Jesus Christ to be scourged at the stake, and afterwards had him brought before the multitude of the Jews, saying, "Fair Sirs, behold your King!" who replied, "let him be crucified!" Then Pilate washed his hands of it, saying "I am innocent of the just blood." And so he delivered our Lord unto them. Much in the like manner did Duke Henry, when he gave up his rightful lord to the rabble of London, in order that, if they should put him to death, he might say, "I am innocent of this deed."[67]

Certainly this text cannot be assumed as a source, but it indicates the existence of another treatment of Richard, this time explicitly as Christ-victim.

From all this material, it would seem that Shakespeare's invented dis-coronation rite belongs to an entire tradition of degradation ceremonies with which a sixteenth-century audience was probably reasonably familiar in at least one of its three forms, chivalric, military, or ecclesiastical. The details of the coronation ritual itself, however, most likely come from Holinshed, whose account of the crowning of Richard II is considered the definitive statement of the ceremony. The idea of a ceremonial unclothing has a parallel in Hall, while the Christological correspondences appear to come from homiletic literature, biblical commonplaces, perhaps also from the Cranmer case and the French chronicle tradition, and finally perhaps even from Bracton, who speaks of kingship in a Christly analogy which sums up the medieval view of the ruler as God's vicegerent, while hinting at the victim equation:

> The king has no equal within his realm, [Subjects cannot be the equals of the ruler, because he would thereby lose his rule, since equal can have no authority over equal.] nor *a fortiore* a superior, because he would then be subject to those subjected to him. The king must not be under man, but under God and under the law, because law makes the king, [Let him therefore bestow upon the law what the law bestows upon him, namely, rule and power.] for there is no *rex* where will rules rather than *lex*. Since he is the

vicar of God, [And that he ought to be under the law appears clearly in the
analogy of Jesus Christ, whose vicegerent on earth he is, for though many
ways were open to Him for his ineffable redemption of the human race
. . . he willed himself to be under the law that he might redeem those who
live under it. . . .][68]

Some of these materials are not sources in the specific sense of the word, but
they are indicative of habits of thought common to Shakespeare's day. Hence
one can understand how Shakespeare could recast Holinshed's account of
Richard's resignation into a quasi-religious returning to God of his kingly
office.[69] But before the actual abdication, or deposition, scene begins, Shakespeare inserts the Bishop of Carlisle's speech on the supremacy of kingly
power, as a means of dictating the tone of the succeeding actions. In actual fact
Carlisle spoke these sentiments to Parliament some weeks *after* Richard's
deposition, but the placing here implicitly questions the legality of the pro-
ceedings and sets up the correspondence between Richard and Christ.[70] Following closely on Carlisle's speech, which approximates to Bracton's comments on kingly prerogative, Richard enters to portray himself as the victim of
Judases and a false Pilate. Then as "priest and clerk" he develops his own
ceremonial. Again, this situation must recall earlier ones: Celestine's unfrock-
ing of himself, and Cranmer's insistence that bishops did not have the power
to degrade their superior.

Richard begins by removing the crown, the last symbol conferred upon a
king, then the scepter, outward signs of "the pride of kingly sway" (IV.i.206).
With his tears he removes the sacred chrism of his anointing; in a sense analogous
to the Segar archetype of knightly degradation, he thus "baptizes" himself
into his new "unkinged" identity.

But the emphasis on anointing raises an interesting point concerning
Richard's own coronation, which Pater also noted without source,[71] and Selden
in *Titles of Honor* (1614) treats in full. Richard was apparently doubtful of
the validity of his anointing because of the provenance of the oil used on that
occasion. According to Selden, there was a legend, presumably arrived at by
analogy with the one concerning the origin of the sacred oil used in crowning
the kings of France at Rheims,

That Our Lady gave *Thomas Becket* Archb. of *Canterbury*, being in banishment vnder *Hen.* II. a Golden Eagle full of precious Ointment, in-
clos'd in a stone vessell, commanding him to preserue it, and foretelling
*quod Reges Anglorum qui vngerentur hoc vnguento pupiles essent Eccle-
siae, & Benigni & terram amissam á parentibus pacificé, recuperarent,
donec Aquila cum Ampulla haberent.* He committed it to safegard in a
Monasterie at Poiters, where *Henry* the first Duke of *Lancaster* vnder
Edward the Third in the warres of *France*, had it deliuered to him, by a
Holy man (they say) which found it by Reuelation. *The* Duke gaue it the
Black Prince. He sent it to the Tower, there to be safely kept in a chest
strongly hoop't with Iron, where *Rich: II.* sonne to the *Black Prince*, in
searching for his fathers Iewels, lighted on it, and much desired to be
annointed with it. But the Archbishop answered him, *sibi sufficere quód
semel per manus suas sacram suscepit in Coronatione pristina Vntionem, quae
habere non debuit iterationam.* The King, notwithstanding, caried it with
him into Ireland, purposing, perhaps, there to haue been annointed with
it, but, in his return to *Chester* he deliuer'd it to the Archbishop, confessing that he did resolue it was decreed, he should not be annointed with it,
and so indeed it fell out. For after him deposd, *Henry* IV. was honor'd
with this suppos'd diuine Ointment in his Coronation.[72]

None of the usual chronicle sources recounts this legend, and certainly Selden
sounds skeptical, but it could explain to some extent Richard's emphasis on
anointment. Shakespeare's knowledge of this matter must, of course, remain
"not proven."

After this, Richard, in repetition, renounces his crown and his "sacred
state," or eleaction by God, and—still inverting the coronation rite—offers to
"release all duteous oaths" of allegiance sworn by those present at his coronation when the Archbishop demanded "of them if they would submit themselues
vnto such a prince & gouernor and obei his commandements."[73] Then he
divests himself of the outward rights and privileges of his kingship, the exterior signs of the wealth, property, revenues, and pageantry of monarchy.
Finally, having disposed of himself as monarch, he denies his "achievements"
as king.

It may be objected that in denying his "acts, decrees and statutes" at this
point, Richard departs from inverted ritual, since these were the actions of his
post-coronation kingship. However, it does constitute an even stronger statement of Richard's total annihilation of his kingly personality: his "body
politic." Since Richard is not merely resigning, but also obliterating himself
as king (and the snowman image supports this interpretation), his actions as
king are similarly to become nonexistent, something that would not follow

from mere abdication. The nullity of Richard as God's vicegerent and law-maker thus logically implies the nullification of all his actions, but Richard, as usual, overstates his case, for not all his statutes were ever repealed. As Hall notes, and the *Statutes of the Realm* confirm, in the first Parliament of Henry IV "wer adnichilate al ye actes passed in the parliament holden by kyng Richard in the .xxi.yere of his reygne, which was called the euyll parliament for the nobilitie, the worse for the menaltie, but worste of all for the com-monaltie."[74] Thus Shakespeare has Richard declare himself someone who has never existed as a legal person. Like a degraded knight or an unfrocked cler-ic, he is equal only to the lowest of laymen—a knave liable to the fullest punishment of the secular arm of the law.

At this point the three rituals of chivalric and clerical degradation and Richard's discoronation come together as one. As with Andrew Harclay, "Nowe arte thou no Knight but a knaue," so with Cranmer, "Nowe are you no lord any more." Similarly, Richard replies to Northumberland's address of "My lord," with total logic:

> No lord of thine, thou haught, insulting man,
> Nor no man's lord. I have no name, no title—
> No, not that name was given me at the font—
> But 'tis usurped. Alack the heavy day.
> That I have worn so many winters out
> And know not now what name to call myself!
> (IV.i.254–259

These lines have been taken to refer to the tale spread by supporters of the house of Lancaster that Richard of Bordeaux was really the illegitimate son of a French canon, something that, according to Froissart, Henry IV alleged to Richard in the Tower.[75] However, they have equal relevance to the degradation of a knight, or, as here, a king, who as a result of treachery to his office and order is "new baptized" and called by his rightful name of "miscreant and false traitor."

And indeed, Richard has already commenced to see himself as a traitor. Shakespeare has now changed the betrayed-Christ image of the deposed king and allows him to play the role of arch-traitor.[76] By his defective rule and his willing deposition of himself, Richard has acted traitorously against the per-son of himself as king, and against the office of kingship. He thus has also betrayed Christ in the image of his vicegerent, and hence has acted even worse than the other traitors. As a result, he begins to look upon himself as damned, and for the next fifty lines or so Shakespeare has Richard speak in terms that seem deliberate echoes of Marlowe's *Doctor Faustus*. The snowman image recalls Faustus' desire for annihilation rather than God's judgment, while "was this the face" ironically echoes Faustus' apostrophe to a devil in the shape of Helen. The farewell scene with Isabella seems to compound these echoes with the exchange of kisses and the undoing of the marriage ritual (V.i.71–75), although the exchange of hearts is also a poetic commonplace.

Richard is then sent to the Tower, and, like degraded knights and clerics, is subject to the secular arm. He is now unadorned *humanum genus*, subject also to the laws of mortality—suffering and death. He is Bolingbroke's "Jack of the clock" (V.v.60), a manikin subject to the will of another, without any power of his own. But even here Richard can pun. He is no king, no knight, no cleric: like Sir Andrew Harclay, he is "but a knave," a Jack. He is deserted even by his horse, and finds charity only in his groom, also a knave. But then Shakespeare makes an important dramatic decision in choosing among the doubtful accounts of the death of Richard II.[77] Instead of following the more common opinion that he was starved to death, or starved himself voluntarily, he shows Richard engaging in the one heroic act of his life, finding a last reservoir of courage in an attempt to cling to life, fighting chivalrously against impossible odds while Sir Piers of Exton and his men hack him to death, as Holinshed records.[78] At that moment, Richard reasserts himself as king in calling down damnation on Exton for his treason, and then dying himself, as a Christian certain of heaven: "Mount, mount, my soul! thy seat is up on high! / While my gross flesh sinks downward, here to die" (V.v.111–112).

Thus, throughout *Richard II* Shakespeare makes use of echoes drawn from many rituals, sources, and commonplaces. Almost every important event in the play is turned by Richard into one of ritual significance. Indeed, he thinks almost entirely in ritual terms, with himself as the versatile leading character with many roles. But nowhere does Shakespeare seem to build on a denser knowledge of background than in the inverted ritual of Richard's un-crowning. This scene was considered politically dangerous in Shakespeare's day, and its significance was well understood, as can be inferred from its connection with the Essex Rebellion of 1601. I believe, too, that an Eliz-abethan audience would also have been able to comprehend and recognize the reverberative echoes of knightly, military, and clerical rituals here outlined. The Elizabethans were skilled in communication by outward symbol and ritual. Even the common people clearly knew how to assess the degree of criminal guilt by the outward rituals of sentencing and execution. Rank was also indicated by outward symbol, and specific offices retained unique costumes. Appearance aimed at reflecting the inward reality of nobility, not only in a Spenserian Neoplatonic sense, but also in daily life, for clothes did indeed "proclaim the man" by identifying his trade and station, as numerous sumptuary laws indicate. Further, the rituals of knighthood were by no means dead, as the accounts of numerous joustings would seem to show, and knightly "courtoisie" was still admired, as the romantic tale of Sir Philip Sidney attests. Certainly a man could prove himself by the nobility of his deeds, but his virtue needed the ratification of a coat of arms from the Royal College of Heralds before he was truly raised in station—something William Shakespeare, Gent., undoubtedly understood.

Hence, in *Richard II*, the ritual stripping away of Richard's symbolic attributes is infinitely more than mere formality. It constitutes his annihilation as a kingly person, his reduction to the rank of knave, the destruction of his achievements, and, as Richard sees it, his excision from the roster of English kings, since he has become a traitor to the office he had held. But then, by making Richard finally nothing more than the naked Everyman who must face death as best he can, Shakespeare has managed to surmount the key difficulty of dealing with the deposition of a monarch. By separating the foolish and inefficient king from the human being, by blaming and humiliating the one while pitying the other, Shakespeare manages to evoke the sympathy of his audience for Richard, a man who at the end of the play achieves a kind of dignity in his sufferings, who by confronting his foes rehabilitates his honor and gains respect by exercise of that personal valor he could not command in his days of power. Stripped to his essential human self, Richard discovers the strength to triumph as man where he failed as king.

CHAPTER IX

"Naked Wretches"—Clothing as Symbol

The ritual degradation and unclothing in *Richard II* has counterparts in other Shakespearean plays, and it is only through a recognition of the essential loneliness and nakedness of human kind, symbolized by an unclothing, that the individuals concerned achieve any kind of spiritual enlightenment. Four representative plays which depend heavily on the symbolic force of clothing and unclothing are *King Lear, Timon of Athens, Macbeth,* and *Henry VIII.* Different in approach though they most certainly are, they all have one important common element: a movement of spirit which centers on the recognition by a central character that he is indeed "naked." As Richard II noted in prison that the rich must divest themselves of all things (referring to Luke 18:25; Matthew 19:24):

> 'Tis as hard to come as for a camel
> To thread the postern of a small needle's eye
> (*RII*, V.iii.17)

so too major characters in these four plays discover the vanity of their human ambitions and achievements, and through their responses to this knowledge they indicate the quality of their own existence.

The most complex of these "clothing motif" plays is, without doubt *King Lear,* and the theme of stripping, of laying aside, is introduced in Lear's opening speech where he uses the word "divest" for his decision voluntarily to lay aside ". . . rule / Interest of territory, cares of state" (I.i.49–50). Then, after Cordelia's disastrous silence, he takes steps to "invest" his elder daughters and their husbands with his powers. Here too, one should notice the use of the personal pronouns. As king, Lear uses the royal "we," but as disappointed father and human being, he uses the singular. This careful distinction between the king's two bodies is scrupulously observed throughout the play. But though divested of actual power, Lear tries to retain its outward appearance, its vesture, in his train of one hundred knights. And again he uses a symbolic reference to clothing in "this coronet part between you" (I.i.139), a remark which is shockingly echoed by the Fool in I.iv.148–149:

> Nuncle, give me an egg, and I'll give thee two crowns.

The stripping metaphor continues throughout the scene as the King of France expresses his amazement that Cordelia could

> Commit a thing as monstrous to dismantle
> So many folds of favor.
>   (I.i.217–218)

But such is his affection that he takes the dowerless Princess as she stands, asking no more than "that little seeming substance" (I.i.198). Like the honest and frank Kent, France sees the reality beneath the appearance: therefore he is worthy of the lady who brings with her only the vesture of her virtue—"she is herself a dowry" (I.i.241).

Clothing remains important in Lear's next scene as Kent enters in disguise to serve his old master in whose countenance he professes to perceive authority. But without the *power*, the outward trappings of that authority, it is nothing more than appearance. One of Lear's knights recognizes this fact quite quickly as he notes the lack of "ceremonious affection" with which the king has been treated. Lear's own self-image is once again clarified here as he refers to himself in this scene almost entirely in the first person singular, for he is no longer the practitioner of the kingly office.

The entry of the Fool further indicates the importance of clothing as symbol, for he immediately offers Kent his coxcomb: Only a Fool is fit to follow a fool like Lear, when he can expect no reward. Likewise, the Fool addresses Lear as an equal, one who deserves motley as a reward for his folly:

> For wise men are grown foppish,
> And know not how their wits to wear
> Their manners are so apish.
>   (I.iv.158–161)

The clothing metaphor is again quite clear, and continually in his topsy-turvy "handy-dandy" manner the Fool returns to describe Lear's action in relieving himself of power as a symbolic stripping: "when thou gavest them [the daughters] the rod and put'st down thine own breeches" (I.iv.164–165). Even the arrival of the frowning Goneril is perceived by Lear in sartorial terms: "What makes that frontlet on?" (I.iv.80), an expression that is indeed worn, a mask for the occasion.

The Fool also continually harps on Lear's giving away of his golden crown, an action which should surely recall the discoronation of Richard II and his recognition that he himself is "nothing." So too the Fool notes that Lear is merely a cipher

> . . . an O without a figure.
> I am no better than thou art now: I am a fool,
> Thou art nothing.
>
> (I.iv.183–185)

Lear is but the shadow of the king without the substance of rule, as he speedily discovers on hearing the ultimatum that he must divest himself of half the trappings of his erstwhile power. The snail and the oyster have houses, but not Lear, a reference not only to the cuckold's horns and dishonest daughters, but also to the fate of Christ himself: "Foxes have holes, and birds of the air have nests; but the Son of man hath not where to lay his head" (Luke 9:58).[1] Such is the loneliness of the human condition.

Even insults are based on dress. Kent's verbal assault on Oswald's gentility calls him a

> . . . three-suited, hundred pound worsted-stocking knave; a . . . glass-gazing, superserviceable finical rogue; one-trunk-inheriting slave.
>
> (II.ii.14–17)

Three suits was the wardrobe generally provided for serving men,[2] while worsted stockings were the sumptuary requirement of the lower classes [Cf. Malvolio's yellow, cross-gartered hose in *Twelfth Night*, the uniform of a yeoman].[3] The sum of one hundred pounds was the minimum standard for the upkeep of gentility, and a single trunk of inherited effects is sufficient insult to Oswald's parentage. He is repeatedly referred to as a knave, a member of the lowest class, and what is worse a knave with pretensions, a narcissistic, mirror-gazing fop, a "cullionly barbermonger," a low-class frequenter of barbershops, the figure of vanity, a man made by a tailor and that badly (II.ii.51–55), a gentleman in appearance only, one who wears the sword to indicate knightly rank, but lacks the honesty attendant upon it. His status is similar to that of Andrew Aguecheek in *Twelfth Night* "dubbed with unhatched rapier and on carpet consideration" (*TN*, III.iv.220–221), one of those knights made so easily and thoughtlessly by King James I after his succession. As Sir Thomas Smith had complained as early as 1585, "as for gentlemen, they be made good cheape in England."[4] Appearance is Oswald's only claim to gentility, and stripped of that he is nothing but a knave, an overdressed puppet, as useless as the letter "Z."

Throughout the play Shakespeare emphasizes matters of clothing and appearance, continually dramatizing the stripping away of King Lear's power in this way, and finally showing the literal removal of his very raiment. After his voluntary divesture of power in Act I, Goneril symbolically strips him of fifty knights; and in II.iv the enraged and powerless monarch goes to Regan, where in a confrontation with both daughters his train of followers is whittled away to twenty-five, ten, five, and finally to the ultimate: "What need one?" (II.iv.258). Lear is now involuntarily divested of all symbols of his former power and is lowered to the status of a beggar-knave, for he is a knight who can no longer support his gentility, and hence would be degraded from any order of knighthood.[5] As Lear in his anguish points out, mere human existence requires very little, but civilization requires more than basic needs. He wants desperately to hold on to the ideals of gentility and civilization which he again expresses in terms of clothing:

> Allow not nature more than nature needs
> Man's life is cheap as beast's. Thou art a lady:
> If only to go warm were gorgeous.
> Why nature needs not what thou gorgeous wear'st,
> Which scarcely keeps thee warm.
>   (II.iv.261–265)

Without some of the outward trappings of wealth to signify the advances made by mankind, one is indeed reeling back to bestiality. That Lear seems to understand this possibility becomes clear through his continual reference to possible madness, to indicate both a fear of becoming representative of the lowest knave in Stuart society—a Bedlam beggar—and also the terror of being stripped of his reason, the one human attribute that distinguishes mankind from the beast.

The climactic scenes on the heath in Act III show the literal degradation, the stripping off of Lear's noble attributes, and those scenes are also an orchestration of madness: the professional sage-fool who speaks truth in his semidivine madness; the dismissed and disguised Edgar, with his mask of madness, and the despised, deeply hurt, and grief-maddened Lear. Each is also an outcast from society: the Fool who is the butt of laughter, Edgar who has voluntarily taken on the guise of a bedlam knave as protection now that he has been stripped of his birthright, and King Lear who in his madness begins to comprehend the horror of his degraded condition. He finds a community of misfortune there on the heath as he moves from angry defiance, to compassion, and finally to acceptance of his fate in three well-defined stages. First, in his curses against the elements (III.ii.), he shows himself as self-centered man, kicking against the goad. Then in III.iv, he strips away futile rage to find pity in his heart for other "poor naked wretches," though he does not yet include himself among their number. Only with the arrival of the almost naked Edgar does Lear perceive what he has become—nothing more than a knave, in fact even less than that—an animal.

Until this time Lear has in fact followed the example of Richard II (*RII*, IV.v). He has given away his crown; he has also voluntarily renounced the exercise of monarchical power, but he has not renounced "the pride of kingly sway." This he now does in the literal stripping off of his clothes. Then in his movement from defiance to despairing insanity he denies all aspects of civilization and addresses Edgar:

> Is man no more than this? Consider him well. Thou ow'st the worm no silk, the beast no hide, the sheep no wool, the cat no perfume. Ha! here's three on's are sophisticated. Thou art the thing itself; unaccommodated man is no more but such a poor, bare, forked animal as thou art. Off, off, you lendings. Come; unbutton here.
>
> (III.iv.97–103)

The Arden Editor, Kenneth Muir, here draws attention to parallel passages from Florio's translation of Montaigne:

> Truely, when I consider man all naked . . . I finde we have much more reason to hide and cover our nakedness than any creature else. We may be excused for borrowing those which nature had therein favored more than us . . . and under their spoiles of wool, of haire, of feathers, and of silke, to shroude us . . . . man is the onely forsaken and out-cast creature, naked on the bare earth . . . having nothing to cover and arme himselfe withall but the spoile of others; whereas Nature had clad and mantled all other creatures, some with huskes . . . with wooll, . . . with hides . . . and with silke . . . : whereas man only (Oh silly wretched man) can neither goe, nor speak, nor shift, nor feed himselfe, unlesse it be to whine and weepe onely, except he be taught.[6]

Here indeed is a pessimistic attitude toward humankind, and iconographically we have the notion of a ritual "stripping off of layers of appearance to arrive at the bare truth."[7] But at the same time it is a purgation, one that carries with it "a possibility of redemption,"[8] for at least Lear has, possibly for the first time, felt compassion—and that for one of the lowest of humanity—a Fool.

The primary instrument of that redemption is Edgar, and then Cordelia. But the important thing to note is that Edgar himself has also been symbolically stripped of his birthright; and by adopting the guise of naked madman, he has himself become almost literally nothing in the eyes of society. Both Edgar and Lear must symbolically "reclothe" themselves in the garments of their virtuous nobility, and their movement toward redemption, reconciliation, justification, what you will, is symbolically shown through their reinvestiture—their return to the society of human beings, in the spiritual and literal clothing of their rank.

Lear's compassion for the Fool begins his journey, which he continues through an act of purgative existential justice, working out his rage by trying his daughters. So far deluded is he that in an "inverted rite" of justice he sees the madman as judge, the Fool his "companion in equity," a joint stool as a daughter, and Persian magnificence and philosophy in Bedlam rags. At this point in the play the Fool disappears, and though on a human level one may wish to know his fate, he is in fact now superfluous. Lear has now become the Fool; he has himself lost his wits; he is "degraded to the status of the meanest of his servants,"[9] and represents "an amazingly daring version of the culminating moment of the sottie: the great reversal when the highest dignitaries appear as fools, and the world, or even Holy Church herself is revealed in cap and bells."[10] However, in his fleeting act of compassion for the faithful motley, Lear reveals his new appreciation of the community of human suffering, a recognition wherein lies the seed of hope, of reconciliation, acceptance, and redemptive love.

However, there is another character who is also symbolically stripped and finally brought to enlightenment, and that is Gloucester who must lose his eyes before he can be taught by Edgar to see with the eye of the spirit and be reconciled to his part in the community of human frailty and suffering. But Edgar's redemptive influence has already been felt by Gloucester, though the newly blinded father does not articulate this fact until he again meets his "Bedlam" son but cannot physically see him. Gloucester then recalls

> I'th' last night's storm I such a fellow saw
> Which made me think a man a worm. My son
> Came then into my mind, and yet my mind
> Was then scarce friends with him. I have heard more since.
>   (IV.i.32–35)

Like Lear, Gloucester has reacted to his initial confrontation with naked, uncivilized man by judging all humanity as animalistic, nothing more than the evaluation given by Job in his despair: "How much less man, that is a worm and the son of man, which is a worm."[11] But also like Lear, Gloucester has begun to learn compassion as he now sees with the eye of the spirit, and he gives money to the Bedlam. Out of his total wretchedness has come something new as he puts on the spiritual vesture of charity, recognizing for the first time the community of human suffering. As Lear perceives his own physical chill and appreciates the mutual physical suffering of the Fool, so Gloucester, repenting of the wrong he has done to Edgar, performs an act of disinterested charity.

After being stripped of material things, the sufferers, in their physical nakedness, which also signifies a spiritual nakedness, attempt to cover themselves with a new, intangible vesture—that of charity. This is similar to the instructions given by Paul in Ephesians 4:24: "And that ye put on the new man, which after God is created in righteousness and true holiness." And again, advice is given which should lead both to a Stoic-Christian resignation: "Let all bitterness and wrath, and anger, and clamor, and evil speaking, be put away from you, with all malice. And be ye kind to one another, tender-hearted, forgiving one another, even as God for Christ's sake hath forgiven you" (Ephesians 4:31–32). Then at Dover Cliff (IV.vi) through an existential experience, Edgar brings his father to an acceptance of his fate in Stoic-Christian resignation to affliction so that he can go on living.

Similarly, Edgar must work out his own salvation, fighting his way from his "Bedlam" nothingness and nakedness back to nobility, which in his case is symbolized by his regaining the right to wear his own coat-armor, a right he earns only after killing Oswald in defense of his father, and again after a *combat à l'outrance* in which he proves his honour by virtuous deeds, defeating the bastard brother who has usurped his title. Thus Edgar receives the reward of earthly justice. W. R. Elton clearly perceives this redemptive quality of Edgar:

> Outwardly he regains his name with his defeat of Edmund, and inwardly, at length, with his descent into feeling. His season in hell begins at the lowest human level, madman and beggar. . . . Edgar conducts erring humanity through the conquest of its despair. In his suffering ascent, Lear's godson, ultimately an inheritor of the kingdom, rises from madman and beggar, retrospectively servant, to rustic countryman, messenger, and armed knight."[12]

And each of these steps is marked by costume changes which reach their peak when he regains the right to his own "blazon of gentrie," his personal banner which is the outward sign of inward nobility, ratified by noble and virtuous deeds. But at the same time, he shows that he wears the inward "blazon" of virtue as he exchanges charitable forgiveness with his half-brother in an act which brings even Edmund to attempt to do good "Despite of mine own nature" (V.iii. 244).

Lear too comes to advance in charity, after his own time in "hell." It is significant that as the "new man" he moves from a literal, earthly crown to the possibility of a spiritual one. Before his appearance in IV.vi, we are told that he is quite mad, crowned with "idle weeds that grow / In our sustaining corn" (IV.iv. 5–6). But even these weeds present the possibility of change, hint at the possibility of development: fumiter, darnel, hemlock, and cuckoo-flowers all have medicinal and narcotic powers, especially the last, the cuckoo-flower. This, identified sometimes with the Bedlam cowslip and with *Cardamine pratensis* would seem fitting, especially since the *Cardamine* "was used by the Greeks and Romans for almost all affections of the head, and according to Farren was used as late as the last century as a remedy for convulsions, epilepsy, and other diseases of the brain."[13] The pathetically crowned Lear reappears, clothed this time, still filled with disgust for humanity, but this time only for women. His comment on the appearance of virtue and its lecherous actuality recalls Hamlet's jigging, ambling, lisping prostitute, with outward innocence covering total corruption:

> . . . Behold yond simp'ring dame,
> Whose face between her forks presages snow.
> That minces virtue, and does shake the head
> To hear of pleasure's name;
> The fitchew nor the soiled horse goes to it
> With a more riotous appetite.
> Down from the waist they are all Centaurs,
> Though women all above.
> But to the girdle do the gods inherit,
> Beneath is all the fiend's.
> (IV.vi. 117–126)

This speech signifies the moral advance that Lear has yet to make towards his ultimate redemption. He must learn that humankind should not be judged solely by its evil examples; he perceives all too clearly the community of human sin, evil, and wrongdoing—all dressed in virtuous appearance. He needs to discover, particularly in the case of Cordelia, the true heart beneath the un-compromising exterior. And, once again the imagery is that of dress:

> Through tattered clothes small vices to appear
> Robes and furred gowns hide all. Plate sin with gold,
> And the strong lance of justice breaks;
> Arm it in rags, a pygmy's straw does pierce it.
> (IV.vi.161–164)

The matter of dress even receives specific reference in the scene of Lear's reconciliation with Cordelia, for "In the the heaviness of sleep / We put fresh garments on him" (IV.vii.21–22). And these garments are more than literally fresh material garments. They are also the garment of the spirit. Lear is rested; he has come from hell, his dark night of the soul; he has emerged from the naked abyss and has come through torture to "bliss" in the presence of Cordelia, who has also operated (like Edgar) as a redemptive influence on him. He kneels before her in a gesture that recalls his kneeling to Goneril in Act II, but this time there is no irony. Lear, as if in a trance, looks on his daughter to confuse his fault with humility and receive the charity of her forgiveness.

At this point Lear has achieved a spiritual freedom, and he has thus gone beyond physical discomfort so that prison has for him neither bars for the body nor fetters for the spirit. Having in effect renounced the world, put off his old garments, he can now rejoice in newfound love and charity. Like Richard II in prison, he finds a certain freedom in resignation when he has lost everything that is material. But such happiness is short-lived, as the world again intrudes upon Lear, and his mind returns to the heath. Once again, Lear is bereft: Cordelia, his "poor fool" is hanged, and the distraught father, perhaps confus-ing and conflating the Fool with his errant daughter, echoes himself on the heath with "Pray you, undo this button." This action seems hardly to indicate Lear's "sense of suffocation"[14] but rather a recollection of the despair on the heath, a remembrance of the naked horror of human existence where he saw man as "worm," and now he asks the question, "Why should a dog, a horse, a rat have life and thou no life at all?" (V.iii.307–308). But then, perhaps perceiv-ing a momentary sign of life upon Cordelia's face, he follows Gloucester, his echo-character, whose fate has continually reinforced Lear's own:

> . . . His flawed heart—
> Alack too weak the conflict to support—
> 'Twixt two extremes of passion, joy and grief,

Burst smilingly.

(V.iii.197–199)

So both Lear and Cordelia, reconciled to each other, leave life together. It is pointless to discuss the possibilities of salvation or damnation for such characters; what is important is to realize that they have gone beyond the outward trappings of human existence. They have understood the physical nakedness of humanity, and they have demonstrated that true love and charity, which exist only in the spirit, are the philosophical heart of human existence. They also demonstrate, like Job, that one comes into the world naked and leaves materially naked, taking only the vesture of charity, forgiveness, and virtue. Perceived in this manner, the play of *King Lear* takes on the universal character of the old morality of *Everyman* and teaches the individual human being where his priorities should lie.

Timon *of Athens* has frequently been noted as having similarities in attitude and even imagery with *King Lear*[15] and certainly the theme of the good man who mistakes appearance for reality pervades both plays. Similarly there is also the theme of aberrant love, or love imperfectly understood. *King Lear* reveals a misunderstanding of the nature of affection, though by the end of the play Lear has developed a recognition of it; but in *Timon of Athens* the theme of love is treated with the utmost bleakness, and the play asks a shocking and appalling question, how does a man live without love? And further, what leads Timon to a complete denial of all the redemptive aspects of human love? Only in the case of the steward, Flavius, is there a love that is honest, free, and generous, totally devoid of self-interest. All other "love" is perverted and degraded. But Flavius's candle is a very tiny one to illuminate a wicked world, and hence Timon's life degenerates into misanthropy, despair, and finally suicide.

To some extent, then, the conflict of *Timon of Athens* presents *King Lear* in reverse. As Lear voluntarily divested himself of power, so Timon willingly denudes himself of his possessions; but when he is left naked by his erstwhile friends, he does not pass through the same stages of spiritual redemption as Lear. However, as H. J. Oliver points out, it is not quite true to say that "where Lear is redeemed by suffering, Timon goes unchanged to his grave."[16] Instead, the play shows "a swift unwrapping of fold on fold of life's significances—civilized man, beasts, the earth, the objective universe itself, until we reach the core of pure and naked significance, undistorted by any symbol, in the nothingness of death."[17] In effect, then, Timon has reached a stage of total contempt of the world, without the hope of eternity attendant upon it in the Judaeo-Christian tradition.

The play itself is based on the overarching action of the stripping away of all aspects of civilization until the hero reaches the state of total nothingness—the result of such voluntary total annihilation being suicide. The contrast between the civilized magnificence at the beginning of the play and the lonely tombstone at the end is indeed total, and a study of this relentless diminishment is most revealing. At the play's opening, Timon displays limitless generosity to all, but his munificence is in fact flawed: It is really *cupiditas*, egocentric eros, self-satisfaction, almost a selfishness, an excess of liberality, a blind prodigality that actually panders to the avarice endemic in Athens. Timon himself also displays a curious kind of greed—for he delights in receiving not monetary or material recompense, but the intangible payment of flattery. He even refuses from Ventidius "the one proffered *exchange* of friendship and mutual honourableness, which he talks so much of."[18] His vaunted generosity is thus so self-centered that he cannot in his inverted selfishness permit competition in the giving of gifts. There is even a touch of snobbery in him:

> Honest Ventidius, You mistake my love:
> I gave it freely ever; and there's none
> Can truly say he gives, if he receives.
> If our betters play that game, we must not dare
> To imitate them; faults that are rich are fair.
> (I.ii.9–13)

The opening of the play shows also the trappings of the civilized world. Poet, painter, jeweler, and merchant all represent the prosperity and the glory of civilization: man's greatest rational achievement which has raised him far above the level of the beasts. The extraordinary splendor of the scene is almost a masque of magnificence, but even at this point, so early in the play, there is a foreshadowing of disaster in the references to fickle Fortune made by the Poet and the Painter, artists who are expected to have the ability to see beneath appearance:

> Poet   When Fortune in her shift and change of mood
> Spurns down her late beloved, all his dependants,
> Which labored after him to the mountain's top
> Even on their hands and knees, let him slip down,
> Not one accompanying his declining foot.
> Painter 'Tis common.
> A thousand moral paintings I can show
> That shall demonstrate these quick blows of Fortune's

> More pregnantly than words. Yet you do well
> To show Lord Timon that mean eyes have seen
> The foot above the head.
>
> (I.i.84–94)

This warning is continued and reinforced by the satiric railing of the cynic, Apemantus. Where Timon is the universal lover, Apemantus is the spirit of universal hate. But nonetheless he has some justice in his pose: he has perceived the heart of the timeserver beneath the fawning exterior. And here the notion of outward appearance commences its development. As Lear was unable to perceive the difference between flattery and true love, so too Timon. The scales must be removed from his eyes, something that occurs only when Timon is so stripped of distractions that he can contemplate mankind in his worst state as well as his best. Timon's generosity is skillfully counterpointed, and even undercut, by Apemantus's cursing, and his sacrificial image of predatory mankind comes with frightening bitterness into the midst of the celebration:

> O you gods, what a number of men eats Timon, and he sees 'em not! It grieves me to see so many dip their meat in one man's blood; and all the madness is, he cheers them up too. I wonder men dare trust themselves with man. Methinks they should invite them without knives: Good for their meat, and safer for their lives.
>
> (I.ii.37–43)

The parallel with the Last Supper is here noteworthy, for at this point Timon indeed seems like a savior figure, only later to become almost an antichrist in his denial of charity.

As the magnificent feast continues with Timon showering gifts upon all, his generosity is seen to be defective. Timon is not the example of the Aristotelian magnanimous man, and he is not practicing liberality, but its excess—prodigality. Here iconography helps to define the difference and indicate the error of Timon's conduct. Cesare Ripa shows Liberality as a woman of virtuous dress, an eagle on her head, and holding two cornucopiae, one of which is inverted, pouring forth precious stones and coins, while the other is upright and full of fruits. In addition, she holds a pair of compasses to signify measure in the giving of gifts, while the two cornucopiae show that simple and costly gifts are equally worthy; the eagle signifies unselfishness, for it hunts for others as well as for itself. Prodigality, on the other hand, is shown as a woman with eyes blinded by a veil who pours precious objects from single cornucopia. The gifts too are those of monetary worth, a situation which also indicates a reckless kind of moral blindness—an inability to perceive true values, a devotion to excess.[19] Prodigality has no measure, no sense of justice, and Timon exhibits this failure in his refusal to admit reciprocity, an attitude which also exhibits contempt and pride, as if no gifts are worthy unless given by the self. Like the veiled woman figure, Timon is blind to the moral consequences of his giving—as being the lover of himself rather than of others.

The problem with this play is to some extent the lack of motivation offered for Timon's extraordinary behavior at the beginning. Are we to assume with Harold Wilson that Timon is "a lofty if impractical idealist who believes that the practice of virtue lies in giving, and who is innocent enough to suppose that other men share his feelings and his aims, who is blind to self-interest because he has little or none of it himself?"[20] If so, a kind of innocence is the cause of Timon's abrupt swing to misanthropy, but such an explanation tends to diminish Timon's misanthropy into mere pique, while the suggestion that from the beginning of the play he is subtly defective in understanding the art of love can also explain why this inherently great man turns to misanthropy and then despair. Practical Athenians, like the Senator, perceive Timon as an innocent dupe, but they underestimate him, seeing only the folly rather than the potential for disaster.

The motif of divesture starts in Act II, and continues throughout the next as well, in the continuous refusal of Timon's erstwhile friends to help him out of his financial embarrassment. Timon tests his definition of virtue as generosity on his friends and finds them wanting in a manner similar to that of *Everyman* who discovers that all fellowship and earthly advantage are useless when the individual comes to face death. But things are even worse for Timon, for even Good Deeds, personified first by Timon and then by Flavius, seems powerless. Thus Timon is stripped of his worldly goods, but it is also a symbolic unclothing of ideals, accomplished indirectly. And it is important to note the order in which Timon's fall is rehearsed. The first to leave is the Senator, a man of politic, predatory qualities, as is well shown in his legalistic distinction between his desire to recoup his investments and his alleged respect for Timon. Shakespeare next strips Timon of all his friends, dissecting them and their motives with almost clinical precision by examining the nature and quality of their refusals—from Lucullus's shock at being asked for a loan when he had expected a gift, through Lucius's transparent excuse of a temporary cash shortage and Sempronius's feigned outrage at being left until last. But what about Ventidius whom Timon had had released from prison, and whose repayment he had then refused? Shakespeare throws this last act of disloyalty away in mere report: perhaps there have been enough refusals, and to some extent Timon had deserved such an answer in retaliation for his own brusque rejection of thanks. Significantly, only his servants show any sympathy for Timon, while his equals and friends treat him like a dog. They who have formerly "eaten" Timon in wealth will now devour him in poverty. This contrast, carefully emphasized by Shakespeare, contributes to an understanding of the essential nobility of Timon, in contradistinction to the proverb that "no man is a hero to his valet," and to quote Jane Austen's Elizabeth Bennet,. "What praise is more valuable than the praise of an excellent servant."[21] Timon, however, unaware of, and later unwilling to admit, the existence of goodness in his world remade by hate, commences to rail against his false friends as he then prepares another feast.

This banquet is the first bitter jest of the erstwhile wealthy man, and it is notably different from its sources where stones painted like artichokes were served. It is also deliberately arranged as a banquet of moderation, in contrast to the banquet of magnificent excess in Act I.[22] The echo-situation is made very specific in Timon's grace, which parallels Apemantus's bitter blessing in Act I, ending with a consigning of the guests to bestiality: "Uncover, dogs, and lap" (III.vi.83). There is, however, one most significant difference between the two railing blessings: where Apemantus adopted an intellectual, almost superior pose, Timon is angry, brutal, personal, and emotionally involved. His rage extends to the whole of humanity: all men are villains, all women whores, and self-interest is the only god. In Shakespeare's addition to the sources, Timon then throws water in the faces of his guests in an action which washes their flatteries from their faces, and administers a symbolic ritual of baptism into a new faith, a new identity.

However, this action is also one of casting out, of degradation, of contempt, for it is analogous to the last quasi-baptismal act in the formal degradation of a knight from the order of knighthood. It should be recalled that when a knight was to be cast out of the order of knighthood, there had to be sufficient reason—usually treason, flying from battle, or perhaps baseness of blood and behavior, even insufficient money to uphold gentility. Here, in this ironic baptism, Timon as the leader of a magnanimous order rechristens his former friends into new identities of "miscreant and false traitor."[23] Thus in his railing at them he baptizes them anew as

> Most smiling, smooth, detested parasites,
> Courteous destroyers, affable wolves, meek
>   bears,

You fools of fortune, trencher-friends, time's
flies,
Cap-and-knee slaves, vapors and minute-jacks.
(III.vi.91–94)

The ephemerality of the steam which arises from the warm water signifies the worthlessness of the friends, and Timon in this speech spews forth a progression of degrading epithets, beginning with degenerate human estate, continuing through animals whose traditional attributes are perverted, to slaves of flattery, evanescent steam, and finally mindless time-markers, mechanical knaves controlled by others, an image that recalls the imprisoned Richard II who identifies himself as Bolingbroke's "Jack of the clock" (*RII*, V.v.60). These friends, like traitorous knights, have been unfaithful to their order—that of friendship and humanity—and are now considered by Timon as knaves, worse than animals, unworthy of all human consideration. He then also renounces humankind, removing himself from all society in a despairing farewell soliloquy of invective that is given form by a carefully orchestrated ritual of inversion and denial of all civilized human values:

. . . Piety and fear,
Religion to the gods, peace, justice, truth,
Domestic night-awe, night-rest and neighborhood,
Instruction, manners, mysteries and trades,
Degrees, observances, customs and laws,
Decline to your confounding contraries
And let confusion live!
. . . .
Timon will to the woods, where he shall find
Th'unkindest beast more kinder than mankind.
(IV.i.15–36)

Like Lear, Timon is reduced to the utter nakedness of the lowest quality of existence, and in his invective he excoriates all mankind. The barest of human needs is all that Timon wants, as he digs for roots like an animal, but ironically finds instead that symbol of man's corruption—gold. His reaction to that discovery does, however, indicate some change in Timon's attitude. Whereas earlier he might have settled for gold and returned to Athenian society once again to distribute largesse, after paying his debts, now he perceives the evil that wealth represents. He knows the corruptive force of gold, and he will therefore use it in an attempt to punish corrupt and venal humanity by working through its weaknesses. Far from learning charity, Timon in his suffering offers the opposite solution, that of hate, and this relentless stripping away of all moral and spiritual human advancement leaves Timon at his most appallingly naked. Here, for the only time in Shakespeare, is a play which strips humanity beyond even its animal essentials. Even where there is charity, in the case of the Steward, Timon steadfastly refuses to recognize it as other than an aberration.

Hatred, the obverse of idealism, has now become for him a philosophical stance, as well as a way of existence. This is shrewdly demonstrated in his altercation with Apemantus in which Timon asserts that he now has the *means* to return to Athens, but his *voluntary choice* is otherwise. He will remain, renouncing even the society of beasts, for they too are as predatory as human beings. This attitude is further clarified in Timon's comparison of himself to a winter tree, denuded of its leaves, for he now puts himself even lower in the great chain of being than animals. Where before he gave gifts to gratify his friends, now he gives gold only to those who will swear to use it to corrupt and pervert Athens to bring it to destruction. Ironically his gift helps to reform a bandit; but the poet and painter, symbolically the prophets and artistic conscience of society, are easily corrupted. Alcibiades, however, though formerly accused as a traitor, is more flexible than Timon and can find in himself the ability to bring about the salvation of Athens.

For such an uncompromising spirit as Timon, there can be only one solution, since the company of neither man nor beast is acceptable to him.[24] He must leave the world. He has come to this nihilistic conclusion in the center of his own private hell. Unlike Lear, who achieves a freedom of spirit such that even a prison is acceptable to him, the loveless Timon chooses to continue in naked misanthropy, turning away all proffers of friendship. He perceives the entire universe as totally abhorrent and refuses any invitations to reenter the society of the world. Thus for him annihilation is the only solution, especially after he has turned away Flavius, the only truly charitable figure of the play. Timon has made what is for him a totally logical, and therefore courageous choice. Since he cannot believe in any goodness, human or animal, death is the only solution. Timon's suicide is also an ultimate act of total defiance, because he has no hope of any life beyond that of the present. Such an answer to the problem of human existence is one which most of us are unable to accept, and therefore we tend to concentrate on Flavius and even Alcibiades as a means of avoiding the question Timon's act raises. Timon, the uncompromising idealist, tries to divest himself of all corrupting influences and discovers that he is totally alone. He has refused to accept or tolerate the limitations of humanity, and his tragedy is that a man of such noble potential can find no answer to the problem of the human condition except to strip himself of his last human attribute—his life.

There is nothing particularly new in drawing attention to clothing as a continuing image in *Macbeth*,[25] but a close examination of the uses to which this image is put is nonetheless revealing. The picture of Macbeth dressed in clothing that neither fits nor becomes him is used almost exclusively by his enemies and becomes more notable as Macbeth's tyranny increases. Similarly, Macbeth's use of the image of "borrowed robes" is an index of his own moral state throughout the play—from his initial astonishment at his elevation to the title of Thane of Cawdor, to his final image of a posturing actor—one who always plays in the borrowed clothing of a role which is but the shadowy imitation of reality.

The first reference to clothing that does not quite fit comes after Ross's announcement of Macbeth's new title, Thane of Cawdor, an instant confirmation of the Weird Sisters' prophecy, and Banquo reinforces the image:

> New honors come upon him
> Like our strange garments, cleave not to their mould
> But with the aid of use.
>
> (I.iii.144–146)

This image, more subtle than Macbeth's "Why do you dress me in these borrowed robes?" (I.iii.109) indicates the virtuous clarity of Banquo's vision, while at the same time Macbeth's use of the same motif indicates his own moral stance. He may already have been tempted, but he has not yet fallen. The same kind of imagery also occurs early in the plotting against Duncan when both the Macbeths, though almost committed to the crime are as yet guilty only in thought, not deed:

> *Macbeth* He hath honored me of late, and I have bought
> Golden opinions from all sorts of people,
> Which would be worn now in their newest gloss,
> Not cast aside so soon.
> *Lady* Was the hope drunk
> Wherein you dressed yourself? Hath it slept since?
>
> (I.vii.32–36)

She, at this point more committed to evil than her husband, takes up the image contemptuously, almost parodically—an indication of the state of her own soul—as she continues to taunt him with cowardice in refusing to go after the crown, "the ornament of life," the outward symbol of kingship. The clothing imagery is curiously revived in Macbeth's panicky and overwrought speech on the death of Duncan, an outburst which threatens to reveal all as he comes to " . . . their daggers unmannerly breecheed with gore" (II.iii.11–112). It takes Lady Macbeth's fainting, whether by accident or design, to create a diversion.

Banquo's comment as the lady is carried out further signifies his moral probity as he speaks of the distinction between appearance and reality, hinting at his own suspicions:

> And when we have our naked frailties hid,
> That suffer in exposure, let us meet
> And question this most bloody piece of work
> To know it further. . . .
>
> (II.iii.122–125)

But Macbeth's reply, in a similar image, has a different subtext. "Let's brief-ly put on manly readiness" (II.iii.130) seems to mean more than merely male attire, instead of a nightshirt, but rather a mask of courage or boldness, as distinct from his just concluded display of *un*readiness. Clothing is now appearance for Macbeth, covering the naked truth of his crime. Macduff also uses a clothing metaphor to signify the unfitness of Macbeth for rule when he bids farewell to Ross as all Duncan's loyal lords prepare to leave: "Adieu, / Lest our old robes sit easier than our new" (II.iv.38–39). He cannot ex-change old robes or habits of loyalty with any ease, without serious qualms of conscience. As usual, it is an enemy of Macbeth and a man of virtue who employs the image.

Macbeth himself returns to the use of clothing in his next notable speech of guilt and self-doubt as he realizes that his crime has brought him but "a fruitless crown" and "a barren sceptre." And again, after the plot against Banquo gets under way; the notion of appearance masquerading as truth takes over, as Macbeth and his lady will make "our faces vizards to our hearts dis-guising what they are" (III.i.34–35). But with his return to the Weird Sisters, Macbeth, now wholly committed to evil, concerns himself only with the literal attributes of rule as they are paraded before him in appearance: crowns, scep-tres, and even "twofold balls and treble sceptres" (IV.i.121).

With the fifth act, clothing metaphors become more and more note-worthy, put as they are most particularly into the mouths of Macbeth's en-emies who divide them into two differing approaches: one of inability to con-fine within limits, and the other its opposite, a dwarf in giant's garments.

Thus Caithness notes of Macbeth that

> He cannot buckle his distempered cause
> Within the belt of rule.
>
> (V.ii.15–16)

Angus, on the other hand, characterizes his situation:

> . . . Now does he feel his title
> Hang loose about him, like a giant's robe
> Upon a dwarfish thief.
>
> (V.ii.20–22)

The deliberate grotesquerie of clothing of the wrong size, whether too small or too large, clearly indicates Macbeth's unfitness for the position he holds, dressed, as he metaphorically is, either in clothes which his spirit is too meager to fill, or conversely, in clothes which are too small to contain the vastness of his vices.

Finally, Macbeth himself in his moment of recognition, his discovery of the futility of his cause, resorts to an image that implicitly recalls that of borrowed clothes, of role-playing, in his most famous speech:

> Life's but a walking shadow, a poor player
> That struts and frets his hour upon the stage
> And then is heard no more.
>
> (V.i.24–26)

And such has been Macbeth's kingship—the rule of an actor, dressed in borrowed robes, playing a role, a series of acts without real legitimacy, a shadow, the appearance without the substance. Macbeth then degrades himself even further in his self-knowledge, pointing out that his life is the equivalent to that of a despised fool, and his achievements offer the same significance as an idiot's tale. Significantly, Macbeth uses this implicit clothing image only in his moment of moral discovery, a time in which he returns to a state analogous to that of his tempted virtue in the first act. And thus he goes out to play his final role, dressed in the armor of a warrior, seeking the appearance of an honorable death with a courage born of despair.[26]

Clothing is also used metaphorically as well as literally in the last of Shakespeare's history plays, *Henry VIII*, and in a manner that recalls the earlier *Richard II*. The contrast between human success, communicated by magnificence in dress and pageantry is contrasted with poverty of appearance and richness in spiritual vesture, while the opposition of earthly and heavenly crowns clearly indicates the force of moral virtue.

Structurally the play is a series of falls and rises, and all are signified by descriptive references to riches and titles. The opening act is full of reported magnificence at the Field of the Cloth of Gold and of power shrewdly exercised. Ceremony is all important, and so is appearance: English "men have broke their backs with laying manors on them" (I.i.84); and the French

> All clinquant all in gold, like heathen gods
> Shone down the English; and tomorrow they
> Made Britain India: every man that stood
> Show'd like a mine. . . .
>   (I.i.18–21)

Pageantry helps to give form to the play, but it is also clearly undercut by the comments of the "walking gentlemen" who play the part of the citizens in earlier history plays. Extreme fashions mask sickness, both physical and moral, imported (with typical English chauvinism) from France. The second scene of the play contrasts rather soberly with the first appearance of Wolsey in ceremonial robes, as Katherine and Henry are seen dispensing justice, while Wolsey represents pride of office. In his next scene, the Cardinal is shown as providing entertainment and offering largesse. But he accidentally initiates his own downfall by being the occasion of the unhistorical appearance of Anne Bullen, fittingly displayed in terms of earthly glory, merriment, and magnificence.[27]

Ritual also has a role, and it is sometimes used to undercut pageantry, as in the immediately following scene where Wolsey's party is contrasted with Buckingham's departure for execution, the axe-blade turned toward him. Here too, for the first time, we have what comes to be an important feature of this play: the brilliantly honest speeches of all those who have fallen from high estate. Divested of their pomp and power they, like Buckingham, are "richer than . . . [their] base accusers" (II.i.104). They are now nothing more than human beings, representative of *humanum genus*, who must learn to die well, giving moral advice to their hearers, urging them to place their trust in God rather than in friendship, human beings, or in kingship. Trials, then, are also frequent throughout the play—five in all, and though justice is not always done, those who lose all in an earthly sense nonetheless gain the moral victory.

As well as being constructed around a series of dramatic and ritualistic courtroom situations, the play, in its contrasting falls and rises has specific contrasts of character: Katherine and Anne, Wolsey and Cranmer, with the final unhistorical joy and prophecy of the glory of the future Queen Elizabeth. Shakespeare shows Anne as the creature of magnificence, of pageant, of fertility, of new honors and titles, though she herself seems not to seek her own advancement in wealth or sovereignty. And as all these are loaded on to Anne, so correspondingly, Katherine is never shown in great worldly splendor, even in her first scene as queen when she thinks only of justice, in contrast to Wolsey. Throughout the play she is gradually divested of everything except her virtue, and she is shown as the instinctive practitioner of Christian charity, thinking always of the sorrows and difficulties of others.

The changing fortunes of both churchmen and women continue to contrast with each other. As Wolsey falls, so does Cranmer rise, and his simple virtue triumphs over his enemies, in contrast to Wolsey, whose pride is suitably punished. Wolsey is portrayed as the villain of the play who opposes the match with Anne in order to gratify his own pride—and at that moment he falls by carelessly leaving an inventory of his wealth, which is also an account of his peculations, for the king to peruse. Henry is ironic in his approach as he greets Wolsey with a compliment before revealing that his proud acquisitiveness and his desire to gain the Papacy have been discovered. But at his trial when he is divested of the great seal, of his wealth, and of his rank, Wolsey handles himself with eloquent dignity. He then starts to reveal the unexpected depth of his character as he exercises philosophical stoicism and Christian charity, avoiding vilification so that even his accusers are forced into reluctant respect and even forgiveness. Finally, he is forced to give up all his property and "to be out of the king's protection" (III.i.343–344). This statement means that he has lost both the immunity conferred by his office and benefit of clergy. He has been degraded, though not formally unfrocked, so that he is but a knave, and subject to the civil arm of the law for it to exercise its justice upon him.

In the depth of his disaster Wolsey perceives his fate as the common state of mankind. This too is his moment of recognition, like that of Richard II, of Lear, and to some extent, of Macbeth. In his self-discovery he calls himself "naked to mine enemies" but he has put on the garb of repentance:

> I know myself now, and feel within me
> A peace above all earthly dignities,
> A quiet conscience.
> (III.iii.378–380)

Similarly, he has also vested himself in solemn, yet effective eloquence, perceiving the futility of earthly things as he gives advice to Thomas Cromwell, the only person who remains by him. As Richard II in prison found only a groom, and Timon a steward, so Wolsey, to his own surprise, has found one servant who is not afraid to stand with him:

> Cromwell, I did not think to shed a tear
> In all my miseries; but thou hast forced me
> (Out of thy honest truth) to play the woman.
> (III.ii.428–430)

His parting advice to Cromwell runs counter to the way he has lived his life, but at the last moment he realizes that his wretched robe, a mere shift to cover his physical nakedness, and his spiritual integrity are all he has left to him, and his good deeds are all he can take with him to the grave:

> Had I but served my God with half the zeal
> I served my king, he would not in mine age
> Have left me naked to mine enemies.
> . . . .
> . . . Farewell
> The hopes of court; my hopes in heaven do dwell.
> (III.ii.455–460)

Once again there is a stripping away of earthly goods and the victim achieves moral enlightenment so that he dies spiritually at ease.

Wolsey's divesture is immediately contrasted with its opposite, a ritual of clothing, as Queen Anne passes over the stage in pageant on her way to her coronation, covered in jewels and surrounded by golden coronets. The Cardinal has learned the lesson of Ecclesiastes, "All is vanity," while Anne is on her way to accept her earthly crown accompanied with brilliant ceremonial and the press of happy crowds. The enthusiastic report of the new queen's progress surrounded by worldly pomp is immediately contrasted with Queen Katherine's final scene in her penurious manor of Kimbolton. Stripped of everything temporal and resigned to death she can now in charity forgive her old enemy, Wolsey. As she sleeps she is granted a heavenly vision in which she is granted a laurel crown, an eternal coronet in place of the earthly one which has been taken from her, and which Anne has achieved. Now, almost liberated from the "mortal vesture" of the body, she can hear celestial music.

After Katherine's death the play turns to the pains of life, as Anne suffers in childbirth, and Cranmer, the representative of the new religion, is persecuted by his enemies. Then the mood alters, and with the presentation of the infant Elizabeth, Cranmer prophesies the glory of the Elizabethan age; reconciliations abound and the play ends in the optimistic manner of the romances.

However, the dominant memory of the play belongs to those who have lost their earthly position. In Katherine's case, her fall from high estate exhibits the strength of her virtue. Wolsey, however, who trusted in his power, his possessions, pomp, and circumstance is brought to a realization that the things of this world are transitory and not to be trusted. In the totality of his loss he is brought to self-knowledge, repentance, and humility. Like the biblical camel, he no longer carries the baggage of wealth or possessions, and passes on his knees through the eye of the needle into the heavenly city. He rediscovers the moral integrity that Katherine had always possessed and he is now ready for death.

In each of the four plays discussed here, clothing, and particularly unclothing, form a clearly defined pattern of imagery. The major characters all undergo a process of reduction in which they lose everything they have cherished and in which they have put their faith. Then in the lowest circle of their private infernos each comes to a recognition, and perhaps an accommodation with the human condition. Edgar is the lone survivor and he has been taught by his suffering. Lear achieves a liberation of spirit in a world forsaken by the gods, and therefore no longer wishes to live. In a specifically Christian context, Wolsey leaves his office to devote himself to God and dies in the hope of eternal salvation, while Katherine dies certain of it. The two bleakest characters of all are Timon and Macbeth who conclude their lives nihilistically, the one dying by his own hand and the other seeking death at the hand of an opponent with the courage that is born of a similar despair. Katherine and Edgar excepted, all these characters have put their faith in false gods, expecting an earthly return on their investments in love or power, with the result that they are degraded from their high estate and lose everything that has mattered to them. But as "naked wretches" they are representatives of *humanum genus*. Their fate is common to us all and in their final realization of the basic impotence of humanity and the folly of pursuing earthly goods they become worthy of respect.

GENERAL CONCLUSION

Through these essays I have attempted to demonstrate the importance of understanding unexpected areas of the contemporary milieu in order to gain further comprehension of Shakespeare's dramatic text. My aim has been to indicate the manner in which the original audience perceived the plays in performance, and curiously this study also has taught me that the very timeliness of a play can also be timeless. Falconry, for instance, has undergone a revival, and its practices are better known; I have even found a student who tamed a wild bird under the tutelage of Bedouins in Israel. This revivified common knowledge even made it possible for the director of an Off-Broadway showcase production of *The Taming of the Shrew* (1977) to develop his entire production around this central image.

I have also tried to illuminate specific passages through study of their context. In this way formerly obscure passages can reveal new meanings, like Richard II and his "usurped" name (V.i.257), or the structural problems of *The Rape of Lucrece* can be explained. These essays also reveal Shakespeare's extraordinary sensitivity to "the woman question," but I do not give him revolutionary credentials as one who continually attacked the *status quo*, though he was a superb observer of it. His comedies and romances do indeed indicate his appreciation of women as teachers of love, as partners in marriage, and above all as friendly equals and companions. However, in the histories and tragedies the feminine characters revert to their more traditional subordinate role and become the victims of masculine power. Comedy remains woman's best friend, as George Meredith said, and his statement is particularly applicable to the comedies of Shakespeare.

What the playwright's *own* opinions were on a given topic are difficult to establish, given his dedication to the creation of viable characters. The comedies of courtship do indeed show a preference for the high-spirited and witty ladies, but after marriage the husband is *primus inter pares*. The partners may engage in the jousts of wit they enjoyed before marriage, but in public the wife submits, and each has a rigidly defined sphere of influence, with specific rights and duties toward the other. Above all, Shakespeare shows concern for the individual human beings he portrays, so that the fate of English kings and queens remains important for the modern audience which may care little for history. Thus his plays deal with the timeless troubles and triumphs of humanity, and even a loveless character like Timon generates some sympathy in his degradation. But even though Shakespeare wrote of the timeless rather than the merely topical, a study of the cultural assumptions and osmotic knowledge of Shakespeare's day leads one to a closer understanding of the play or the poem which was written to elicit a specific audience response. In this way we draw closer to a study of the dramatist in his workshop with renewed respect for the majesty of a mind which could seize so brilliantly on matters commonplace or esoteric, transmuting them through the philosopher's stone of his imagination into precious permanence.

NOTES

General Introduction

1. Lawrence Stone, *The Family, Sex and Marriage in England 1500–1800* (New York: Harper and Row, 1977); Irene G. Dash, *Wooing, Wedding, and Power: Women in Shakespeare's Plays* (New York: Columbia University Press, 1981); Coppélia Kahn, *Man's Estate: Masculine Identity in Shakespeare* (Berkeley and Los Angeles: University of California Press, 1981); Suzanne W. Hull, *Chaste, Silent, & Obedient: English Books About Women* (San Marino, Calif.: Huntington Library, 1982); Linda Woodbridge, *Women and the English Renaissance: Literature and the Nature of Womankind, 1540–1620* (Urbana and Chicago: University of Illinois Press, 1984); *The Woman's Part: Feminist Criticism of Shakespeare*, eds. Carolyn Ruth Swift Lenz, Gayle Greene, and Carol Thomas Neeley (Urbana: University of Illinois Press, 1980).

PART ONE

CHAPTER 1. Matrimonial Law and the Education of Lovers

A longer, more comprehensive study of this subject has already appeared in *Shakespeare Quarterly*, 30 (1979), 68–81, under the title "'As Marriage Binds, and Blood Breaks': English Marriage and Shakespeare." Material from this article is used by permission.

1. Mary Edmond, "In Search of John Webster," *Times Literary Supplement*, December 24, 1976, pp. 1621–22, convincingly identifies him with the carriage-building family of Smithfield, and Mark Eccles, "John Webster," *Times Literary Supplement*, January 21, 1977, p. 71, recalls the existence of a John Webster who entered the Middle Temple in 1598 from New Inn. This may be the playwright.

2. W. Nicholas Knight, *Shakespeare's Hidden Life: Shakespeare at the Law 1585–1595* (New York: Mason and Lipscomb, 1973), offers the controversial thesis that Shakespeare's knowledge of the law was quite extensive and probably obtained through his working as a scrivener, and also through participation in his father's lawsuits.

3. W. W. Lawrence, *Shakespeare's Problem Comedies* (London: Macmillan, 1931). Lawrence's view has been refuted by Davis P. Harding, "Elizabethan Betrothals and *Measure for Measure*," *Journal of English and Germanic Philology*, 49 (1950), 139–158; Ernest Schanzer, "The Marriage Contracts in *Measure for Measure*," *Shakespeare Survey* 13, ed. Allardyce Nicoll (Cambridge: Cambridge University Press, 1960), pp. 81–89; S. Nagarajan, "*Measure for Measure* and Elizabethan Betrothals," *Shakespeare Quarterly*, 14 (1963), 31–38; J. Birge-Patil, "Marriage Contracts in *Measure for Measure*," *Shakespeare Studies* 5, ed. J. Leeds Barroll, III (Dubuque, Iowa: Wm. C. Brown Co., 1969), pp. 106-111.

4. See Raphael Holinshed, *Chronicles* (London, 1587; rpt. London, 1807–09; rpt. New York: AMS Press, 1965), III, 392. *Richard III*, III.vii.4–6.

5. Holinshed, III, 207; *1 Henry VI*, V.v.25–29.

6. See also Jason P. Rosenblatt, "Aspects of the Incest Problem in *Hamlet*," *Shakespeare Quarterly*, 29 (1978), 349–364.

7. Frederic William Maitland, *Roman Canon Law in the Church of England*, 2nd rev. ed. (London: Methuen, 1898), p. 1.

8. Maitland, p. 2.

9. *The Book of Common Prayer 1559: The Elizabethan Prayer Book*, ed. John E. Booty (Charlottesville: University Press of Virginia for the Folger Shakespeare Library, 1976), p. 290.

10. Chilton Latham Powell, *English Domestic Relations 1487–1653* (New York: Columbia University Press, 1917), p. 58.

11. The dispensability or otherwise of this impediment was the basis for the divorce of Henry VIII and Katherine of Aragon. See also Powell, p. 9. For an excellent Tudor summary of both prohibitive and diriment impediments see William Harrington, *In this Boke Are Conteyned the Commendacions of Matrymony, the Maner and Fourme of Contractyng Solempnysynge and Lyuyng in the Same. . . .* Imprynted at the Instaunce of Mayster Polydore Vergyl Archdeaken of Welles (London, 1528). This book had offi-

cial sanction and was reprinted several times in its first year of publication.

12. For a detailed account see Rosenblatt, Note 6 above.

13. Since 7 Edward VII (1907), c.47, commonly known as "The deceased wife's sister act" in England, this impediment has become dispensable in England, but prior to that date such a relationship would have been both incestuous and adulterous. Roman canon law considered affinity dispensable much earlier than England.

14. See Henry Swinburne, *A Treatise of Spousals, or Matrimonial Contracts* (London, 1686), p. 228. This exhaustive account by the judge of the Prerogative Court of York was written around 1600 and published posthumously.

15. J. J. Scarisbrick, *Henry VIII* (1968; rpt. Berkeley and Los Angeles: University of California Press, 1970), p. 8. For a discussion of public honesty see John Foxe, *Ecclelsiastical History . . .* (London, 1596), II, 732.

16. This act was repealed by 28 Henry VIII, c.7, "An Acte for the establishmente of the Kynges succession," which listed the Levitical degrees and bastardized both Mary and Elizabeth.

17. Swinburne, pp. 14, 56–57, 75.

18. Swinburne, pp. 114–119.

19. Some earlier scholars misunderstood the situation. See particularly W. W. Lawrence, Note 3 above. See also J. W. Lever, Introduction to *Measure for Measure*, New Arden Edition (London: Methuen, 1965), pp. liii–lv.

20. Alexander W. Renton and George G. Phillimore, *The Comparative Law of Marriage and Divorce* (London: Sweet and Maxwell, 1910), p. 18.

21. Swinburne, pp. 227–228.

22. Reginald Haw, *The State of Matrimony . . .* (London: S.P.C.K., 1952), p. 143.

23. Joel Hurstfield, *The Queens Wards* (Cambridge, Mass.: Harvard University Press, 1958), p. 143.

24. H. J. Schroeder, *Canons and Decrees of the Council of Trent: Original Text with English Translation* (St. Louis, Mo.: Harder, 1941), p. 183.

25. George S. Howard, *A History of Matrimonial Institutions* (Chicago: University of Chicago Press, 1904), I, 316, together with numerous other authorities, is wrong in stating that *Tametsi* was not "accepted" in England.

26. Frederick J. Furnivall, ed., *Child-Marriages, Divorces, and Ratifications &c in the Diocese of Chester, A.D. 1561–66*, Early English Text Society, OS 108 (London: Kegan Paul, 1897), pp. 140–141.

27. J. H. Crehan, S.J., "Shakespeare and the Sarum Ritual," *The Month*, 218, N.S. 32 (Jul.–Aug., 1964), pp. 47–50.

28. Hugh M. Richmond, *Shakespeare's Sexual Comedy: A Mirror for Lovers* (Indianapolis, Ind.: Bobbs-Merrill, 1971), p. 71.

29. Francis Fergusson, *The Human Image in Dramatic Literature* (Garden City, N. Y.: Doubleday Anchor, 1957), p. 157.

30. Thomas Marc Parrott, ed., *Shakespeare: Twenty-Three Plays and the Sonnets* (New York: Scribner's, 1938), p. 480; Mary Augusta Scott, "*The Book of the Courtyer*, a Source for Benedick and Beatrice," *PMLA*, 16 (1901), 475–502.

31. John Dover Wilson, ed., *Much Ado About Nothing*, New Cambridge Edition (Cambridge: Cambridge University Press, 1923), Introduction, p. ix, and pp. 92–102;

Allison Gaw, "Is Shakespeare's *Much Ado* a Revised Earlier Play?" *PMLA*, 50 (1935), 715–738.

32. Walter N. King, "Much Ado About Something," *Shakespeare Quarterly*, 15 (1964), 143–155.

33. David L. Stevenson, *The Love-Game Comedy* (New York: Columbia University Press, 1946), pp. 208–209.

34. Nadine Page, "The Public Repudiation of Hero," *PMLA*, 50 (1935), 739–744.

35. Charles Tyler Prouty, *The Sources of "Much Ado About Nothing"* (New Haven, Conn.: Yale University Press, 1950), p. 63.

36. Sherman Hawkins, "The Two Worlds of Shakespearean Comedy," *Shakespeare Studies* 3, ed. J. Leeds Barroll, III (Cincinnati, Ohio: The Center for Shakespeare Studies, 1968), pp. 62–80.

37. Barbara K. Lewalski, "Love, Appearance and Reality: Much Ado About Something," *Studies in English Literature*, 8 (1968), 237.

38. See Neville Coghill, "The Basis of Shakespearian Comedy," in Anne Ridler, ed. *Shakespeare Criticism 1935–1960*, The World's Classics (London: Oxford University Press, 1963), pp. 201–227. Originally published 1950.

39. Barnabe Rich, *The Excellencie of Good Women* (London, 1613), p. 29.

40. Juan Luis Vives, *A Very Frutefull and Pleasant Boke Callyd the Instruction of a Christen Woman*, trans. Richard Hyrde (London, 1541), fol. 60.

41. Vives, fol. 60.

42. Stefano Guazzo, *The Civile Conversation*, trans. George Pettie and Barth. Young, Tudor Translations, Second Series, Vols. VII & VIII (London: Constable, 1925; rpt. New York: AMS Press, 1967), VII, 174–175, 190.

43. See Ruth Kelso, *The Doctrine of the English Gentleman in the Sixteenth Century*, University of Illinois Studies in Language and Literature Vol. XIV, Nos. 1–2 (Urbana: University of Illinois Press, 1929; rpt. Gloucester, Mass.: Peter Smith, 1964).

44. Robert Grams Hunter, *Shakespeare and the Comedy of Forgiveness* (New York: Columbia University Press, 1964). pp. 85–105, disagrees with my emphasis on social conventions, saying "In fact, Claudio's crime is being human" (p. 105). He also wonders whether one does leave the play "untroubled by doubts as to Claudio's worthiness" (p. 105). I do, however, agree with him in his comments on the religious connotations and orthodoxy of Claudio's penitential journey toward forgiveness.

45. Alexander Niccholes, *A Discourse of Marriage and Wiving* (London, 1615), p. 48.

46. For the form of spousals see Swinburne, pp. 11–15, 205.

47. Harrington, sig. Aiiii.

48. Swinburne, p. 15.

49. R[obert] C[leaver], *A Godly Forme of Householde Government* (London, 1598), p. 137; see also William Perkins, *Christian Oeconomie*, . . . trans. Thomas Pickering (London, 1609), p. 77.

50. Prouty, p. 46.

51. Page, p. 744. King (p. 150) also comments on this marketplace attitude which makes virginity the most important attribute for a bride.

52. John Cordy Jeaffreson, *Brides and Bridals*, 2nd ed. (London: Hurst & Blackett, 1873), I, 88; Edward J. Wood, *The Wedding Day in All Ages and Countries* (New York: Har-

per's, 1869), pp. 248–249.

53. See *The Book of Common Prayer, 1559: The Elizabethan Prayer Book*, ed. John E. Booty, p. 291.

54. Harrington, sig. Aiiii^v.

55. Vives, fol. 32. See also Joyce Hengerer Sexton, "The Theme of Slander in *Much Ado About Nothing* and Garter's *Susanna*," *Philological Quarterly*, 54 (1975), 419–433.

56. Guazzo, VII, 174–175, 190.

57. Heinrich Cornelius Agrippa von Nettesheim, *A Treatise of the Nobilitie and Exellencye of Woman Kynd*, trans. David Clapham (London, 1542), sigs. Aiiii^v-Biii^v; see also Guazzo, VIII, 26.

58. William Bercher, *The Nobylytye of Wymen, 1559*, ed. R. Warwick Bond (London: Roxburghe Club, 1904), p. 96.

59. Guazzo, VIII, 7.

60. Guazzo, VII, 240.

61. Barbara Everett, "*Much Ado About Nothing*," *Critical Quarterly*, 3 (1961), 319–335, draws attention to this fact, noting that this is the first Shakespeare play "in which the woman's world predominates" (p. 320).

62. Lewalski, p. 244.

63. Lewalski (p. 242) remarks on the way in which "Beatrice and Benedick endeavor to come to terms with the world through wit, intellect, reason."

64. Robert Burton, *The Anatomy of Melancholy*, ed. Floyd Dell and Paul Jordan-Smith (New York: Tudor Publishing Co., 1941), Part 3, Sect. 2, Memb. 3, p. 742.

65. Lewalski, p. 250; Robert Grams Hunter suggests that Claudio's path follows that of Thomas Aquinas, contrition, confession, and satisfaction. Lewalski's terminology, however, follows more closely that of the two homilies on Repentance, which raise interesting questions about the efficacy of good works.

66. Robert Grams Hunter (pp. 104–105) professes some doubts over the audience's forgiveness of Claudio.

67. Michael Taylor, "*Much Ado About Nothing*: The Individual in Society," *Essays in Criticism*, 23 (1973), 153, says "Benedick and Beatrice *must* change; they must learn to live with each other, for an independence such as theirs is heretical when it denies the value of the pact which binds society together."

68. This section appeared in somewhat different form as "The Betrothals of *All's Well That Ends Well*," *Huntington Library Quarterly*, 26 (1963), 179–192. Used by permission.

69. Robert Grams Hunter, p. 130.

70. For detailed treatment of *Measure for Measure* and its betrothals see the sources cited in Note 3 above.

71. *All's Well That Ends Well*, New Arden Edition, ed. G. K. Hunter, 3rd ed. (London: Methuen, 1962), pp. 6–7; see also Muriel C. Bradbook, "Virtue Is the True Nobility: A Study of Structure in *All's Well That Ends Well*," *Review of English Studies*, N.S.., I (1950), 289-301.

72. G. Wilson Knight, "The Third Eye: An Essay on *All's Well That Ends Well*," in *The Sovereign Flower* (London: Methuen, 1958), pp. 95–160.

73. Robert Grams Hunter, pp. 121–126.

74. G. K. Hunter, Introduction to "*All's Well That Ends Well*," p. xxxvii. On the matter of

social class see John M. Love, "'Though Many of the Rich are Damn'd': Dark Comedy and Social Class in *All's Well That Ends Well*," *Texas Studies in Literature*, 18 (1977), 517–527.

75. E. M. W. Tillyard, *Shakespeare's Problem Plays* (London: Chatto & Windus, 1954), p. 89.

76. Madeleine Doran, *Endeavors of Art: A Study of Form in Elizabethan Drama* (Madison: University of Wisconsin Press, 1954), p. 251, says that "the only 'problem' is Helena's getting the man she wants for a husband." See also John F. Adams, *"All's Well That Ends Well*: The Paradox of Procreation," *Shakespeare Quarterly*, 12 (1961), 262.

77. Cesare Ripa, *Iconologia* (Padua, 1611; rpt. New York: Garland Publishing, 1976), pp. 73–75.

78. On Bertram's attainment of sexual maturity see William Babula, "The Character and the Conclusion: Bertram and the Ending of *All's Well That Ends Well*," *South Atlantic Bulletin*, 42 (1977), 74–100. See also Richmond, p. 71.

79. For an excellent summary of criticism of this play, see Joseph G. Price, *The Unfortunate Comedy* (Toronto: University of Toronto Press, 1968), pp. 75–129.

80. John C. Bean, "Comic Structure and the Humanizing of Kate in *The Taming of the Shrew*," in Carolyn Ruth Swift Lenz, Gayle Greene, and Carol Thomas Neely, eds., *The Woman's Part: Feminist Criticism of Shakespeare* (Urbana: University of Illinois Press, 1980), p. 75. He also asserts (pp. 74–75) "She is unquestionably his most erotic heroine, and her femininity is magically potent."

81. See also Albert H. Carter, "In Defense of Bertram," *Shakespeare Quarterly*, 7 (1956), 21–31.

82. See Hurstfield, p. 139.

83. Hurstfield, p. 139.

84. Hurstfield, p. 141.

85. Harrington, Sig. Aiii.

86. George Hayward Joyce, S.J., *Christian Marriage: An Historical and Doctrinal Study*, Heythrop Series I (London: Sheed and Ward, 1948), p. 80. The impediments of force and lack of free consent were those employed to secure the religious annulment of the marriage of Consuelo Vanderbilt to the Duke of Marlborough, a union that had manifestly been consummated. However, canon law did not extend to a civil annulment, and the two were divorced under that rubric and the succession to the title left undisturbed.

87. Glenn H. Blayney, "Wardship in English Drama (1600–1650)," *Studies in Philology*, 53 (1956), 478.

88. Knight, p. 143.

89. Swinburne, p.206.

90. See Harding and Schanzer.

91. Harrington, sig Aii^v.

92. See *Much Ado About Nothing*, IV.i.46–48, and p. 21 above.

93. Joyce, pp. 75–82; Swinburne, pp. 236–239.

94. Swinburne, p. 237.

95. See John Arthos, "The Comedy of Generation," *Essays in Criticism*, N.S. 5 (1955), 97–117.

96. New Arden Edition, pp. 103–104. Swinburne (p. 209) believes that the exchange of

rings confirms whatever contract the words then spoken import. Should there be any doubt whether the contract be considered matrimony or espousal "it is to be judged matrimony" in law.

97. Swinburne, pp. 150–151.

98. Harold S. Wilson, "Dramatic Emphasis in *All's Well That Ends Well*," *Huntington Library Quarterly*, 13 (1950), 239.

99. Kenneth Muir, *Shakespeare's Sources*, I (London: Methuen, 1957), 100–101. See also Carl Dennis, "*All's Well That Ends Well* and the Meaning of Agape," *Philological Quarterly*, 50 (1961), 75–84.

100. Blayney (p. 478) maintains that "The reconciliation of Bertram and Helena is not the triumph of romantic love, but obedience to a royal command at the time of their marriage."

101. See Robert Grams Hunter, pp. 121–126.

102. Glenn H. Blayney, "Enforcement of Marriage in English Drama (1600–1650," *Philological Quarterly*, 38 (1959), 463–464, remarks that "Shakespeare in *All's Well That Ends Well* fused realism and romance by adapting two romantic plots to disguise and yet illustrate the social problems of wardship and resulting enforced marriage." I think this view is too reductive and consider that these aspects are useful for character motivation and development, but, like Shakespeare's use of matrimonial law as plot device, they are not the primary topics of the play.

CHAPTER II. Trouser Roles and the Teachers of Love's Truth

1. Linda Woodbridge, *Women and the English Renaissance: Literature and the Nature of Womankind, 1540–1620* (Urbana and Chicago: University of Illinois Press, 1984), p. 155. For a well-documented account of female transvestism see J. W. Binns, "Women or Transvestites on the English Stage? An Oxford Controversy," *Sixteenth-Century Journal*, 2 (1974), 95–120.

2. Juliet Dusinberre, *Shakespeare and the Nature of Women* (London: Macmillan, 1975), p. 241.

3. Dusinberre, p. 245.

4. Dusinberre, p. 233.

5. Hugh M. Richmond, *Shakespeare's Sexual Comedy: A Mirror for Lovers* (Indianapolis, Ind.: Bobbs-Merrill, 1971), p. 140.

6. Paula S. Berggren, "The Woman's Part: Female Sexuality as Power in Shakespeare's Plays," in Carolyn Ruth Swift Lenz, Gayle Greene, and Carol Thomas Neely, eds., *The Woman's Part: Feminist Criticism of Shakespeare* (Urbana: University of Illinois Press, 1980), p. 19.

7. Berggren, p. 20.

8. Anne Barton, Introduction to *The Two Gentlemen of Verona*, *The Riverside Shakespeare* (Boston: Houghton Mifflin, 1974), p. 143.

9. Alexander Leggatt, *Shakespeare's Comedy of Love* (London: Methuen, 1974), p. 33. See also the whole of his illuminating essay on this play, pp. 21–40.

10. Leggatt, pp. 37–39.

11. Erwin Panofsky, *Studies in Iconology* (New York: Oxford University Press, 1939), has an excellent account of "Blind Cupid," in his fourth chapter, where he makes this distinction admirably clear.

12. H. B. Charlton, *Shakespearian Comedy* (London: Methuen, 1966), pp. 38–39.

13. Leggatt, pp. 39–40.

14. For stage history see the excellent introduction by John Russell Brown to the New Arden Edition (London: Methuen, 1959), pp. xxxii—xxxvi. The summary of critical comments throughout is admirable. Shylock criticism is too voluminous to summarize here, but two book-length studies should be mentioned: Herman Sinsheimer, *Shylock: The History of a Character* New York: Benjamin Blom, 1947); Bernard Grebanier, *The Truth about Shylock* (New York: Random House, 1962).

15. The quaintly sexist language of *Black's Law Dictionary*, 4th ed. (St. Paul, Minn.: West Publishing Co., 1951), is taken from the definition of "Equity," p. 634.

16. Lawrence W. Hyman, "The Rival Lovers in *The Merchant of Venice*," *Shakespeare Quarterly*, 20 (1970), 109–116 (p. 109); this suggestion is also supported by Robert Hapgood, "Portia and *The Merchant of Venice*: The Gentle Bond," *Modern Language Quarterly*, 20 (1967), 19–32. Graham Midgely, "*The Merchant of Venice*: A Reconsideration," *Essays in Criticism*, 10 (1960), 119–133, suggests that Antonio is an unconscious homosexual facing a rival.

17. Richmond, p. 136.

18. John Russell Brown, *Shakespeare and His Comedies*, 2nd ed. (London: Methuen, 1962), pp. 61–75.

19. Leggatt, p. 147.

20. Brown, *Shakespeare* . . . , pp. 64–67 gives an excellent analysis of the commercial imagery of Bassanio.

21. Barbara K. Lewalski, "Biblical Allusion and Allegory in *The Merchant of Venice*," *Shakespeare Quarterly*, 13 (1962), p. 343.

22. Leggatt, pp. 129ff. writes shrewdly on this topic.

23. Leggatt, p. 133.

24. Cesare Ripa, *Iconologia* (Padua, 1611; rpt. New York: Garland Publishing, 1976), p. 509.

25. Sigmund Freud suggests that the importance of the choice of lead represents a "displacement" from the metal of death to the discovery of what is most precious. See "The Theme of the Three Caskets," in *The Standard Edition of the Complete Psychological Works of Sigmund Freud*, trans. James Strachey (London: Hogarth Press, 1958), Vol. 12, 291–301 [orig. pub. 1911–13].

26. Leggatt, pp. 133–134, also makes this his observation.

27. T. E., *The Lawes Resolutions of Womens Rights: or the Lawes Prouision for Women* (London, 1632), p. 125.

28. Sigurd Burckhardt, "*The Merchant of Venice*: The Gentle Bond," *English Literary History*, 29 (1962), 239–262, is right in seeing the match as one of "bonded" love, and it does parallel the Shylock contract, but he errs in not connecting it with English matrimonial law. See also Keith Thomas, "The Double Standard," *Journal of the History of Ideas*, 20 (1959), 195–216.

29. Lewalski (p. 341) notes that in cases of forced conversion from Judaism converts were usually allowed at least a stipend on which to live and even to begin their business once again.

30. For an account which touches on some of the same points made here see Alice N. Benston, "Portia, the Law, and the Tripartite Structure of *The Merchant of Venice*," *Shakespeare Quarterly*, 30 (1979), 367–385.

31. Bertrand Evans, *Shakespeare's Comedies* (Oxford: Clarendon Press, 1960), p. 97, suggests that in this matter she looks toward Prospero; but I should also like to add that the next such manipulative character is Helena.

32. Anne Barton, Introduction to *As You Like It*, *The Riverside Shakespeare*, (Boston: Houghton Mifflin, 1974), p. 365.

33. Richmond, p. 123.

34. See Robert M. Kimbrough, "Androgyny Seen through Shakespeare's Disguise," *Shakespeare Quarterly*, 33 (1982), 17–33, particularly, pp. 23–27.

35. Nancy K. Hayles, "Sexual Disguise in *As You Like It* and *Twelfth Night*," *Shakespeare Survey* 32, ed. Kenneth Muir (Cambridge: Cambridge University Press, 1979), pp. 63–72, speaks at length of the complexity of this "layering," see particularly, p. 65.

36. Hayles (p. 66) suggests that the lioness "evoke[s] the possibility of female engulfment," and the snake "the threat of phallic invasion."

37. Hayles, p. 64.

38. John Earle, "A Younger Brother," in *Micro-cosmographie*, ed. Gwendolen Murphy (London: Golden Cockerel Press, 1928), p. 15. See also John W. Draper, "Orlando, the Younger Brother," *Philological Quarterly*, 13 (1934), 72–77.

39. Stefano Guazzo, *The Civile Conversation*, trans. George Pettie and Barth. Young. Tudor Translations, Second Series, Vols. VII & VIII (London: Constable, 1925; rpt. New York: AMS Press, 1967), VII, 182–183.

40. Kimbrough, p. 23.

41. Hayles, p. 64.

42. Leggatt, p. 190.

43. Evans, p. 93.

44. Though this appearance was customarily considered evidence of a true lover, there was another, completely opposed one. Robert Burton, for instance, believed that careful dress was the hallmark of the lover. In *Much Ado About Nothing* Shakespeare makes use of this latter tradition. See Marie Channing Linthicum, "Benedick's Love-Symptoms: Cosmetics and Costume," *Modern Language Review*, 22 (1927), 442–444.

45. See Thomas Overbury, *The Overburian Characters*, ed. W. J. Paylor. The Percy Reprints (Oxford: Basil Blackwell, 1936), XIII, 10–11.

46. Pierre de la Primaudaye, *The French Academie* (London, 1618), p. 207.

47. Leon Battista Alberti, *Hecatonphila. The Arte of Loue* (London, 1598), fols. 23, 24.

48. Agnes Latham, Appendix B, *As You Like It*, New Arden Edition (London: Methuen, 1975), pp. 133–135, agrees with this comment.

49. Edward Gosynhill, *Here Begynneth a Lytle Boke Named the Schole House of Women . . .* (London, 1561?), sig. Aii.

50. Desiderius Erasmus, "Marriage" ["Conjugium," orig. pub. 1523], in *The Colloquies of Erasmus*, trans. Craig R. Thompson (Chicago: University of Chicago Press, 1965),

250 NOTES TO PAGES 87–94

p. 119.

51. It may be objected that the ladies of *Love's Labour's Lost* contract a similar kind of spousals with their men, but the canonical terminology is not present. Not until *Measure for Measure* does Shakespeare make major use of this form of spousing, in the match of Angelo and Mariana.

52. M. C. Bradbrook, *The Growth and Structure of Elizabethan Comedy* (London: Chatto and Windus, 1961), p. 91, does not believe that these plays should be taken quite so seriously.

53. T. W. Craik, Introduction to *Twelfth Night*, New Arden Edition (London: Methuen, 1975), p. xxxiv.

54. Anne Barton, Introduction to *Twelfth Night*, *The Riverside Shakespeare* (Boston: Houghton Mifflin, 1974), p. 403.

55. The title *Twelfth Night* may also signify the date of its first performance. J. Leslie Hotson, *The First Night of "Twelfth Night"* (London: Hart-Davis, 1954) argues an attractive, though not convincing case for January 1600–01.

56. Leggatt, p. 226.

57. D. J. Palmer, *"Twelfth Night* and the Myth of Echo and Narcissus," *Shakespeare Survey* 32, ed. Kenneth Muir (Cambridge: Cambridge University Press, 1979), pp. 73–78, discusses the use of this myth as structural device.

58. Peter G. Phialas, *Shakespeare's Romantic Comedies: A Study of Their Form and Meaning* (Chapel Hill: University of North Carolina Press, 1966), p. 270; Herschel Baker, Introduction to *Twelfth Night*, *The Complete Signet Shakespeare* (New York: Harcourt Brace Jovanovich, 1972), p. 878, denies any such development to both Orsino and Olivia.

59. Barton, p. 405.

60. Barton, p. 406.

61. Leggatt, p. 222.

62. Paul Mueschke and Jeannette Fleisher, "Jonsonian Elements in the Comic Underplot of *Twelfth Night*," *PMLA*, 48 (1933). 722–740.

63. Alan S. Downer, "Feste's Night," *College English*, 13 (1952), 258–265.

64. Anne Barton (p. 407) also notes this point.

65. Ngaio Marsh, "A Note on a Production of *Twelfth Night*," *Shakespeare Survey* 8, ed. Allardyce Nicoll (Cambridge: Cambridge University Press, 1955), pp. 69–73. I can personally verify the extraordinary effect of this stage business.

66. New Arden edition, p. 8n.; see also William C. Carroll, "The Ending of *Twelfth Night* and the Tradition of Metamorphosis," in *Shakespearean Comedy*, ed. Maurice Charney and Jeanine Parisier Plottel (New York: New York Literary Forum, 1980), pp. 49–61; and M. E. Lamb, Ovid's *Metamorphoses* and Shakespeare's *Twelfth Night*," also in Charney and Plottel, pp. 63–77.

67. See particularly John W. Draper, *The "Twelfth Night" of Shakespeare's Audience* (Stanford, Calif.: Stanford University Press, 1950) and Richard Levin, "Viola: Dr. Johnson's 'Excellent Schemer'," *Durham University Journal*, 71 (1979), 213–222.

68. See New Arden edition, p. 10n., and C. J. Sisson, *New Readings in Shakespeare*, (Cambridge: Cambridge University Press, 1956), I, 185.

69. Ernst H. Kantorowicz, *The King's Two Bodies: A Study in Medieval Theology* (Princeton, N.J.: Princeton University Press, 1957), pp. 284, 283; see also pp. 273–302,

passim.

70. Hayles, p. 71.

71. Plato, *Symposium*, trans. B. Jowett, ed. Louise Ropes Loomis; in *Five Great Dialogues* (New York: Walter J. Black for the Classics Club, 1942), pp. 178–179. See also Kimbrough, pp. 17–33, particularly p. 22, which draws attention to the *Symposium* and p. 28, which comments on Viola and the necessity of developing "psychic androgyny."

72. Plato, p. 181.

73. Kimbrough, p. 31. He also considers Viola "Shakespeare's furthest venture into androgyny as seen through disguise" (p. 29).

74. Leggatt, p. 223.

75. See Barnabe Riche, *Rich, His Farewell to Militarie Profession* (London, 1581).

76. Evans, p. 121; also Leggatt, p. 233, who remarks on the "catty" nature of Viola's remark.

77. Alexander Niccholes, *A Discourse of Marriage and Wiving* (London, 1615), p. 48.

78. Hayles, p. 71.

79. Richmond, p. 180.

80. Despite the New Arden note (p. 57) I do not believe that this line refers to physical beauty, but rather to the emotional stability the editors note earlier. Additionally, one should recall the feminist view of the Garden of Eden which maintained that woman was created out of Adam's rib so that she would be perceived as his equal.

81. Louis B. Wright sees Malvolio as the exaggerated embodiment of the perfect servant as described by Walter Darell, *A Pretie and Short Discourse of the Life of Seruingmen* (London, 1587); see Louis B. Wright, "A Conduct Book for Malvolio," *Studies in Philology*, 31 (1931), 115–137.

82. Hayles, p. 271n. views Antonio's dilemma here as similar to that of his namesake in *The Merchant of Venice*, indicating the difficulty of homoerotic love in a heterosexual society, for both love another man and lose him to a woman.

PART TWO

CHAPTER III. Society's Conventions and *The Comedy of Errors*

1. Alexander Leggatt, *Citizen Comedy in the Age of Shakespeare* (Toronto: University of Toronto Press, 1973), p. 149. For an important psychoanalytically oriented study on adultery and cuckoldry see Coppélia Kahn, *Man's Estate: Masculine Identity in Shakespeare* (Berkeley and Los Angeles: University of California Press, 1981).

2. For discussion of *Lucrece*, see Part Three, Chapter VI.

3. The work sounds much more affirmative than it actually is. Basically, it is an account of the laws affecting women from medieval times through Bracton and Coke to the present time (1632). Some of it is heavily influenced by Thomas Smith and Henry Swinburne. The relative simplicity of the explanations indicates T. E.'s assessment of his audience, for he takes care to write in English, not "an uncouth language, cleane abstruded from their sex" (p. 403), a comment that says a great deal about the decay of classital learning among women. The family of Thomas More and the famous Coke sisters would not

have needed such condescension.

4. I take this title from the admirable summary of books about women by Suzanne W. Hull, *Chaste, Silent, & Obedient: English Books for Women*, 1475–1640 (San Marino, Calif.: Huntington Library, 1982). Other related studies on feminine conduct are: Ruth Kelso, *Doctrine for the Lady of the Renaissance* (Urbana: University of Illinois Press, 1956); Diane Bornstein, *The Lady in the Tower: Medieval Courtesy Literature for Women* (Hamden, Conn.: Archon, 1983); Linda Woodbridge, *Women and the English Renaissance: Literature and the Nature of Womankind* (Urbana and Chicago: University of Illinois Press, 1984); and the pioneering study by Carroll Camden, *The Elizabethan Woman* (Houston, Texas: Elsevier Press, 1952). See also Ruth Kelso, *The Doctrine of the English Gentleman in the Sixteenth Century*, (1929; rpt. Gloucester, Mass.: Peter Smith, 1964).

5. Pierre Charron, *Of Wisdom*, trans. Sam[p]son Lennard (London, [1627]), pp. 487–488.

6. R[obert] C[leaver], *A Godly Forme of Householde Government* (London, 1598), p. 230.

7. Charron, p. 487. The differing emphasis on books of female and male conduct can be gauged from an examination of the publication history of the two important works of Juan Luis Vives. *A Very Frutefull and Pleasant Boke Called the Instruction of a Christen Woman. . . .* Trans. Richard Hyrde (London, 1529) was reprinted nine times, but *The Office and Duetie of an Husband* (London, 1555) exists in a single edition.

8. Thomas Smith, *De Republica Anglorum* (London, 1583), p. 101. This situation remained unaltered until the passage of the Married Women's Property Acts of 1883 and 1893.

9. Smith, p. 105.

10. Smith, p. 105.

11. Keith Thomas, "The Double Standard," *Journal of the History of Ideas*, 20 (1959), 200–201.

12. Smith, p. 104.

13. Smith, pp. 101–102.

14. T. E., p. 141.

15. Lest one become smugly superior, in State v. Rhodes, 61 N.C. 453 (1868) the following statement appears in the ruling: "We will no more interfere where the husband whips the wife than where the wife whips the husband, and yet we would hardly be supposed to hold that a wife has a right to whip her husband. We will not inflict upon society the greater evil of raising the curtain upon domestic privacy to punish the lesser evil of trifling violence."

16. K. B. Smellie, *The British Way of Life* (London: Heinemann, 1955), pp. 31–32.

17. T. E., pp. 128–129.

18. W[illiam] H[eale], *An Apologie for Women . . .* (Oxford, 1609), p. 26.

19. See Geoffrey Bullough, ed. *Narrative and Dramatic Sources of Shakespeare* (London: Routledge & Kegan Paul, 1964), I, 9–10. R. A. Foakes, ed., *The Comedy of Errors*, New Arden Edition (London: Methuen, 1962), pp. 113–115, gives a detailed account of the biblical material.

20. This colloquy was frequently translated and printed in England. See also *A Mery Dialogue Declaringe the Propertyes of Shrowde Shrewes and Honest Wyues* (London, 1557);

Robert Snawsel, *A Looking Glasse for Maried Folkes* (London, 1610). For information on Snawsel and his translation, based on my original identification of the Erasmus connection, see Andrew McLean, "Another Translation of Erasmus's *Coniugium*: Snawsel's *Looking Glasse for Maried Folkes* (1610)," *Moreana*, 43–44 (1974), 55–64. *Note*: This colloquy also contains the celebrated tale of Jane Colt's brief rebellion against the rule of her husband, Thomas More.

21. See H. B. Charlton, *Shakespearian Comedy* (London: Methuen, 1938), pp. 68–72.
22. Charles Brooks, "Shakespeare's Romantic Shrews," *Shakespeare Quarterly*, 11 (1960), 351–356, compares Adriana with Kate and sees them as women of spirit rather than true shrews.

CHAPTER IV. The Manning of the Haggard:
or *The Taming of the Shrew*

This chapter appeared in a slightly different form in *Essays in Literature*, I (1974), 149–165. Used by permission.

1. George R. Hibbard, "*The Taming of the Shrew*: A Social Comedy," in *Shakespearean Essays*, ed. Alwin Thaler and Norman Sanders, Tennessee Studies in Language and Literature, 2 (Knoxville: University of Tennessee Press, 1964), p. 16; see also Coppélia Kahn, "*The Taming of the Shrew*: Shakespeare's Mirror of Marriage," *Modern Language Studies*, 5 (1975), 88–102.
2. See Ruth Kelso, *Doctrine for the Lady of the Renaissance* (Urbana: University of Illinois Press, 1956), pp. 96, 108, and elsewhere in Chapter V, "Vocation." Also see Carroll Camden, *The Elizabethan Woman* (Houston, Texas: Elsevier Press, 1952), Chapter V, "Domestic Relationships."
3. Germaine Greer, *The Female Eunuch* (New York: McGraw-Hill, 1971), p. 206, makes a brief note of this point: "He wants her spirit and energy because he wants a wife worth keeping. He tames her as he might a hawk or a high-mettled horse, and she rewards him with strong sexual love and fierce loyalty." T. H. White, *The Goshawk* (New York: Putnam's, 1951), p. 158, agrees that "Petruchio tames his Kate as an austringer did his hawk, and he was conscious of the fact."
4. M. C. Bradbook, "Dramatic Role and Social Image: A Study of *The Taming of the Shrew*," *Shakespeare Jahrbuch*, 94 (1958), 134.
5. See Betty Bandel, "Shakespeare's Treatment of the Social Position of Women," M. A. Thesis, Columbia University, 1951; Jean E. Gagen, *The New Woman: Her Emergence in English Drama, 1600–1730* (New York: Twayne, 1954). Irene G. Dash, *Wooing, Wedding and Power: Women in Shakespeare's Plays* (New York: Columbia University Press, 1981) devotes a perceptive chapter to *The Taming of the Shrew* (pp. 33–64), drawing attention to the carefully orchestrated contrast between Katharina and Bianca through which each woman is defined by the other. On p. 60, however, she misunderstands my approach by reading literally what was meant to be taken figuratively.
6. Greer, p. 205.
7. White, pp. 16, 25, 28, 36. All the following representative books on falconry work implicitly from this general premise. See also Juliana Berners, *The Book Containing the*

Treatises of Hawking, Hunting . . . [The Boke of St. Albans] (London, 1496); George Turbervile, *The Book of Falconry or Hawking* (London, 1611); Simon Latham, *Lathams Falconry or the Faulcons Lure and Cure* (London, 1614); Frederick II of Hohenstaufen, *The Art of Falconry*, Being the *De Arte Venandi cum Avibus*, trans. and ed. by Casey A. Wood and F. Marjorie Fyfe (Stanford, Calif.: Stanford University Press, 1943). For a very personal account of hawk-taming see T. H. White. This book discusses from deeply felt experience the mutuality of necessary cruelty and the battle of wills, together with the suffering and psychological interdependence experienced by both hawk and tamer.

8. Latham, p. 66.
9. White, p. 126, especially of goshawks.
10. At a falconry meeting some years ago, a noted European hawkmaster observed as his prize bird flew away that even he had found it impossible to hold a falcon more than four years or so. Then its natural wildness would assert itself, and the bird would leave. Constant vigilance is therefore essential.
11. Latham, p. 67; see also Turbervile, pp. 26, 33.
12. Turbervile, p. 77.
13. Turbervile, p. 79.
14. Latham, p. 67.
15. Bradbrook, pp. 140–141.
16. C. C. Seronsy, "'Supposes' as a Unifying Theme in *The Taming of the Shrew*," *Shakespeare Quarterly*, 14 (1963), 19.
17. Seronsy, p. 19.
18. Latham, p. 67.
19. James E. Harting, *The Ornithology of Shakespeare* (London: J. Van Voorst, 1871), p. 43; Frederick II, p. 255.
20. Harting., p. 48; also see the *OED*.
21. Frederick II, p. 157.
22. Charles Brooks, "Shakespeare's Romantic Shrews," *Shakespeare Quarterly*, 11 (1960), 356, notes that the shrewishness of both Adriana and Kate "results from will and spirit, which properly controlled can make valuable wives out of them."
23. Hibbard, p. 65.
24. Hibbard, p. 65.
25. See Desiderius Erasmus, "A Marriage in Name Only, or The Unequal Match," *Colloquies*, trans. Craig R. Thompson (Chicago: University of Chicago Press, 1965), pp. 403–412.
26. See Pierre de la Primaudaye, *The French Academie* (London, 1618), p. 203, among many others.
27. Henry Swinburne, *A Treatise of Spousals or Matrimonial Contracts* (London, 1686), Section XVII, "Of the Effects of Spousals," pp. 222–235.
28. Swinburne, p. 236.
29. Lists of husbandly and wifely duties are legion in conduct books. One good source is Guillaume de la Perrière, *The Mirrovr of Policie* . . . (London, 1598), sigs. Aa4^v-Dd4^v. Significantly, the wife's list is much longer than the husband's.
30. La Primaudaye, p. 207. This matter of physical violence is where the Zeffirelli-Burton-Taylor film went astray, resorting to action where Shakespeare opted for intel-

lectual subtlety.

31. John W. Draper, "Kate the Curst," *Journal of Nervous and Mental Diseases*, 89 (1939), 757–764, attempts to prove Kate a clinical study of the choleric personality. For the matter of humor regulation by diet see, among many others, Vives, fol. 20ᵛ.

32. Berners, sig. Bj.

33. See White, pp. 33, 38, 50, 92, for a falcon's diet.

34. White, p. 16.

35. Richard Blome, *Hauking or Faulconry* (1683; rpt. London: Cresset, 1929), p. 47.

36. Latham, p. 18.

37. See Neville Coghill, "The Basis of Shakespearian Comedy," in *Shakespeare Criticism, 1935–1960*, ed. Anne Ridler (London: Oxford University Press, 1963), p. 209.

38. Brooks, p. 354.

39. Stefano Guazzo, *The Civile Conversation*, trans. George Pettie and Barth. Young, 1581 and 1586, Tudor Translations, Second Series, Vols. VII–VIII (London: Constable, 1925; rpt. New York: AMS Press, 1967), VII, 27.

40. John C. Bean, "Comic Structure and the Humanizing of Kate in *The Taming of the Shrew*," maintains that in this speech Kate indicates that she is "liberated into the bonds of love" (p. 66): See Carolyn Ruth Swift Lenz, Gayle Greene, and Carol Thomas Neely, eds., *The Woman's Part: Feminist Criticism of Shakespeare* (Urbana: University of Illinois Press, 1980), pp. 65–78; see also Brooks, p. 354.

41. Frederick II, p. 160.

42. "The State of Matrimonie," *The Seconde Tome of Homilies* (London, 1595), sig. Gg6ᵛ.

43. Michael West, "The Folk Background of Petruchio's Wooing Dance: Male Supremacy in *The Taming of the Shrew*," *Shakespeare Studies* 7, ed. J. Leeds Barroll, III (New York: Burt Franklin, 1974), pp. 65–73, notes this partnering aspect, remarking (p. 72) that "indeed, properly understood, the play's ideals may not be so hostile to those of a modern feminist."

44. Jeanne Addison Roberts, *Shakespeare's English Comedy: "The Merry Wives of Windsor" in Context* (Lincoln: University of Nebraska Press, 1979), p. 73.

45. Alexander Leggatt, *Citizen Comedy in the Age of Shakespeare* (Toronto: University of Toronto Press, 1973), pp. 146–149.

CHAPTER V. The Indiscretions of Desdemona

1. This chapter appeared in different form in *Shakespeare Quarterly*, 14 (1963), 127–139. Used by permission.

2. Susan Snyder, *The Comic Matrix of Shakespeare's Tragedies: "Romeo and Juliet," "Hamlet," "Othello," and "King Lear"* Princeton, N.J.: Princeton Universtiy Press, 1979), p. 73.

3. Carol Thomas Neely, "Men and Women in *Othello*: ' what should such a fool / Do with so good a woman?' " *Shakespeare Studies* 10, ed. J. Leeds Barroll, III (New York: Burt Franklin, 1977), p. 136.

4. A. C. Bradley, *Shakespearean Tragedy* (1904; rpt. London: Macmillan, 1951), pp. 201–206; Neely, p. 133.

5. Leslie A. Fiedler, *The Stranger in Shakespeare* (New York: Stein and Day, 1972), pp.

141–142, 148.

6. Georges Bonnard, "Are Othello and Desdemona Innocent or Guilty?" *English Studies* [Amsterdam], 30 (October 1949), 183.

7. John W. Draper, *The "Othello" of Shakespeare's Audience* (Paris: J. Didier, 1952), p. 72. In his earlier study, "Desdemona, a Compound of Two Cultures," *Revue de Littérature Comparée*, 13 (1933), 344, Draper also notes the dichotomy in the character of Desdemona and suggests that Shakespeare deliberately anglicized her in order to gain added realism.

8. Irene G. Dash, *Wooing, Wedding and Power: Women in Shakespeare's Plays* (New York: Columbia University Press, 1981), p. 104.

9. Dash, p. 104.

10. H. B. Charlton, "Shakespeare's *Othello*," *Bulletin of the John Rylands Library*, 31 (1948), 47.

11. Carroll Camden, "Iago on Women," *Journal of English and Germanic Philology*, 48 (1949), 70, 71.

12. Bonnard, p. 179.

13. Dash, p. 104.

14. Fiedler, p. 155. Both A. H. Gilbert, "Scenes of Discovery in *Othello*," *Philological Quarterly*, 5 (1926), 119, and S. A. Tannenbaum, "The Inception of Othello's Jealousy," *Shakespeare Association Bulletin*, 10 (1935), 178–179, draw attention to Iago's misinterpretation of Desdemona's actions, but neither treats the subject in detail.

15. Jacob Rathgeb, "A True and Faithful Narrative of the Bathing Excursion . . .", trans. and quoted in William Brenchley Rye, *England as Seen by Foreigners in the Days of Elizabeth and James the First*, (London: John Russell Smith, 1865), p. 7.

16. For more detailed studies, see Carroll Camden, *The Elizabethan Woman* (Houston, Texas: Elsevier Press, 1952); Ruth Kelso, *Doctrine for the Lady of the Renaissance* (Urbana: University of Illinois Press, 1956); Louis B. Wright, *Middle-Class Culture in Elizabethan England* (Chapel Hill: University of North Carolina Press, 1935), p. 465ff.

17. Keith Thomas, "The Double Standard," *Journal of the History of Ideas*, 20 (1959), 210–211.

18. Juan Luis Vives, *A Very Frutefull and Pleasant Boke Called the Instruction of a Christen Woman* (London, 1541), fol. 54.

19. Vives, fol. 57^v. See also Kelso, pp. 48–50, 55.

20. Vives, fol. 60. See also Kelso, p. 56; Camden, *The Elizabethan Woman*, pp. 65–66.

21. Church of England, *Constitutions and Canons Ecclesiasticall*, 1604, with Introduction and notes by H. A. Wilson (Oxford: Clarendon Press, 1922), Canon C.

22. William Harrington, *In This Boke Are Conteyned the Commendacions of Matrymony*, (London, 1528), sigs. Eii–Eii^v. See also Camden, *The Elizabethan Woman*, pp. 92–93.

23. Church of England, *Constitutions*. . . . , Canon LXII.

24. Church of England, *Constitutions*. . . , Canons LXIII, CI–CIII.

25. Guillaume de la Perrière, *The Mirrovr of Policie* . . . trans. from *Le Miroir Politique*, (London, 1598), paraphrase of sigs. Ddi–Ee2^v; see also Kelso, pp. 95–107; Camden, *The Elizabethan Woman*, pp. 131–133.

26. Fiedler, p. 157.

27. Camden, "Iago on Women," p. 65.

28. Neely, p. 139.

29. Draper, "Desdemona, a Compound of Two Cultures," pp. 337–351; see also, *The "Othello"*

of Shakespeare's Audience, p. 59.

30. Thomas Coryat, *Crudities, Hastily Gobled Vp in Five Moneths Trauells* . . . (London, 1611), p. 265.

31. Draper, "Desdemona, a Compound of Two Cultures" (p. 337, n. 2), notes the unsavory reputation of Venetian gondoliers.

32. Snyder (p. 84) draws attention to the fact that Othello is "middle-aged, thick-lipped—everything that Desdemona is not." This is visual evidence of the "disjunction of love" that lies at the center of the play.

33. It is important to note that Venetian acceptance of the legality of Desdemona's clandestine marriage is in effect a statement of Othello's baptism as a Christian. Otherwise the diriment impediment of *disparitas cultus* would exist, since a marriage between an infidel and a Christian was invalid.

34. Here is another tragic inversion of a traditionally comic situation.

35. See my note, "Not Shakespeare This Time," *Word Study*, 26 (1961), 7–8.

36. Pierre de la Primaudaye, *The French Academie*, trans. by T. B. (London, 1618), p. 212.

37. R[obert] S[nawsel], *A Looking Glasse for Maried Folks*, . . . (London, 1610), p. 54.

38. La Primaudaye, p. 211.

39. Camden, "Iago on Women," pp. 58–59.

40. Draper, *The "Othello" of Shakespeare's Audience*, p. 262, believes that the English self-assertive Desdemona is gradually replaced by the Venetian Desdemona of Cinthio, and it is this latter character rather than Shakespeare's that has been admired by the critics. Stephen Reid, "Desdemona's Guilt," *American Imago*, 27 (1970), 257, thinks she has an obscure sense of guilt beneath her virtue, possibly arising from her relationship to her father (p. 258) whom she did, in fact, betray (p. 261) and hence Othello's treatment of her, even her murder, is justified (p. 262).

41. Alexander Niccholes, *A Discourse of Marriage and Wiving* . . . (London, 1615), p. 48.

42. Coryat, p. 261.

43. Coryat, pp. 264–265.

44. Coryat, p. 263.

45. Lily B. Campbell, *Shakespeare's Tragic Heroes, Slaves of Passion* (Cambridge: Cambridge University Press, 1930), pp. 148–174.

46. Neely, pp. 137–138.

47. Reid (p. 246) notes Desdemona's denial of her very real "carnality."

48. Robert Dickes, "Desdemona: An Innocent Victim," *American Imago*, 27 (1970), 280–281, sees an incest-motif in her relationship with Brabantio, so that she marries Othello, the devil, as father substitute. Fiedler (p. 142) offers some similar comments, as does Reid (pp. 258–260) who considers her elopement as an act of revenge against her father.

49. Dickes (p. 279) suggests that "Finally she wanted death. This wish, however, was not made explicit by Shakespeare and must be assumed as an unconscious one based on superego demands."

50. Dash, p. 123.

51. Ernest Brennecke, "'Nay That's Not Next': The Significance of Desdemona's 'Willow Song,'" *Shakespeare Quarterly*, 4 (1953), 36.

52. Fiedler, p. 155–156.

53. Neely, p. 139.

258 NOTES TO PAGES 153–159

PART THREE
CHAPTER VI. The Siege of Lucrece

1. Susan Brownmiller, *Against Our Will* (1975: rpt. New York: Bantam, 1976), p. 23.
2. United States Army, *The Geneva Conventions of 1949 and Hague Convention No. IV of 1907*. Army Subject Schedule 27–1 (Washington, D. C.: HQ, Department of the Army, 8 October 1970), p. 5.
3. M. H. Keen, *The Laws of War in the Late Middle Ages* (London: Routledge and Kegan Paul, 1965), p. 119.
4. Keen, p. 119.
5. Keen, pp. 120–121.
6. United States Army, *The Law of Land Warfare*, FM 27–1, Department of the Army, July 1956 (Washington, D.C.: U. S. Government Printing Office, 1956), p. 21.
7. Alberico Gentili, *De Jure Belli Libri Tres* (1612), trans. John C. Rolfe. The Classics of International Law, No. 16 (Oxford: Clarendon Press for the Carnegie Endowment for International Peace, 1933), II, 215.
8. Raphael Holinshed, *Chronicles* (1587; rpt. London, 1807–09; rpt. New York: AMS Press, 1976), III, 91.
9. Holinshed, III, 103.
10. *The Law of Land Warfare*, p. 20.
11. Balthasar Ayala, *De Jure et Officiis Bellicis et Disciplina Militari, Libri III* (1582), trans. John Pawley Bate. The Classics of International Law (Washington, D. C.: Carnegie Institution, 1912), II, 233.
12. Ayala, II, 235–236.
13. Edward Davies, *The Art of War and Englands Traynings* (London, 1619), pp. 66–67.
14. Davies, p. 66.
15. Keen, pp. 128–129.
16. Keen, p. 124.
17. Keen, pp. 124–125.
18. Holinshed, III, 280.
19. Gentili, II, 213.
20. Hugo Grotius, *De Jure Belli ac Pacis Libri Tres* (1646), trans. Francis W. Kelsey. The Classics of International Law, No. 3 (Oxford: Clarendon Press for the Carnegie Endowment for International Peace, 1925), II, 739.
21. James Hamilton Wylie and William Templeton Waugh, *The Reign of King Henry the Fifth* (Cambridge: Cambridge University Press, 1929), III, 349–351. It is interesting to note that Holinshed does not record this singular lapse on the part of the monarch *sans peur et sans reproche*.
22. Keen, p. 133.
23. Nancy Cotton Pearse, *John Fletcher's Chastity Plays: Mirrors of Modesty* (Lewisburg, Pa.: Bucknell University Press, 1973), p. 90.
24. Augustine, *The City of God*, trans. Henry Bettenson, ed. David Knowles (Harmondsworth, Middlesex: Penguin, 1972), as quoted by Brownmiller, p. 365. I disagree with her assess-

ment of the Augustinian comment as "witty scorn," agreeing with Pearse that Augustine neither praises nor condemns Lucrece (p. 92n.).

25. William Tyndale, *The Obedyence of a Chrysten Man* (London, 1561), fol. 39.

26. Pearse, p. 91.

27. William Shakespeare, *The Poems*, ed. F. T. Prince, New Arden Edition (London: Methuen, 1960, p. xxxv.

28. Juliet Dusinberre, *Shakespeare and the Nature of Women* (London: Macmillan, 1975), p. 280.

29. Dusinberre, p. 279.

30. J. R. Hale, *The Art of War and Renaissance England*, Folger Booklets on Tudor and Stuart Civilization (Washington, D. C.: Folger Shakespeare Library, 1961), p. 26, says that "Siege accounts were eagerly read, and travelers came to inspect fortifications as naturally as they looked at churches or paintings." *All's Well That Ends Well*, ed. G. K. Hunter, New Arden Edition (London: Methuen, 1962), 10n. comments "The comparison of wooing to besieging is, of course, commonplace." See also p. 35 above.

31. *The Law of Land Warfare*, p. 22.

32. See Coppélia Kahn, "The Rape in Shakespeare's *Lucrece*," *Shakespeare Studies* 9, ed. J. Leeds Barroll, III (New York: Burt Franklin, 1976), pp. 45–72.

33. Kahn notes the eroticism of this description and also the martial and political undertones of Tarquin's language, (p. 57).

34. Pierino Belli, *De Re Militari et Bello Tractatus* (1563), trans. Herbert C. Nutting. The Classics of International Law, No. 18 (Oxford: Clarendon Press for the Carnegie Endowment for International Peace, 1936), II, 326. The translator notes that the reading is uncertain in the 1563 original, "Roch a parlamentare e mento reduta," I, 144.

35. Belli, II, 325.

36. Hallett Smith, *Elizabethan Poetry* (Cambridge, Mass.: Harvard University Press, 1952), pp. 113–117, gives an admirable short account of the backgrounds of the "plaints" of Lucrece. R. Thomas Simone, in his full length study gives an analysis of some of the rhetorical figures: *Shakespeare and "Lucrece": A Study of the Poem and Its Relation to the Plays*. Elizabethan and Renaissance Studies, ed. James Hogg (Salzburg: Institut für Englische Sprache und Literatur, Universität Salzburg, 1974), pp. 58–75.

37. Belli, II, 240, and Ayala, II, 233.

38. Bracton, fol. 45, cited in T. E., *The Lawes Resolutions of Womens Rights* (London, 1632), p. 396. See also Kahn, pp. 61–63.

39. Kahn, p. 64.

40. Douglas Bush, *Mythology and Poetry in the Renaissance* (Minneapolis: University of Minnesota Press, 1932), p. 153.

41. Kahn maintains that Lucrece puts the guilt on Tarquin for the rape, but accepts the sacrificial responsibility of a married woman—"to keep herself sexually pure for the sake of her husband and of Rome."

42. Kahn, p. 64.

43. Geoffrey Fenton, *Tragicall Histories* (London, 1572).

CHAPTER VII. A "SMOKE OF WORDS":
THREE HISTORICAL LADIES

1. An earlier version of this chapter appeared under the title "Women and Political Power in Shakespeare's English Histories," in *Topic: A Journal of the Liberal Arts* 36, "The Elizabethan Woman," ed. Anne Parten (Washington, Pa.: Washington and Jefferson College, 1982), 54–65. Used by permission.

2. Irene G. Dash. *Wooing, Wedding and Power: Women in Shakespeare's Plays* (New York: Columbia University Press, 1982), p. 207.

3. Juliet Dusinberre, *Shakespeare and the Nature of Women* (London: Macmillan, 1975), p. 278.

4. Madonne Miner, "'Neither Mother, Wife, Nor England's Queen': The Roles of Women in *Richard III*," in Carolyn Ruth Swift Lenz, Gayle Greene, and Carol Thomas Neely, eds., *The Woman's Part: Feminist Criticism of Shakespeare* (Urbana: University of Illinois Press, 1980), p. 48.

5. Robert B. Pierce, *Shakespeare's History Plays: The Family and the State* (Columbus: The Ohio State University Press, 1971), p. 85 and elsewhere.

6. David M. Bevington, "The Domineering Female in *1 Henry VI*," *Shakespeare Studies* 2, ed. J. Leeds Barroll, III (Cincinnati: The Center for Shakespeare Studies, 1966), pp. 151–158.

7. Raphael Holinshed, *Chronicles* (1587; rpt. London, 1807–09; rpt. New York: AMS Press, 1965), III, 207.

8. Bevington, p. 56; See also *1 Henry VI*, ed. A. S. Cairncross, New Arden Edition (London: Methuen, 1962), p. 114n: "It is no accident that, as one captured French 'enchantress' is led off prisoner, another, her direct successor, is led on, 'prisoner'."

9. Dash, p. 160. However, by overlooking Shakespeare's use of structural resonance in the play, she passes over the manner in which Shakespeare deliberately introduces her with undertones of hostility, in this manner controlling the reaction of the audience.

10. Edward Hall, *The Union of the Noble and Illustre Famelies of Lancastre and York* (London, 1550), Henry VI, fol. clvj^b.

11. Hall, Henry VI, fol. cli^b.

12. Hall, Henry VI, fol. clx^b.

13. Holinshed, III, 236. Jean Morris, *The Monarchs of England* (New York: Charterhouse, 1975), p. 131, wittily retells the old story that Henry, who had retreated into incapacity, "did however emerge . . . into perfect lucidity when . . . his wife Margaret had a son. He said the child must have been conceived by the Holy Ghost. Margaret ignored questions of the child's legitimacy; he was her son, and his defense her first object."

14. There are in fact very few domestically oriented scenes between mothers and children in Shakespeare. The following come to mind: Lady Capulet and Juliet, Lady Macduff and her children, Hermione and Mamillius. While *Coriolanus* includes some notably domestic scenes, children (to include the hero) are not part of them.

15. Dash, p. 182, suggests that Margaret retains a belief in these feminine virtues and hence is vulnerable to York's attacks on her womanhood.

16. Hall, Henry VI, fol. clxiii^b.

17. Margaret's historical fate is not without pathos. She was ransomed back to France by Louis XI, after four and a half years of imprisonment in the Tower, leaving England towards the end of January 1476. Before the month was out she had been forced to renounce all her rights in Anjou, and within a few months her father was forced to disinherit his grandson in favor of his nephew. By secret convention of May 25, 1476, this heir, Charles II of Maine, agreed to bequeath his whole estate to the King of France. Margaret retired to a small castle, but on her father's death, 10 July 1480, Louis XI seized everything, leaving her penniless. She was saved from beggary by "the feudal chivalry of a country gentleman, Francis Vignolles, lord of Morains . . . [who] offered the daughter of his liege lord hospitality in his castle of Dampierre," until her death in August 1482. Philippe Erlanger, *Margaret of Anjou, Queen of England* (London: Elek Books, 1970), p. 244.

18. See Miner, pp. 41, 48. She also suggests this scene "leads to the formation of bonds against a mutual foe," pointing out an unnoticed theme of "women aiding women," with which I cannot fully agree.

19. *King John*, ed E. A. J. Honigmann, New Arden Edition (London: Methuen, 1954), p. 32n.

20. New Arden Edition, p. 54n.

21. See M. M. Reese, *The Cease of Majesty* (London: Edward Arnold, 1961), pp. 283–284; Michael Manheim, *The Weak King Dilemma in the Shakespearean History Play* (Syracuse, N. Y.: Syracuse University Press, 1973), p. 143.

22. E. A. J. Honigmann percipiently reminds us (New Arden Edition, p. lxvi) that the Elizabethans were trained in rhetoric and "the refinements of debate." Hence the response of an Elizabethan audience to Constance's lamentations must have been very different from our own.

23. Arthur has said little in the play, usually a few words in an attempt to silence Constance, but in the justly famous scene with Hubert (IV.i), he develops into eloquence as he pleads for his eyes. Once again, words, the weapons of the weak, are all that he can muster, and his success is only temporary, since death comes soon.

24. Manheim, p. 143.

25. For an account of the disputed authorship see *Henry VIII*, ed. R. A. Foakes, New Arden Edition (London: Methuen, 1964), pp. xv–xxviii.

26. For some illuminating comments on this play see G. Wilson Knight, "Henry VIII and the Poetry of Conversion," in *The Crown of Life* (1947; rpt. London: University Paperbacks: Methuen, 1965), pp. 256–336, esp. for Queen Katherine, pp. 289–296.

27. Knight, p. 289.

28. Holinshed, III, 737–740, gives a very full account of Katherine's trial, her life, her confrontation with Cardinal Campeius, and her death. Shakespeare draws very heavily on that account and the one in Foxe's *Actes and Monumentes*, both of which treat Katherine and her cause with respect. She never lost the love of the people of London, and these accounts corroborate that fact.

29. See Part One, Section 1, particularly p. 7, for an account of the relevant legalities.

30. Holinshed, III, 739.

31. Holinshed, III, 739.

32. Holinshed, III, 785–796. Shakespeare violates historical fact for dramatic emphasis by

having Katherine die just before the birth of Queen Elizabeth. In fact she lived until 1536, and on the day of her death it is recorded that Queen Anne wore yellow. Henry's joy at the birth of the young Elizabeth is, of course, historically unfounded, but it emphasizes the redemptive theme.

PART FOUR

CHAPTER VIII. The Degradation of Richard II

—An Inquiry into the Ritual Backgrounds

1. This chapter originally appeared in *English Literary Renaissance*, 7 (1977), 170–196. Reprinted by permission.

2. Walter Pater, *Appreciations* (1889; rpt. London: Macmillan, 1910), p. 198.

3. Raphael Holinshed, *Chronicles* (London, 1587; rpt. London, 1807–09; rpt. New York: AMS Press, 1965), III, 165. Edward Hall, *The Union of the Noble and Illustre Famelies of Lancastre and York* (London, 1550), Henry VI, fol. xxvi[b]; Enguerrand de Monstrelet, *Chronicles*, trans. Thomas Johnes (Hasod, 1809), II, 507; George F. Beltz, *Memorials of the Most Noble Order of the Garter from Its Foundation to the Present Time* (London, 1841), pp. lxivn–lxvn.

4. William A. Shaw, *The Knights of England*, 2 vols. (London: Sherratt and Hughes, 1906), I, 13–24.

5. See also note 12. The ostensible reason for Paget's degradation was lack of noble blood on his mother's side.

6. William Segar, *The Booke of Honor and Armes* (London, 1590), pp. 10–11. For a possible Shakespeare connection I have the support of Diane Bornstein, "Trial by Combat and Official Irresponsibility in *Richard II*," *Shakespeare Studies* 8, ed. J. Leeds Barroll, III (New York: Burt Franklin, 1975), pp. 136–137.

7. John Stow, *Annales* (London, 1592), pp. 861–862.

8. See Brit. Lib. Harl. MS. 6064, fol. 39[v]. I owe this reference to William Green.

9. Elias Ashmole, *The Institution, Laws and Ceremonies of the Most Noble Order of the Garter* (London, 1672), p. 622.

10. William Green, *Shakespeare's "Merry Wives of Windsor"* (Princeton, N.J.: Princeton University Press, 1962), p. 112. This account is based on that of the *Blue Book* of the Garter, which is in the custody of the Dean of Windsor.

11. Ashmole, p. 622, notes that by the Garter Statute of 32 Henry VIII, traitors' names were merely identified in marginal notes, to avoid the untidiness of erasure.

12. Ashmole, p. 621. See also note 5.

13. M. H. Keen *The Laws of War in the Late Middle Ages* (London: Routledge and Kegan Paul, 1965), p. 89.

14. In this context it is interesting to note that in 1915 the banners of Kaiser Wilhelm II, his Crown Prince, and the Emperor Franz Josef, together with the banners of five other German princes and dukes, were removed from their respective stalls. However, their stallplates were permitted to remain and no formal degradation ceremony was performed. See Edmund H. Fellowes, *The Knights of the Garter (1348–*

1939)(London: Pub. for the Dean and Canons of St. George's Chapel, Windsor Castle, by S.P.C.K., 1939). Similarly, the Keeper of the Muniments, Windsor Castle, has informed me that in 1942 the banner of Emperor Hirohito was removed without ceremony, "and the only one to go." This disagrees with Anthony Bailey (*New Yorker*, April 11, 1977, p. 59), who says that Victor Emmanuel III was removed from the roster. I have found no record of his membership.

15. Hall, Edward IV, fol. ii.

16. Stow, p. 685. This account is repeated in full by John Selden, *Titles of Honor* (London, 1614), pp. 338–339. For the ritual of degradation from the Bath see also William Segar, "The Opinion of Norroy King of Armes Touching the Precedencye of the Knightes of the Bath," Folger MS. Xd.282. Note that the master cook's function here is taken as that of knave. For the question of adequate defense see Keen, *The Laws of War* . . . , pp. 124–127n; and above, pp. 157–158.

17. Hall, Edward IV, fol. iii.

18. Hall, Henry VII, fol. xliii. See also Keen, *The Laws of War* . . . , p. 54, and M. H. Keen, "Treason Trials under the Law of Arms," *Transactions of the Royal Historical Society*, 5th ser., 12 (1962), 92.

19. In *Stuart Plays*, ed. Arthur H. Nethercot, Charles R. Baskervill, and Virgil B. Heltzel (New York: Holt, Rinehart and Winston, 1971).

20. Stow, pp. 334–335. Note here Stow's confusing repetition, since "drawing" in the sense of disemboweling while still living naturally precedes beheading. But "drawing" has also another meaning, that of being drawn on a hurdle to the place of execution. The differentiation is not always precise, but "drawn, hanged, and quartered" would not generally be taken to mean disembowelling. See *OED*.

21. Segar, p. 65.

22. Keen, *The Laws of War* . . . , pp. 58, 19; John Barnie, *War in Medieval Society: Social Values in the Hundred Years War 1337–99* (Ithaca, N.Y.: Cornell University Press, 1974), p. 67.

23. Pierino Belli, *De Re Militari et Bello Tractatus* (1563), trans. Herbert Nutting. The Classics of International Law, No. 18 (Oxford, Clarendon Press for the Carnegie Endowment for International Peace, 1936), 2 vols., Part VIII, cap. 6; Balthazar Ayala, *De Jure et Officiis et Disciplina Militari*, Libri III (1582), trans. John Pawley Bate. The Classics of International Law (Washington, D.C.: Carnegie Institution, 1912), 2 vols., Bk. III, gives a very full account of military discipline which is particularly relevant since Ayala was jurisconsult and judge advocate general of the Spanish forces in the Low Countries. See also Alberico Gentili, *De Juri Belli Libri Tres*, (1612), trans. John C. Rolfe. The Classics of International Law, No. 16 (Oxford: Clarendon Press for the Carnegie Endowment for International Peace, 1933), Bk. II, chs. XIV–XVI *passim*.

24. In G. D. Squibb, *The High Court of Chivalry* (Oxford: Clarendon Press, 1933), pp. 18–19.

25. Squibb, pp. 123–127.

26. Squibb, p. 8.

27. Charles M. Clode, *The Military Forces of the Crown: Their Administration and Government*, 2 vols. (London: John Murray, 1869), I, 18.

28. Squibb, p. 51.

29. Squibb, pp. 50–51, notes that the High Court of Chivalry had jurisdiction over "actuall degradation" of an individual, presumably for dishonorable or treasonous behavior, but that it could not question the granting of a patent of nobility under the Great Seal.

30. Apparently the attack on the baggage train was an unauthorized free-booting expedition mounted by a few knights and some local peasants, not the major attack Henry feared. For comments on the sequence of events, see Sir Charles Oman, *The Art of War in the Middle Ages*, 2 vols. (1924; rpt. New York: Burt Franklin, 1969), II, 385, and John Keegan, *The Face of Battle* (New York: Viking, 1976), p. 111. For the rulings of military lawyers see Gentili, II, 212, and Ayala, II, 46. For the massacre at Smerwick see the comment by J. Dover Wilson in the New Cambridge Shakespeare edition of *Henry V* (1947), pp. xxxv–xxxvi. I owe these last three references to a former student, Edward A. Rauchut, Jr.

31. For a fine discussion of Shakespeare's military knowledge, see Paul A. Jorgensen, *Shakespeare's Military World* (Berkeley and Los Angeles: University of California Press, 1956).

32. Francis Grose, *Military Antiquities*, 2nd ed., 2 vols. (London, 1812), II, 107. Originally published 1786. An eyewitness has informed me that substantially the same ritual was performed (though quite illegally) in the United States Army as late as World War II. It is now forbidden by the article of military justice entitled "Limits of Punishment." See United States Army, *Manual for Courts-Martial*, 1951, ch. xxv.

33. Grose, II, 107.

34. Earl of Northumberland, *Lawes and Ordinances of Warre Established for the Better Conduct of the Services in the Northern Parts* (London, 1640), sig. C2ᵛ.

35. *An Abridgement of English Military Discipline* (London, 1686), p. 271.

36. Squibb, p. 23n.

37. For a singularly complete account of the rules covering trial by combat see John Ferne, *The Blazon of Gentrie* (London, 1586), Part I, "The Glorie of Generositie," pp. 308–341.

38. Segar, pp. 83–84.

39. Henry Bracton, *Bracton on the Laws and Customs of England*, ed. George E. Woodbine, trans. with revisions and notes by Samuel E. Thorne, 2 vols. (Cambridge, Mass.: Belknap Press of Harvard University Press, 1968), II, 385, 386.

40. Squibb, p. 23.

41. Squibb, p. 25.

42. Stephen W. Findlay, O.S.B., *Canonical Norms Governing the Deposition and Degradation of Clerics: A Historical Synopsis and Commentary*, The Catholic University of America Canon Law Studies, No. 130 (Washington, D. C.: Catholic University of America Press, 1941), p. 245.

43. John Foxe, *Actes and Monumentes* (London, 1583), pp. 517, 879–880, 1508, 1524, 1555, 1767–1768.

44. Holinshed, IV, 83, erroneously places both events on March 21.

45. Foxe, pp. 1887–1888.

46. Jasper Ridley, *Thomas Cranmer* (Oxford: Clarendon Press, 1962), p. 3.

47. Ridley, pp. 3–4.

48. Holinshed, II, 869.

49. The idea of a possible connection between Cranmer's degradation and Shakespeare's treatment of the discoronation of Richard II was suggested to me by Fr. Eric McDermott, S. J., of Georgetown University.

50. Foxe, pp. 2133–2135, 517.

51. Findlay, p. 103.

52. Findlay, p. 103.

53. Findlay, p. 206.

54. Foxe, p. 1883.

55. Foxe, p. 1881.

56. Foxe, p. 1883.

57. Foxe, pp. 1883–1884.

58. Foxe, p. 1883.

59. Ernst H. Kantorowicz, *The King's Two Bodies: A Study in Medieval Political Theology* (Princeton, N. J.: Princeton University Press, 1967), p. 36.

60. Foxe, p. 1883. In a parallel account on p. 1882 Foxe violates the order of ritual by having the bishops begin with the crozier.

61. Geoffrey Bullough, ed. *Narrative and Dramatic Sources of Shakespeare*, 8 vols. (London: Methuen, 1966), III, 90.

62. Foxe, p. 2132.

63. Foxe, p. 2126. The text of the *Forma degradationis* is on pp. 2133–2135.

64. Kantorowicz, pp. 35–40.

65. Hall, Richard II, fols. viii[b]–ix. In view of the fact that Hall on other occasions seems to use the phrases "scepter and diademe" and "croune and sceptre" as synecdoche, I occasionally wonder whether his "ceremonial" account might not be suspect.

66. Holinshed, II, 863.

67. "Translation of a French Metrical History of the Deposition of King Richard the Second, Written by a Contemporary," ed. John Webb, *Archeologia*, 20 (1824), 179.

68. Bracton, II, 33. The bracketed sentences are Bracton's, as translated by Thorne: "additional matter, afterthoughts, placed in [the MS's] margins" ("Translator's Introduction," p. x).

69. Kantorowicz, p. 36.

70. Shakespeare takes this speech from Holinshed, who by way of Hall was influenced by the *Chronicque de la Traïson et Mort de Richard Deux Roy Dengleterre*. See M. V. Clarke and V. H. Galbraith, "The Deposition of Richard II," *Bulletin of the John Rylands Library*, 14 (1930), 154. For remarks on the chronology of events see *Richard II*, ed. J. Dover Wilson, New Cambridge Edition (1939), p. 200.

71. Pater, p. 196.

72. Selden, p. 134.

73. Holinshed, II, 713.

74. Hall, Henry IV, fol. x[b].

75. Jean Froissart, *Chronicles*, trans. John Bourchier, Lord Berners (London, 1525), p. 314.

76. Kantorowicz, pp. 38–39.

77. See Appendix VII, "The Death of Richard II," *Archeologia*, 22 (1824), 282–292, note

67, above.
78. Holinshed, III, 14.

CHAPTER IX. "Naked Wretches"—Clothing as Symbol

1. See also Matthew 8:20.
2. William Shakespeare, *King Lear*, ed. Kenneth Muir, New Arden Edition (London: Methuen, 1959), p. 68n.
3. John W. Draper, *The "Twelfth Night" of Shakespeare's Audience* (Stanford, Calif.: Stanford University Press, 1950), p. 106, believes that these specifically denoted a member of the lower classes.
4. Thomas Smith, *De Republica Anglorum* (London, 1585), sig. Eii.
5. See Chapter viii, p. 195.
6. Florio's Montaigne, iii. 250, 268, vi. 189–190; III. 215–216, as quoted in New Arden ed., p. 122n.
7. Theodore Spencer, *Shakespeare and the Nature of Man* (New York: Macmillan, 1942), p. 150.
8. Spencer, p. 150.
9. Enid Welsford, *The Fool* (1935; rpt. Garden City, N. Y.: Doubleday, 1961), p. 264.
10. Welsford, p. 265.
11. Job 25:6. For man's kinship with the beasts see G. Wilson Knight, "The Lear Universe" in *The Wheel of Fire* (1930; rpt. London: University Paperbacks, Methuen, 1961), pp. 181–186.
12. William R. Elton, *King Lear and the Gods* (San Marino, Calif.: Huntington Library, 1966), pp. 85–86.
13. New Arden ed., p. 164n.
14. New Arden ed., p. 218n.
15. See, for instance, Spencer, p. 181; William Shakespeare, *Timon of Athens*, ed. H. J. Oliver, New Arden Edition (London: Methuen, 1963), pp. xli–xlii; and Geoffrey Bullough, *Narrative and Dramatic Sources of Shakespeare* (London: Routledge and Kegan Paul, 1966), VI, 234–235.
16. New Arden ed., p. xli.
17. G. Wilson Knight, "The Pilgrimage of Hate: An Essay on *Timon of Athens*," in *The Wheel of Fire*, pp. 232–233.
18. David Cook, "*Timon of Athens*," *Shakespeare Survey* 16, ed. Allardyce Nicoll (Cambridge: Cambridge University Press, 1963), pp. 83–94.
19. Cesare Ripa, *Iconologia* (Padua, 1611; rpt. New York: Garland Publishing, 1976), pp. 311, 438.
20. Harold Wilson, *On the Design of Shakespearian Tragedy* (Toronto: University of Toronto Press, 1957), p. 146. Rolf Soellner, "*Timon of Athens:*" *Shakespeare's Pessimistic Tragedy* (Columbus: Ohio State University Press, 1979), pp. 122–125, sees this as a perversion of charity.

21. Jane Austen, *Pride and Prejudice* (Boston: Houghton Mifflin, 1956), p. 185.

22. John W. Draper also suggests that it may be meant to recall the Elizabethan custom of feasting one's creditors, "The Theme of *Timon of Athens*," *Modern Language Review*, 129 (1934), 29.

23. Chapter viii, pp. 193–194.

24. Wolfgang Clemen, *The Development of Shakespeare's Imagery* (1951: rpt. New York: Hill and Wang, n.d.), p. 175, notes the way "the world of animals and plants . . . informs the language of the play in the last acts."

25. Caroline Spurgeon, *Shakespeare's Imagery and What it Tells Us* (1935; rpt. Boston: Beacon Press, 1958), pp. 324–327.

26. I do not fully agree with Lily B. Campbell, *Shakespeare's Tragic Heroes: Slaves of Passion* (1939; rpt. New York: Barnes and Noble, 1959), pp. 208–239, in which she portrays *Macbeth* as "A Study in Fear." Nonetheless, her comments on Macbeth's last battle merit consideration.

27. Surprisingly little has been written on *Henry VIII*, but one suggestive piece is by G Wilson Knight, "*Henry VIII* and the Poetry of Conversion," in *The Crown of Life* (1947; London: University Paperbacks, Methuen, 1965), pp. 256–336.

BIBLIOGRAPHY

This bibliography lists only those works actively used in the preparation of this study and cited in the footnotes. An exhaustive bibliography including all works consulted might rival the length of the text itself.

An Abridgement of Military Discipline. London, 1686.

Adams, John F. "*All's Well That Ends Well*: The Paradox of Procreation." *Shakespeare Quarterly*, 12 (1961), 261–270.

Agrippa von Nettesheim, Heinrich Cornelius. *The Commendation of Matrimony*. Trans. D[avid] Clapham. London, 1540.

A Treatise of the Nobilitie and Excellencye of Woman Kynde. Trans. David Clapham. London, 1542.

Alberti, Leon Battista. *Hecatonphila. The Arte of Loue*. London, 1598.

Arthos, John. "The Comedy of Generation." *Essays in Criticism*, 5 (1955), 97–117. [*All's Well That Ends Well*.]

Ashmole, Elias. *The Institutions, Laws, and Ceremonies of the Most Noble Order of the Garter*. London, 1672.

Augustine. *The City of God*. Trans. Henry Bettensen, ed. David Knowles. Harmondsworth, Middlesex: Penguin books, 1972.

Austen, Jane, *Pride and Prejudice*. Boston: Houghton Mifflin, 1956.

Ayala, Balthazar. *De Jure et Officiis Bellicus et Disciplina Militari*, Libri III (1582). Trans. John Pawley Bate. 2 vols. The Classics of International Law. Washington, D. C.: Carnegie Institution, 1912.

Babula, William. "The Character and the Conclusion: Bertram and the Ending of *All's Well That Ends Well*." *South Atlantic Bulletin*, 42, No. 2 (1977), 94–100.

Bailey, Anthony. "Profiles: The Elder Daughter." [Queen Elizabeth II] Part I. *New Yorker*, April 11, 1977, pp. 42–83.

Baker, Herschel. Preface to *Twelfth Night*. In *The Complete Signet Shakespeare*. New York: Harcourt Brace Jovanovich, 1972.

Bandel, Betty. "Shakespeare's Treatment of the Social Position of Women." M. A. Thesis. Columbia University, 1951.

Barnie, John. *War in Medieval Society: Social Values in the Hundred Years Wars 1337–1399*. Ithaca, N. Y.: Cornell University Press, 1975.

Barton, Anne. Introductions to Shakespeare's Comedies. In *The Riverside Shakespeare*. Boston: Houghton Mifflin, 1974.

Bean, John C. "Comic Structure and the Humanizing of Kate in *The Taming of the Shrew*." See Lenz and others, pp. 65–78.

269

Belli, Pierino. *De Re Militari et Bello Tractatus* (1563). Trans. Herbert C. Nutting. 2 vols. The Classics of International Law, No. 18. Oxford: Clarendon Press for the Carnegie Endowment for International Peace, 1936.

Beltz, George F. *Memorials of the Most Noble Order of the Garter from Its Foundation to the Present Time*. London, 1841.

Bentson, Alice N. "Portia, the Law and the Tripartite Structure of *The Merchant of Venice*." *Shakespeare Quarterly*, 30 (1979), 367–385.

Bercher, William. *The Nobylytye of Wymen (1559)*. Ed. R. Warwick Bond. London: Roxburghe Club, 1904.

Berggren, Paula S. "The Woman's Part: Sexuality as Power in Shakespeare's Plays." See Lenz and others, pp. 17–34.

Berners, Juliana. *The Boke Containing the Treatises of Hawking, Hunting . . .* [The Boke of St. Albans]. London, 1496.

Bevington, David M. "The Domineering Female in *I Henry VI*." *Shakespeare Studies* 2, ed. J. Leeds Barroll, III (Cincinnati, Ohio: The Center for Shakespeare Studies, 1966), pp. 151–158.

The Bible, King James Translation.

Binns, J. W. "Women or Transvestites on the English Stage? An Oxford Controversy." *Sixteenth-Century Journal*, 2 (1974), 95–120.

Birge-Patil, J. "Marriage Contracts in *Measure for Measure*." *Shakespeare Studies* 5, ed. J. Leeds Barroll, III (Dubuque, Iowa: Wm. C. Brown Co., 1969), pp. 106–111.

Black's Law Dictionary. 4th. ed. St. Paul, Minn.: West Publishing Company, 1951.

Blayney, Glenn H. "Enforcement in English Drama (1600–1650)." *Philological Quarterly*, 38 (1960), 459–472.

————. "Wardship in English Drama (1600–1650)." *Studies in Philology*, 53 (1956), 470–484.

Blome, Richard. *Hawking or Faulconry* (1683). London: Cresset, 1929.

Bonnard, Georges. "Are Othello and Desdemona Innocent or Guilty?" *English Studies* [Amsterdam], 30 (1949), 175–184.

Bornstein, Diane. *The Lady in the Tower: Medieval Courtesy Literature for Women*. Hamden, Conn.: Archon, 1983.

————. "Trial by Combat and Official Irresponsibility in *Richard II*." *Shakespeare Studies* 8, ed. J. Leeds Barroll, III (New York: Burt Franklin, 1975), pp. 136–141.

Bracton, Henry. *Bracton on the Laws and Customs of England*. Ed. George E. Woodbine. Trans. with revisions and notes by Samuel E. Thorne. Cambridge, Mass.: The Belknap Press of Harvard University in association with the Selden Society, 1968.

Bradbrook, M. C. "Dramatic Role and Social Image: A Study of *The Taming of the Shrew*." *Shakespeare Jahrbuch*, 94 (1958), 132–150.

————. *The Growth and Structure of Elizabethan Comedy*. London: Chatto & Windus, 1961.

————. "Virtue is the True Nobility: A Study of Structure in *All's Well That Ends Well*." *Review of English Studies*, N. S. 1 (1950), 289–301.

Bradley, A. C. *Shakespearean Tragedy*. London: Macmillan, 1904.

Brennecke, Ernest. "'Nay, That's Not Next': The Significance of Desdemona's Willow Song'." *Shakespeare Quarterly*, 4 (1953), 35–38.

Brooks, Charles. "Shakespeare's Romantic Shrews." *Shakespeare Quarterly*, 11 (1960),

351–356.

Brown, John Russell. *Shakespeare and His Comedies*. 2nd ed. London: Methuen, 1962.

Brownmiller, Susan. *Against Our Will*. 1975; rpt. New York: Bantam, 1976.

Bullough, Geoffrey, comp. and ed. *Narrative and Dramatic Sources of Shakespeare*. 8 vols. London: Routledge and Kegan Paul, 1957–75.

Burckhardt, Sigurd "*The Merchant of Venice*: The Gentle Bond." *English Literary History*, 29 (1962), 239–262.

Burton, Robert. *The Anatomy of Melancholy*. Ed. Floyd Dell and Paul Jordan-Smith. New York: Tudor Publishing Co., 1941.

Bush, Douglas. *Mythology and Poetry in the Renaissance*. Minneapolis: University of Minnesota Press, 1932.

Camden, Carroll. *The Elizabethan Woman*. Houston, Texas: Elsevier Press, 1952.

———. "Iago on Women." *Journal of English and Germanic Philology*, 48 (1949), 57–71.

Campbell, Lily B. *Shakespeare's Tragic Heroes: Slaves of Passion*. 1939; rpt. New York: Barnes and Noble, 1959.

Carroll, William C. "The Ending of *Twelfth Night* and the Tradition of Metamorphosis." See Charney and Plottel, pp. 49–61.

Carter, Albert H. "In Defense of Bertram." *Shakespeare Quarterly*, 7 (1956), 21–31.

Charlton, H. B. "Shakespeare's *Othello*." *Bulletin of the John Rylands Library*, 31 (1948), 28–53.

———. *Shakespearian Comedy*. London: Methuen, 1938.

Charney, Maurice, and Jeanine Parisier Plottel, eds. *Shakespearean Comedy*. New York: New York Literary Forum, 1980.

[Church of England.] *The Book of Common Prayer, 1559: The Elizabethan Prayer Book*. Ed. John E. Booty. Charlottesville, Va.: The University Press of Virginia for the Folger Shakespeare Library, 1976.

———. *Constitutions and Canons Ecclesiastical*, 1604. Introduction and Notes by H. A. Wilson. Oxford: Clarendon Press, 1922.

———. *Homilies*. London, 1595.

C[leaver], R[obert]. *A Godly Forme of Householde Gouernment*. London, 1598.

Clemen, Wolfgang. *The Development of Shakespeare's Imagery*. 1951; rpt. New York: Hill and Wang, n.d.

Clode, Charles M. *The Military Forces of the Crown: Their Administration and Government*. 2 vols. London: John Murray, 1869.

Coghill, Neville. "The Basis of Shakespearean Comedy." In *Shakespeare Criticism, 1935–1960*. Ed. Anne Ridler. London: Oxford University Press, 1963.

Cook, David. "*Timon of Athens*." *Shakespeare Survey* 16. Ed. Allardyce Nicoll (Cambridge: Cambridge University Press, 1963), pp. 83–94.

Coryat, Thomas. *Crudities, Hastily Gobled Vp in Fiue Moneths Trauells. . . .* London, 1611.

Crehan, J. H., S. J. "Shakespeare and the Sarum Ritual." *The Month*, 218, N. s. 32 (Jul–Aug., 1964), 47–50.

Darell, Walter. *A Pretie and Short Discourse of the Life of Seruingmen*. London, 1587.

Dash, Irene G. *Wooing, Wedding and Power: Women in Shakespeare's Plays*. New York: Columbia University Press, 1981.

Davies, Edward. *The Art of War and Englands Traynings*. London, 1619.

Dennis, Carl. *"All's Well That Ends Well* and the Meaning of Agape." *Philological Quarterly*, 50 (1961), 75–84.

Dickes, Robert. "Desdemona: An Innocent Victim." *American Imago*, 27 (1970), 279–297.

Doran, Madeline. *Endeavors of Art: A Study of Form in Elizabethan Drama*. Madison: University of Wisconsin Press, 1954.

Downer, Alan S. "Feste's Night." *College English*, 13 (1952), 258–265.

Draper, John W. "Desdemona, a Compound of Two Cultures." *Revue de Littérature Comparée*, 13 (1933), 337–351.

———. "Kate the Curst." *Journal of Nervous and Mental Diseases*, 89 (1939), 757–764.

———. "Orlando, the Younger Brother." *Philological Quarterly*, 13 (1934), 72–77.

———. *The "Othello" of Shakespeare's Audience*. Paris: J. Didier, 1952.

———. "The Theme of *Timon of Athens*." *Modern Language Review*, 29 (1934), 20–31.

———. *The "Twelfth Night" of Shakspeare's Audience*. Stanford, Calif.: Stanford University Press, 1950.

Dusinberre, Juliet. *Shakespeare and the Nature of Women*. London: Macmillan, 1975.

E., T. *The Lawes Resolutions of Womens Rights: Or the Lawes Prouision for Women*. London, 1632.

Earle, John. *Micro-cosmographie*. Ed. Gwendolen Murphy. London: Golden Cockerel Press, 1928.

Eccles, Mark. "John Webster." *Times Literary Supplement*, January 21, 1977, p. 71.

Edmond, Mary. "In Search of John Webster." *Times Literary Supplement*, December 24, 1976, pp. 1621–1622.

Elton, William R. *"King Lear" and the Gods*. San Marino, Calif.: Huntington Library, 1966.

Erasmus, Desiderius. *The Colloquies of Erasmus*. Trans. Craig R. Thompson. Chicago, Ill.: University of Chicago Press, 1965.

Erlanger, Philippe. *Margaret of Anjou, Queen of England*. London: Erlek Books, 1970.

Evans, Bertrand. *Shakespeare's Comedies*. Oxford: Clarendon Press, 1960.

Everett, Barbara. *"Much Ado About Nothing."* *Critical Quarterly*, 3 (1961), 319–335.

Fellowes, Edmund H. *The Knights of the Garter (1348–1939)*. London: S. P. C. K. for the Dean and Canons of St. George's Chapel, Windsor Castle, 1939.

Fenton, Geoffrey. *Tragicall Histories*. London, 1572.

Fergusson, Francis. *The Human Image in Dramatic Literature*. Garden City, N. Y.: Doubleday Anchor, 1957.

Ferne, John. *The Blazon of Gentrie*. London, 1586.

Fiedler, Leslie A. *The Stranger in Shakespeare*. New York: Stein and Day, 1972.

Findlay, Stephen W., O.S.B. *Canonical Norms Governing the Deposition and Degradation of Clerics: A Historical Synopsis and Commentary*. The Catholic University of America Canon Law Series No. 130. Washington, D. C.: Catholic University of America, 1941.

Foxe, John. *Actes and Monumentes*. . . . London, 1583.

———. *Ecclesiastical History*. London, 1596.

Frederick II of Hohenstaufen. *The Art of Falconry*, Being the *De Arte Venandi cum Avibus*. Trans. and ed. Casey A. Wood and F. Marjorie Fyfe. Stanford, Calif.: Stanford University Press, 1943.

Freud, Sigmund. *The Standard Edition of the Complete Psychological Works of Sigmund Freud*. Trans. James Strachey. London: Hogarth Press, 1958.

Froissart, Jean. *Chronicles*. Trans. John Bourchier, Lord Berners. London, 1525.

Furnivall, Frederick J., ed. *Child-Marriages, Divorces, and Ratifications, &c in the Diocese of Chester, A. D. 1561–66* . . . . Early English Text Society Publications. Original Series No. 108. London: Kegan Paul, 1897.

Gagen, Jean Elisabeth. *The New Woman: Her Emergence in the English Drama, 1600–1730*. New York: Twayne, 1954.

Gaw, Allison. "Is Shakespeare's *Much Ado* a Revised Earlier Play?" *PMLA*, 50 (1935), 715–738.

Gentili, Alberico. *De Jure Belli Libri Tres* (1612). Trans. John C. Rolfe. The Classics of International Law, No. 16. 2 vols. Oxford: Clarendon Press for the Carnegie Endowment for International Peace, 1933.

Gilbert, A. H. "Scenes of Discovery in *Othello*." *Philological Quarterly*, 5 (1926), 119–130.

Gosynhill, Edward. *Here Begynneth a Lytle Boke Named the Schole House of Women*. . . . London, 1561?

Grebanier, Bernard. *The Truth About Shylock*. New York: Random House, 1962.

Green, William. *Shakespeare's "Merry Wives of Windsor."* Princeton, N. J.: Princeton University Press, 1962.

Greer, Germaine. *The Female Eunuch*. New York: McGraw-Hill, 1971.

Grose, Francis. *Military Antiquities*. 2nd ed. 2 vols. 1786: rpt. London, 1812.

Grotius, Hugo. *De Jure Belli et Pacis Libri Tres* (1646). 2 vols. Trans. Francis W. Kelsey. The Classics of International Law, No. 3. 2 vols. Oxford: Clarendon Press for the Carnegie Endowment for International Peace, 1925.

Guazzo, Stefano. *The Civile Conversation*. Trans. George Pettie and Barth. Young, 1581 and 1586. The Tudor Translations. Second Series Nos. 7–8. London: Constable, 1925; rpt; New York: AMS Press, 1967.

Hale, J. R. *The Art of War and Renaissance England*. Folger Booklets on Tudor and Stuart Civilization. Washington, D. C.: Folger Shakespeare Library, 1961.

Hall, Edward. *The Union of the Noble and Illustre Famelies of Lancastre and York*. London, 1590.

Hapgood, Robert. "Portia and *The Merchant of Venice*: The Gentle Bond." *Modern Language Quarterly*, 28 (1967), 19–32.

Harding, Davis P. "Elizabethan Betrothals and *Measure for Measure*." *Journal of English and Germanic Philology*, 49 (1950), 139–158.

Harrington, William. *In This Boke Are Conteyned the Commendacions of Matrymony, the Maner & Fourme of Contractyng Solempnysynge and Lyuyng in the Same*. . . . London, 1528.

Harting, James E. *The Ornithology of Shakespeare*. London: J. Van Voorst, 1871.

Haw, Reginald. *The State of Matrimony: An Investigation of the Relationship between Ecclesiastical and Civil Marriage in England after the Reformation, with a Consideration of the Laws Relating Thereto*. London: S.P.C.K., 1952.

Hawkins, Sherman H. "The Two Worlds of Shakespearean Comedy." *Shakespeare Studies* 3, ed. J. Leeds Barroll, III (Cincinnati, Ohio: The Center for Shakespeare Studies, 1968), pp. 62–80.

Hayles, Nancy K. "Sexual Disguise in *As You Like It* and *Twelfth Night*." *Shakespeare Survey*

32, ed. Kenneth Muir (Cambridge: Cambridge University Press, 1979), pp. 63–72.

H[eale], W[illiam]. *An Apologie for Women, or an Opposition to Mr. Dr. G[ager] His Assertion. Who Held in the Act at Oxforde. Anno 1608. That It Was Lawfull for Husbands to Beate Their Wiues*. Oxford, 1609.

Heilbrun, Carolyn G. *Toward a Recognition of Androgyny*. New York: Harper Colophon, 1973.

Hibbard, George R. "*The Taming of the Shrew*: A Social Comedy." In *Shakespearean Essays*. Ed. Alwin Thaler and Norman Sanders. Tennessee Studies in Language and Literature, No. 2 (Knoxville: University of Tennessee Press, 1964), pp. 15–28.

Holinshed, Raphael. *Chronicles*. 6 vols. London, 1587; rpt. London, 1807–09; rpt. New York: AMS Press, 1965.

Hotson, J. Leslie. *The First Night of "Twelfth Night."* London: Hart-Davis, 1954.

Howard, George E. *A History of Matrimonial Institutions*. Chicago, Ill.: University of Chicago Press, 1904.

Hull, Suzanne W. *Chaste, Silent, & Obedient: English Books for Women, 1475–1640*. San Marino, Calif.: Huntington Library, 1982.

Hunter, Robert Grams. *Shakespeare and the Comedy of Forgiveness*. New York: Columbia University Press, 1960.

Hurstfield, Joel. *The Queens Wards: Wardship and Marriage Under Elizabeth I*. London: Longmans, Green & Co., 1958.

Hyman, Lawrence W. "The Rival Lovers in *The Merchant of Venice*." *Shakespeare Quarterly*, 20 (1970), 109–116.

Jeaffreson, John Cordy. *Brides and Bridals*. 2nd. ed. 2 vols. London: Hurst & Blackett, 1873.

Jorgensen, Paul A. *Shakespeare's Military World*. Berkeley and Los Angeles: University of California Press, 1956.

Joyce, George Hayward, S.J. *Christian Marriage: An Historical and Doctrinal Study*. Heythrop Studies I. London: Sheed and Ward, 1948.

Kahn, Coppélia. *Man's Estate: Masculine Identity in Shakespeare*. Berkeley and Los Angeles: University of California Press, 1981.

————. "The Rape in Shakespeare's *Lucrece*." *Shakespeare Studies* 9, ed. J. Leeds Barroll, III (New York: Burt Franklin, 1976), pp. 45–72.

————. "*The Taming of the Shrew*: Shakespeare's Mirror of Marriage." *Modern Language Studies*, 5 (1975), 88–102.

Kantorowicz, Ernst H. *The King's Two Bodies: A Study in Medieval Political Theology*. Princeton, N.J.: Princeton University Press, 1967.

Keegan, John. *The Face of Battle*. New York: Viking, 1976.

Keen, M. H. *The Laws of War in the Late Middle Ages*. London: Routledge and Kegan Paul, 1965.

————. "Treason Trials under the Law of Arms." *Transactions of the Royal Historical Society*, 5th Ser.,12 (1962), 85–103.

Kelso, Ruth. *The Doctrine of the English Gentleman in the Sixteenth Century*. University of Illinois Studies in Language and Literature, Vol. 14, Nos. 1–2. Urbana: University of Illinois Press, 1929; rpt. Gloucester, Mass.: Peter Smith, 1964.

————. *Doctrine for the Lady of the Renaissance*. Urbana: University of Illinois Press, 1956.

Kimbrough, Robert M. "Androgyny Seen through Shakespeare's Disguise." *Shakespeare Quarterly*, 33 (1982), 17–33.

King, Walter N. "Much Ado About Something." *Shakespeare Quarterly*, 15 (1964), 143–155.

Knight, G. Wilson. *The Crown of Life*. 1947; rpt. London: University Paperbacks, Methuen, 1965.

———. *The Sovereign Flower*. London: Methuen, 1958.

———. *The Wheel of Fire*. 1930; rpt. London: University Paperbacks, 1961.

Knight, W. Nicholas. *Shakespeare's Hidden Life: Shakespeare at the Law, 1585–1595*. New York: Mason and Lipscomb, 1973.

Lamb, M. E. "Ovid's *Metamorphoses* and Shakespeare's *Twelfth Night*." See Charney and Plottel, pp. 63–77.

La Perrière, Guillaume de. *The Mirrovr of Policie*. [Trans. from *Le Miroir Politique*.] London, 1598.

La Primaudaye, Pierre de. *The French Academie; Fully Finished in Foure Bookes*. Trans. by T. B. London, 1618.

Latham, Simon. *Lathams Falconry or the Faulcon's Lure and Cure*. London, 1614.

Lawrence, William Witherle. *Shakespeare's Problem Comedies*. New York: Macmillan, 1931.

Leggatt, Alexander. *Citizen Comedy in the Age of Shakespeare*. Toronto: University of Toronto Press, 1973.

———. *Shakespeare's Comedy of Love*. London: Methuen, 1974.

Lenz, Carolyn Ruth Swift, Gayle Greene, and Carol Thomas Neely, eds. *The Woman's Part: Feminist Criticism of Shakespeare*. Urbana: University of Illinois Press, 1980.

Levin, Richard. "Viola: Dr. Johnson's 'Excellent Schemer'." *Durham University Journal*, 71 (1979), 213–222.

Lewalski, Barbara K. "Biblical Allusion and Allegory in *The Merchant of Venice*." *Shakespeare Quarterly*, 13 (1962), 327–343.

———. "Love, Appearance and Reality: Much Ado About Something." *Studies in English Literature*, 7 (1968), 235–251.

Linthicum, Marie Channing. "Benedick's Love-Symptoms: Cosmetics and Costume." *Modern Language Review*, 22 (1927), 442–444.

Love, John M. "'Though Many of the Rich Are Damn'd': Dark Comedy and Social Class in *All's Well That Ends Well*." *Texas Studies in Language and Literature*, 18 (1977), 517–527.

Maitland, Frederic William. *Roman Canon Law in the Church of England*. 2nd. rev. ed. London: Methuen, 1898.

Manheim, Michael. *The Weak King Dilemma in the Shakespearean History Play*. Syracuse, N. Y.: Syracuse University Press, 1973.

Marsh, Ngaio. "A Note on a Production of *Twelfth Night*." *Shakespeare Survey* 8, ed. Allardyce Nicoll (Cambridge: Cambridge University Press, 1955), pp. 69–73.

McLean, Andrew. "Another Translation of Erasmus's *Coniugium*: Snawsel's *Looking Glasse for Maried Folkes* (1610)." *Moreana*, 43–44 (1974), 55–64.

A Mery Dialogue, Declaringe the Propertyes of Shrowde Shrewes and Honest Wyues. London, 1557. [A very free translation of Erasmus's *Coniugium*.]

Midgely, Graham. "*The Merchant of Venice*: A Reconsideration." *Essays in Criticism*, 10

(1960), 119–133.

Miner, Madonne. "'Neither Mother, Wife, Nor England's Queen': The Roles of Women in *Richard III*." See Lenz and others, pp. 35–55.

Monstrelet, Enguerrand de. *Chronicles*. Trans. Thomas Johnes. 2 vols. Hasod, 1809.

Morris, Jean. *The Monarchs of England*. New York: Charterhouse, 1975.

Mueschke, Paul, and Jeannette Fleisher. "Jonsonian Elements in *Twelfth Night*." *PMLA*, 48 (1933) 722–740.

Muir, Kenneth. *Shakespeare's Sources*. Vol. I. London: Methuen, 1957.

Nagarajan, S. "*Measure for Measure* and Elizabethan Betrothals." *Shakespeare Quarterly*, 14 (1963), 31–38.

Neely, Carol Thomas. "Women and Men in *Othello*: 'what should such a fool / Do with so good a woman?'." *Shakespeare Studies* 10, ed. J. Leeds Barroll, III (New York: Burt Franklin, 1977), pp. 133–158.

Nethercot, Arthur H., Charles R. Baskervill, Virgil B. Heltzel, eds. *Stuart Plays*. Rev. ed. New York: Holt, Rinehart and Winston, 1971.

Niccholes, Alexander. *A Discourse of Marriage and Wiving: and of the Greatest Mystery Therein Contained: How to Choose a Good Wife from a Bad*. London, 1615.

Northumberland, Earl of. *Lawes and Ordinances of Warre Established for the Better Conduct of the Services in the Northern Parts*. London, 1640.

Oman, Charles. *The Art of War in the Middle Ages*. 2 vols. 1924; rpt. New York: Burt Franklin, 1969.

Overbury, Thomas. *The Overburian Characters*. ed. W. J. Paylor. The Percy Reprints, No. 13. Oxford: Basil Blackwell, 1936.

Page, Nadine. "The Public Repudiation of Hero." *PMLA*, 50 (1935), 739–744.

Palmer, D. J. "*Twelfth Night* and the Myth of Echo and Narcissus." *Shakespeare Survey* 32, ed. Kenneth Muir (Cambridge: Cambridge University Press, 1979), ₚp. 73–78.

Panofsky, Erwin. *Studies in Iconology*. New York: Oxford University Press, 1939.

Pater, Walter. *Appreciations*. 1898; rpt. London: Macmillan, 1910.

Pearse, Nancy Cotton. *John Fletcher's Chastity Plays: Mirrors of Modesty*. Lewisburg, Pa.: Bucknell University Press, 1973.

Perkins, William. *Christian Oeconomie: Or a Short Survey of the Right Manner of Ordering a Familie According to the Scriptures*. Trans. Thomas Pickering. London, 1609.

Phialas, Peter G. *Shakespeare's Romantic Comedies: The Development of Their Form and Meaning*. Chapel Hill: University of North Carolina Press, 1966.

Pierce, Robert B. *Shakespeare's History Plays: The Family and the State*. Columbus: The Ohio State University Press, 1971.

Plato. *Symposium*. Trans. B. Jowett, ed. Louise Ropes Loomis. In *Five Great Dialogues*. New York: Walter J. Black for the Classics Club, 1942.

Powell, Chilton Latham. *English Domestic Relations 1487–1653*. New York: Columbia University Press, 1917.

Price, Joseph G. *The Unfortunate Comedy: A Study of "All's Well That Ends Well" and Its Critics*. Toronto: University of Toronto Press, 1969.

Prouty, Charles Tyler. *The Sources of "Much Ado About Nothing."* New Haven, Conn.: Yale University Press, 1950.

Ranald, Margaret Loftus. "'As Marriage Binds, and Blood Breaks': English Marriage and Shakespeare." *Shakespeare Quarterly*, 30 (1979), 68–81.

_____. "The Betrothals of *All's Well That Ends Well*." *Huntington Library Quarterly*, 26 (1963), 179–192.

_____. "The Degradation of Richard II: An Inquiry into the Ritual Backgrounds." *English Literary Renaissance*, 7 (1977), 170–196.

_____. "The Indiscretions of Desdemona." *Shakespeare Quarterly*, 14 (1963), 127–139.

_____. "The Manning of the Haggard: Or *The Taming of the Shrew*." *Essays in Literature*, 1 (1974), 149–165.

_____. "Not Shakespeare This Time." *Word Study*, 26 (1961), 7-8.

_____. "Women and Political Power in Shakespeare's English Histories." *Topic: A Journal of the Liberal Arts*, 36, "The Elizabethan Woman," ed. Anne Parten (Washington, Pa.: Washington and Jefferson College, 1982), 54–65.

Rathgeb, Jacob. "A True and Faithful Narrative of the Bathing Excursion. . . ." See Rye.

Reese, M. M. *The Cease of Majesty*. London: Edward Arnold, 1961.

Reid, Stephen. "Desdemona's Guilt." *American Imago*, 27 (1970), 245–262.

Renton, Alexander W., and George Phillimore. *The Comparative Law of Marriage and Divorce*. London: Sweet and Maxwell, 1910.

Rich, Barnabe. *The Excellencie of Good Women. The Honor and Estimation That Belongeth unto Them. The Infallible Markes Whereby We Know Them*. London, 1613.

Richmond, Hugh M. *Shakespeare's Sexual Comedy: A Mirror for Lovers*. Indianapolis, Ind.: Bobbs-Merrill, 1971.

Ridley, Jasper. *Thomas Cranmer*. Oxford: Clarendon Press, 1962.

Ripa, Cesare. *Iconologia*. Padua, 1611; rpt. New York: Garland Publishing, 1976.

Roberts, Jeanne Addison. *Shakespeare's English Comedy: "The Merry Wives of Windsor" in Context*. Lincoln: University of Nebraska Press, 1979.

Rye, William Brenchley. *England as Seen by Foreigners in the Days of Elizabeth and James the First*. London: John Russell Smith, 1865.

Scarisbrick, J. J. *Henry VIII*. 1968; rpt. Berkeley: University of California Press, 1970.

Schanzer, Ernest. "The Marriage Contracts in *Measure for Measure*." *Shakespeare Survey* 13, ed. Allardyce Nicoll (Cambridge: Cambridge University Press, 1960), pp. 81-89.

Schroeder, H. J. *Canons and Decrees of the Council of Trent; Original Text with English Translation*. St. Louis, Mo.: Herder, 1941.

Scott, Mary Augusta. "*The Book of the Courtyer*: A Possible Source for Benedick and Beatrice." *PMLA*, 16 (1901), 475–502.

Segar, William. *The Booke of Honor and Armes*. . . . London, 1590.

_____. "The Opinion of Norroy King of Armes Touching the Precedencye of the Knightes of the Bath." Folger Shakespear Library MS. Xd.282.

Selden, John. *Titles of Honor*. London, 1614.

Seronsy, Cecil C. "'Supposes' as a Unifying Theme in *The Taming of the Shrew*." *Shakespeare Quarterly*, 14 (1963), 15–30.

Sexton, Joyce Hengerer. "The Theme of Slander in *Much Ado About Nothing* and Garter's *Susanna*." *Philological Quarterly*, 54 (1975), 419–433.

Shakespeare, William. *All's Well That Ends Well*. Ed. G. K. Hunter. New Arden Edition.

3rd ed. London: Methuen, 1962.

————. *As You Like It*. Ed. Agnes Latham. New Arden Edition, London: Methuen, 1975.

————. *Henry V*. Ed. J. Dover Wilson. New Cambridge Edition. Cambridge: Cambridge University Press, 1947.

————. *1 Henry VI, 2 Henry VI, 3 Henry VI*. Ed. A. S. Cairncross. New Arden Edition. London: Methuen, 1962, 1962, 1964.

————. *Henry VIII*. Ed. R. A. Foakes. New Arden Edition. London: Methuen, 1964.

————. *King John*. Ed. E. A. J. Honigmann. New Arden Edition. London: Methuen, 1954.

————. *King Lear*. Ed. Kenneth Muir. New Arden Edition. London: Methuen, 1959.

————. *Measure for Measure*. Ed. J. W. Lever. New Arden Edition. London: Methuen, 1965.

————. *The Merchant of Venice*. Ed. John Russell Brown. New Arden Edition. London: Methuen, 1959.

————. *Much Ado About Nothing*. Ed. J. Dover Wilson. New Cambridge Edition. Cambridge: Cambridge University Press, 1923.

————. *Much Ado About Nothing*. Ed. A. R. Humphreys. New Arden Edition. London: Methuen, 1981.

————. *The Poems*. Ed. F. T. Prince. New Arden Edition. London: Methuen, 1960.

————. *Timon of Athens*. Ed. H. J. Oliver. New Arden Edition. London: Methuen, 1963.

————. *Twelfth Night*. Ed. M. A. Lothian and T. W. Craik. London: Methuen, 1975.

————. *The Complete Signet Classic Shakespeare*. Gen. Ed. Sylvan Barnet. New York: Harcourt Brace Jovanovich, 1972.

————. *The Riverside Shakespeare*. Boston: Houghton Mifflin Co., 1974.

————. *Twenty-Three Plays and the Sonnets*. Ed. Thomas Marc Parrott. New York: Scribners, 1938.

————. *William Shakespeare: The Complete Works*. Gen. Ed., Alfred Harbage. The Pelican Shakespeare. Baltimore, Md.: Penguin Books, 1969.

Shaw, William. *The Knights of England*. 2 vols. London: Sherratt and Hughes, 1906.

Simone, R. Thomas. *Shakespeare and "Lucrece": A Study of the Poem and Its Relation to the Plays*. Elizabethan and Renaissance Studies. Ed. James Hogg. Salzburg: Institut für Englische Sprache und Literatur, Universität Salzburg, 1974.

Sinsheimer, Hermann. *Shylock: The History of a Character*. New York: Benjamin Blom, 1947.

Sisson, Charles J. *New Readings in Shakespeare*. 2 vols. Cambridge: Cambridge University Press, 1956.

Smellie, K. B. *The British Way of Life*. London: Heinemann, 1955.

Smith, Hallett. *Elizabethan Poetry*. Cambridge, Mass.: Harvard University Press, 1952.

Smith, Thomas. *De Republica Anglorum*. London, 1583.

S[nawsel], R[obert]. *A Looking-Glasse for Maried Folkes*. London, 1610.

Snyder, Susan. *The Comic Matrix of Shakespeare's Tragedies: "Romeo and Juliet," "Hamlet," "Othello," and "King Lear."* Princeton, N.J.: Princeton University Press, 1981.

Soellner, Rolf. *"Timon of Athens": Shakespeare's Pessimistic Tragedy*. With a Stage History by Gary Jay Williams. Columbus: The Ohio State University Press, 1979.

Spencer, Theodore. *Shakespeare and the Nature of Man.* New York: Macmillan, 1942.

Spurgeon, Caroline. *Shakespeare's Imagery and What It Tells Us.* 1935; rpt. Boston: Beacon Press, 1958.

Squibb, G. D. *The High Court of Chivalry.* Oxford: Clarendon Press, 1933.

State v. Rhodes, 61 (North Carolina) 453 (1868).

Stevenson, David Lloyd. *The Love-Game Comedy.* New York: Columbia University Press, 1946.

Stone, Lawrence. *The Family, Sex and Marriage in England, 1500–1800.* New York: Harper and Row, 1977.

Stow, John. *Annales.* London, 1592.

Swinburne, Henry. *A Treatise of Spousals, or Matrimonial Contracts.* London, 1686.

Tannenbaum, S. A. "The Inception of Othello's Jealousy." *Shakespeare Association Bulletin*, 10 (1935), 178–179.

Taylor, Michael. "*Much Ado About Nothing*: The Individual in Society." *Essays in Criticism*, 23 (1973), 146–153.

Thomas, Keith. "The Double Standard." *Journal of the History of Ideas*, 20 (1959), 195–216.

Tillyard, E.M.W. *Shakespeare's Problem Plays.* London: Chatto & Windus, 1954.

Trent, Council of. See Schroeder, H.J., *Canons and Decrees of the Council of Trent.*

Turbervile, George. *The Book of Falconry or Hawking.* London, 1611.

Tyndale, William. *The Obedyence of a Christen Man.* London, 1561.

United States Army. *The Geneva Conventions of 1949 and Hague Convention No. IV of 1907.* Army Subject Scedule 27–1. Washington, D. C.: HQ, Department of the Army, 8 October 1970.

———. *The Law of Land Warfare.* FM 27–1, Department of the Army. Washington, D.C.: U.S. Government Printing Office, 1956.

———. *Manual for Courts Martial.* Washington, D. C.: Department of the Army, 1951.

Vives, Juan Luis. *The Office and Duetie of an Husband.* London, 1555.

———. *A Very Frutefull and Pleasant Boke Callyd the Instruction of a Christen Woman.* Trans. Richard Hyrde. London, 1541. [Orig. pub. in Latin with dedication to Queen Katherine of England, 1523.]

Webb, John, ed. "Translation of a French Metrical History of the Deposition of King Richard the Second, Written by a Contemporary." *Archeologia*, 20 (1824), 1–423.

Welsford, Enid. *The Fool.* 1935; rpt. Garden City, N. Y.: Doubleday, 1961.

West, Michael. "The Folk Background of Petruchio's Wooing Dance: Male Supremacy in *The Taming of the Shrew*," *Shakespeare Studies* 7, ed J. Leeds Barroll, III (New York: Burt Franklin, 1974), pp. 65–73.

White, T. H. *The Goshawk.* New York: Putnam's, 1951.

Wilson, Harold S. "Dramatic Emphasis in *All's Well That Ends Well*." *Huntington Library Quarterly*, 13 (1950), 217–240.

———. *On the Design of Shakespearian Tragedy.* Toronto: University of Toronto Press, 1957.

Wood, Edward J. *The Wedding Day in All Ages and Countries.* New York: Harper's, 1869.

Woodbridge, Linda. *Women and the English Renaissance: Literature and the Nature of Womankind, 1540–1620.* Urbana and Chicago: University of Illinois Press, 1984.

Wright, Louis B. "A Conduct Book for Malvolio." *Studies in Philology*, 31 (1931), 115–132. See also Darell.

————. *Middle Class Culture in Elizabethan England*. Chapel Hill: University of North Carolina Press, 1935.

Wylie, James Hamilton, and William Templeton Waugh. *The Reign of King Henry the Fifth*. 3 vols. Cambridge: Cambridge University Press, 1929.

Index